Workin' on the Railroad

WORKIN'
on the
RAILROAD

Reminiscences
from the
Age of Steam

Edited with commentary by
RICHARD REINHARDT

WEATHERVANE BOOKS
NEW YORK

For my father, Emil Reinhardt—
not because he is especially fond of railroads,
but because I am especially fond of him.

Acknowledgments

The editor is grateful to a number of persons and institutions for their help in assembling the ingredients of this volume. He would like to thank, in particular, the staffs of the San Francisco Public Library; the General Library of the University of California, Berkeley; the Bancroft Library of the University of California, Berkeley; the Wright Memorial Library of Parsons College, Fairfield, Iowa; the Enoch Pratt Free Library of Baltimore, Maryland; the Library of the Cooper Union for the Advancement of Science and Art, New York City; and Roger Olmsted for his collection of *Scribner's Magazines.*

For permission to make use of copyrighted material, the editor wishes to thank:

McGraw-Hill Book Company for "I grabbed the handhold" and "I decided to stop sleeping on coal cars," from *Clear the Tracks!* by Joseph Bromley, as told to Page Cooper. Copyright 1943 by Joseph Bromley.

Stoyan Christowe for "As I touched the steel," from *My American Pilgrimage,* by Stoyan Christowe, Little-Brown & Co., Boston, 1947. Copyright 1947 by Stoyan Christowe.

University of Oklahoma Press for "The murky atmosphere . . . the faint light" and "I wore two pairs of pants," from *From Cab to Caboose: Fifty Years of Railroading,* by Joseph A. Noble. Copyright 1964 by the University of Oklahoma Press.

Crown Publishers for "Right after we pulled out, I started my campaign," from *The Story of American Railroads,* by Stewart H. Holbrook. Copyright 1947 by Crown Publishers.

The *American Mercury* for "Few of them ever came back a second time," from the article "Railroad Boom-Town," by Laurence Bell. Copyright 1938 by the *American Mercury.* And for "A tip is not a humiliation," from the article "The Art of the Pullman Porter," by H. N. Hall. Copyright 1931 by the *American Mercury.*

The California Historical Society for "The boardwalk of Auburn," from Clarence M. Wooster's "Railroading in California in the Seventies," published in the *Quarterly of the California Historical Society.* Copyright 1939 by the California Historical Society.

Caxton Printers, Ltd., for "The nearest peace officer to my camp was 125 miles away," from *End of Track,* by James H. Kyner with Hawthorne Daniel. Copyright 1937 by Caxton Printers.

Contents

Introduction

THE AGE OF THE STEAM RAILROAD lasted here in North America for 104 years, nine months, and eighteen days, give or take a few weeks for disputed historical claims,

It began on a Saturday morning in August, 1829, when a self-assured young mathematician, recently out of Columbia College, climbed onto an outlandish, piston-driven carriage, took a firm grip on the throttle, and rattled away, with a hiss of steam and a creak of wooden rails, into the forest of eastern Pennsylvania. It ended, symbolically, on the opening day of the second year of the Century of Progress Exposition in Chicago in May, 1934, when two stream-lined, petroleum-powered passenger trains, the first of their kind in the world, rolled onto an enormous outdoor stage while several thousand spectators roared with excitement. Technology had overreached technology: the Age of the Diesel had begun.

During the hundred-and-some-odd years between these two events, the United States spread from sea to sea, fell apart, pulled itself back together, transformed its deserts into farms and its farms into factories, and closed the curtain on its last frontier; and, all the while, the mighty railroad occupied the undisputed center of American public life. The railroad founded cities, populated states, created governments, destroyed the wilderness. It was the great speculator, the political tyrant, the recruiter of immigrants, the opener of new lands, the cynosure of poets and pioneers, the symbol of adventure, opportunity, escape, and power. Not even the government was more ubiquitous, more tangible, more influential than the railroad.

Naturally, this all-pervasive institution became a vast abstraction, vaguely but deeply engraved on the mind of the American people. Like "Wall Street,"

"Hollywood," and "The Underworld," the railroad was part dream, part substance. Its familiar human components developed into abstractions, too: The
Engineer, The Fireman, The Conductor, The Ticket Agent, The Surveyor, The
Telegrapher, The Porter, The Brakeman, The Capitalist, The Construction
Worker, The Tramp. At least one of these—The Engineer—clearly was an immortal archetype. As the late Lucius Beebe put it: "Perhaps no other occupation
ever fetched the American fancy as did that of the locomotive engineer. Not
even the cowboy, the Indian scout, the Godlike vision of Washington at Valley
Forge or the swift facility of 'Tinker to Evers to Chance' quite so effectively
captured the national imagination." Working on the railroad was the most
virile, challenging, and exciting career a man could follow.

Yet, the railroad man, for all his historic importance, his archetypal
stature, and his economic power, has achieved only a minor position in American literature. Back in 1950 the *New Yorker* magazine took notice of this
deficiency in a short essay about Casey Jones, the "Brave Engineer," published
in its "Talk of the Town" department. According to the *New Yorker,* hardly
anyone knew the true story of this famous railroad hero, or realized that Casey
Jones had been an actual person.

After reading the *New Yorker* item, Dr. Henry Steele Commager, the
historian, remarked to some of his colleagues that he, too, had been struck by
the dearth of folklore, as well as of formal literature, about railroaders and
railroading. Whereas all manner of other men and vocations had won a place
in the sagas of the United States—buffalo hunters, mountain men, covered-
wagon emigrants, seamen, whalers, Mississippi steamboatmen, river gamblers,
outlaws, pony express riders, cowboys, lumberjacks, gold miners—not many
railroad men, outside of Casey Jones (and John Henry, whom Dr. Commager
apparently overlooked), had made the grade into the fraternity of folk heroes.

For several months afterward, the *New Yorker* was bombarded with
manuscript accounts of real and spurious railroad characters, but this belated
homage failed to significantly improve the public standing of the railroad man.

This persistent neglect is rather mysterious, but it obviously is not the
result of a shortage of printed words about railroads. From the very beginning
of the steam locomotive, railroading has inspired an astonishing output of
learned monographs on rolling stock, locomotive parts, machine tools, couplings, switches, tunnels, bridges, and so forth; an equally prodigious number
of annual reports, stock prospectuses, operating statements, and the like; and
a mountainous accumulation of legal opinions, waivers, claims, contracts, regulations, congressional hearings, commission findings, grand jury indictments,
and other more or less tedious public documents.

Along with all this recondite, technical material, there are countless
millions of words in the language of laymen and in the form of travelers'

journals, company histories, novels, biographies, short stories, ballads, poems, and plays, not to mention guidebooks, timetables, anniversary brochures, souvenir pamphlets, rule books, instruction manuals, and advertisements.

Unfortunately, a huge amount of this written matter, including most of the fiction, is flat and stale and lifeless. Frank P. Donovan, the most diligent bibliographer of American railroading, undertook several years ago to survey "The Railroad in Literature," and he concluded that the four all-time outstanding writers of American railroad fiction were Cy Warman, Frank H. Spearman, Francis Lynde, and Frank L. Packard. All of these men wrote strong, authentic novels and short stories, but none is in the class of Nathaniel Hawthorne, Walt Whitman, Herman Melville, or Mark Twain. More important, the masters of the "Railroad School" of fiction are not even in the class of the lesser writers who formalized the myths of the cowboy, the Indian, the gunfighter, and the frontier marshal. The best novels of the "Railroad School" have been out of print for decades and have vanished from most library shelves. The best short stories, alas, are as dated as the dusty back files of the magazines they appeared in: *McClure's, Munsey's, Collier's, American,* and the *Saturday Evening Post.*

What happened, according to Donovan, is that a minor sort of "golden age" of railroad fiction flourished between about 1890 and 1910. Then, as automobiles came into general use, editors and writers lost interest in stories about

A breakdown sometimes interrupted a routine run.

George's *Forty Years on the Rail,* 1887

the lives of railroad men. The railroad genre went out of style and never revived. In fact, the whole subject of railroading remained almost moribund until the late 1940's, when publishers sensed the growing interest of locomotive buffs, historians, and antiquarians, and began again to publish railroad lore.

Still, it would take more than a mere change of fashion to account for the chronic inadequacy of railroad literature. Volumes and volumes appear nowadays on the subject of locomotives, short lines, main lines, and parlor cars. But on the subject of the railroad man—practically nothing. One is forced to the conclusion that there must be some intrinsic quality in railroading itself that has resisted literary exploitation.

Perhaps the problem is that working on the railroad, unlike cowpunching or administering pistol justice, is a complex business. Its patterns have been shaped by such intangible forces as social caste, tradition, regulations, and the interplay of men and machines within the structure of large corporations. These elements do not lend themselves to facile literary interpretation, nor can they easily be boiled down into simple tales of confrontation between good and evil, personified by men in white hats and black hats.

Not only is railroading technically and socially complicated, it also is relatively monotonous. Dramatic incidents do occur: a new line is built across the continent, surmounting enormous obstacles; a winter storm swoops down on the prairie, stranding a passenger train; armed bandits raid a baggage car; a locomotive races against time to save the life of a child; an engineer ties down his whistle, orders his fireman to jump, and murmurs a prayer as the cab disintegrates into a seething cloud of flame. But these are isolated moments in a vast routine of quiet runs and ordinary days. A railroad, after all, is a means of transportation, not a chivalric battlefield. The sound and smell of the locomotive, the thunder of wheels, and the panorama of changing scenery are exciting to a romantic passenger; but the internal dynamics of the railroad business are precise, prosaic, and repetitive.

Then, too, the railroad man himself (excepting, of course, the Brave Engineer of fable) seems to lack the solitary, fatalistic, picaresque code of behavior that gives a heroic dimension to the cowboy. Railroad men are conservative and fraternal. Their community life is introverted, closely woven, and deep-dyed with tradition. To an old-fashioned railroader, honor consists in starting young and working one's way up the ladder. In the Age of Steam, it was axiomatic that the best locomotive engineers previously had been firemen, the best conductors had risen from brakemen, and the best executives had started at the bottom as callboys, telegraphers, switchmen, or section hands. Railroading was not a temporary pastime for soldiers of fortune but a lifetime commitment for strong, dedicated men.

At his worst, the old-time railroader was a narrow-minded, unimaginative functionary, more frightened of being fired than of dying in a flaming wreck. He had worked for the railroad since his early boyhood, and he had never known another career. Isolated in some small town or shabby, brick-paper neighborhood surrounding the divisional terminal, he lived in psychological exile from the general American community, chained to his job, a Babbitt-on-wheels. To challenge the traditional assumptions and practices of railroading was unthinkable; to desert the railroad was impossible.

While these institutional qualities of railroad men—including respect

Flagging in winter was uncomfortable and unromantic.

Clarke's *The American Railway,* 1897

for authority, conformity to routine, and pride in technical skill—are admirably suited to the business of moving vehicles, they make for a formidably exclusive profession that is proof against the intrusion of literary men. A would-be writer could become an expert in the landmarks and lingo of the Alaska gold rush, for example, by spending a few months in the Klondike. Without the need of any long apprenticeship, he could join a wagon train, a fishing boat, a lumber camp, or an autumn roundup. The railroad, on the other hand, was far out of reach. If you were willing to peddle peanuts in the day coaches or drive spikes along the roadbed, you could work a short hitch on some great trunk line across the western plains; but your experience was not likely to provide a quick initiation into the mysteries of the profession. Railroading was too thick to be devoured by an ambitious young man just out of college.

As a result of these intrinsic peculiarities of the railroad profession, the American trainman passed through the Age of Steam, his era of greatest importance, relatively unsung. Most of the material that masqueraded as "railroad fiction" was pseudo-literature, peopled by stock characters who moved mechanically through a railroad setting that was as thin and flat as the scenery of a play. The so-called trainmen of fiction were really cowboys or Indians, dressed in oily coveralls and red bandannas, mouthing railroad slang, and falling in love with petal-cheeked Pullman passengers. When the railroad genre went out of fashion, the cowboys climbed back into the saddle, the Indians boarded biplanes, and nobody noticed the difference. Only two characters out of the whole marvelous adventure of railroading remained clearly defined in the public mind: the ruthless railroad promoter and the fearless railroad engineer.

Now, having admitted that good railroad literature is rare and scattered, the editor of this volume of reminiscences would like to add hastily—all-in-one-breath-before-you-go-away—that such literature is by no means nonexistent. At about the time that Dr. Commager was bemoaning the scarcity of railroad folklore, three excellent books were published, each contributing proof that there was an abundance of anecdote and legend lying around, waiting to be gathered and retold: Stewart H. Holbrook's *The Story of American Railroads* (1947), Freeman H. Hubbard's *Railroad Avenue* (1945), and B. A. Botkin and Alvin F. Harlow's *Treasury of Railroad Folklore* (1953). Each of these books is the work of an editor, historian, or folklorist with a lively talent for picking out the best stories in American railroad history and presenting them accurately and well. One does not have to be a railroad buff or an afficionado of American history to find them fascinating.

Still, it seems to me that no editor has yet pursued the simple course of letting the American railroad man tell his historic story in his own way; and that is what I have tried to do in this book. *Workin' on the Railroad* is nothing more or less than a carefully selected scrapbook of personal memories of old days on the railroad. To find these reminiscences, I have had to dig back into sources that were long neglected or overlooked: diaries, autobiographies, magazine articles, after-dinner speeches, local histories. I have avoided the stories of once-in-a-lifetime exploits and have sought out recollections of the everyday life of railroaders. That daily routine was often exciting enough to bristle up the hair on the back of your neck, and, viewed with our present wisdom, appears to have been considerably wilder than is the daily routine of an astronaut. Several pieces of putative "fiction" got into the book because they clearly were based on observed fact; and two or three on-the-scene reports by non-railroad people qualified because it seemed to me that the writers had captured the flavor of a unique experience.

As autobiographers, the railroad men in this book turn out to be a little grumpy, distinctly braggy, and exceedingly hard-boiled. Charm does not flow out of them like holy chrism as it does when actresses, trial lawyers, and professional football players sit down to the tape recorder in the presence of well-trained ghost-writers. Even when the guiding hand of the ghost is visible in these selections (and it is obvious here and there), the grimy knuckles of the real railroad man always show through. This is a tough life, a long day, "a game that calls for all the stuff a man has in him," as one locomotive manufacturer puts it.

Most of the stories are what you might call "grandfather tales." They reek the odors of the past: coal smoke and waiting-room ink, spittoons and dried apple pie. Reading them, one feels himself drawn backward into the tightly ordered, masculine society of the railroad. Even though the writer of the piece may be a "boomer," drifting six months here and six months there; one senses the grip of the railroad upon him. He drifts within a stratified community, like the army, the diplomatic corps, or the ranks of a large, paternalistic corporation. The influence of the railroad is stronger upon him than that of a personal god; and he has more in common with a man of his own calling from across the country than he does with the grocery clerk next door.

Inarticulate? Well, yes. These are the ruminations of telegraphers, porters, and section hands.

Harsh and callous? Yes, that too. Early railroading was almost unbearably uncomfortable and dangerous. Death haunted the switchyards, the icy tracks, the slippery car tops, the moving couplers with their lethal link-and-pin clasps. To be crippled, scalded, crushed between the cars—this was the future that waited for the average trainman. For the surveyor and the construction worker, fate was an Indian arrow, a blizzard, a landslide, a stroke of blinding sun.

But romantic? Yes, truly these are romantic tales. For if railroading was inaccessible, complex, and cold-blooded to outsiders, it remained for three-quarters of a century or more the most glamorous adventure on earth for the men who built the tracks and ran the trains. The long-drawn whistle of a passing freight called hundreds of thousands of small-town boys from the hills and prairies, and the reality of working on the railroad seldom disappointed those who survived its hazards. That reality is still alive and visible to anyone who will look at old-time railroading through the eyes of those who lived it.

Scribner's Monthly, 1888

Three Witnesses at the Birth of the Iron Horse

I

*"I had never run a locomotive or any other
engine before; I have never run one since;
but on that eighth of August, 1829, I was
the first locomotive engineer on this continent."*

SEVERAL YEARS AGO a weekly magazine that dotes on quaint and picturesque detail made a conscientious effort to pin down the origins of Santa Claus—not Nicholas of Myra, the Christian saint, but Jolly Old St. Nick, the Santa Claus of commerce, the bearded New Amsterdam burgher who works in department stores at Christmas time.

The results of the search were disappointing. Apparently, no contemporary witness foresaw the extraordinary development of the Santa Claus profession when it was only a merry twinkle in a sales manager's eyes. Nobody took notes, drew a sketch, or summoned the newspapers. The only way to fix the date of Santa's installation in the toy department is to work backwards, as lexicographers do in establishing the age of a word.

Fortunately for thousands of writers, mural painters, anthology-gatherers, and other seekers after historic truth, this sort of indifference did not greet the first manifestation of professional railroading in North America. On the contrary, nearly everyone who was remotely involved in the advent of the Iron Horse (or "steam pot," as canalboat men and stage drivers contemptuously called it) realized that this event might be the start of the millennium. Unlike the department store Santa, the American railroad man came on strong, accompanied by cannon fire and whistles and libations of rum punch. The only difficulty one finds in tracing him back to his roots is to select the most authentic claimant out of an embarrassing richness of "firsts."

Did the first railroad man appear in the person of Oliver Evans of Philadelphia, who built the First Steam-Propelled Carriage in America in 1804?* Or was he actually Colonel John Stevens of Hoboken, New Jersey, whose rack-rail engine was the First Steam Machine to Carry Passengers on a Track in the United States in 1825?

Was the primordial railroader a hostler on the three-mile, wooden-tracked, horse-drawn, granite-hauling line between the quarries at Quincy, Massachusetts, and the banks of the Neponset River, over which the builders of the Bunker Hill Monument lugged blocks of stone to Boston in 1826? Or was he one of the promoters of the Mohawk & Hudson between Albany and Schenectady, the First Railroad to Be Chartered (although not the first to be built) in America in 1826?

Granting that each of these pioneers deserves (and undoubtedly has received) a monument, suitably inscribed, one still can maintain that *the* very first American railroad man, symbolically at least, was a young civil engineer named Horatio Allen, not long out of Columbia College, who had the sense to see that the future of transportation lay with some peculiar steam-powered vehicles then being tested in the coalfields of northern England and who crossed the Atlantic in midwinter to find out what was going on.

Horatio Allen had been working as a resident engineer on the Delaware & Hudson Canal, a great commercial venture of the day. The Delaware & Hudson would carry anthracite coal (a somewhat rare commodity) from the mines at Carbondale, in northeastern Pennsylvania, to the Hudson River and New York. When the chief engineer of the project, John B. Jervis, decided to build a pair of rails between the coalfields and the western end of the canal, he commissioned the twenty-five-year-old resident engineer to buy iron tracks and experimental locomotives in England.

Allen left for Liverpool in January, 1828. Within two weeks after reaching England, he found his way to the office of George Stephenson, the prophet and fanatic of steam locomotion. Stephenson was chief engineer of the Liverpool & Manchester Railroad, then under construction, and he was doing his best to introduce self-propelled steam locomotives on the line, over the objections of advocates of horsepower, mule power, stationary engines, canvas sails, canal barges, and staying-at-home. Stephenson cheerfully welcomed a Yankee convert and sent young Allen around to look at crude installations of track among the English collieries.

Although Allen found ample evidence of the practicality of locomotives, he also ran into a good deal of disagreement over how locomotives should be

---

*Its horrible name was Oructor Amphibolis—sometimes, even more repulsively, *Eructor Amphibolis*—and it was used to power a river dredge.

constructed. He concluded it would be sensible to order two models from Stephenson, to be built at Newcastle, and one from John U. Rastrick, to be built at Stourbridge.

More than fifty years later, Allen recounted the results of his experiment:

HE THREE LOCOMOTIVES arrived in New York in the winter of 1828–29. One of each type was set up with the wheels raised off the ground, and every operation except onward motion was fully tested.

But it was not until spring that we could have access to the railroad track at Honesdale, Pennsylvania, the head of the canal, for river and canal were closed by ice. During the winter, therefore, I resumed my connection with the Delaware & Hudson Canal Company in a new capacity—giving testimony before the legislature of the state of New York in behalf of a $300,000 loan to complete the construction of the railroad.

When the time came at last for one of the locomotives to be dispatched from New York by river and canal to Honesdale, it was the *Stourbridge Lion,* the engine built by Foster, Rastrick & Co., that was sent. This locomotive had received its name because of the fancy of its painter, who had embellished the circular, slightly convex surface of the boiler end with the brightly colored head of a lion.

How it happened that the *Stourbridge Lion* was chosen for this crucial test I do not know. It is to be regretted that one of the Stephenson locomotives was not sent, for these were prototypes of the locomotive *Rocket,* whose performance in October of the same year astonished the world. Had one of the Stephenson engines been selected, the feat of the *Rocket* would have been anticipated in the United States.*

Being at liberty in July and August from my other engineering work, I volunteered to go to Honesdale and take charge of transferring the *Stourbridge Lion* from the canalboat to the railroad track, which was some twenty feet inland and eighteen feet above the level of the canal. From this point, the railroad ran straight for about six hundred feet, parallel with the canal, then crossed Lackawaxen Creek on trestlework that formed a curve nearly a quarter of a mile long. After the curve the line ran almost straight into the woods of Pennsylvania. The rails were six-by-twelve inch hemlock timbers. On the surface of each rail was spiked the "track"—a bar of rolled iron, two-and-a-quarter inches wide and a half inch thick.

THE DELAWARE & HUDSON COMPANY chose a Saturday morning in midsummer for the trial run. Market-day crowds flocked into Honesdale to stare at

---

*Actually, Stephenson's famous *Rocket* was in many respects an improvement on the *America,* the first engine he had sent to New York. At the Rainhill trials beginning October 8, 1829, the *Rocket* went up to 24 miles an hour pulling a train and 60 miles an hour without a train. This celebrated machine is preserved in London's South Kensington Museum.

the strange, horizontal boiler-on-wheels with its tall smokestack, its two angular grasshopper beams, and its bizarre red lion's head, like the sign in front of some English tavern. The townspeople set up a cannon to salute the monster. After a few rounds, the artillery piece exploded, mutilating the arm of one of the men in command.

W HILE THE LOCOMOTIVE was being lifted in midair between the canalboat and the road, we had an opportunity to see that the axles had an unyielding position. There was no kingbolt that would allow the axles to swing when the locomotive was passing round the curve. The four wheels, holding their rigid position, were to be forced round the curve by the power of the engine. The locomotive also impressed the lookers-on by its great weight. [It weighed seven tons.]

Under these circumstances, the lookers-on concluded the road would break down under the weight of the locomotive or else the train would derail on the curve and hurtle off the trestle into the creek, thirty feet below.

On my part, I knew that the road would carry the locomotive safely. It was too late to consider the possibility of disaster. There was no other course but to have a trial made of the strange animal that had been brought there at great expense.

When the steam had reached the right pressure and all was ready, I took my position on the platform of the locomotive alone, placing my hand on the throttle valve handle, and told the other men it was not necessary that the life and limbs of more than one should be subjected to any danger. Having no doubts about the railroad, I would take the ride entirely alone. I knew the time would come when I should look back with great interest to the ride that was now before me.

I was at first undecided whether to move slowly or with a fair degree of speed. But preferring, if we did go down, to go handsomely and without any evidence of timidity, I started with considerable velocity. The locomotive, having no train behind it, answered at once to the movement of my hand on the throttle valve. Without showing any evidence of distrust, I ran the straight line, reached the curve, and passed it before there was time to think of its safety. Soon I was out of sight on the three miles' ride through the woods.

After losing the cheers of the lookers-on, the only sound I heard was the exhaust steam and the creaking of the timber structure under the wheels. I had never run a locomotive or any other engine before; I have never run one since; but on that eighth of August, 1829, I was the first locomotive engineer on this continent—and not only engineer, but fireman, brakeman, conductor, and passenger.

I ran that locomotive three miles out and three miles back and stopped it at the starting place.

Over fifty years later I revisited the scene of that first ride. I walked over it in the early morning so that nothing should interfere with the thoughts and feelings that rose to the surface, bringing me recollections of the past, realization of the present, and anticipation of the future. It was a morning of wonderful beauty, and that walk will hold its place in my memory beside that lone ride more than half a century before.

—Adapted from Horatio Allen's reminiscences, "The First Five Years of the Railroad Era," in *Railroad Gazette*, New York, April 4 and 11, 1884.

ALTHOUGH THE *Stourbridge Lion* had passed its test without taking the life of Horatio Allen (he lived to age ninety-seven), the directors of the Delaware & Hudson were not convinced that their railroad was suited to the steam locomotive—or it to their road. After a few more trials, they ran the awkward engine off the tracks and left it standing forlornly beside the canal; and Horatio Allen went down to Charleston to take up his new duties as chief engineer on the ambitious South Carolina Railroad, which was just getting started on its 136-mile course from the sea to the Savannah River.

At the approach of winter, the company had a shed built over the *Lion*. But curious visitors tore away planks to peek at the relic inside, souvenir-hunters carried off valves, and rain blew in on the driving rods. For fourteen years, the *Lion* rusted there. Finally, the company consigned the sturdy boiler to the repair shops in Carbondale, where it supplied steam for a stationary engine; and when even the boiler was rusted out, it went to the scrap heap.

When Horatio Allen was eighty-one, he reexamined the assembled scraps of the *Lion* at an exhibition of railroad equipment in Chicago. He was astonished to find that John Rastrick had built the boiler on entirely different principles from those he had agreed to follow.

As for the Stephenson engines, mouldering in a warehouse in New York, Allen lost track of them, the Delaware & Hudson forgot them, and their remains have disappeared from history.

Oliver Evans's Oructor Amphibolis (1804) was an ancestor of the steam locomotive.

*At the Maryland Institute, John Latrobe lectured on
the beginnings of the Baltimore & Ohio Railroad.*

King's *The Southern States*, 1875

II

*"No one dreamed of steam upon the road.
Horses were to do the work."*

HORATIO ALLEN'S lone ride, like the space trip of the first astronaut 140 years later, depended upon the work of many other men. Railroads never were built by solitary geniuses in attic laboratories but by stock companies, committees of bankers, ambitious town councils, well-greased legislatures, and cabals of prosperous merchants with friends in Washington, D.C. Never has this communal aspect of railroading been more obvious than in the early days of the Baltimore & Ohio Railroad, the first general freight and passenger line in America.

The B&O was the forlorn hope of a community of merchants who were trying to resist commercial stagnation. This group of Baltimore businessmen had begun to sense in the mid-1820's that their city was being squeezed out of the rich trade developing in the new lands west of the Alleghenies—even though Baltimore was farther west than the rival ports of New York and Philadelphia. The problem was transportation. In 1825, the Erie Canal had opened, linking New York and the Hudson Valley to the shores of the Great Lakes at Buffalo. Philadelphia, too, had developed an east-west canal. But the syndics of Baltimore discovered, to their dismay, that it would be prohibitively expensive to build a canal of their own. In desperation, they turned to the new and untried technology of the rails: they would build a set of tracks three hundred miles long, from Chesapeake Bay to the banks of the Ohio River.

Among the enthusiasts who helped draft the charter for the Baltimore & Ohio in 1827 was a brilliant, twenty-four-year-old lawyer named John Hazelhurst Boneval Latrobe, whose father had been a successful architect and whose brother was later to be chief engineer of the B&O. Using the charters of old turnpike companies as a model, Latrobe worked with other lawyers to shape the legal framework of the greatest enterprise Baltimore had ever attempted. In March, 1827, the company was in business, with a capital of $1.5 million.

A year later, Latrobe was retained by the railroad to negotiate rights-of-way; and from then until his death in 1891, he was connected with the B&O.

For sixty years or so he served as the railroad's general counsel, finding time also to write books and speeches, paint landscapes, invent a patented stove, design monuments, found an African colonization society for freed slaves, establish the Maryland Institute, sit on innumerable boards and commissions, and father eight children.

When he looked back upon the beginnings of the B&O, John Latrobe remembered, above all, the naive enthusiasm of a simpler day.

E VERYBODY WANTED STOCK. Parents subscribed in the names of their children and paid the dollar on each share that the rules prescribed. Before a survey had been made—even before common sense had been consulted— the possession of stock was regarded as a provision for old age; and great was the scramble to obtain it. The excitement in Baltimore roused public attention elsewhere, and a railroad mania began to pervade the land.

Then came the surveys. Jonathan Knight, the chief engineer of the greatest work in the country, the National Road from Washington to Wheeling, was brought into the service of the new company. Engineers from the United States Army brought West Point to bear upon the road; and a mission of engineers was sent to England. Everything was done with an eager enthusiasm that was unexampled even in our enterprising annals. The directors gratified their subscribers by permitting them to double their stock.

And yet, with the best skill of the country at work, the vaguest ideas prevailed. I well remember lending a hand in the preparation of a drawing suggested by one of the engineers, showing how the railroad would cross the mountains. A double track was to be constructed up and down the slope as straight as an arrow. The upper end of one set of tracks would be close to a stream, which was to be used to fill water cars. The weight of these, as they descended on one track, would drag up the passenger cars on the other track, the two trains being connected by a rope passing around a pulley at the summit. At the bottom of the mountain, the water cars were to be emptied; but the engineer had forgotten to provide a way for getting them back to the top for the next trip. Nonetheless, with some facility in watercolors, I put down the notions of the distinguished gentleman in as florid a style of art as the modern illustrations of Jack the Giant Killer.

On the Fourth of July, 1828, in bright sunshine, a glittering procession assembled to bury the cornerstone of the railroad where Mount Clare Station now covers acres of ground with shops and enginehouses. First came the Masons with banners and music. Then came the trades with anvils ringing, types setting, vats smoking, labor of all kind in full operation, and banners and music, too. Then came the good ship *Constitution* with sails set, streamers floating, and guns run out. Then came Charles Carroll of Carrollton, the last surviving signer of the Declaration of Independence: a spare, attenuated old man, verging on four score years and ten, small in size but active in his movements, with eyes still bright and sparkling, and a voice now thin and feeble, but clear and distinct. In emphatic utterances, this venerable and venerated man prophesied the success of the great work on whose cornerstone he struck the gavel and applied the square.

THE B&O's ground-breaking ceremonies set high standards for pomp and ingenuity. On horse-drawn floats, millers ground wheat, stonecutters chipped granite, and brewers brewed brew. During the procession, the guild of weavers manufactured a bolt of cloth which the tailors then fashioned into a coat that was presented to Charles Carroll of Carrollton as he hefted his dedicatory spade.

Turning to a friend at his side, the ninety-year-old statesman remarked: "I consider this among the most important acts of my life, second only to my signing of the Declaration of Independence, if second even to that."

That night, Baltimore resounded with toasts and songs, but it was observed that Charles Carroll of Carrollton, while visiting a model ship that had been rigged up as a bar, sipped only water.

A S SOON AS the grading was completed for a mile west of Mount Clare, the iron strap, then called a rail, was laid down, and a car built, not unlike a country market wagon without a top. In this car Charles Carroll of Carrollton, Alexander Brown, William Patterson, Philip E. Thomas, other directors of the company, and leading citizens of Baltimore made trips forward and backward, drawn by a single horse and filled with the elation of boys lucky enough to secure a ride on the platform of a passenger car as it passes along the streets. After the directors were served, the public was permitted to enjoy the same luxury, at (if I recollect aright) twelve-and-a-half cents a head, round trip.

In the beginning, no one dreamed of steam upon the road. Horses were to do the work. Even after the line was completed to Frederick, relays of horses trotted the cars from place to place. In this way, the Relay House, at the junction of the Washington Branch, obtained its name. One of the early locomotives was known as a "horsepower." A horse was placed in a car and made to walk on an endless belt that communicated to the wheels. The machine worked, after a fashion; but on one occasion, when drawing a car filled with editors and representatives of the press, it ran into a cow. The passengers, after having been tilted out and rolled down an embankment, were, naturally enough, unanimous in condemning the contrivance.

Following the horsepower car came the *Meteor*, a sailing vehicle, the invention of Evan Thomas. It required a good gale to drive it and would run only when the wind was what sailors call "abaft" or on the quarter. Head winds were fatal to it, and Mr. Thomas was afraid to trust a strong side wind lest the *Meteor* might upset. So it rarely made its appearance unless a northwester was blowing, when it would be dragged out to the farther end of the Mount Clare embankment and come back, literally, with flying colors.

A great desideratum of the railroad was to reduce the friction of the axles. Ross Winans made his appearance in Baltimore and instantly became a celebrity with his friction wheel, an ingenious and beautiful contrivance. I can remember as though it were yesterday seeing Charles Carroll of Carrollton, who was the great man on all great occasions in Baltimore, seated on Winans' little car in one of the upper rooms of the Exchange, being drawn by a ridiculously small weight attached to a string passing over a pulley and dropping into the hall below. Around him were all the prominent men in Baltimore, as pleased as children with a new toy. In fact, there was a verdant freshness about railroad things in those days that is wonderful to recollect.

Not only was friction to be avoided in the cars, but the road itself became the subject of experiment. Miles and miles of iron straps were laid on stone curbs, to the great edification of the public. To ride in a railroad car in those days was to go literally thundering along. The roll of the wheels on stone and iron was almost deafening. In due season it was discovered that the wheels were hammering the iron straps out of existence. When this became known, after tens of thousands of dollars had been thrown away, one of the directors (a man of general information) proposed to lay a thin slab of lead between the iron and the stone to relieve the concussion. Luckily, this costly experiment, which would have furnished the sportsmen of the interior with slugs and bullets without cost, was not carried into effect.

When steam made its appearance on the Liverpool & Manchester Railroad, it attracted great attention here. But there was this difficulty about introducing an English engine on an American road: An English road was virtually straight, whereas an American road had curves of as small a radius as two hundred feet. There was not capital enough in the United States to justify engineers in defying nature. If a tunnel could be avoided, the tunnel was postponed and a circuitous route adopted, although the distance was increased in consequence; similarly, embankments were avoided by heading valleys instead of crossing them. This led to sharp curves here, where there would have been straight lines in England.

For a brief season, it was believed that this feature of the early American roads would prevent the use of locomotive engines. The contrary was demonstrated by a gentleman who was later distinguished for his private worth and public benefactions, one of those to whom wealth seems to have been granted by Providence that men might know how wealth could be used to benefit one's fellow-creatures: Peter Cooper of New York. Mr. Cooper believed that steam might be adapted to the curved roads which he saw would be built in the United States and that the reciprocating motion of a steam cylinder could be converted to rotary motion without a crank. He built an engine called *Tom Thumb* to demonstrate both articles of his faith; and this was the first locomotive for railroad purposes ever built in America.

—From "The Baltimore & Ohio Railroad Company: Personal Recollections," a lecture before the Maryland Institute, delivered by John H. B. Latrobe on March 23, 1868.

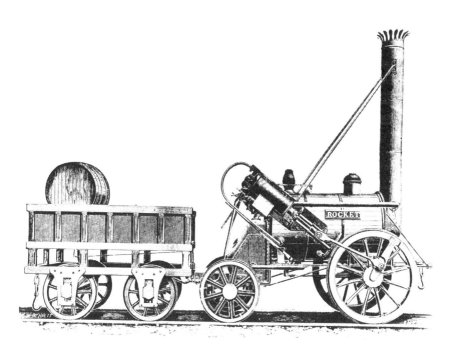

Rastick's Stourbridge Lion *(top) and Stephenson's*
Rocket *proved the practicality of railroad locomotives.*

Scientific American, 1894 and 1897

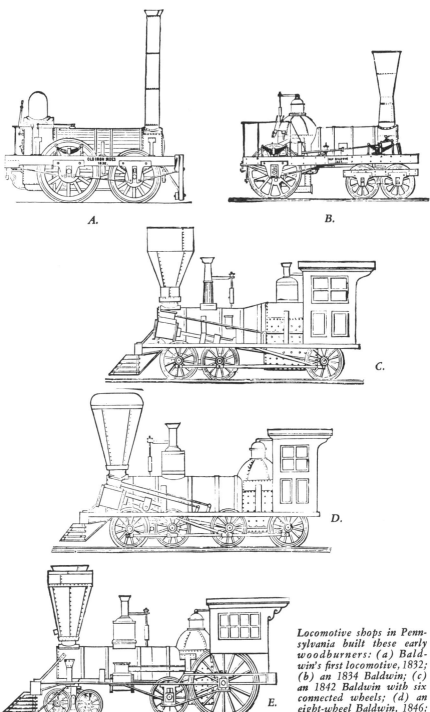

A.

B.

C.

D.

E.

Locomotive shops in Pennsylvania built these early woodburners: (a) Baldwin's first locomotive, 1832; (b) an 1834 Baldwin; (c) an 1842 Baldwin with six connected wheels; (d) an eight-wheel Baldwin, 1846; (e) Baldwin's fast passenger engine, 1848.

Scientific American, 1884

III

*"Insignificant as that little engine was,
we made the trip of thirteen miles
in an hour and twelve minutes."*

DURING THE COURSE of his ninety-two years, Peter Cooper lived half a dozen abundant lives. He was a prolific inventor, an imaginative businessman, a multi-millionaire, a philanthropist and educator (he founded the Cooper Union of New York), the patriarch of a talented, public-spirited family, a beloved civic figure in his native city.

Born in 1791, when New York was a sprightly town of twenty-seven thousand at the foot of Manhattan Island, he lived to see the largest and most important city in the Western Hemisphere crowding from central Long Island to the New Jersey marshes. His business career was a series of daring adventures: he was successively a hatter, a carriage-builder, a machinist, machine-maker, grocer, iron-founder, glue manufacturer, real estate developer, and the promoter and financial backer of the Atlantic cable. His inventions, like those of Benjamin Franklin, were protean, eccentric, marvelous: a mechanism to harness the currents of the East River to run machinery; a chain-power system for the Erie Canal; a shore-controlled torpedo boat for the Greek insurgents of 1821; an aerial freight cable; a method for mortising the hubs of wheels; a machine to drive a ferry boat by compressed air; a contrivance for shearing the nap from cloth; a device that simultaneously rocked a cradle, fanned away flies, and played a lullaby.

But no single invention or enterprise with which Peter Cooper was associated—excepting possibly the founding of Cooper Union—brought him so much lasting fame as the experimental engine he built for the Baltimore & Ohio Railroad. As a recent biographer commented: "The whole episode was characteristic of him in a dozen ways. He entered it partly, as he says, as a purely business proposition to save his investment, partly to test out his favorite scheme for changing rectilinear to rotary motion, and partly, in the spirit of adventure, to see if he couldn't solve a practical problem that was baffling others. He carried it out almost entirely by himself, pitting his ingenuity—he calls it his 'knack of contriving'—and his craftmanship against established theories and routine practice. And he remained the amateur to the end: his locomotive was frankly an experiment, never intended to be run as a working engine on the line."*

T
OM THUMB was a very little, insignificant locomotive that I made, I think, in the year 1829.†

At about that time, I had been drawn into a speculation in Baltimore with two men who represented that they had very large means. We bought together three thousand acres of land, extending some three miles along Fells Point Dock on the north side of the harbor at Baltimore. After I had been in partnership with them a little while and had paid my portion of the purchase money (we bought the whole tract for $105,000), I found that they had paid nothing and that I was even then paying their board bills.

I insisted at once that they either pay up or sell out. I was willing to buy or sell, whichever they chose. They could not buy, and so, after a good deal of bargaining, one man was induced to take ten thousand dollars for his share, which I paid to him at once. The other, after a while, agreed to go out for a little less.

After purchasing their interests, however, I had an elephant on my hands. The question was what to do with it.

At the same time, the Baltimore & Ohio Railroad Company, which had started with high expectations of fortune, had run into trouble. I can remember Mr. William Patterson's telling me that the company had expected the road to be so prodigal in its returns that they could afford to make the rails of silver. Instead, they found at the end of one year that they had spent their first 5 percent of capital and had demonstrated only that they must change the location of their road to avoid the short turns they had adopted to save expense. They had learned from their own experience, as well as from the opinions of competent engineers from England, that no road could be successfully run with locomotives on which there were curves of less than 300 feet radius. On the Baltimore & Ohio, they had curves of 150 to 200 feet radius, and there were many of them.

The company was plunged into despair, and the principal stockholders determined that they would no longer pay the assessment on their stock. In the abandonment of that railroad, I saw the defeat of my own enterprise, for the growth of the city of Baltimore depended upon the success of that road, and I had purchased that tract of land to take advantage of the rapid growth of the city. If the Baltimore & Ohio could not use locomotives on the road they had constructed, my land was not likely to be of much value for a long time to come. So I told the president and a few of the directors that if they would hold on and not

---

*Edward C. Mack, *Peter Cooper, Citizen of New York*, Duell, Sloan & Pearce, New York, 1949; p. 109.

†It was 1830.

sacrifice their stock, I would put together a small locomotive that could pull a train around those curves.

I happened to have in my factory a peculiar kind of an engine that I had gotten up to experiment with an idea that is perhaps worth noticing. I had the idea that there must be a very great loss attending the application of steam power by a crank. In my opinion, the steam piston could be made to transmit its power directly into rotary motion without the use of a crank. To test this, I had had a small brass engine made, with a 3¼-inch bore and 14-inch stroke. When the engine was completed, I got permission to try it in comparison with another engine that was being used to bore a steam cylinder. Whenever the shackle bar was thrown off the large engine, my little engine would take over the work and go on with it. There was an English engineer standing by, waiting to see the experiment, and when he saw the larger engine stopping and the other going on with the work, he remarked that if anybody should ever have told him that this little engine would carry that work, he would have told them they knew nothing about mechanics. And when he saw the engine actually working he said, "I now see that we shall cross the ocean in six days by the power of steam."

Afterwards, I took that little engine from the Sterling Works in Stanton Street, in New York, and used it in my factory for pumping water and other purposes.

When I found it necessary to do something to encourage the construction of the Baltimore & Ohio Railroad, I took the small engine, frame and all, to Baltimore, where I went into a coachmaker's shop [the B&O's Mount Clare railroad shop] and got permission to build a locomotive. I got some boiler iron and made a boiler about as high as an ordinary wash boiler. How to connect the boiler with the engine, I didn't know. I couldn't find any iron pipes. The fact was, there were none for sale in this country. So I took two muskets, broke off the wooden parts, and used the barrels for tubing, one on one side and the other on the other side of the boiler. I called this locomotive the *Tom Thumb*, because it was so insignificant. I didn't intend it for actual service, but only to show the directors what could be done.

One Saturday evening, just about sundown, I got up steam, ready to make a start. The president of the road, Philip E. Thomas, and one or two other gentlemen stepped onto the locomotive, and we went out a few miles and returned. This was the first effort I had made with *Tom Thumb*, and the only one I made with the engine in that particular shape. On Monday morning, I found that some unprincipled person had got in and wrung off and stolen all the copper pipes!

It took me a week or more to repair the machine; then someone got in and broke a piece out of the wheel, experimenting with it; and then two wheels, cast one after another, were damaged by the carelessness of the turner. Thought I: the fates are against me! I was thoroughly disgusted and discouraged; but being determined that I would not be balked entirely, I changed the engine so that the power could be applied through the ordinary connection with a crank.

At last all was ready; and I again invited the directors to come and witness the start. I got thirty-six persons in one car. The locomotive carried six men, besides its own fuel and water. You would think that so small a cylinder would not be able to do the work, with a boiler only about as big as a flour barrel! I had feared that I would not be able to get enough steam out of that boiler, so I had attached a blower, such as you never saw, I guess, to a crooked joint on the top of the smokestack. From there I carried a belt down over a wheel on the shaft. When I got up enough speed, the belt ran a blower. I found that I had sufficient power to draw the shavings right through the boiler.

I acted as engineer. Before long, I found that the springs I had placed to govern the pressure of steam in the boiler were not strong enough. The steam was being blown to waste, and I was afraid all the water would go out of the boiler. Since I could not conveniently alter the safety valves, I took a wire that was on the engine, fastened the safety valves down, and held it there in my hand. No one can ever know the difficulties I encountered and the anxiety I passed through that day!

Insignificant as that little engine was, we made the trip of thirteen miles to Ellicott's Mills in an hour and twelve minutes, and we demonstrated that a locomotive could be made which could go around those short curves—the thing that I had set out to do. We had it downhill coming back and made the run in fifty-seven minutes.

—Collated from the manuscript "Reminiscences of Peter Cooper," in the Cooper Union, New York; and from Peter Cooper's address to the Master Mechanics Association of New York, May 12, 1875.

IV

"Away went horse and engine,
the snort of the one and the puff
of the other keeping time and tune."

JOHN LATROBE went out to the Mount Clare shops with the president, the treasurer, and other officers of the B&O to watch Peter Cooper raise steam in the boiler of the *Tom Thumb.* Cooper's "crank-substitute," which Latrobe could not properly describe nor precisely understand, made a clacking noise as the machine moved across the platform of the roundhouse—"a lilliputian affair, indeed, compared to the revolving platforms now in use." To the young Baltimore lawyer, the most impressive qualities of Cooper's invention were its feeble substance and its puny size.

THE MACHINE was not larger than the handcars used by workmen to transfer themselves from place to place. As I recall its appearance, my only wonder is that so apparently insignificant a contrivance should ever have been regarded as competent to the smallest results.

The boiler was not as large as the kitchen boiler attached to many a range in modern mansions. It stood upright in the car. The furnace occupied the lower section; the upper part was filled with vertical tubes. The cylinder was only three and one-half inches in diameter, and speed was gotten up by gearing.

On Mr. Cooper's first trip to Ellicott's Mills, an open car—the first used upon the road—was attached to his engine and filled with the directors and some friends, myself among the rest. We passed the curves without difficulty at a speed of fifteen miles an hour. We ascended the grades with comparative ease. The day was fine, the company in the highest spirits. Some of the excited gentlemen of the party pulled out memorandum books and, at the highest speed, which was eighteen miles an hour, wrote their names and some connected sentences to prove that it was possible to do so, even at that great velocity.

But the triumph of *Tom Thumb* was not altogether without a drawback. The great stage proprietors of the day, Stockton & Stokes, drove out from town on one occasion [September 18, 1830] with a gallant gray horse of great beauty and power attached to another car on the second track (for the company had made two tracks to the Mills). They met the engine at the Relay House on its way back. From this point it was determined to have a race home. The start was even. Away went horse and engine, the snort of the one and the puff of the other keeping time and tune. At first the gray had the best of it, for *his* steam would be applied to the greatest advantage on the instant. The horse was perhaps a quarter of a mile ahead when the safety valve of the engine lifted, and the thin blue vapor issuing from it showed an excess of steam. The blower whistled, the steam blew off in vapory clouds, the pace increased, the passengers shouted, and the engine gained on the horse. Soon it lapped him; the silk was plied; the race was neck and neck, nose and nose—then the engine passed the horse, and a great hurrah hailed the victory. But it was not repeated, for just at this time, when the gray's master was about giving up, the band that drove the pulley that drove the blower slipped off its drum. The safety valve ceased to scream, and the engine for want of breath began to wheeze and pant.

In vain Mr. Cooper, who was his own engineman and fireman, lacerated his hands in attempting to replace the band upon the wheel. In vain he tried to urge the fire with light wood. The horse gained on the machine and passed it; and, although the band was presently replaced, and steam again did its best, the horse was too far ahead to be overtaken. He came in the winner of the race.

But the ultimate victory was with Mr. Cooper, notwithstanding. He had held fast to the faith that was in him and had demonstrated its truth beyond per-adventure. In a patent cause, tried many years afterwards, the boiler of Mr. Cooper's engine became, in some connection that has been forgotten, important as a piece of evidence. It was hunted for and found among some old rubbish at Mount Clare. It was difficult to imagine that this boiler had even generated steam enough to drive a coffee mill, much less perform the feats here narrated.

—From "The Baltimore & Ohio Railroad: Personal Recollections," a lecture before the Maryland Institute, delivered by John H. B. Latrobe on March 23, 1868.

PETER COOPER never would admit defeat, even by a good gray horse. Half a century afterward, he said of *Tom Thumb's* humiliation: "They tried a little race one day, but it didn't amount to anything. It was rather funny; and the locomotive got out of gear."

When Baltimore celebrated its centennial in 1880, Peter Cooper, approaching ninety, rode in the festive parade with a model of the original *Tom Thumb*. The horse was not honored.

As for the B&O, it continued to entertain passengers with horse-drawn carriage rides for a few months, meanwhile advertising for full-size steam locomotives adapted to its curving route; and shortly, Phineas Davis, of York, Pennsylvania, began supplying working engines for the road.

The commercial objectives of the project were not so quickly attained. It was a quarter of a century before the tracks reached the Ohio River at Wheeling, West Virginia, and a decade after that before the B&O began to fulfill its great promise of profit and economic stimulation. By that time, the railroad had cost more than $31 million—considerably more than the total valuation of all the earthly goods in Baltimore.

Had the city fathers suspected how long it would take and how much it would cost to build an iron trail across the Alleghenies, they might all have given up and moved to New York.

CHAPTER TWO

Whale Oil, Pitch Pine, and Ingenuity

I

"To start with, I worked at seventeen dollars a month, which seemed a princely sum."

A FEW YEARS AGO, a group of American scholars made an effort to determine whether or not there is an historical analogy between the current space program and the development of railroads in the nineteenth century.[*]

As a starting premise, the professors agreed that the coming of railroads was a technological innovation that had radical consequences for all segments of society. The railroad profoundly affected the average person's attitudes toward space and time. It altered the political and economic structure of the country. It created new ways of business organization, changed the uses of manpower and money, and governed the geographic distribution of population until the automobile began to dominate American demography in the 1920's.

The question that had to be answered was, to what extent does history repeat itself? Does modern space technology bear any significant resemblance to the railroad technology of the past? If so, can we use the experience of the railroad to predict the social effects of space exploration?

As you might have expected, the results of the study turned out to be strong on historical data and weak on prognostication. Most of the professors admitted they knew more about economic history than they did about the Apollo moon shot. They hesitated to make comparisons and refused to make predictions.

---

[*]Their conclusions appear in *The Railroad and the Space Program: An Exploration in Historical Analogy*, edited by Bruce Mazlish, professor of history at the Massachusetts Institute of Technology, and published by the M.I.T. Press at Cambridge, Massachusetts, in 1965. The American Academy of Arts and Sciences sponsored the project under a grant of financial aid from the National Aeronautics and Space Administration.

But the group effort did serve a useful purpose. It documented the some-times forgotten fact that the development of the Iron Horse was more than just a series of daring and peculiar public appearances by Peter Cooper, Horatio Allen, and some quaint little engines that are now in museums. Rail-road building, from the beginning, was really a massive and serious enterprise. Like the space program, it required an immense national expenditure of energy and money. Its apparent quaintness is only an optical illusion caused by the mists of time.

Scientific wonders of the past seem odd and frivolous when you look back on them, like a flickering old film of horseless carriages, crank-operated tele-phones, and biplanes with paper fuselage; and our current advances in space, which appear to us incredibly marvelous, will look similarly crude and funny to our grandchildren. The early technicians of railroading took themselves and their work quite as seriously as do today's astronauts. The most talented engineers and businessmen on the continent were at work, trying to develop steam power into a magnificent means of transportation. Every person of scientific imagination knew that the railroad, properly equipped and managed, would surpass every existing form of movement. The only problem was to smooth out a few wrinkles in the track.

Take night operations, for example. It was Horatio Allen, the pilot of the *Stourbridge Lion,* who launched the first engine of the Charleston & Ham-burg Railroad into South Carolina's inky darkness, lighted by a pyramid of blazing pine knots piled on a mound of sand atop a flatcar and pushed along ahead of the locomotive.

Somebody else devised a simple hopper to dribble sand onto the track whenever the rails were slippery with oil drippings, frost, or the crushed bodies of grasshoppers. And still another resourceful mechanic, unforgettably named Isaac Dripps, found a solution to the problem of cattle on the tracks of the Camden & Amboy.

The C&A, which long ago became a minor spur of the Penn-Central, had suffered persistent interference from domestic animals. Once a hog got under a locomotive and was instantly decapitated, derailing the engine and shaking up the passengers, especially an unidentified man who turned a somersault out an open window. Isaac Dripps proposed to get rid of intrusive livestock by attaching a pair of outthrust, wrought-iron bars to the front of the engine to impale a wandering beast before it could slip under the wheels. This cow-prong worked so well that a bull was carried along for several hundred yards, wedged between the tines, and had finally to be removed with block and tackle. This encounter induced the inventor to modify his basic design into a sort of down-thrust metal comb, the predecessor of all the cowcatchers that later became standard equipment on American locomotives.

The need of a cowcatcher quickly became apparent.

George's *Forty Years on the Rail*, 1887

. . . so did the need of a wrecking crew.

Howland's *Steamboat Disasters*, 1840

It also was along the route of the Camden & Amboy that the enterprising children of Bordentown, New Jersey, made a significant technological advance in passenger comfort by selling hot bricks wrapped in blankets on winter days.

Without insisting that each of these accomplishments bears direct analogy to recent advances in space flight, one can suggest that they are at least small steps of man. Charles George, a long-time conductor on the Chicago & Northwestern, clearly remembered many such steps and recorded them in his memories of forty years as a railroad man:

IN 1847, when I was a country boy in my teens, I gathered a few dollars I had saved, said good-bye to my native village, and went to try my luck in the busy city of Boston. I found a place where I could lodge at ten cents a night and took my meals wherever I could get food cheapest. My money was gradually melting away, however, and my enthusiasm was on the wane when I ran across Charles Minot,* who had known me when he was practicing law in my hometown of Haverhill. Now he was superintendent of the Boston & Maine Railroad and was known as one of the most capable and progressive men in Massachusetts.

"Hello, Charley," he said. "When did you leave Haverhill? What are you here for?"

"Looking for something to do," I answered gloomily, "and I'm tired of asking for a place."

"Got any money?"

"Not very much."

"Cheer up, my boy," he said cheerily, slipping a five-dollar bill into my hand. "How would you like to be a railroad man?"

"Like it?" I echoed. "Just give me a chance, sir."

As a result of our meeting, I became baggagemaster of the train to Medford, about five miles out of Boston. To start with, I worked at seventeen dollars a month, which seemed a princely sum to a poor boy who had been walking about the streets, homeless and almost penniless, a few days before. In four or five months my salary was raised. I drew thirty-five dollars a month, and I felt richer than I ever have felt since.

In those days railroading had only started on its career. Our trains would be laughed at by the present generation, so accustomed to more scientific methods. Railroad cars were nothing more than stagecoaches on trucks, coupled together with chains. When the locomotive started, it took up the slack in the link chains

---

*Charles Minot was a trained lawyer who developed into one of the country's most imaginative railroad managers. Son of a justice of the Massachusetts Supreme Court, he became interested in the Boston & Maine Railroad during its construction period and took a job as a survey chain-carrier to learn engineering. He quickly advanced to a managerial position. In 1850 the nearly completed Erie Railroad, stretching from the Hudson River to the Great Lakes, hired him as general superintendent. Minot was probably the first railroad manager to use the Morse telegraph to control and direct train movements.

with a series of jerks that sent passengers headlong and caused many bruises. The original coaches had room for only four to six passengers inside and two outside on seats at each end. This plan was soon modified by building a car with the capacity of several coach bodies and dividing it into compartments with two transverse seats in each. The conductor collected fares by climbing along a footboard outside. It was hard to crowd more than twenty passengers into one of these boxes.

I can remember an excursion on the Fourth of July when many of these cars were used. They were lighted with whale oil lamps, which made the tops of the cars smoky and spattered the sides with grease. The seats were stiff and uncomfortable, covered with horsehair. Small sheet-iron stoves were used for heating, though many cars were without them. The only way to get a breath of fresh air was by opening the windows. To these discomforts were added showers of cinders and dense smoke, for early engines were without spark arresters. Flames often streamed back as far as the rear car. Pitch pine was largely used for fuel, and the amount of smoke, sparks, and cinders may be imagined.

Freight cars were called "burthen cars," and trains were known as "brigades." Freight cars were mere boxes, a little longer than wide, with a wheel at each corner. They had doors on each side, and we trainmen had to walk around the sides on a footboard, holding on by an iron rod running the whole length of the car. Freight cars were so small that we reported two as one, reporting a train of forty cars, for instance, as twenty. I remember a freight collision in 1849 when the cars were so small and light that many of them were thrown over a fence and scattered all over the neighboring farms.

The brakes of all cars were on top. The brakeman sat in that elevated position in a little cab, using a foot lever as is now used on omnibuses and heavy wagons.

It was before the days of telegraphy. In case of a breakdown or wreck, the only way help could be brought, or other trains warned, was by sending a handcar or a messenger.

The bell cord ran along the top of the cars and was wound on a reel. We had to climb up to the top, no matter how fast the train was running, to use the cord or adjust it in case of mishap.

Some of the old strap-rails were still in use on the Boston & Maine. These were wooden rails on which strap iron was spiked. The iron often curled up, owing to heat or frost, and when the wheels struck the end of one of these curved straps, the other end would be forced up through the bottom of the car. Passengers were often hurt by these "snakeheads," as they were called. We frequently had to stop and pound down the iron or hold it down until the train had passed over. The first iron rails were not much better. They were only twelve feet long and weighed just thirty to forty pounds a yard. A man on our road could lift two of them at once. Gradually they were made larger and heavier, and finally steel rails were introduced.

Railroad stations were mere sheds, open on two or more sides to wind and rain. A pine box, set by the side of the track to serve as a ticket case, often was the only landmark for a station. The little sheltering places built for the engines were playhouses. Sidetracks connected with the main track at one end only, and when we took a car out, we had to push it by hand. Switch engines had not been thought of.

On the Boston-Medford line we had a small, cabless engine, weighing about five tons. The train was made up of a single car, which was baggage and passenger car combined. Crude as our service was, however, out-of-town residents were eager to persuade railroads to stop at their nearby stations.

A little group of people who had settled about a mile out of Medford, or six miles from Boston, waited on Superintendent Minot one day with a request that he stop the train at their settlement. He refused, thinking the venture would not pay, but they persisted in their demand and declared they would make him stop his train whether he wanted to or not.

Next day, as we began to climb a heavy grade just outside Medford, the wheels of the engine slipped. After a moment or two, we came to a full stop where several of the settlers were standing. They jumped aboard while the engineer got out to investigate the cause of our delay. He found that the track had been smeared with molasses. He had to back up to get enough momentum to carry him over the hill. In the face of such persistence, there was no use trying to run past that station any longer.

Within a few months, I transferred to the Portland run of the Boston & Maine, and a few years later I became one of three conductors on the Western Vermont Railroad. The work was often hard, but seldom did it lack an element of fresh adventure.

My work on the Portland train was particularly heavy and fatiguing. In those days the baggagemaster had to take a turn at the brakes as often as the brakeman and to keep his own car clean, inside and out, as car cleaners were then unknown. The wheels had to be wiped with waste, which was no small task, splashed as they were with whale oil. Part of the baggageman's equipment was a long-nosed oil can, from which we had to oil the wheels at nearly every station. Still, we boys enjoyed a liberty of action that would drive a man out of the profession in our present times of perfect order and discipline. Two other baggagemasters and I once took it into our heads to change off trains without saying a word to Superintendent Minot about it. It took Mr. Minot a day to discover that something was wrong.

"What does this mean?" he demanded, as he looked over the schedule and saw that none of us were on the right train.

Naturally we could give him no satisfactory explanation, and he summarily discharged every one of us. However, he punished us merely as a lesson, for we were all reinstated after a few days.

My misdemeanor gave me an unexpected increase in pay. When I went to Mr. Minot to ask him to take me back, I jokingly remarked that I had heard that when a man was discharged and hired over again it was a custom to raise his pay. Mr. Minot laughed heartily and then said, "All right, Charley, I will give you five dollars more per month. I guess you have had discipline enough to earn it this time."

One day on the Western Vermont, we accomplished a remarkable and daring feat, the like of which was probably never known before and doubtless has not been since. The train consisted of a baggage car and two passenger coaches, with the engine *General Stark*, recently built at the Lawrence Locomotive Works. The engineer was Dick Allen, known to the world as Richard Norton Allen, the inventor of the paper car wheel called by his name, and a wealthy capitalist of Cleveland.

About five miles from Bennington, the train ran over a steer and the engine and two cars were thrown off the track. It seemed to me that the only way to get another engine was to run a handcar or walk.

"What's to be done?" I asked my friend George Dunlap, who was conductor on this run.

"I'll tell you," he replied. "It's nearly all downgrade to Bennington, so let's uncouple the last car and run her back to the station."

In these days, anything like that would cost a man his position; but in the olden time, quick expedients and great risks were often necessary. When the passengers had gotten out of the rear coach, Dunlap, a brakeman named Downer, and I took the uncoupled car and started off.

We went along fine from the first, half wondering what we should do when we got to a piece of upgrade that must be passed. However, fortune was in our favor. The momentum we had gained took us over the rise of ground and on to the downgrade again. A wandering cow next threatened us. We stood on the platform with shouts and gesticulations, and managed to frighten off the intruding animal. Soon afterward, our car rolled into Bennington station. With a relief engine, we went back to the scene of the accident, pulled the other engine onto the track, and went on to Rutland at terrific speed. The *General Stark* did nobly, for we made our time and connection with the Rutland and Burlington train going north; and our daring deed was the talk in railroad circles far and near.

—Condensed from Charles George's *Forty Years on the Rail*,
R. R. Donnelly & Sons, Chicago, 1887.

An inventor named Townsend found a solution to the problem of smoke and cinders, but it never caught on.

Scientific American, 1847

II

"It may seem incredible, but it is nevertheless the fact, that ten miles of rail are to be handled and laid down this day by these eight white men and these crews of Chinese laborers."

IF THE DEVELOPMENT of the railroad was really a prototype of the space program, then the space program is likely to be full of inconsistencies. Inconsistency was the outstanding characteristic of the young science of railroad engineering. Railroads grew and spread capriciously, like trees in an irregular climate, thrusting out long, sturdy branches in favorable years and leaving strange, empty gaps during periods of drought. Many railroads were still struggling with such primitive problems as snakeheads and cattle on the tracks when out popped one of those long, substantial limbs—the transcontinental railroad.

This great mechanical link-up between the Atlantic and the Pacific had been a subject of dreams and propaganda and congressional argumentation for two decades. The project finally got started during, and because of, the Civil War; and the last track was put down in 1869. This date probably would be considered a high point in railroad technology were it not for the fact that railroads, generally, were at a rather low point. They had not yet developed a safe type of car coupling, a secure brake, a uniform gauge for trackage, a universal time standard, or most of the other attributes of a sound transportation system.

In any case, the principal accomplishment of the great transcontinental line (aside from the remarkable success of its builders in laying hold of public lands and money), was not in applied science but in logistics. The Central Pacific Railroad, building east from California, had no local supplies of coal, iron, or manpower; and, after crossing the Sierra Nevada range, it had practically no water. The Union Pacific, en route west from Omaha, found absolutely no lumber but a superabundance of unfriendly Indians. On both sides, the contractors had to move large numbers of men and vast quantities of material through a harsh and desolate territory and to try to make money while doing it.

It was natural that reporters on the scene should compare the huge construction crews to armies. The whole project had a military aspect. The Union

*Chinese laborers—in camp, at work, and buried in
strangely marked graves—were scattered along the
transcontinental lines from the mid-1860s to 1880s.*

Harper's Weekly, 1869 and 1883

Pacific even put a general, Grenville Dodge, in charge. And it was equally natural that spectators should view the enterprise as a battle between the Central Pacific and the Union Pacific. Both railroads wanted to build as many miles of government-subsidized track as possible before meeting the end of the other line.

Ultimately, the government put a stop to the wildest manifestations of this rivalry, which included grading parallel roadbeds and staging pick-handle fights between the work crews. The meeting place was arbitrarily set at Promontory, Utah.

But the habit of competition between the two lines died hard. The brothers Jack and Daniel Casement, contractors for the Union Pacific, had succeeded in laying seven miles, 800 feet of track in a single day; and Thomas C. Durant, the vice president of the company, let it be known that he would bet ten thousand dollars that no one could exceed that record.

In late April, 1869, when the two lines were only twenty-five miles apart, the builders of the Central Pacific reckoned it was a good time to take up the challenge. If they could set a new record, the Casement brothers would have no time or space in which to better it. J. H. Strobridge, the construction superintendent of the Central, picked out a crew of eight Irish tracklayers, had two miles of rails loaded onto a train, and hitched two engines double-head to push the materials to the end-of-track.

But, as the engines moved forward, a push bar broke. The train derailed, and the rest of the day was lost in curses and repairs.

Next morning, April 29, the Central Pacific crew started again, with the engines pulling instead of pushing the supply train. A correspondent of the leading newspaper in San Francisco, the daily *Alta California,* was on hand to watch this demonstration of technological virtuosity. To anyone interested in historical analogies, this reporter's ecstatic dispatch on the "conquest of that old enemy of mankind, space," bears comparison with certain reportorial essays that blossomed exactly one hundred years later, in the early summer of 1969, when Neil Armstrong set foot on the moon.

IT IS DAYBREAK in the valley of the Great Salt Lake. Standing here, on rising ground, we look down upon a field of combat. It stretches the length of a plain that must have been at some remote period the shore of a great inland sea. Yonder is the lake, which is all that remains of this vast, landlocked ocean. The water is glistening in the morning sun. Along the line of the railroad are the white camps of the Chinese laborers, and from every campground squads of men are marching out to battle with that old enemy of mankind, space.

There is a jaunty air about the Oriental workman as he marches along. He wears a peaked woolen cap with ear flaps, and his appearance brings to mind an ancient Crusader rather than a coolie laborer. The enthusiasm of the occasion evidently has brought even him under its influence. As for the Caucasian members of the force, they are worked up to the highest pitch of enthusiasm.

Yesterday's failure has nerved every man to such exertion that no accident can possibly occur. Do you see that platform car, loaded with iron, coming up the track? It is wheeled along by a pair of horses, hitched in tandem, galloping at the side of the track in the manner of a tow-team hauling a canalboat. They are met by another car, returning after having left its burden of iron rails at the front. This car is bowling along the downward slope, pushed by men on each side, using their feet like oars. Surely, there must be a contretemps, for vehicles cannot pass on a single track.

But wait! The downhill car is stopped in an instant. The men lift it off the track and stand it on the edge, and the loaded car slips past without delay.

Arrived at the front, two men throw a wooden bar beneath the wheels to stop the car. The horses are detached and gallop to the rear. On either side of the car, four men seize hold of a rail with iron nippers, haul it forward off the flatcar, and lay it on the waiting ties. The car moves forward. After it comes a gang of men who halfway drive the spikes and screw on the first bolts. At a short interval behind this group comes a squad of Chinamen to hammer home the spikes. Behind these is a second squad of Chinamen, two deep, on either side of the track. The outer line, armed with picks, loosens the dry earth; the inner line, with shovels, scrapes up the soil and throws it around the ties.

I timed the whole movement twice. First time, 200 feet of rail laid in one minute and twenty seconds. Second time, 200 feet in one minute, fifteen seconds. This is about as fast as a leisurely walk—as fast, in other words, as the early ox teams used to travel across the plains. It may seem incredible, but it is nevertheless the fact, that ten miles of rails are to be handled and laid down this day by these eight white men and these crews of Chinese laborers.

But we have taken in only a portion of the scene. Along the line are overseers, galloping up and down, seeing that everything is properly done. In a carriage right at the front sits Mr. Charles Crocker, the general superintendent of construction for the Central Pacific Railroad, and Mr. J. H. Strobridge, his first officer. They are the generals of this engagement. The eye of Mr. Crocker takes in every detail of the operation, and his merry laugh wakens the echoes when anything amusing takes place.

Nothing ever appears to depress Mr. Crocker. On Tuesday, after the first attempt had failed, I went to talk with him. I found him shooting at the end of a cigar box set on the ground a hundred yards away. He had sent a bullet through it five times out of nine; and one of the shots was almost in the center. His face clouded for a moment when he heard that the engine had gone off the track, and the great feat on which he had set his heart was impossible—at least for that day. But his face soon regained its jovial aspect, and his laugh rang out again as clearly as if nothing had occurred that might annoy him.

By 6:00 A.M., two miles of rail have been laid. A train containing two more miles of iron is pushed forward from the rear. As it steams up to the last rail, a squad of men rushes forward, and in exactly ten minutes the train has been completely unloaded: 200 tons of iron rails and ten tons of spikes. Then the small horse-drawn cars are loaded with iron and start ahead, one after another. Meanwhile, the ties are being hauled along a parallel route on the right, while water carts and tool wagons move forward on the left.

By noon it begins to appear that the great feat will be successfully accomplished. In six hours and forty-two minutes, the Central Pacific has laid six miles of track. But here are 1,200 to 1,400 men to be fed—and they are six miles from the "home" they left at dawn. Far to the rear, one can behold a strange sight. It looks like a village in motion. It is the boardinghouse train, composed of a number of plain, wooden house cars with peaked roofs. Inside are the bunks of the workers, arranged in the manner of the steerage of a ship, and also the dining rooms, where these men are fed like fighting cocks. The bread and meat are of the very best.

As soon as the boardinghouse train is at hand, implements are thrown down and the white laborers retire to their dinner. The Chinamen bring their food with them and dine on the line of the work.

So far as I have been able to observe, there is not the slightest antagonism between these two races engaged in the work of the Central Pacific. Passing along the line of Chinamen, the Caucasian commander of the gang sings out: "Hurry up there, ye divils, shure we have no time to lose!" And the answer, coming from the whole squad, in a laughing manner: "Tach I yah!" (This, I inferred, meant: "Ready and begorra, we do that.")

It was refreshing to see how well the races got along together. The idea probably is beginning to dawn on the mind of the white laborer that John Chinaman, instead of competing with him or pulling him down, is shoving him up the social scale. John has to do the hard work, while Patrick generally commands and directs. He shouts aloud, "Look alive there, ye scalpeens," and John's fellow countryman sings out, "Why you no dig faster?"

A large delegation of gentlemen from the Union Pacific had been with us all the forenoon. They were exceedingly skeptical that this feat could be performed. In fact, they were willing to bet largely on certain failure. Now, at lunch with us at one o'clock, with six miles already accomplished, their ideas were completely changed. A head man among them admitted that the organization of the Central Pacific is far superior to his own.

From my observation, the camps of the Union Pacific (except for the Mormon camps, which are models of order and sobriety,) suffer from the demoralizing influence of hundreds of desperadoes who have been expelled from neighboring territories by vigilance committees and have crawled along with the advancing army of workers from the East, setting up tent towns devoted to gambling and prostitution. By contrast, neither whiskey nor places of dissipation are permitted by the Central Pacific within their lines. Of course, the Central Pacific has no legal right to prevent free American citizens from selling rum—or poison, for that matter. But the company has found it to be in their own interest to take the law into their own hands in this regard. Out in these untamed wilds, it is better to pay a fine, if any should be levied, than to allow a vast army of employees to be demoralized by rum. The consequence is that sobriety, a strict attention to duty, order, and regularity pervades all their camps. Their workers also enjoy the full fruits of their earnings; for the proceeds of the sweat of their brows do not go to increase the gamblers and prostitutes. Mr. H. H. Minkler, the chief tracklayer, told me he has often had as much as seventy-five thousands dollars deposited at Wells, Fargo & Co. to the credit of his white laborers.

As for the Chinamen, they do for themselves. They are unpleasant and repulsive pagans, but they are not given to rum. They are on hand when they are wanted. They work faithfully and steadily. The delegation from the Union Pacific were specially loud in their praise of the organization of the Chinese.

The Union Pacific men were interested spectators of the afternoon's work. Sitting apart on their horses, they alone seemed to feel no share of the excitement that is now boiling over in these men of so many different races. The sense of expectation mounts as the shadows begin to lengthen. With dinner over, we can look back on a morning of great accomplishment and forward to an evening of triumph. We have now, after a full and hearty meal, only four more miles of track to lay. The iron is all well up to the front. Even if an engine were to run off a track, the accident could not retard us now.

I say "us" because I have been infected by the prevailing enthusiasm. I no longer look upon these gymnastic tracklayers with the cold eyes of a mere outsider. By some unreasoning process, I have become merged into the busy mass around me.

The music of the regular blows of the spike drivers falls deliciously on my ear. The steady advance of the ballasters excites me to lively cheers. I look back and watch the splendid drill of the supply trains as something in which I have a personal interest. I have become a CP of the most uncompromising kind. It is only with difficulty that I can restrain myself from a demonstration of triumph that will compel the UP men to sink right into their boots. The pride that a Californian feels on this occasion is entirely justifiable, for this is, to some extent, a contest between the East and West. The ostensible combat is with the old demon of space. But the real battle, at least today, is between the old, worn-out, debauched, and dissipated East and the young, vigorous, organizing, audacious West.

Nearly an hour is lost in bending the rails for a great curve that will complete the day's work. The rails must be placed on blocks and, with the blows of heavy hammers, forced into the desired form. But this delay does not thwart us in obtaining our objective. It merely shows that, if the line had been perfectly straight and level, the men would easily have accomplished much more.

Onward moves the army of workers. The engines puff. The platform cars roll past. "*Klink, klink,*" go the hammers. Before the night comes on, the great job is completed. The last two rails are laid, the last spike is driven, and the conquering army returns to its quarters.

No such day has ever passed before in the history of railroading. Heretofore, the building of a railroad has been regarded as the slowest kind of work. Now we see a line stretching across a vast continent, completed inside of five years, and today has brought extraordinary proof that it is possible to lay rail at the rate of a leisurely walk.

The transcontinental railroad is the greatest work of its kind that ever has been built. Other railroads of equal extent may later be constructed, but the world is not big enough to admit of much greater enterprise than this.

—Adapted from the report of a correspondent of the San Francisco daily *Alta California*, May 1 and 3, 1869.

Scribner's Monthly, 1892

Champagne, oratory, and the driving of a "Last Spike"
marked the completion of track from coast to coast in 1869.

AT SIX IN THE EVENING, when the tired laborers stopped work, the Central Pacific had added ten miles, two hundred feet of track to the wealth of its owners, four Sacramento merchants and a handful of bankers in New York and Boston.

"Nobody was crowded, nobody was hurt, nobody lost a minute," J. H. Strobridge recalled years later. "Every bolt was screwed on, every spike driven home." It was a day to live forever in a construction superintendent's heart.

The workmen rode back to their boardinghouse train on the empty flatcars. The Union Pacific engineers who had measured the work with rod and chain rode home to certify that there had been no guesswork and no fraud. And the names of the eight men who had lifted something over 1,800,000 pounds of iron that day were marked down in the time book for double pay. (Their names, variously spelled and misspelled, appear today in the historic records of the first transcontinental railroad: Mike Shay, George Eliott, Edward Kileen, Thomas Daley, Mike Sullivan, Mike Kenedy, Fred McNamare, and Patrick Joice.)

This had been the finest moment in the great endeavor to lay tracks across the continent. It was a stagy, overtly contrived moment, a form of publicity stunt; yet, it was the real climax of the project, and more significant than the famous Last Spike ceremony a few days later.

Unfortunately, the ten-mile day also was a peak point in the public's innocent enthusiasm for railroads; for the Iron Horse and the iron trail were proving to be a questionable boon to many communities and classes.

If everyone had paid attention to the wise old philosophers of the past, no one would have been surprised that the railroad brought painful consequences along with all its blessings. Philosophers had been teaching for thousands of years the axiom that applied science, and even applied magic, always has detrimental effects as well as benefits. The myth of King Midas is a nightmarish warning against the dangers of overly successful alchemy; and Mary Wollstonecraft Shelley's *Frankenstein,* published in 1818, stands as a classic literary caveat against creating a scientific monster that can overpower its master.

But human beings tend to ignore warnings. It is unpleasant to be continually on guard, easier to accept each new technological achievement on its own terms—that is, to accept the stated objectives of technology and not to question the secondary consequences. This is how it was with the railroad. This is how it has been with automobiles, airplanes, television, and chlorinated hydrocarbon pesticides; and this is how it will be with space travel. Nobody could foresee that the railroad would become a political tyrant and an economic bully, or that it would reconstruct American geography. Nobody can really foresee what space travel will do to our lives and minds, either. All major technological accomplishments have results that are alien to their main purposes, but knowing this fact does not make those results predictable.

With all due respect to the professors who struggled to find an analogy between the railroad and the space program, we are still lost in the stars. We cannot even guess what future generations will think of our splendid accomplishments in space. It is quite possible that history will place a lesser value on the technological achievements of Wernher Von Braun, the rocket man, than on those of Isaac Dripps, of cowcatcher fame.

CHAPTER THREE

Pathfinders and Rock Pushers

I

*"When I realized I had been in this valley
many times...the full dangers
of this country dawned on my mind."*

NOWADAYS, NOBODY THINKS of a surveyor as a railroad man. A surveyor is a highway man. He stands there, on the gravel shoulder of an eight-lane freeway, dressed in white levis, yellow boots, a hard hat, and a fluorescent crimson jacket, peering through a telescope on a tripod and making windmills with his arms. It is a job without romance, without heroic pretensions. Who expects to find immortal adventure locating off-ramps and plotting overpasses?

Carrying a rod and chain for the railroad in the Age of Steam was a quite different matter. It was not only adventurous but frequently hazardous and even heroic. Furthermore, it was a work of transcendant importance to the future of the railroad. A badly surveyed route was like a congenital malformation that would permanently cripple its victim. Once in a while, a railroad might deliberately choose a steep, meandering, expensive route to serve a political purpose, secure a subsidy, or fatten the purse of a construction company that had been set up to milk the capital out of the venture; but, as a rule, a bad route was an irremediable mistake. Any engineer who could save his employers from such a disaster was a hero, indeed. The bronze statue of an engineer who found a low pass through the Rocky Mountains stands beside the tracks of the Great Northern Railroad in Montana.

During the fever of railroad construction in the 1880's, locating parties swarmed through the West, searching for level valleys dotted with deep artesian wells, hunting for new passes, rafting down river canyons, triangulating lines across the open prairie. To a banker, a real estate promoter, or a small-town newspaper editor, the sight of a survey crew was as welcome as the first robin of spring. If the survey came, could the right-of-way buyer and the grading contractor be far behind?

Among the surveyors in this competitive era was a young New Englander named Edward Gillette, who had been schooled as a civil engineer at the Sheffield School at Yale and had worked as a topographer for the Coast Survey and the Army Engineers before taking a railroad survey job in 1881. Gillette was dedicated to the simple principle that a straight line is the shortest disance between two points—and that the shortest railroad between two points is likely to have the most profitable operations. This theorem, applied in the deserted dunes of northwestern Nebraska, resulted in considerable savings to Gillette's railroad. In appreciation, the Burlington system named a town for him—but Gillette preferred the climate and companionship in Sheridan, Wyoming. He made his home there for many years before his death, at eighty-two, in 1936. It was in Sheridan that he put down his memoirs of working on the railroad:

OUT IN THE SAND HILLS of Nebraska in 1884, the Burlington and the Union Pacific were in sharp competition for new territory. When I joined the Burlington as a survey engineer that December, they put me in charge of a party whose work was to locate as quickly as possible a line from Aurora to Hastings. There was reason to fear that the Union Pacific was trying to secure this route, so I was given only two days to locate ten miles of line and make maps for the company's agent to use in purchasing right-of-way.

The company had furnished us with maps and profiles of previous surveys between the two towns. These surveys had been made at various times, but all of them wandered around, following a stream called Blue River. It seemed to me that the country was almost flat—at least it was flat compared to the land I had seen along the route of the Denver & Rio Grande—so I simply drew a straight line on the map between Aurora and Hastings and then rode out, following section lines and noting where the straight line would run. It missed most of the farmhouses, was on good ground, and did not cross anything bigger than a small drainage ditch.

After inspecting this line for twelve miles, I rode back to my party and we started locating. We finished twelve miles in two days. On the third day, the right-of-way agent began buying land. Those were the greatest days of railroad building the country has ever known, and you can see the speed at which we sometimes had to move.

Our party consisted, besides myself, of a transitman, head chainman, rear chainman, back flagman, stake marker, stake driver, levelman, rodman, topographer, assistant topographer, draftsman, two line teamsters, a supply teamster, and a cook. We also had to have a dog, for a camp without one was, to us, the same as a home without children.

Living in camp was no hardship, even in winter. The tents were of heavy canvas, closed by a fly that was used as an awning in summer. They were well staked to the ground, and a ditch was dug around the sides to drain the water away. Earth was heaped around the base to keep out the wind, and a small sheet-iron stove gave all the warmth and hot water desired. A board divided the space inside. Half was used for sleeping quarters. On the frozen ground we piled up a foot or more of straw, covered it with a wagon sheet, and spread out our tarpaulins and blankets. The blankets were spread one on top of the other and folded over to keep our feet snugly pocketed. There is nothing more uncomfortable in camp —or at home, for that matter—than to find one's feet sticking out of the bedclothes on a cold night.

Each of the boys would take his turn for a week making a fire in the stove fifteen minutes before rising time, so that the tent would be warm and hot water would be available for the others. This was not so bad a task, since each fellow taking his turn had the satisfaction of knowing that someone else would be making fires for him for the next five or six weeks.

The corner opposite the stove was enclosed with a bed tarp. With some hot water and a tub borrowed from the cook, this created a well-patronized bathroom. The cook, who had plenty of spare time between breakfast and supper, while the rest of the party was out in the field, would do the men's laundry for a small charge. This kept him in funds. He always had money for all his expenses, yet he once showed me all the checks he had received for nearly two years. He had not been obliged to cash a single one.

With our good shelter and good food, we were much better off than the neighboring settlers in their log cabins and sod shanties. We got so accustomed to a warm tent that we found it very uncomfortable to sleep in any of the frontier hotels, which were the coldest places on earth. Travelers stopping at these flimsy places used to make a grab for their clothes in the morning and rush to the office, where there would be a big box stove with a roaring fire to keep a man from freezing. One very cold morning a farmer came into the office with icicles dangling from his whiskers, and a salesman who had spent the night in the hotel asked him, "Which room did you have?"

The cook or one of the teamsters (generally known as "mule skinners") would act as barber for the survey party. It was a common sight on Sundays to see one of the boys sitting outdoors on a camp stool, having his hair cut by one of the teamsters who had learned this trade by roaching, or trimming, the manes of horses so that the hair would stand straight up.

In January, 1885, we started a line northwest from Broken Bow, Nebraska. The weather was extremely cold, and blizzards were frequent. Corn, which was selling at ten and twelve cents a bushel, was the cheapest available fuel.

The weather was not allowed to interfere with our work. We were on line every day, and soon we had pushed the survey to the middle fork of the Loup River, where we came to Stem's Ranch, sometimes called Rankin's Ranch. The cowboys were amazed to see a railroad party. No one could believe that a railroad would penetrate that wild region. We were getting so far from our base of supplies that we had to cache enough provisions to last for several months before we dared to venture further into the sand hills.

The cowboys gave valuable information about the country to the west. They told us about a cabin at Dock Lake, about thirty miles west, where a range rider sometimes spent the winter. Since the cabin was not in use that year, we arranged to take in a wagon outfit loaded with blankets and provisions, find the cabin, and use it as a supply base. Fuel would be of critical importance, for the cowboys told us there was nothing to burn in the sand hills except buffalo chips and a few cherry roots. I arranged to have several loads of dry ash wood hauled up from the banks of the river. Without it, our survey crew could not have got along.

Early one morning, the teamster started for Dock Lake. I was to follow a little later on horseback, but I was delayed in camp, and it was late in the afternoon before I got started on the track of the wagon. Riding as fast as possible and striking matches to see the trail in the gathering darkness, I pushed along until about ten o'clock at night, when I saw a reflection in the sky ahead of me. I had hurried in that direction for some distance before realizing it was northern lights and not the reflection from a campfire.

At that point, I endeavored to retrace my route back to the wagon trail. Having counted the divides and valleys I had crossed, I hoped to be able to find my way back by the motions of the horse climbing and descending the slopes. It soon began to snow, however. Giving up my effort to find the trail, I unsaddled and picketed my horse where there was feed. With the saddle for a pillow and the saddle blanket for covering, I lay down like a cowboy and tried to sleep. It was too cold to sleep for any length of time. I kept busy running up and down hills to get my blood circulating, lying down to sleep, getting up again to shake off the snow, repeating the exercise, and lying down again. Finally, I found the horse, who had tired of grazing, standing over me, and I decided it would be more comfortable in the saddle than trying to rest under these conditions; so I resumed my trip.

In my abrupt departure from camp, I had neglected to bring along my compass. I hoped to get my bearings from the sun at dawn. In this, too, I was disappointed. It snowed so hard that the sun was not visible until ten o'clock. Then, looking back, I was able to see a faint outline of the sun, and I turned back toward camp. The horse was showing signs of being tired, and it was essential to reach shelter that day.

About noon, I came upon the cabin at Dock Lake. Apparently I had passed through a valley to the north of it during the night. The teamster had spent the previous night there and had already started back to camp. I caught up with his wagon late in the afternoon. As my horse was about all in, I rode with the driver, happy to satisfy my hunger with several postponed meals.

I had been lost overnight in both New Mexico and Colorado, but conditions in the sand hills were entirely different. There were no woods, no streams, no shelter; and the only guide to direction was a hollow, called a "blowout," carved on the northwest side of the hills by the prevailing winds. The sand hills region was, and still is, a dangerous place in which to be lost in winter.

Once while prospecting the country for a good line, I rode into a long, smooth valley that looked ideal for a railroad route. I determined to run a survey line there the next day. As it was beginning to snow, however, I started back towards camp, following my tracks in the old snow. Soon I ran across one of our own survey stakes, and I realized I had been in this valley many times. Then the full dangers of this country dawned on my mind.

I told the men my own experience in getting lost and warned them to exercise great care. If a man should get lost in a blizzard, there would be small chance of his living through it. We took special precautions to make our tents withstand the blizzards. The guy ropes were tied through holes bored in a heavy plank that was buried deep in the sand: ordinary tent stakes were of little use. Since the blizzards usually came from the northwest, we faced the openings of the tents to the southeast, and, during fierce winds, we gave the back poles extra bracing.

Despite these warnings and precautions, trouble developed during our move to Dock Lake. I had ordered all the men to stay with the wagons to steady the load on sidehills, and specifically told them not to go hunting, as we had plenty of fresh meat. We succeeded in reaching Dock Lake by nightfall and pitched our tents; but at the supper table I noticed that one of the men in the party did not appear. It turned out that Jack had taken his rifle shortly after lunch and had gone over toward the next valley, saying he would join the party further on.

After supper, we built a big fire outside and put a lantern on top of a pole on a sand hill near the camp. When the boy did not turn up, we fired a gun at intervals and kept lights on in the tents all night.

In the morning I found that Jack had not returned. We organized four hunting parties. A wagon went with each group. This would be left on the top of a hill where it could be easily seen. Snow had fallen during the night, and we had to take care that others did not get lost.

After three days' hunting without result, I enlisted some cowboys to help, although they said it was no use. By now, wolves or coyotes would have picked Jack's bones. But when I returned to camp after a discouraging search, I learned that one of the parties had found the boy, wandering in a demented condition, still holding onto his rifle. He was too far gone to give an account of his experience, and it was several days before his system would stand anything but the lightest food.

When Jack had recovered sufficiently to recall his wanderings, he told us he had intended to follow a valley parallel to our course but had gotten lost trying to rejoin the survey party. After two nights in the open, during which he had a hard time to keep from freezing, he determined to take a due easterly course at sunrise and keep to it all day, hoping by this means to reach assistance. As the sun set that day, he realized that he was going west. He had followed the sun all day. That was as far as he could remember.

Apparently, he had never been a great distance from our camp, but the snow that had fallen each night had covered the tracks we made each day. For many nights Jack talked in his sleep, repeating the words, "Won't they ever find me?"

As spring came on, mosquitoes and horseflies became such pests that all the game—elk, deer, and antelope—left the country, and our horses suffered so much that we had to cover them with grain sacks. I was riding a white horse, and at times he looked almost black. He was worn out fighting the flies, and finally would not even switch his tail to get rid of them. Once, on clapping my hand to his nose, I killed fourteen horseflies.

It had taken us all winter and a good part of the spring to get through the sand hills. In all that time, we had not met anyone outside our own party except for a few cowboys and some Indians. Now, as the survey party approached the first sod shanty on the Box Butte Table, a woman came to the door. She did not realize what a curiosity she would be to the boys. They stopped work, lined up, and gave her three cheers, much to her astonishment.

There on Box Butte, a townsite had been surveyed on the claim of one of the settlers, and he had started a newspaper to boost the new town. The editor of the paper rode out to investigate the various surveys we had made. He came upon some of our location stakes. On preliminary lines, these stakes were customarily

*Surveyors were often forced to make
their sightings from a precarious perch.*

marked *1, 2, 3*, etc. or *a, b, c*, while on location lines they were designated *AL*, *BL*, etc., with the initials of the chief of the party on the opposite side. One of the stakes on Box Butte Table happened to be marked *BBL*, with my initials, *EG*, on the back of the stake.

The editor announced in large headlines that he had solved the secret of the railroad route. His town was going to get the railroad, as evidenced by a location marked *BBL* for "Box Butte Line" and *EG* for "Easy Grade."

We had an ideal camp near the Table. It was just out of sight of a spring where antelope came every day to drink, and we had plenty of fresh meat with little effort. But our course lay onward, toward the southern entrance to the Black Hills.

By January, 1888, the railroad had been constructed to Alliance, Nebraska. My party headed back to Lincoln, and we had the novel experience of riding back through the sand hills on the train.

A wonderful transformation had taken place. Towns with courthouses, churches, stores, and residences had sprung up, apparently overnight, near our old campsites. The railroad had opened an uninhabited region, and although it was an unfavorable place, thousands of persons had found homes, and the claims of settlers had gained financial value.

—Condensed from Edward Gillette's *Locating the Iron Trail*.
Copyright 1925 by the Christopher Publishing House, Boston, Mass.

II

"I wore two pairs of pants, three pairs of
heavy wool socks, and overshoes—
and even so I froze the tips of my toes."

IN CERTAIN WAYS, the railroad surveyor was the last authentic hero in the epic of the American frontier. Long after the buffalo grass had succumbed to the plows of sodbusters and nesters, the railroad survey engineer was still drifting around, living his ultra-masculine idyll of hardship, simplicity, and rustic adventure. He had all the essential adolescent attributes of a classic western cavalier: he was youthful, uncivilized, impermanent; he was completely free of female influence; his style of life was comradely and courageous; and his work always ended before it could turn stale and routine or be circumscribed by domestic responsibilities.

A magazine writer, describing railroad operations in the early 1890's, got soft and misty at the very thought of a tired survey crew at twilight:

"When they get back to camp and, after a wash in the nearest creek, find a smoking-hot supper ready—even though it consist of fried pork and potatoes, corn bread and black coffee—their troubles are all forgotten, and they feel a true satisfaction which the flesh-pots of Delmonico's cannot give. One greater pleasure remains—to fill the old pipe and recline by the campfire for a jolly smoke."

To an audience of Americans who felt guilty about Delmonico's and nostalgic about campfires, the surveyor's life had a deep, dream-like allure. Tracks and locomotives, roundhouses and repair shops—those aspects of the railroad were permanent, practical, and unromantic. But the wilderness survey —ah! *that* was an ephemeral activity, a fragile enterprise to which a man might devote the energies of his youth and the memories of his old age.

Happily, surveying went on and on, long after the other realities of pioneering were over, long after even the retinal shadows had faded, and Buffalo Bill's Wild West Show had played its last performance in the capital cities of Europe.

When a young engineer named Joseph Noble went to work for the Atchison, Topeka & Santa Fe out in the Far West in 1907, the Indian wars, cattle drives, land rushes, and gold digs were past; yet, Noble's recollections of his work in a survey crew are infused with the same sense of frontier adventure that pervades those other great incidents of our national experience.

THERE ISN'T MUCH railroad construction going on nowadays, and what little there is consists mainly of relocating existing lines or building branches to serve mines or other industrial developments. The proposed route is looked over from an automobile or helicopter, and if topographic maps are available for the area involved, a preliminary line can be laid out in the office that will be very close to the final route. If the country is difficult and no good maps can be had, they can readily be produced from aerial photographs.

Living conditions for engineering field parties have been correspondingly improved. Ordinarily they can count on staying at an air-conditioned motel with private bath and TV, eating in an establishment approved by Duncan Hines, and riding to and from work listening to the car radio.

Fifty years ago, working conditions on a surveying party were a little more rigorous. The area through which the line would run was first looked over by an engineer, using a buckboard or saddle horse for transportation; and if his report was favorable, surveying parties were put in the field. A full-size surveying party in open country ordinarily consisted of from thirteen to sixteen men. Their function was to produce a map and profile of the line, together with topographic information, including the location of adjacent land corners and the probable size of required bridge openings. From this information the length of the route, necessary gradients, and maximum curvature could be determined and the construction costs estimated.

Between 1907 and 1913, I worked on surveys extending over a thousand miles of line, mainly for the Santa Fe, in West Texas, eastern New Mexico, western Oklahoma, and Kansas. The country looked to me about as I understood it did when they shot the last buffalo. It was well supplied with coyotes, rattlesnakes, blue quail, prairie chickens, jack rabbits, prairie dogs, and antelope, and on the big ranches there were a lot of cattle.

Some of these cows had seen a man on foot so seldom they didn't know what he was. Many times, when I was several thousand feet from the remainder of the party, a bunch of cattle would charge across the prairie toward me, come to a sliding stop about a hundred feet away, lower their heads, regard me with apparent wonder for a few seconds, then turn tail and depart as rapidly as they had come. The first time this happened, I thought maybe I had got in the wrong business. But I jerked off my coat, waved it at them, and yelled, "Git along, little dogies," or the 1908 equivalent, and they took off with tails lashing. The present generation of cows seems to have become accustomed to the sights and sounds of civilization, and I don't imagine they would look up from their grazing if John Glenn floated down in the middle of the herd.

Coyotes never annoyed us, except they might wake you up with their yelping. They loved to howl at night, particularly just before daybreak. On one occasion they stole a ham which the cook had left lying on the dining table. I have seen them chasing jack rabbits, and they never seem to be in any hurry: just loping along after the rabbit, keeping him in sight. Cowpunchers have told me it was fairly common for two coyotes to take turns chasing a jack rabbit. While one ran the rabbit in circles, the other sat on his haunches and watched the proceedings until his turn came.

You might find a rattlesnake anywhere. They were mostly sidewinders, three or four feet long, and we frequently found them around prairie dog towns. A prairie dog town might cover several acres. The dogs lived in holes about six inches in diameter, each hole surrounded by a mound of dirt four or five inches high. Presumably, these mounds were intended to keep water out of the holes. As you approached, you would generally find the dogs scattered over the prairie foraging. When they recognized you as a possible enemy, they would retreat to their holes and sit on their hind legs watching you until they determined what your intentions were or you got too close. Then they dived into their holes.

A surveying party working in this country had to operate a good deal like an exploring expedition in the days of Coronado, except, of course, you were not as likely to get scalped.

We lived in tents. I have forgotten the exact size, but I believe the office and sleeping tents were about twelve by sixteen feet and the cook tent a little larger, as it had to accommodate the cookstove, dining table, supplies, work tables and the cook's bed. I never knew a cook who didn't sleep in the cook tent. Maybe it was warmer and more convenient for him, or possibly he had lost confidence in humanity and wanted to be where he could keep an eye on his supplies.

The locating engineer and instrumentmen slept in the office tent, so called because it contained a knockdown drafting table, a couple of high stools and a chest for storing engineering and office supplies. The remainder of the party slept in the other tents.

The tents had no floors, so whenever we could we pitched them on grassy

In a survey camp the scenery was often spectacular,
but the diet was always heavy on canned tomatoes.

spots, which helped to keep down the dust. Contrary to what might be expected, the tents were surprisingly comfortable in cold weather if properly pegged down and banked with earth around the bottom on the outside. On one job in southwestern Kansas I lived in a tent without experiencing any particular discomfort during a blizzard that dropped the temperature to twenty degrees below zero.

The cooks on these parties were generally pretty good, and the food was plentiful. Necessarily, where refrigeration was impracticable, fresh meat was not always on the menu, but there was plenty of ham, bacon, and canned meat of various kinds.

For breakfast we usually had pancakes with butter and syrup; ham, bacon, or sausage; eggs; stewed fruit (apricots, peaches, or prunes); oatmeal; and, of course, coffee. The milk was canned. I used plenty of it on oatmeal and in my coffee but I never learned to like it.

Lunch we carried with us: boiled eggs, ham sandwiches, maybe pear or apple pie, the crust of which was usually soggy, sometimes apples or oranges, and always canned tomatoes. We had coffee a few times, but we seldom stopped long enough to build a fire during the winter, and in hot weather, water tasted better. A good many times when we stopped for lunch on the prairies, I just ate a can of tomatoes and lay down with my head behind a clump of bear grass to get out of the wind.

Supper was always a good meal: ham or fresh beef, pork, or lamb; boiled cabbage; boiled potatoes; cole slaw; stewed tomatoes; butter; jam or preserves; bread (baked by the cook); canned apricots, plums, cherries, or peaches; all kinds of condiments; pie; and coffee.

And of course, there was often the pinto bean, the Mexican *frijol*, which is cultivated extensively in the high country of the Southwest. This bean, cooked with salt pork and flavored with chilis, is a gastronomic delight. I never saw a man who didn't like it. Back in the days when I could eat what I liked, two or three plates full of *frijoles* at supper would make up for all the day's hardships.

Most of the camp cooks I knew could turn out good meals, but it was exceptional to find one who didn't have an irascible disposition. Maybe it was the gang they had to cook for, or the lonely life they led—they were in camp all day by themselves—or perhaps they drank too much coffee or vanilla extract. Whatever caused it, they were, as a class, hard to get along with.

One morning during the cold winter of 1911/12, when I was running a survey party about fifty miles southwest of Dodge City, Kansas, one of the chainmen burst into my tent and demanded, "Say, Noble, can you get along without a cook?"

I stopped lacing my boots. "I guess I didn't understand you. What did you say?"

He repeated the question. I said, "Of course not. What brought this up?"

"Well," he said, "my feet were pretty cold when I got up so I went in the cookshack, turned down the oven door on the cookstove, and was warming my feet and lacing my boots when Franklin began cursing me and yelling for me to get out of his kitchen. What he said to me I won't take from anybody, and if it will not inconvenience you, I'll just kill the bastard."

He was deadly serious, so I said, "It would inconvenience me considerably. We are fifty miles from a town or the railroad, in the middle of a blizzard, and have fifteen men to feed. Besides, you would get into a lot of trouble, and I think we ought to try to settle this some other way. Let's go talk to Franklin."

He agreed, and we went over to the cookshack. There were a good many abandoned farmhouses in the area where we were working, left by settlers who had given up and gone Back East, and we had set up the kitchen in one of these houses instead of in a tent. I told the cook exactly what Jones had said to me. His face turned about the color of the snow outside, and he fingered a meat cleaver nervously, but after a few seconds he laid it down and said he had flown off the handle and was sorry about the whole thing. After some further apologies, I asked Jones if he was satisfied and he said just forget it.

Two weeks later, we moved in to the railroad at Hartland. The cook left the same day under his own power.

The work, especially on preliminary surveys, went forward rapidly, sometimes as much as ten or twelve miles in one day. Since our transport was all horse drawn, we had to move camp frequently to avoid wasting a lot of time traveling to and from work. Personal equipment was necessarily limited. Mine consisted of a folding cot, a bedroll, and a suitcase. On one job I had a guitar, bought from some troubadour who was leaving the party.

Everybody had a tarp—cow country for tarpaulin—which, together with two or three blankets or quilts, make your bedroll. The tarp was essential. It was about six feet wide and fourteen feet long and went under and over your bedding, protecting you against the weather if you were sleeping outside, and keeping out some dust if your bed was in a tent. The usual grade of canvas in these tarps was about twelve ounces per square yard. The best grade was twenty ounces, which was practically waterproof but very difficult to roll up when wet. A twenty-ounce tarp was a sort of status symbol, like having a cake of Pear's soap or a Rolls Royce.

The cots were army style, three feet wide by six and a half feet long, made of heavy canvas on a wood frame, and with X-shaped legs. By taking out the wooden end pieces, the cot could be folded into a compact bundle about three feet long and rolled up in your bedroll, a handy arrangement when moving camp. Chairs were rare. The dining table had seats made of two-by-twelve plank bolted to the table, and in the other tents we sat on our cots or an empty box.

Actually, we didn't have much time for sitting around. We ate breakfast before daybreak and supper, usually, after dark. Bedtime came pretty early except to the instrumentmen and locating engineer. They worked in the office tent until around ten or eleven o'clock, platting the day's work on a map and profile and laying out the next day's work. There was no work on Sunday. You could do your washing, take a bath in a washtub, shave if you had the nerve, or just walk around and look at the country.

Strange as it may seem for men who spent ten or eleven hours in the field every working day, some of us never tired of looking at new country. One Sunday morning when we were camped near Mount Dora, New Mexico, I decided to climb a mountain we could see on the western horizon. The Colorado & Southern had a water tank at Mount Dora. I hid behind the pump house while a freight train was taking on water. When the train started to pull out, I climbed into a coal car and rode to Des Moines, which was on the flank of the mountain. The train stopped there to do some switching, so I had no trouble getting off.

I enjoyed the trip up the mountain and was ready to go back to camp about the middle of the afternoon. Pretty soon an eastbound freight stopped to pick up some cars. My luck was holding, or at least I thought it was. The conductor looked like an amiable individual. I told him I was also a railroad man. "How about letting me ride back to Mount Dora?" He said OK, if I thought I could get off. Without pondering, I climbed on top of a box car and sat down on the running board.

We went down the hill at about thirty miles an hour. I enjoyed the scenery until I noticed the engine was already by the water tank at Mount Dora. Suddenly, I realized the train wasn't going to stop. I could either unload right then or go on to Clayton, in which case I would have no way to get back.

I figured out the answer to this one pretty quick. When the car passed over a cinder fill about fifteen feet high, I hit the ground running. I did pretty well for the first few steps, which were about five yards apart. Then my feet couldn't keep up with the rest of me, and I started a combined slide and roll, finally coming to a stop near the right-of-way fence. The cinders I dug out of my hide impressed on me the fact that steam locomotives going downhill don't stop for water as often as they do going uphill.

As for entertainment in camp, it was more or less confined to reading, pitch, and poker, or listening to some frontier virtuoso give out with "Abdul Abul-Bul Ameer" or "The Chisholm Trail" to an improvised guitar accompaniment. We generally had a set of boxing gloves around the camp, and occasionally some of the hardier individuals would spar a few rounds. Once I made the mistake of putting on the gloves with a cook we found out (too late) had been a sparring partner of Jess Willard. Fortunately, he didn't dislike me, or I probably wouldn't be here today.

There was one ceremony—I guess it would come under the heading of entertainment—that we sometimes used to introduce a tenderfoot to the Wild West. If we were sleeping in the open, we would wait until the new arrival had gone to sleep, then drag a saddle and a couple of trace chains across his tarp to the accompaniment of loud shouts of "Whoa!" The victim came out of his bedroll as if he had been fired out of a cannon.

The cook tent was heated by the cookstove. When we needed heat in the other tents, we used a Sibley stove, a metal cone that sat on the ground. It had a door in one side and a small opening at the bottom to afford draft. We cut our own wood, if available, and on the plains we burned cow chips and mesquite roots.

Cow chips were easy to pick up, and you could carry a tow sack full of them without difficulty; but they didn't burn too well, and you usually had to cover considerable territory to find enough. Mesquite roots, on the other hand, were fairly plentiful and made a good fire; but digging them up with an ax and grubbing hoe was really work. We ordinarily compromised and collected some of each.

Cow chips made a smoldering fire, especially if they were damp. We often gave them a little added zip with kerosene. This was safe enough if you poured the oil on *before* the fire was lighted. But working on the Texico-Lubbock line, we had a young cook straight from New York City who had never seen—and probably had never heard of—a cow-chip fire. On his very first night with the party, we slept on the ground in the open, and I awakened just before daylight to discover that he had a cow-chip fire going. The chips were smoking and not burning very well. Just as I sat up, the cook threw, or rather poured, some kerosene on the fire from a five-gallon can. Instantly the can exploded, throwing burning oil over him and setting his clothing afire. He started to run, which, of course, was the worst thing he could have done. I jumped up and grabbed a blanket and put out the fire.

He was seriously burned, and we took him to a hospital in Lubbock. He didn't want to go to a hospital and kept telling me they gave patients like him a drink out of a "black bottle" when they got tired of them. I told him this was not the way we treated burnt cooks in Texas, but he didn't believe me. I think he eventually got well.

A field party didn't use much water but we always made camp near a stream or well. There were few streams in the territory whose water was fit to drink, and so, for the most part, we depended on wells, always pumped by a windmill.

Sheep ranches usually had metal windmills, but in the cattle country the standard mill was a Fairbanks Morse "Eclipse," with a twelve-foot wooden wheel on a twenty-five-foot wood tower. If the wind stopped blowing, which it occasionally did, you had to climb the tower and turn the wheel by hand. Fortunately, all wells discharged into a pond or galvanized metal storage tank, so we didn't have to pump water by hand for the horses and mules.

A couple of two-horse spring wagons provided the transportation for an average party. Sometimes we had a buckboard or hack, also pulled by two horses. A hack had side curtains that could be rolled down in bad weather, but the wagons were open top. If it rained or snowed, you just hoped you'd brought your slicker.

For some reason, every surveying party I worked on was in a hurry to complete the job, and the weather had to be pretty bad to keep us in camp—raining or snowing so hard you couldn't see through a level or transit. It seems to me the wind blew nearly all the time. In the winter it froze you; in the summer it burned like the sun; and at any time it was likely to give you a good sandblasting with gravel about the size of BB shot. It made accurate instrument work very difficult. Unless the tripod legs were well spread, the wind could blow the instrument over.

The well-dressed young man wore a wide-brim Stetson, buckskin gloves, flannel shirt, corduroy trousers (and coat if needed), wool socks, and fourteen-inch laced boots. I wore heavy woolen union suits in the winter and light wool or cotton in hot weather. A yellow "Fish brand" slicker was standard.

I always carried two red bandanna handkerchiefs, one for the customary use, the other to tie over my face, outlaw style, in warm weather. The wind could burn you as badly as the sun, and a hat wasn't much protection. Bandannas also were handy for giving signals to the head chairman or back flagman. Incidentally, we found that a bright orange flag could be seen better against most backgrounds than any other color we tried.

For severe winter weather you needed a sheepskin coat or its equivalent, a sweater, four-buckle overshoes, and a cap that could be pulled down over your ears. On one job in Kansas I wore two pairs of pants, three pairs of heavy wool socks, and overshoes—and, even so, I froze the tips of my toes and fingers. On another job, in Arkansas, we worked so often in waist-deep water that I discarded my boots and wore ordinary, high-top shoes; boots were just a dead weight. The mosquitoes were so bad that I had to wear a veil, gloves, and denim jumper over my flannel shirt. They would bite right through a heavy shirt.

In a construction camp, life was more settled than it was in a locating party. Some installations were in one place for several months, or even a year. A few concessions could be made to civilization.

The first one that comes to my mind is that we had wood floors and sidewalls in the tents. The floors were one-inch boards and were warmer than the ground, or seemed so, and they could be swept out easily. Also, anything dropped on them was easier to find—that is, unless it fell through a crack.

Board sidewalls were also a real convenience. You could drive nails in them and hang up all kinds of things, such as calendars and clothing. Some dudes even put up a mirror.

The work consisted principally of setting stakes for the contractor's guidance, measuring drainage areas to determine the size of bridge openings, keeping track of the grading classification (i.e., how much rock was being moved), computing the grading quantities, and giving the work general supervision.

The matter of classification meant a good deal to a contractor, as he might be paid fifteen cents a cubic yard for moving earth and thirty-five or forty cents for taking out loose rock. Sometimes the determination of a category required considerable judgment on the engineer's part, and his decision did not always satisfy the contractor.

On one job I worked on in East Texas, there were a number of clay cuts, some of them twenty or twenty-five feet deep. The clay was soft on top, but as you went deeper it hardened into a sort of hardpan or shale. Material was classified on this job as earth, loose rock, and solid rock. The definition of loose rock was anything that was not solid rock and yet could not be plowed with a six-mule team. There was no clear line of demarcation between soft and hard material. When measuring a cut for classification, you just had to use your best judgment as to where the earth stopped and rock began.

Naturally, the resident engineer got into a lot of arguments with contractors about the amount of loose rock he was allowing; but there was one contractor who never mentioned classification. He must have been a student of applied psychology. One day when we stopped at his camp for dinner, he said: "I've been thinking about you boys, eating with all them mule skinners, and it ain't right. I've fixed up a place here where you can eat by yourselves, and from now on I want you to leave your lunch at home and eat dinner with me." The resident engineer protested mildly that this was too much of an imposition, but the contractor was insistent, and at last we reluctantly agreed.

The contractor then led us to a small tent equipped with a table and two benches, told us to make ourselves at home, dinner would be over shortly, and left. The table had a checkered red and white oilcloth cover. Sitting on it, along with the salt, pepper, catsup, and pickles, were three tin cups, a pitcher of water and a quart of Four Roses whiskey. The dinner arrived from the cook tent in due course, and after a leisurely meal, we went on about our business, which included some measurement of classification.

After such treatment I imagine we were inclined to look on this contractor's problems with a kindly eye. While I have no reason to believe his interest in our welfare was prompted by anything other than his generous nature, I'm reasonably sure the bread he cast upon the waters—or in this case put on the table—was returned to him in the predicted fashion.

—Abridged from *From Cab to Caboose: Fifty Years of Railroading*, an autobiography by Joseph A. Noble. Copyright 1964 by the University of Oklahoma Press, Norman, Oklahoma.

III

"The nearest peace officer to my camp was 125 miles away. It was up to the contractor to be the law for his own men."

IF THE RAILROAD SURVEYOR was a figure of romance, the grading contractor who followed after him was the personification of mischief. In the public mind, every contractor was either a rapacious crook, a political opportunist, or a cruel slave driver, bossing an enormous toiling army of Irish tarriers, Chinese coolies, and other anonymous navvies fresh from the steerage of immigrant ships.

There was some justice in the stereotype. During the quarter century of frenzied railroad construction after the Civil War, many so-called road builders were actually irresponsible, ill-equipped amateurs, while others were really railroad owners in corporate disguise, milking capital out of their own companies and skimming off government construction subsidies. Their sense of duty to the republic and to their own employees was informal, not to say negligent. Chortling Charley Crocker, the major general of construction on the Central Pacific, told a newspaper reporter in 1868 that he really had no idea how many men he had on the payroll: they mustered each day in squads, not as individuals, because all Chinese and Indians looked so much alike that "no human being could tell them apart." Crocker also had no idea how much money he was making because the office records of the Central Pacific burned up before a congressional committee could investigate the operations of the construction subsidiary.

As for the construction workers, they belonged to that great mass of the poor whose historic annals are short. Their labor was hard, unprofitable, and mostly unsung. A Swedish immigrant named Hans Mattson left this commentary on his work as a bridge builder near Galesburg, Illinois, in 1852:

"During my healthy days I stood on the bottom of Rock River from seven o'clock in the morning until seven at night, throwing wet sand with a shovel onto a platform above, from which it was thrown onto another, and from there to terra firma. The most disagreeable part of the business was that one-quarter of each shovelful came back on the head of the operator.... After a couple of weeks the company's paymaster came along, and upon settling my board bill ($1.50 a week) and deducting for the [days I spent in bed, shaking with ague and fever,] I made the discovery that I was able to earn only fifteen cents net per week in building railroad bridges."*

Not every contractor was a villain, of course—nor did every contractor get rich. The very nature of the country through which the railroad passed could ruin an inexperienced contractor on his first job. Everything depended on unpredictable, uncontrollable factors: the quality of the soil, the weather, the distance from supplies, the depth of cuts and fills, the availability of manpower, the presence or absence of wild animals, bandits, and hostile Indians.

In evidence of this is the testimony of James H. Kyner, a railroad contractor whose business career began with a plum of patronage that rapidly withered into a prune.

Kyner had been a soldier in an Ohio regiment during the Civil War and had lost a leg at Shiloh. With a small pension and a young wife, he settled in Omaha, where he happened to make some speeches in praise of railroads.

*Hans Mattson, *Reminiscences: The Story of an Emigrant*, St. Paul, 1892, pp. 29–30.

Kyner's politics attracted the notice of officials of the Union Pacific, who saw to it that he was elected to the state legislature and later was rewarded with a grading contract on a UP spur line in the Loup River valley. This job was rewarding enough; but when Kyner then contracted to grade a section of the Oregon Short Line in southern Idaho, the fun ended. Almost every problem that could bedevil an unlucky contractor tumbled onto his head.

I WAS JUST COMPLETING my first twenty-five miles of work as a railroad contractor, along in the 1880's, when I learned of an opportunity to continue on the Oregon Short Line, which was then being built through southern Idaho. I went out to Ogden, Utah, and from there to the end-of-track at American Falls. The bridge across the Snake River had been completed, but the track reached only a short way beyond it to a little camp of railroad engineers on the farther side. I drove out for eighty miles across the desert, looking over the land, preliminary to choosing some section of it to build. A good deal of the route was going to involve rock cuts and other work for which I had no equipment and no experience, so I chose an easy-looking, eight-mile stretch down Wood River from the town of Shoshone.

The question of getting supplies bothered me, for the end-of-track was eighty miles away. Everything would have to be freighted across that waterless desert of lava rock and sagebrush. But when I raised that question in Omaha, I was told that the track would be laid in another thirty days. Thereafter, moving supplies would be far simpler.

I shipped my equipment from Nebraska to Idaho at once, even sending along some of the men who had worked for me in the North Loup Valley. I had much to learn. It isn't every mile of track that is laid on the easily graded, sandy loam of the North Loup.

Instantly, I ran into a hundred difficulties. The section I had chosen, which looked so simple, turned out to be made of difficult, unyielding lava rock. Men were hard to get—and what tough customers many of them were! No mild Nebraska farmers here, save the few I took with me. Heavy fists and six-shooters were the ordnance, and the commonest liquid was whiskey, straight, in large quantities. After the first payday, my camp was overrun with drunken men, full of fight.

The work was horribly difficult. A fool man with a twelve-mule team broke a brand new plow that had cost me a hundred dollars before it had done a dollar's worth of work. I was angry and worried, and as I got into my buckboard to drive back to camp that day, a tremendous "hammer man," who could swing an eight-pound hammer all day long, came up to me with some grievance of his own. I put him off and picked up the reins, but he swore at me.

"You're a —— —— coward!"

The man was standing near the buckboard, his great six-foot body a mass of muscle and sinew. I am not a small man, but he was larger and infinitely stronger than I. Still, no man could be permitted to talk to the boss like that. I leaped, and with all my weight behind the blow, I struck him in the face. Down he went. Knowing that I was gone if he ever rose again, I leaped astride him, quite consciously bent on closing both his eyes before he could recover. I had fairly well succeeded, too, before I was hauled off. From that time I was boss. Pick handle justice reigned.

The next payday even more men were drunk, though I could not imagine where they got their liquor, way out there, miles and miles from anywhere. Finally I discovered that a man had pitched a tent at the far end of camp and had brought in a considerable store.

I went down to see him, told him how much trouble he was making, and asked him to move. He refused, pointing to a license that he had tacked to his tent pole. It was a government license, and this was government land. Legally, he was within his rights, and I could see that there was no way to get rid of him except by force.

I went back to where the dynamite was stored, got out a stick and cut it in two, picked up a fuse and cap, and started back. On the way I bored a hole in the dynamite with my pencil. I put the cap and fuse on the dynamite and lit a cigarette before I reached his tent.

Dynamite was essential to a well-run construction job.
Harper's Weekly, 1883

Once again I asked the fellow if he would move and was told very positively that he would not.

"All right," I said. "If you won't move, I'll move you."

I fuzzed out the fuse, lit it from my cigarette, and held the stick in my hand.

"When this fuse gets down to the point where you won't dare pick it up, I'll toss her in."

"I'll move!" he cried. "I'll move!" And he began to scurry around.

The fuse by now was getting short, and I tossed it not far from his tent. It went off with a roar. The tent shook, and his horses, breaking loose, ran off a way.

"I'm going back to get another stick of dynamite," I shouted as the man ran to get his horses. But I didn't need another. He packed up as quickly as he could and disappeared, license and all.

The nearest peace officer to my camp at that time was 125 miles away. It was up to the contractor to be the law for his own men. We knew that bad men were about. John Crowe, who kept books for me, told me that every month when he opened a new time book, many of our own men changed their names. Often they changed their jobs as well. From being a teamster they might turn to shovel-and-pick work. It was obvious that these men were hiding from the law.

The country was infested with highwaymen, and every construction camp had men who served as informers for gangs of ruffians who were plotting to steal the payroll. Holdups were so frequent that the stages gave up carrying "treasure boxes," and this made the task of bringing in cash for a payroll extremely difficult.

Five men—that seemed to be the usual number, all on horseback—would come riding along the road. There was no ambush among the sagebrush and the boulders. The bandits merely jogged along in all innocence toward the approaching vehicle. When it reached them, two men would rein out to one side of the road and three to the other. Then, as the stage started past, the driver suddenly would find four rifles pointing at him. He would stop, of course, and the fifth member of the gang would take the money. Nothing was ever done about it by "the law."

As for myself, I had never carried a gun, and I had no desire to carry one now, but I had to. I bought a handsome, single-action .44 the very next time I went to Omaha and began to practice, very privately, until I learned to use the weapon.

Quickness is essential if a revolver is to be of service in a pinch. I practiced pulling the trigger as I swung the gun down. The amount of powder I burned in practice was enormous. From the commissary I obtained circular pieces of cardboard that came between the layers of crackers in a barrel, and, hanging one of these on a greasewood branch, I'd pace off twenty or thirty steps and go to work.

It took me a long time to get the hang of it, but finally I could hit those cardboard targets a good deal oftener than I missed them. Still, I had no desire to be a gunman. I thought that if the men about knew I could shoot, there would be less likelihood of my being called on to do so seriously.

I began to conduct my target practice more openly. On Sundays and other times when the men were not at work, I would take my target into the sagebrush, as if in search of seclusion. A few shots would attract attention, of course, and before long a good-sized audience would collect while I did my best to fill that cardboard full of holes. Fifteen or twenty holes in such a target could make it look very impressive. I got what I was really aiming at when I heard a man say to his partner, "By God, Bill, I wouldn't want the old man to be a-shootin at me."

During all the time I was railroading in the West, I never drank or sat at a gambling table. Countless times, however, I had to visit saloons, for that was where everyone congregated, and I was forever hunting for men to work for me. On several occasions, after a payday had reduced my force, I took a teamster and a wagon and went into the town of Shoshone.

At that time, there were said to be about five thousand people in Shoshone, and it was a commonplace remark that there was not a respectable woman among them. Men who knew the mining camps, cow towns, and railroad villages of the West far better than I did assured me that Shoshone was the toughest of the lot. Stabbings and shootings were common occurrences, and the cemetery in the sagebrush was well populated by men who had died with their boots on.

The most spectacular saloon in the town was Pink's Place. In the same room as the bar were a wheel of fortune, faro games, and stud-poker tables. Upstairs was the rookery occupied by the girls of the place.

The owner was one Pinkston, who was recognized throughout the country as the head of an organized band of gamblers and highwaymen. Pinkston was not a large man. He was clean, trim, active, and was, I think, the handsomest man I ever saw. I remember talking to him only twice, both times when I entered his place in search of men. But from those two conversations, it seemed obvious to me that he was well bred and well educated. He was smooth-shaven, and when he drank, his face, instead of growing red, turned as pale as that of a woman. His gun, if he wore one (and I have no doubt he did), was never in evidence.

Going to Pink's Place for men, I met the person known as "Pink's woman." Whether she was his wife or not I do not know, but in some ways she was like him. Among the painted creatures that filled the place, she stood apart—soft-spoken, rather pretty, pleasantly dressed. When I asked for Pinkston, she said he was busy and nodded to where he sat in a game of cards. She asked if she could do anything for me. I told her I needed men. Very quietly and efficiently, she rounded some up for me.

It is hard to believe that these two people, with their apparent gentility, were leaders of a criminal element that caused me great anxiety as a railroad contractor; but I have told all this to show that building railroads in Idaho in the eighties presented other problems than those imposed by lava rock.

Of itself, the lava rock would have been difficult enough. As I have said, I chose my section because the work appeared light. But the moment we started, we learned something about that rock. To move it required the use of enormously high explosives. Black powder did little but to heave up blocks too big to handle. The rock had to be shattered by a sharper explosion, and even then the stuff seemed to be keyed together. It was almost impossible to load and haul it away. Blasts sometimes barely cracked the surface, blowing down, instead, into openings —ancient bubbles, perhaps, in the lava.

To make things worse, men were getting harder and harder to get. After every payday there would be a troublesome shortage of manpower. The railroad shipped hundreds from the East; but when they reached the railhead, many of those fellows drove straight on to Oregon and Washington, having gotten free transportation to the end-of-the-track.

Freighting in supplies was another grave problem. For every dollar that I spent in the purchase of case goods, more than two dollars was spent getting it to camp. Baled hay that cost six dollars a ton in Nebraska had cost me a hundred dollars a ton by the time it was piled in my camp. Often, despite the high rates we paid, professional freighters could not be found at all, and I would have to take men off the work, send them to American Falls, and wait four or five days for their return.

It is no wonder that throughout the building of that eight-mile stretch on Wood River I constantly lost money. With every setting of the sun my load of indebtedness was growing. Time after time my payroll fell behind the estimates. Finally, I had to go to Omaha to borrow some money in order to continue. My wife came back with me. We had quite a sum with us—thousands of dollars—and naturally wondered how it could be guarded. Ultimately, we divided it. My wife pinned some currency to an inner garment, and I rolled up all I could and stuffed it down into the cavity of my artificial leg.

We reached the camp with the money, but my wife was almost ill with exhaustion, and I was ready to get into bed myself. The physical strain of sixteen hours in a rattling, swaying, jerking coach and eight more in a bouncing, careening buckboard would have been enough to tire us out, but the strain of carrying that money through such a land was even worse.

The roughness of life in Idaho in those days can hardly be exaggerated. The high, dry plains were extraordinarily hot almost every summer day, with the thermometer often registering 120 degrees. So dry was the air that horses working at the heavy task of loading scrapers seemed never to sweat enough to wet a hair. The nights, at the same time, were very cold. In the morning following a day when the temperature had gone far above a hundred, I often found a thin coating of ice on the water pail that sat beneath the fly of my tent. By throwing a double blanket over the pail I could keep the water cool all day. By midday the surface of the ground would be so hot that dogs would whimper, picking up their feet as if on coals. If a person stopped for more than a few seconds, he'd have to kick away the soil to get his feet under that thin, overheated surface.

It took tough, hardy men to stay in such a land. No wonder so many ringtailed roarers were about. Gentleness and consideration were almost unknown.

Thick skins, brute force, and constant determination were almost essential, and they were common enough attributes around our camps in those days.

Because of the large number of bad men in the area, Bob Kilpatrick, of the contracting firm of Kilpatrick Brothers & Collins, never went anywhere without a bodyguard—a swarthy, black-haired, black-eyed Mexican, who invariably trailed behind his boss, wearing a heavy cartridge belt from which hung two loaded holsters.

The Kilpatrick camp was among the largest in that country, and it had more tough men about it than smaller camps like mine. I had been at Kilpatrick's often, for there were many things to learn there; but I learned one trick that I did not imitate.

In the Kilpatrick camp, one big cook tent supplied all the food for several dining tents, in each of which were several long tables with boards along each side as seats. Entering one of these tents one day, just after the noon meal, I saw the tin plates spaced with such extraordinary precision as to arouse my curiosity. In my camp, the tables always looked as if a hurricane had just passed through.

A man appeared with a pail of water and a stick with a rag attached to the end. He soused the swab into his pail, wiped out a plate or two without lifting them from the table, dipped the swab again, and continued along the line, giving each tin plate a lick and a promise.

Never had I seen such a cleaning up as that before. I was amazed at the man's ability to swab out a tin plate, which is very easily moved, without disturbing it a fraction of an inch. Looking down into one of the swabbed-out plates, on which the dirty rag had left a spiral of food particles, I saw the reason. Every one of those tin plates was nailed securely through its bottom to the table.

After finishing up at Wood River—which nearly finished me—I got a contract for thirty miles of construction far up the main line, beyond Mountain Home and not too far from Boise. It was the biggest job I had ever tackled, but easier than that awful lava rock. I almost danced with delight when I went to look it over.

How we made that Idaho dirt fly! We ran into a little hardpan we could not plow, and we "shot" it. But once a little powder had been used, it went perfectly. I greatly enlarged my outfit and had so many horses at work that it took three tons of oats a day to feed them. We worked ten hours a day, six days a week, with scrapers and wheel scrapers doing most of it, but what a relief it was to move from Wood River to Indian Creek!

At last we came to the end of it. The engineers made their last inspection, and we had only to pay off our men and ship that greatly enlarged outfit to the next job, in Colorado. But then I faced a final problem that was not so simple to solve.

The payroll had grown enormously. It would take the better part of twenty thousand dollars to pay the men for the last month, and the country was swarming with bad men from all over the United States and Mexico. It was inconceivable that any payroll could be brought in without those gunmen knowing it was due. The only possibility was to try to dodge them—or, failing that, to fight it out with them.

The prospect was not pleasant. I had to go to Ogden, myself, to bring the money back, and my companion would be Stitt, my bookkeeper. Stitt was not a timid soul. But he was a bookkeeper, not a wielder of six-shooters. Still, he had to go, so that his records could be examined, and so did Doty, who was a kind of partner on that work. Doty was a good man at moving dirt—or, rather, at making other men move it—but he was nervous and far from handy with a gun. I was as much afraid of Doty's shooting as of any bandit.

Fortunately, Frank Luddington, a resourceful fellow whose nerves and aim were steady, was still working with me as a subcontractor.

"Lud," I said, "I've got to go to Ogden with Doty and Stitt, and I'd like you to come with us."

He nodded, and it was not necessary for me to enlarge on the problem. Frank had taken on such tasks before, and he had a sawed-off shotgun that he carried on such errands, its walnut stock tucked up against his right arm. I got him a round-trip pass, and, having some affairs of his own in Ogden, he went off a day or two ahead of us.

Doty, Stitt, and I left camp in my buckboard, with Jim, a pacer, and Frank, a trotter, hitched to it. Hundreds of men saw us drive away from camp, and the departure of the bookkeeper fairly shouted that we were going for the final settlement, especially as payday was only four days off. All we could do was to hope we would be able to dodge a holdup on our return.

Nine or ten hours later, we arrived at end-of-track. There was, of course, no town there, but men were constantly going and coming, with the result that a kind of tent village had been set up. A couple of men had set up a business with two tents—one a stable tent, where horses were stabled for their absentee owners, and the other a bunkhouse or flophouse where, within the confines of the tent, the sagebrush and cactus had been cleared away so that men could spread their bedrolls on the ground. There was a charge of one dollar for bunking there. I have forgotten what fantastic figure was set upon the "stabling" of horses in the stable tent. However, we left the wagon and horses and climbed aboard the caboose of an empty construction train that was heading back to Shoshone.

We reached Ogden that evening and registered at the Depot Hotel. This hostelry, at which all railroad employees obtained a special rate, stood not far from where the Utah Northern crossed the Union Pacific, a good half-mile from the business section of the town. We met Luddington there. Immediately after breakfast the next morning, all of us went down to the disbursing office on the second floor of the building next door to the bank of Guthrie, Dooly, and Company.

The disbursing clerk had been expecting us, and the estimate, with the final check pinned to it, was waiting. The necessary accounting was simple. Within a few minutes the clerk had recorded what he needed and handed me a check for a little over $23,600.

It was hardly more than nine o'clock. A train for Pocatello was due to leave within the hour. We went at once to Guthrie, Dooly, and Company, on whom the check was drawn. Mr. Dooly, with a face as expressionless as a pan of dough, looked at the check and examined my endorsement. Putting it aside, he swung open the wicket, stooped down and lifted out, one by one, four canvas bags of gold, on each of which was stamped, $5000.

"Oh, Mr. Dooly," I began, "don't give me that. We have to carry this money a long way. Let me have it in currency."

He stood back with his hands on the shelf in front of him, still with no expression on his face.

"That's legal tender, sir," he said, clipping his words off short.

I saw I could do nothing. Train time was near.

"Well," I said, "let me have the six hundred-odd in dollars, halves, and quarters."

We had to have that much change, despite its weight. He handed it out in rolls, finally placing the remaining three thousand dollars, in currency, on the pile, and dropping a folded canvas treasury bag on top of it.

I handed one of the bags to each of my companions, stuffed the currency into my inside coat pocket, and dropped the silver and the fourth bag of gold into the treasury sack; and off we went.

The other three, each with a bag of gold on his shoulder, walked along readily enough; but, having that weighty sack of gold and silver on my back, I needed help long before we had walked the rather considerable distance to the station. Luddington traded with me, finally, and we reached the station a little before the train backed in. Had we had more time, we probably could have exchanged that gold for currency at some other bank, but we were anxious to get back to camp. The sooner we completed that round trip, the more unexpected our return would be.

Having boarded the train, however, we began to worry. We did not take a Pullman—perhaps there was no Pullman on the train—but rode instead in a day coach, 120 miles to Pocatello. There, by a stroke of luck, we were in time to catch a loaded construction train that was starting at once for the end-of-track. Had we taken a passenger train to Shoshone, we would have had to parade the station platform with all that money in plain sight. As it was, we rode in the construction train caboose—the only passengers. None of Pinkston's hangers-on got a glimpse of those canvas bags as we rattled slowly through Shoshone and out over the rough roadbed that lay behind it. Just over Canyon Creek, our buckboard and horses were waiting in the stable tent.

Never in my life had I been so keyed up. All the way from Ogden my every sense was alert. Hundreds of men in Ogden had seen us with that gold. Scores more in Pocatello had seen us just as plainly, and telegrams of seeming innocence could easily have carried the news ahead. But the news did not need to be carried at all: the poorest fool in camp knew what we had gone for.

I was thoroughly convinced—in fact, I positively *knew*—that somewhere between end-of-track and my camp, someone would attempt to take that money from us. I was determined to shoot it out when those five men should come. Only a few months back I had been $63,000 in debt, all but ruined, and now, after working and struggling, I had paid all those debts except this payroll that I had still to meet. Once that was paid, I would be clear again, with my outfit larger than it had ever been and with several thousand dollars of that money we were carrying left for me.

The construction train rattled and bumped to a stop just after the sun had set. We had come to end-of-track. Quickly, we shouldered our money and strode off toward the stable tent. There, in the dusk, my buckboard was standing.

"Doty," I said, as we were putting the money in, "You go over there and cut me an armful of willow branches. Lud, you get the horses. Stitt and I will wait."

They hurried off. Stitt suggested we get a bite to eat at a tent not far off, but I would not hear of it. We had a nine-hour drive ahead, and I did not propose to waste time with food. Our horses were well fed, and that was all that mattered.

Doty came back with the willow branches and Lud led out the horses. The neck yoke and traces were hooked in place. We climbed in—Doty on my left, Stitt on the low, slat bed of the buckboard, with his feet hanging off behind, and Lud with his sawed-off shotgun behind me.

"Now listen," I said. "The minute I see 'em coming, I'll start shooting. If it's a bunch, I'm going to make 'em all get off the trail to the east. I'm not going to let 'em separate. And Doty, when I start shooting, you keep out of my way. Dive into the sagebrush if you want to, but don't get in front of me or you'll get shot. Lud, I expect you to stay with me."

"By God, I will," he said.

"But if you start using that shotgun, you get off the buckboard. Don't shoot past me. Get off and get out to the side."

He agreed, and I tightened the reins.

"Now remember," I went on, keyed to such a pitch as I had never been before, "if this money don't reach camp, it'll be because I'm dead!"

I took one of Doty's willow branches and began to lash those willing horses. There was more than $20,000 under Doty's feet and mine, another $3,000 in my coat pocket, and the barrel of a .44 beneath my thigh, with its butt turned up where I could grasp it quickly.

We drove three miles or four before darkness came. The tents at end-of-track faded away behind us. The sagebrush and greasewood melted into the oncoming night. The horses, on whom I constantly used that willow branch, settled into their stride. Jim swayed a little from side to side as he paced through the deep sand, and Frank's feet touched almost noiselessly on the trail.

After a while, the trail got rougher, and I turned the horses up onto the graded right-of-way, which had no tracks on it yet. Now and again, we would come to a place where a bridge was yet to be built across a dry creek, and down we would go, rattling through the gully, then bouncing and careening up again.

These breaks in the level right-of-way grew more frequent, and in the dark we almost overturned in crossing one of them. At that point, I went back to the sandy trail once more.

I strained my eyes to watch the faint horizon. The sky was dark, but the earth lay darker. Any instant, I might see the silhouettes of horsemen against that pale line. Now and then my hand leaped to my upturned revolver when I caught sight of some piece of wind-blown sagebrush that resembled the figure of a man.

I wore a willow branch to shreds on the backs of the horses. Throwing it away, I took another from Doty, who sat silently beside me. Stitt scratched a match to see what time it was, and I swore at him: A match in the clear air on that level plain could be seen a mile.

Mile after mile rolled past. I sat tensely upright on the seat, leaning forward a little, always conscious of the heavy butt of my revolver there between my legs. More miles, more hours, and still those horses kept their stride. I took the last of Doty's willow branches.

In the east the sky was turning faintly gray. We swayed and bounced across a gully that I knew—a welcome one, for it was close to camp. The grade rose gradually, and I saw the ghostly shapes of silent tents. The faint light of a lantern showed through the canvas of the commissary tent.

I pulled up the horses. We stiffly got down. Without a word, we pulled out our load of gold and carried it over to the entrance of the tent.

As we reached it, the canvas flap drew back suddenly. There stood Crowe, looking keenly at us.

"What are you up so early for?" I asked.

Crowe beckoned me in.

"I've been up all night," he said.

"What for?"

He raised his finger and beckoned me over to the side wall of the tent. There he pulled the loose canvas down an inch or two and pointed out. I stared out into the feeble gray light.

There, not thirty feet away, stood five horses, their saddles and their bridles on. I drew in my breath and asked what they were doing.

"Perhaps they thought you wouldn't be in so soon," Crowe whispered. "Anyway, they got up a poker game. One of our men got roped into it and came to me for some money. He told me they were playing. I didn't try and stop 'em, you can bet."

I took a long breath.

"Don't charge the money up to him," I said.

I sat down weakly on a trunk. Where Lud and Stitt and Doty went, I do not know. I went to sleep there on the trunk and didn't wake up for hours.

—Abridged from *End of Track*, the autobiography of James H. Kyner, with Hawthorne Daniel. Copyright 1937 by Caxton Printers, Caldwell, Idaho.

CHAPTER FOUR

The Brakeman's
Glorious, Rowdy Life

I

"It was four or five months before I 'got it.'"

ALMOST WITHOUT EXCEPTION, old-time railroad men begin their stories on a wistful note, in sentimental recollection of a little boy who loved to watch the trains go by, savoring the symbols on the boxcars like candy on his tongue: the Grand Trunk Line, the Erie Road, the Great Northern, the Burlington, the Santa Fe...

Take, for example, the story of Daniel Willard, a New England farm boy who developed into one of the most distinguished presidents of the Baltimore & Ohio Railroad. For him, the first taste of that irresistible railroad confection was carried by the old, wood-burning locomotives of the Vermont Central, which used to cut across his father's pasture on the banks of the Connecticut River, trailing clouds of white smoke through the meadows and setting the calves and colts scampering off the tracks.

For Samuel Vauclain, a tough, resourceful chief executive of the Baldwin Locomotive Works in Philadelphia, the same enticing flavor lurked in the miasma of coal smoke and valve oil that hung about the roundhouse of the Pennsylvania Railroad in the Allegheny Mountain town where he was born. For Herbert Hamblen, the adventurous New Yorker who wrote the classic of railroad biography called *The General Manager's Story,* the enticement was a freight train, puffing slowly and laboriously up a heavy grade, "the brakemen sitting—if it happened to be pleasant weather—on their brake wheels, with folded arms and hat brims flapping in the breeze."

Often, it was these rough young brakemen who captured the imagination of the boy by the side of the tracks and infected him with an incurable longing to work on the railroad. The brakeman's job was dangerous, as any trackside boy could easily see; but at least it was attainable, comprehensible. It seemed to consist primarily of skipping from car to car, setting brakes, ducking for tunnels, and sometimes going back with a flag to protect the train from the following express.

For all the simplicity of their work, however, brakemen had every attractive attribute of professional railroad men. They spoke a spicy slang, smelled of beer and tobacco, and had been everywhere. When they walked downtown, they wore new black suits with a woven-in pattern of one-inch squares, trimmed around the lapels and pocket-flaps with heavy satin braid; and their spring-bottom pants flared out below the ankles, forming bells that extended to the toes of their high-heeled boots.

Obviously, braking was the place for an ambitious young man to begin his railroad career. As Herbert Hamblen tells it, the job was easy enough for any boy to learn. The main problem was staying alive to enjoy it.

"VERY WELL," said the young man at the center of the railroad yard, "I am the yardmaster here, and as I'm rather short of brakemen and you appear to be a likely young fellow, I will give you a job. Keep your eyes and ears open. Obey orders strictly, *whether you can or can't*, and—" he grabbed me by the arm and pulled me back just as I was about to step into the path of a rapidly approaching car, which would certainly have put an abrupt end to my railroading career "—be careful, never, never, under any circumstances, to step onto a railroad track *anywhere* without first looking both ways, and always give everything on wheels the right of way."

And he added: "When will you be ready to go to work?"

"Right away," I said.

The yardmaster looked at his watch.

"Well, I don't know but that you had better get your dinner first. It's now eleven-thirty. There's no use of your getting killed on any empty stomach."

Away I went to my hotel, highly elated at my success. I was now a genuine railroad man, I thought. To be sure, I didn't like all those references to killing and maiming, but I thought they had been thrown out only to try my nerve. I congratulated myself that I had shown no sign of flinching.

I was wrong in my conjecture, of course. Like all railroad yards, this was more or less a slaughterhouse, and one poor fellow's life was crushed out of him that afternoon, although I did not hear about it until the next day—which was just as well, I guess, for if I had known of it at the time, I dare say I should have lost some of the nerve I felt so proud of.

Ten minutes ahead of time, I reported to the yardmaster. Sticking his head out of the door, he called:

"Hey, Simmons!" And a fine, large, sunburned, black-bearded man appeared. "Here's a green man I want you to break in. Put him on top and let him pass the signal for a day or two until he can handle himself."

Simmons, who was the conductor of a "drill"—a switch-engine crew—took me out to the engine and said to the engineer, a grimy, greasy individual:

"Bill, here's a fresh fish Dawson wants to break in. I'll put him on the head car and let him pass the signal."

Bill watched sourly while Simmons instructed me to climb onto the car next to the engine and repeat the signals of the man in the middle of the train. That seemed simple enough, but I hadn't been doing it for more than ten minutes when the engine stopped and Bill called out: "Hey! Hey! You, there! Dominie? Parson?"

Seeing that he was addressing his remarks to me and not liking his impertinence, I said:

"Well, what is it? Are you talking to me?"

"Yes, I'm talkin' to you, and ye better keep a civil tongue in your head. What kind of a signal is that ye're givin' me? Wha'd'ye want me ter do, anyway?"

"I don't want you to do anything, and I don't care what you do. I'm giving you the signal just as I get it."

"No, ye hain't nuther, an' don't ye give me no back talk. Say, where do you come from?"

"I'm from Walton," I said.

"I thought so. Another Walton punkin husker. Say, Simmons, take this blamed ornament o' yours down off here an' give me a man that knows one signal from another, or I'll smash all the cars in the yard." And he gave the engine a jerk back that nearly threw me off the car.

"Oh, he's all right," Simmons said. "He's a little green, but he'll get over that." Then, to me: "Be careful how you pass the signals, bub, or the engineer can't tell what he's doing."

I said I was doing them just exactly as the other man did.

"Well, that's all right," Simmons said. "Bill is kinder cranky, but you mustn't mind that."

But we hadn't worked ten minutes more, and my arms were beginning to ache from the continuous motion, when Bill roared out:

"Say, you infernal counter jumper, will you git out of the way so I can see that man's signals? Set down, fall down, git off o' there. You'll scare the engine off the tracks the way you're flappin' your wings." And then, having occasion to go to the other end of the yard, he pulled her wide open, drenching me with soot and water from the stack. I had my best clothes on, and they were ruined.

When we were relieved at six o'clock, I was tired, dirty, disgusted with railroading, and firmly determined to quit at once. During the evening, however, I scraped up acquaintance with a young fellow about my own age, who, like myself, was a "boy from home," although not so green as I. He had been on the railroad for a whole year and liked it, and he predicted that inside of thirty days, I would, too. He said he wouldn't go back to the farm for anything. Although he admitted that the talk about killing and maiming was by no means exaggerated, he hoped to escape that almost universal fate by being careful. Poor fellow! He was blown from the top of his train a few months later and found by the section crew, frozen stiff.

Considerably cheered by my new friend's advice, I reported again for duty at six o'clock the next morning and worked all day with no more thrilling adventure than an occasional cursing from sooty Bill.

Before I had been a week in the yard, I was well broken in and had acquired the reckless air that is the second stage in a greenhorn's experience. It is characteristic of the period *before* he gets hurt.

I delighted in catching and riding on the most swiftly moving cars, became an expert at making quick couplings and flying switches. Occasionally an old hand would say, with a shake of the head: "You'll get it bime'by." But I only laughed.

It was four or five months before I "got it." I was making a coupling one afternoon. I had balanced the pin in the drawhead of the stationary car and was running along ahead of the other car, holding up the link. Just before the two cars were to come together, the one behind me left the track, having jumped a frog. Hearing the racket, I sprang to one side, but my toe caught the top of the rail. I was pinned between the corners of the cars as they came together. I heard my ribs cave in like an old box smashed with an ax.

The car stopped and held me like a vise. I nearly fainted with pain, quite unable to breathe. Fortunately, Mr. Simmons was watching. With the presence of mind that comes of long service, he called at once for the switch rope, and he would not allow the engine to come back and couple the car again, as that would surely have crushed out my life.

It seemed to me that I would surely suffocate before they got that switch rope hooked onto the side of the car, although I knew the boys were hustling for dear life. I tell you, when your breath is shut off, seconds are hours. My head was bursting. I became blind. There was a terrible roaring in my ears. And then, as the engine settled back on the switch rope, I felt a life-giving relief as I fell, fainting, into the arms of the boys.

They carried me into the yardmaster's office. Every step of the way the jagged ends of my broken ribs pricked and grated as though they would punch holes in me. My breath came in short, suffocating gasps.

The company's doctor, a young fellow fresh from college, who was paid twenty-five dollars a month to tend damaged employees, cut my clothes off, half murdered me with punching and squeezing, and finally remarked: "There's nothing much the matter with him. Few of his slats stove in, that's all."

He bandaged me, and a couple of the boys half led, half carried me to the boardinghouse, where I lay, unable to move without help, for six weeks.

The boys cheered me up greatly by telling of their own various mishaps. Few of them had escaped broken bones and smashed fingers; and I was assured that broken ribs were nothing, absolutely nothing. Their talk restored my spirits wonderfully, for I had been disconsolately thinking that I was now a physical wreck, fit only for a job of flagging on some road crossing at twenty dollars a month. Even Simmons, who appeared to be a particularly fine specimen of manhood, told me he once had fallen while running ahead of a car, just as I had been doing, and twelve cars and the engine had passed over him, rolling him over and over, breaking both his legs, and, as he said, mixing up his insides so his victuals didn't do him much good for a year afterward.

Shortly after I returned to work, Simmons got one side of a new freight train, and, to my great delight, he took me with him on the road. I was not only glad to get out of the slaughterhouse with all my limbs, but also pleased at the prospect of learning the practical railroading that I had heard so much about.

We had a fine, big, eight-wheel caboose, right out of the paint shop, red outside and green inside. There were six bunks in her, a row of lockers on each side to sit on and keep supplies in, a stove and table, and a desk for the conductor. We furnished our own bedding and cooking utensils, and, as Simmons would not have any but nice fellows around him, we had a pleasant and comfortable home on wheels. We each contributed to the mess, except the flagman, who did the cooking. He messed free. We took turns cleaning up. As the boys had good taste, we soon had the car looking like a young lady's boudoir. We had lace curtains in front of the bunks, a strip of oilcloth on the floor, a mat that the flag-man had swiped from a sleeping car, a dog, and a canary.

Since a younger man than I had been assigned to the crew, I was second man. I rode at the head of the train, on the engine, and was the engineer's flag. I opened and closed switches, cut off and coupled the engine, held the train on downgrades, watched out for the caboose on curves, took water, shoveled down coal to the fireman, rang the bell at crossings, put out the blower, oiled the valves, ran ahead with my flag to protect our end, and handed the engineer oil cans, wrenches, and lights for his pipe.

I made acquaintance now with that formidable document, the timetable. I heard train orders and the officers who issued them discussed by such high authorities as conductors and engineers; and I listened in astonishment at the erudition these men displayed. The officers of our road, I soon learned, "didn't know nothing" and should not have been allowed to sit on the fence and watch the trains go by—whereupon I conceived a great wonder as to how the railroad survived under such densely incompetent management.

My greatest delight was riding the engines. The engineers and firemen were fine, sociable fellows. When we were a little late, the engineer would sometimes say, "Don't you set no brakes goin' down here—I got to git a gait on 'em." Then, as the train pitched over the top of the hill, he would cut her back a notch at a time, until he got her near the center, and gradually work his throttle wide open.

How she would fly downhill, the exhaust a steady roar out of the stack, the connecting rods an indistinguishable blur! The old girl was rolling and jumping as if to leave the track, with the train behind half hidden in dust, and I hanging onto the side of the cab for dear life, watching out ahead, and hoping, oh so much, that he'll shut her off before we get to that sharp reverse curve.

Petrified, I watch the engineer's grimy left hand on the throttle, waiting to see the preliminary swelling of muscles that will show me he is taking a grip to shove it in. But there is not a sign. His head and half his body are out the window. And now we are upon that curve! I give a frightened glance at the too-convenient ditch where I expect to land, and I take a death grip on the side of the cab.

Whang! She hits the curve. I am nearly flung out the window in spite of my good grip. Before she has half done rolling (how do the springs stand it?) she hits a reverse. I am torn from my grip on the window and slammed against the boiler; and the engine, having passed this most uncomfortable place, flies on, rolling and roaring down the mountain. The engineer has not moved an eyelid, nor has the fireman interrupted for an instant the steady, pendulum-like swinging of the fire door and the scoop. Fifteen minutes afterward, safe in the siding with switches locked, nobody seems to remember that we have done anything particular.

At first, I considered the locomotive too complicated to understand. But, gradually, I learned its various parts. When I learned that most engineers and firemen had risen from brakemen like myself, I took heart and began to hope that someday I might sit on the right side of the cab, to be spoken to with some slight deference by the officials of the road and stared at in open-mouthed admiration by small boys at country stations.

—From Herbert E. Hamblen's *The General Manager's Story.*
The Macmillan Company, New York, 1898 and 1907.

A diligent trackwalker,
alert to obstacles in the
right-of-way, could save
a train from derailment.
Scribner's Monthly, 1888

Coupling with the link-and-pin was the most hazardous of the brakeman's duties.

Clarke's *The American Railway, 1897*

II

"We lived on the car tops. Weather did not count."

DURING THE FIRST fifty or sixty years of steam, thousands of brakemen lost their lives to the peculiar hazards of their work. There simply was no way for a man to avoid danger while coupling cars with a link and pin or setting hand brakes on the top of a swaying, windswept boxcar on a freezing winter night. A brakeman who escaped being hurled to the ground or crushed between moving freight cars could thank his stars more than his own skill.

Presumably, it was this constant exposure to mayhem and death that caused many old-time brakemen to develop a callous, pessimistic outlook and a reckless style of behavior. Brutalized by the hardship of their work, brakemen became the worst drunkards, gamblers, and rowdies in a profession that was infamous for drinking, drifting, and disorder. When preachers and social reformers decried the moral degradation of railroad men, it was railroad brakemen they had in mind—although, as a matter of fact, the tough, fatalistic attitude of the brakemen permeated the entire railroad fraternity.

Nowhere on the continent was the life of a brakeman more difficult than out on the cattle frontier of Kansas in the 1870's. The cars and locomotives were old and cheap; the roadbeds were new and lightly ballasted; the winter storms were horrendous; the cargoes of longhorn cattle were intractable; and at the end of every line of track there was a frontier cow town, inhabited by belligerent, gun-carrying horsemen who turned out to be the natural enemies of railroad brakies.

To endure the cattle run, a brakeman needed exceptional courage and unusual luck. Even so, there were railroad men who found this precarious assignment exactly to their taste. Among these bravoes was a young boomer named Harry French, straight from the switching yards at K.C., with a rudimentary mustache sprouting on his lip and a confident smile at the corners of his mouth. The gambling tables of Dodge City, the respect of his peers, and sixty-five dollars a month in salary made life on the prairie quite acceptable to Harry French. He rambled joyfully from Topeka to Hunnewell, out at the edge of the Indian Territory; and the only thing that irritated him was a yen for more adventure. His memoirs, dictated in the 1930's to his son, Chauncey Del French, are an evocative record of the brakeman's life.

I WAS HIRED by the Santa Fe as a brakeman on the Kansas prairie in 1876 and detailed to run between Newton and Topeka. The population of Topeka at that time was close to fifteen thousand. It was a clean town with decent hotels and good food at reasonable prices. It also was the home of a number of skilled poker players. I have always believed that I should have liked to live there permanently.

As for Newton, its site had been open prairie five years earlier. To capture some of the cattle trade of Abilene, the Santa Fe had decided to build a new town about seventy-five miles farther southwest. In less than sixty days Newton had a population of over two thousand souls.

From all reports most of them were mighty tough souls. As usual in a cow town, there was open season on the marshal. That individual had to be quicker on the draw than any drunken tough looking for trouble. If the marshal wasn't quicker, he was soon run out of town—or dead. It was in 1871 or 1872 that the border saying originated: "No Sundays west of Newton. No God west of Pueblo."*

Newton's rise marked the decline of Abilene. Then Newton, in turn, was supplanted by Caldwell as the railroads extended their lines farther into the Southwest. Caldwell had its day as a cattle metropolis before being dethroned by Dodge City. The Newton I knew in 1876 was quiet. A church had taken over a former saloon, and it was possible for the congregation, when they directed their gaze heavenward, to see bullet holes in the ceiling.

The railroad man and the cowboy shared a dread of the winter months. Longhorns and buffalo had a habit of drifting before the icy blasts of a Kansas norther. For the cowboy, the drifting meant the loss of control of the herd under his care; for the railroad man, it meant an extra hazard when stray herds sought shelter in the railway cuts. Many wrecks were caused by trains plowing into packed masses of animals.

---

*Every western town that has ever been worth shooting up on a Saturday night ornaments itself with some variation of this proverb, for example: "There's no railroad west of Junction City, no law west of Kansas City, and no God west of Hays City."

Like the cowboy, the railroad brakeman dreaded winter.
Harper's Weekly, 1880

I was introduced to a Kansas blizzard the first winter I worked for the Santa Fe. There was a light fall of snow, and then the wind started—a wind such as I had never known before. The chill of its snow-laden blast seemed to make paper of warm garments. I made my way with considerable difficulty from my boarding-house to my favorite saloon. Only my anticipation of an evening of poker made me struggle against that powerful blast of icy, sleet-laden wind. I had just thawed out beside a roaring fire and got nicely started in the game, a noggin of warm whiskey by my elbow, when a callboy tapped me on the shoulder.

"French," he said, "the dispatcher wants you right away."

"What's up?" I demanded. I had been congratulating myself on the fact that I did not have to go out on a run for another twelve hours. I was hoping Mr. Blizzard would have blown himself away before I had to decorate the top of a boxcar.

"You're going out with a light engine, ahead of the regular passenger train. There's a freight engine broke down somewhere beyond Cimarron."

"Why did you pick on me?" I grumbled.

"That's easy," the callboy replied, grinning. "I knew where to find you."

There was nothing to do but sign his greasy book. An hour later our freight engine rumbled over the last switch and headed out into the open prairie.

"It sure is a nasty night," I remarked to the engineer as I thawed my half-frozen fingers on the boiler head.

"You ain't seen it all yet, kid," he replied. "Wait till we hit them big cuts around the Arkansas."

I climbed over onto the front end of the fireman's seatbox. The half-warm cab was a great deal better than a boxcar top on this particular night. There was one other consolation—I would get to deadhead back on a passenger train. But I had a few worries. There was enough snow on the rails to retard our engine noticeably, whereas the passenger train behind us would have no snow to buck. It would probably follow us closely all the way. Should the cuts be blocked with snow—or animals—I would have some fast flagging to do.

When we hit the first of the cuts, all three of us breathed a sigh of relief. There was no snow in them; the wind had swept them thoroughly. I climbed off the seat box and took a position close to the tank brake. Suddenly, the engineer let out a yell. "Cattle!" I spun the hand brake on, swung on it, locked it, and dived up onto the woodpile on the tender. There was a queer bumping noise as we plowed into the herd, then a real crash as the engine plunged off the rails and tipped partly over.

I was thrown—a dizzy, whirling sensation—and lit on thin ice at the edge of the Arkansas. The water was not deep; I escaped with a wetting. Longhorns and buffalo were thrashing about as I climbed the low bank. The fireman was helping the injured engineer back out onto the tender. The fireman's arm hung loosely by his side. I located my lanterns. They were both out. Only the red light was in serviceable condition.

"Matches," I gasped through chattering teeth. My clothes were freezing to me. I accepted a handful from the fireman, tilted the lantern upside down, and held a match under the wick.

"Be ready to unload," I warned. "They might get by me."

There were plenty of animals milling around the engine, but they seemed puzzled by the red light and made no attempt to charge me. I dodged and twisted to get free of them. Once clear of the herd, I ran as fast as I could. After a few minutes of sprinting, I could see the headlight of the passenger train.

My frantic signals were answered by a call for brakes. The staccato snorts of the engine in reverse were sweet music to my ears. When the engine passed me, her drivers were turning as fast in reverse as they had been in forward motion a few seconds previously. I could see the brakeman and conductor twisting on brakes between the coaches. Less than twenty feet separated the two engines when the passenger train stopped.

Wrapped in blankets and nursing a bottle of whiskey that a sympathetic passenger gave me, I spent the rest of that night hovering over a stove in the baggage car, trying to get the chill out of my bones.

It was a few months afterward that the division superintendent called me in and offered me a run between Dodge City, Granada, and Pueblo. Dodge City, Queen of the Cow Towns! If he could have guessed how much I wanted to see it! I left as soon as possible, riding deadhead on a pass.

Shortly after the rain left Newton, the passenger brakeman was injured making a coupling. The conductor asked me to take charge of the rear end of the train. He offered to pay me out of his own pocket, but I refused to accept his money. I was glad to be of service—and curious for this experience.

The rear car was one of the newfangled "Pullmans." The seats were a rich-looking plush material. I watched the Negro porter transforming one seat into a comfortable-looking bed. The washbowls were a fine grade of mottled marble. Water was supplied to each bowl by an individual pump. The car was loaded to capacity with wealthy stockmen, and, I suspect, a number of fancy women. In the cramped quarters of the men's smoking room, a high-play poker game was in progress. Gold pieces and bills were the stakes, and they were very much in evidence.

I was particularly interested in one of the players. Fine clothes, careful barbering, diamond-decked fingers marked him as a gambler. His eyes spotted the lantern on my arm as I entered.

"Are you the brakeman?" he asked softly. He stopped the game and sent the porter for more wine.

"Just until we get to Dodge City," I replied. "The regular man got his arm broke making a coupling."

"Tough for him, but it gets you some extra money."

"He'll be laid up for a couple of months," I said. "I'm just helping out because the train would be shorthanded. I don't get paid. That'll go to the injured man."

The players seemed interested in the conversation. One of them, a cattle owner, paid for the wine. He was wearing a buckskin vest with a huge golden chain and fob ornamenting it. Pearl-handled six-shooters nestled in inlaid holsters just below his fancy vest. Black broadcloth coat and trousers plainly indicated that he was a man of considerable wealth. I stared at the huge quantity of money displayed so carelessly on the table. When the players were ready to resume their game, I turned to leave the smoking room.

"Wait a few minutes if you can, young feller," the cattleman suggested. Then, turning to his companions: "Let's split a pot with the man who got hurt." His eyes glanced around the table.

"I'll add to it," the gambler said in his soft, whisper-like voice. "Aces or better to open the pot—half to the injured man, ten percent to the kid who works in his place for nothing."

Again the nod went around the table. I watched the cards dealt. Hand after hand passed. The deal went around again and again. Steadily the pile of currency grew. Other passengers crowded around to watch the betting. The cattleman finally opened the pot (it may have been just a coincidence that the gambler dealt him the hand) and a three-cornered duel of wits began between the cattleman, the gambler, and a funeral-faced man dressed in somber black, whom I knew afterwards as a lawyer in Dodge City. Under fire the lawyer dropped out. When the showdown finally came, the cattleman laid down three queens and two jacks. The gambler exposed three kings and the other two jacks.

"Count the pot," was the cattleman's only comment. There was a trifle over eight hundred dollars.

The gambler beckoned me to his side. "Here's four hundred dollars for that hurt man—an' here's your ten percent." He handed me two twenty-dollar bills. I stammered my thanks to the players and assured them that the injured man would be given the money as soon as possible. (He had been given an opiate and taken off the train at Hutchinson.) I shall always remember that circle of smiling faces as I wished them luck.

I have forgotten the name of that injured brakeman, but I can never forget the unbelief with which he listened to my tale of where all that money came from.

"A godsend," he muttered over and over.

I certainly found my own forty dollars a godsend. The Santa Fe was three months in arrears on wage payment. An employee could sign up for meal tickets at company eating houses, but the landlord and all other bills had to be "stood off" for long periods at a time. It was not a very satisfactory way of working but common to all railroads in the earlier stages of their development. In cases of injury this "no pay on pay day" policy often worked real hardship on the affected families.

With the exception of a rousing fist fight in one of the day coaches, the rest of the trip to Dodge City was uneventful. The fight was apparently a sudden flare-up of temper that spread like a forest fire—only the diplomacy of the conductor calmed it. Absolutely fearless himself, he pried apart combatants, sometimes appealing to reason, sometimes threatening retribution. At any rate, he quieted the near-riot without bloodshed or gunfire.

We arrived in Dodge City at 2:00 A.M. I expected that the streets would be deserted; instead, they were crowded with men and women. Most of the women, of course, were of the half-world that flourished around the dance halls. Most of them carried small derringers—wicked-looking little pistols even when attached to the lady by silken thongs. These firearms were carried mostly for effect. No one could have been safer than those women. To offer an insult by even so much as a raised eyebrow meant shoot, fight, or apologize at once.

The streets were lit with coal-oil lamps. At least, that was the intention— most of them had been shot out. Shooting out a light was the height of cowboy humor. Not even the train lights or our hand lanterns were safe from the cowboys' casual practice shots.

Board sidewalks lined the two main streets. Ponies were tied to hitching racks in front of saloons and dance halls. Fiddles wheezed in the dance halls, and an occasional organ droned out dance music. Entrance to a dance hall was a simple matter: you tossed a dollar into a whiskey barrel that had already served its joyous purpose.

I made the round of the streets, looking for a place to sleep. One street was about four blocks long and ran east and west. Another street ran from the depot, north and south, and divided the main east-west street about the middle. Alongside one of the east-west streets was a sidetrack used for passing trains. The street facing the railroad tracks was thick with saloons and dance halls. A spur track led off from the main line to the stock corrals and loading pens, which were about a mile from the town proper.

Long-horned Texas cattle were carried eighteen head to a railroad car, and the stock corral at Dodge City held eighteen carloads—324—at a time. These loading pens were always busy. A single shipment might require several trains. Cowboys on horseback went on the gallop to and from the herd out on the prairie. Drovers, buyers, inspectors, cowboys, railroadmen labored, cursed, and fought during the rush season.

As the flood of cattle headed for Dodge City, it became necessary for the herds to stay farther out on the prairie. A herd and its chuck wagon might be parked ten miles from Dodge City while the drover made arrangements to ship or sell. From the boxcar tops at night, one could see the campfires far out on the prairie. Oftentimes there were so many that it was not possible to count them accurately. Since the average herd numbered about three thousand head, with many herds totaling ten thousand head, it is easy to believe that many times there were a hundred thousand cattle within ten miles of Dodge City.

During the time I worked out of Dodge City, I grew to know the cowboys at work and at play. I saw cowboys ride herd when the dust must have made the air almost unbreathable. I knew their courage with the herd when the electric storms "made forked lightnin' play ring-around-a-rosy on m' hat," as one described it.

Most of the cowboys of that time were young, stamped with the indefinable good looks that the South seems to place, like a mark of quality, on its sons and daughters. Older men were usually Confederate veterans—TNT dressed in buckskin. They would not swerve an inch to make trouble—or to avoid it.

Gunfights were common. We dreaded trips on cattle trains that included two or more different outfits. On such trains, the crews prudently stayed out of the caboose. Fights and gunfights started over trivial or fancied insults. One fight that left our caboose a total wreck started when a cowboy remarked, "I don't like to play cards with a dirty deck." One of the rival outfit understood him to say "dirty neck." This man had been forced to make the trip without an opportunity to clean up, and he resented the implication that his neck was dirty. When the struggle had finally quieted and the smoke cleared away, three cowboys were badly wounded. The fourth got his neck washed by the coroner.

The train to which I had been assigned arrived in Dodge City a couple of hours after I did. My new conductor's name was Hirene. A miscue on a link-and-pin coupling had cost him most of the fingers of one hand, and this injury had not completely healed. The loss of his braking help threw considerably more work upon me. I was the only brakeman. My duties included everything that pertained to the movement of the train. I drew supplies for the caboose, filled its water tank and coal bins. I also shoveled coal to the engine tender—about three tons to the coaling. There were three coalings between Dodge City and Granada, two between Granada and Pueblo. After getting the engine coaled, I would take my telegraph instrument, cut in on the box relay to get all necessary train orders, and deliver these to the conductor and engineer. I was earning every penny of my sixty-five dollars a month.

None of the duties, of course, was out of the usual routine. We lived on the car tops. Weather did not count.

The proper speed for a freight train had been set at eighteen miles per hour, and that speed was checked by a recording device in each caboose. This device, known as a "Dutch clock," was probably the most unpopular invention known to train crews. There was no acceptable alibi for failing to keep within the speed limit recorded by the clock. It was not long, however, before we discovered that the Dutch clock could be jimmied. After we had started our run, about the first sidetrack out of the terminal, we would uncouple the caboose and give it a good, hard slam into the standing train at eighteen miles per hour. The clock thereafter would continue to register eighteen miles per hour, irrespective of what speed we developed during the rest of the run.

Trains breaking in two were the bane of our existence. The link-and-pin couplings were liable to break under a pull or become uncoupled when slack ran forward. We worked with our ears cocked. A sudden change in the sound of the engine's exhaust meant trouble. At night, this change in exhaust effort was our only warning.

Break-in-twos called for every bit of railroading that was in a man. If the train broke apart in just one place, the action was simple. The brakeman "tied down" (stopped with his hand brakes) the section he happened to be riding on. The other section then backed up and coupled on to it. If the train broke in more than one place, however, the action became fast and complicated.

Another worry that aged trainmen prematurely was that we were held responsible for "flat wheels." This rule was never enforced to the limit, but for a number of years it was possible for a railroad company to deduct from the train-man's pay any damage he might have caused by setting the brakes too tight. The rule was finally broken by the railroad unions and by a lawsuit started by a trainman. He proved that, after he had paid for a set of damaged wheels, the railroad had retreaded them and used them under a boxcar. The man collected a large sum as "rent" for the use of his wheels.

For all the problems and discomforts we experienced, I liked the prairie run with its ever changing conditions. Dodge City was more than just a town to me: it was a real fusion of the deep South and the West, and no one could walk its turbulent streets without feeling the glamor of that meeting.

But I had a bitter falling out with the new general superintendent, a man by the name of H. R. Nickerson. So I walked out on my job with the Santa Fe, my first real big-time railroad, and hired out as a brakeman on the Lawrence, Leaven-worth & Galveston—the "Lazy, Lousy, & Greasy," in the railroadese of that time.

My first run was from Olathe to Ottawa, my next from Ottawa to Indepen-dence. When the railroad was finally completed through to Wellington, I was promoted: Conductor Harry French—just old enough to vote.

I was a freight conductor, of course, but I felt like a veteran railroad man. I had succeeded in raising a very authentic mustache, and I was popular in Ottawa, numbering friends by the dozen. Any railroad man was popular. The railroad meant prosperity to the community, and this reflected back in goodwill upon all railroad employees.

My favorite barbershop actually capitalized on my patronage. In this swanky shop an ornate rack (placed in plain view of the street) displayed the shaving mugs and razors of its patrons. Each mug and razor bore the name of its owner in shining gilt Germanic lettering. Those aspiring to real fame could press their noses against the somewhat wavy glass window and ascertain that Conductor Harry French of the LL&G was shaved in that shop. A railroad conductor or engineer had about as much prestige, and about the same amount of public atten-tion, as a crack airline pilot of today. The comparison would be in favor of the railroad man, because the railroad man was in close contact with more people.

Freak storms and unusual occurrences then, as now, were accepted as usual in Kansas. On one run south, Ottawa to Independence, we were stalled by a migration of grasshoppers. Great clouds of them actually darkened the sky, and masses piled on the tracks, making traction impossible for our locomotive. We shoveled and scraped to get by huge drifts of insects.

We also had horse trouble—a bank of eleven that seemed to think the railroad tracks were their special pasturage. Our train struck and killed seven on one trip. The return trip, northbound, eliminated the remaining four. It was impossible to stop the train soon enough with hand brakes. All the train crews were glad to be rid of those horses, even though the company had to pay for them.

I am sure our system of train handling and train orders would be considered very sketchy today. Rules were not standardized, and much confusion existed.

A regular train might be ordered "canceled" for one day. If a need for that train developed, the "cancel" order might be "repealed." The train would then be sent out on its regular run.

One such series of orders—"cancel and repeal"—caused a head-end collision to my train between Lenexa and Rosedale. We were carrying stock and running under orders to make all speed possible. In its hurry to get that stock delivered, the company even waived a check of the Dutch clock. The opposing train was a Missouri, Fort Scott & Gulf regular that my train orders showed as "canceled" for that day.

The wreck occurred in one of those blinding, whirling snowstorms that only Kansas can produce. Both engine crews jumped before the impact, and no one was seriously hurt. But the engines collided with terrific force, and immediately afterwards the wreck caught fire. The impact ditched a lot of our stockcars. Those that were not ditched were shaken enough to open the doors. Out poured a flood of longhorns, bawling with fright and rage. Some were injured, all were crazy-mad. The right-of-way was fenced with barbed wire, and the terrified cattle raged up and down the narrow space between the tracks and the fence.

The engineer on our train, having sprained his ankle in "unloading," hobbled up to see how much damage had been done to his beloved engine. He was a short, fat man with a protruding stomach and a thick, bush-beard that reached almost to the summit of the stomach. He had just about reached the engine when he heard the thud of hoofs behind him. Glancing over his shoulder, he beheld the glitter of long horns through the swirling snowflakes. Forgotten was the beloved engine, the sprained ankle—he sprinted for the nearest telegraph pole with the grace and speed of a ten-second man. He actually gained on the steers. Grasping the pole with both hands, he went up it. Had he been a trained acrobat, he couldn't have shown more dexterity. He seemed to use that little round stomach as a sort of fulcrum for each upward heave.

Much of my engineer's fear of longhorns was entirely justified. Longhorns were wild Spanish cattle. The long trek to the North made them "trail-broke," but it did not make them noticeably tamer. There was no joke about the "long-horned" part of their description. Many is the time I have seen cowboys twist a steer's head to pass him through a stockcar door.

From the crossarm at the top of the pole, the engineer had a bird's-eye view of not only the herd but also the fireworks that came as the third act. The train we had hit was carrying a carload of oil directly behind the engine. As the barrels of oil grew hot, they exploded, scattering bursts of sparks and flame across the snowy countryside.

The cowboys in the caboose had been badly shaken up by the collision. They joined the train crews on the tops of the cars that remained upright. As fire spread through the wrecked trains, the cowboys made heroic efforts to free the steers imprisoned in the stockcars. No bullfighter ever faced a tougher spot. In groups of three or four, the cowboys would climb down off the car tops and open the doors that were still closed.

*In pleasant weather the brakeman enjoyed a way of life
that was the envy of every small boy.*

Clarke's *The American Railway,* 1897

It must have taken iron nerve to get into those cars, amid those thrashing feet and tossing horns. If a steer was too badly injured to get up, a bullet put him out of his misery at once; otherwise, that steer was routed out of the car. Most of the cars nearest the engine were on their sides, or nearly so, and here the cool nerve of those trained men saved a lot of beef. While a couple of them worked desperately to open the doors, two others would stand guard against the milling herd that wanted to charge everything that moved. If a steer went crazy, as many of them did, one shot stopped his charge. With the coming of daylight, the herd quieted. They strayed back along the right-of-way and made things miserable for the wrecking crew that arrived just before dawn.

Hunnewell was the shipping point for all the LL&G's cattle trade. The location of this cow town gave it many advantages for cattlemen shipping directly to the stockyards in Kansas City. The saving in time on the train (as compared to Dodge City) became an important factor, and Hunnewell flourished.

The downtown section, as I remember it, had one hotel, two stores, one barbershop, a couple of dance halls, and eight or nine saloons. The town was Dodge City on a smaller scale. There was no Bat Masterson to control the casual use of firearms, and there was more shooting than I ever saw in Dodge City. Because of the nearby Indian reservation, the cowboys took more liberties than they would have elsewhere. They could not be pursued into Indian Territory by law enforcement officers. The cowboys of Hunnewell more than lived up to their reputation as hell-raisers.

As railroad men, we had the usual trouble keeping lights lit at night when cowboys were on a rampage. We would often get messages from the agent at Hunnewell, advising us to show no lights entering town. These were not idle warnings. A bevy of saloons faced the railroad tracks. A light on our train— headlight, hand lantern, or caboose marker—was almost certain to draw a few practice shots.

While running into Hunnewell, I recommended the hiring of my elder brother as a brakeman. He was detailed to my crew, and I used up about three months making a passably good brakeman out of him. He had been warned about showing a light in Hunnewell; but one night when we entered the town, he forgot to put out his hand lantern. As he started to climb down off a boxcar, a pistol roared. The shooter must have been a couple of blocks away. Brother's light went out. He always claimed that the bullet had to pass between his legs in order to hit his lantern, but this point is debatable.

Brother threw the switch, and after our train was sidetracked, he reset it for the main line. We put our engine away in total darkness and then cleaned up ready for supper, but my brother did not show up. My other brakeman, a former cowboy, after a tour of all the saloons, notified me that he could not find him. An intensive search of the town failed to locate him. Daylight the next morning brought him walking into town carrying his bedroll. He had passed the night in a culvert a couple of miles from that "shootin'est" town.

And it *was* a shooting town. It was not uncommon for a group of whiskey-mad cowboys to take a violent dislike to some particular saloon or store. They would mount their ponies, shoot up the town, and ride their horses full tilt into the offending saloon or place of business. Bartenders and clerks made themselves scarce. One spree lasted for three days and nights. It was more than a riot. The cowboys owned the town. They knocked the heads off sugar barrels so that the ponies might eat their fill. Guns blazed day and night.

Finally, the agent sent a wire to Wellington advising the sheriff of conditions. The sheriff assembled a few militia and a number of deputies. I was the conductor of the special train. Arriving there, the sheriff lined up the militia and deputies, and ordered the cowboys to disperse. He and his "tin soldiers and toy men" were roundly jeered. Some fool fired a gun and a real fight started. The militia's first volley killed several cowboys and took much of the fight out of the others. By sundown the fight was over, and most of the cowboys were in Indian Territory.

My return trip to Wellington was to be on a fast stock train. ("Fast" was about thirty miles an hour.) Leaving town, I climbed into the cupola, where I could have the train under observation. On top of the caboose there was a stranger. I climbed out and asked him where he was going.

"As far as your damn train goes," was the surly reply.

I told him what the fare would be. Passengers on freight trains were not uncommon, and riding was permitted. But this stranger's hand slid down to his hip to produce the longest, ugliest six-shooter I have ever seen.

"This is my fare, runt," he growled.

While I did not like the reference to my size (my height has always been limited to five feet six inches), that gun and his disposition were all the fare he needed. I told him so.

My rear brakeman, who had been building a fire in the caboose stove, missed me. Thinking something might be wrong with the train, he climbed the ladder on the front end of the caboose. This put him behind the gunman. When the brakeman's head cleared the top of the caboose, he saw the man toying with his huge shooting iron. That gun was a particularly vicious-looking affair. The trigger had been wrapped with rawhide so the weapon could be fired by merely snapping the hammer. I could imagine a slug the size of my thumb being coughed out of the muzzle if that hammer snapped.

My brakeman took no chances. Softly, he continued climbing. A short brake club dangled at his wrist. The roar of the train silenced his two swift steps, and he swung his club in a short arc, ending on the gunman's derby hat. Mr. Gunman went down. His weapon dropped to the roof of the caboose and fired as it hit. The bullet made a hole in the cupola but did no other damage. I grabbed him to keep him from rolling off the speeding train, and we tied him, unconscious, to the running board on top of the caboose. There he rode until we arrived at Wellington. Some of his language when he regained consciousness was highly descriptive. It was a shame that it had to be wasted on the prairie air.

The sheriff came down at our invitation and looked over the prisoner.

"Which one of you took him?" he asked.

I motioned to the brakeman. "He was the artist with the brake club," I said. "All I did was look at the gun."

"You'll get a big share of the reward," the sheriff told the brakeman. "There's about two thousand dollars on his head."

The brakeman had been very unconcerned about his prisoner until he found out that he had captured a genuine badman, one that was wanted in several localities for murder. Only then was he afraid. The day that the reward was divided marked the end of my brakeman's railroading. He took his share (about fifteen hundred dollars) and purchased a whole farm outfit—teams, wagons, horses, plows. The last I heard, he was located on a homestead at Burden, Kansas.

I kept the gun as a souvenir. At least I kept it until luck ran against me in a poker game. Easy come—easy go.

—Excerpted from Chauncey Del French's *Railroadman*,
copyright 1938 by the Macmillan Company, New York.

III

*"Shorn of his usefulness by the air brake,
he has been left a victim of evolution,
an organ without a purpose."*

OLD-TIME BRAKIES, like sergeants in the army, exerted an influence on their profession far greater than their rank. This came about because brakemen substantially outnumbered other members of the train crew and also supplied a large proportion of the recruits to higher levels of railroading. All freight conductors began as brakemen, and so did most passenger conductors; and as a result of this pattern of advancement the insolence, profanity, and derring-do of the braking vocation were spread throughout the entire railroad system, even into the upholstered interior of the parlor car, where passengers were thus enabled to enjoy a rough approximation of the social graces atop a boxcar.

The person who was chiefly responsible for bringing all brakemen permanently down from the roof and installing them in the caboose and chair car was George Westinghouse, Jr., the protean inventor and businessman who developed the air brake. Westinghouse was one of those restless geniuses who goes out searching for a necessity to mother his inventions. At age twenty-two, when he began experimenting with the uses of compressed air, he had already patented several inventions, including a railroad frog and a water meter. He had wound up his service in the Union Army and was back home in upstate New York, casting around for something necessitous to invent, when he read an article about the use of compressed air drills to bore a tunnel through the Alps. After a series of unproductive experiments, he found a way to stop a train by running a hose from a compressed-air tank in the engine back to the brakes on the cars; and he talked the officers of the Pennsylvania Railroad into letting him try it on their passenger train from Pittsburgh to Steubenville, Ohio.

The engineer of the Steubenville train was suspicious and reluctant to rely on the Westinghouse brake. Fortunately for the inventor, a farmer stalled a wagon on a crossing ahead of the train, and the engineer, after giving his habitual whistle for hand brakes, remembered the new device in time to jerk open the hand valve. The air brakes brought the train to a stop just short of the terrified farmer and his balky horse.

This first successful Westinghouse brake, patented in 1868, transmitted air pressure from a single tank to activate the brake shoes on every car. The greater the number of cars, the weaker would be the pressure on the rear brakes. Four years after his first patent, however, Westinghouse perfected a new system that reversed the principle of the original air brake. It was now the *release* of air pressure, rather than the application of pressure, that activated the brakes. A compressed-air tank was installed in every car and connected by hose to the locomotive. If one tank should fail, it would not cause the whole system to fail.

After these innovations had been tested, the Pennsylvania Railroad promptly installed air brakes on its passenger trains, and other railroads soon adopted the same or equivalent braking systems.

One might have supposed that the whole rowdy gang of old-fashioned brakemen, with their baneful morals and salty tongues, would then have vanished like the canalboat men and stagecoach drivers of yore; but for technical and economic reasons this did not happen. It was fifteen years before freight trains received the benefits of air brakes, and almost two decades before federal legislation made air brakes mandatory on trains moving from state to state.

The technical problem was that air brakes took longer to affect the rear cars of a lengthy freight train than they did the front cars. The front cars would grind to a halt before the rear cars had even slowed down. The train would crumple up in a series of front-to-rear collisions, like a monstrous end-to-ender on a crowded automobile freeway. Men in the rear of the train would be injured, cargo damaged, couplings smashed and destroyed.

The economic argument against air brakes was even more persuasive. Air brakes were expensive; the lives and limbs of railroad men were cheap.

Finally, an Iowa farmer named Lorenzo Coffin, who had dedicated himself to the cause of railroad safety, hounded the Master Car-Builders Association into making a full test of air brakes on freight trains. The first fifteen days of testing in 1886 merely confirmed what was already known: air brakes could not stop a long freight train without folding it up like a concertina. The second series of tests, in the spring of 1887, again showed that no mechanically coupled air brake then in production could halt the rear of a train at the same time as the front—but they also demonstrated that an electrical coupling could activate air brakes almost simultaneously the full length of the train. By the third set of tests, in autumn, 1887, Westinghouse had modified his designs so that a train of fifty cars could be stopped safely in two seconds.

Although the railroads were in no hurry to install air brakes merely for the safety and convenience of their employees, the U.S. Railway Safety Appliance Act of 1893 made air brakes and safety car couplings mandatory on interstate runs. Hand-operated brakes became a quaint anachronism, seen only on rural short lines.

The "brakeman," of course, has continued to exist, at least in name. He rides the diesel-powered, piggyback, containerized freights and serves as an assistant to the conductor in the dwindling passenger service. But his old, irascible temperament, soured by the hazards of the car tops, has mellowed. His original savagery had begun to soften even in 1893, when they put the air brake on all the trains. It was, as *Harper's Weekly* put it, "an instance of degeneration."

T HIS YEAR, 1893, will undoubtedly be the greatest year for railroad travel ever known in this country. With the stimulus of the Columbian Exposition in Chicago to woo people forth upon the rail, the increase over any previous year's travel must prove to be simply enormous. What fact in connection with the railroads will most strongly impress itself upon this great army of travelers? Will it be the elegance and comfort of the coaches, the speed of the trains, or the ease with which great crowds are handled and close connections made? Indeed, these things have their importance, but we believe that the one fact which will most forcibly strike the clear thinker and trained observer will be the frightful decadence of the American passenger train brakeman.

A person does not need to be very old to remember when a railroad brakeman was something besides an ornament. It was before the introduction of air brakes. This sort of brakeman was still numerous, perhaps universal, twenty years ago, in the 1870's. In those days a brakeman, as it were, broke. It was the Heroic Age of the brakeman.

How easy to conjure up pictures of him! He was, in the first place, a full-sized man physically. Often he might have gone on the police force, had he not scorned the life as effeminate and calculated to take the spirit out of a man. His lower jaw was invariably inclined to be heavy, indicating the firmness which was always his. He seldom made any pretensions to beauty of face. Such things were beneath him. There was a slight cynical cast to his countenance; and he had, when speaking to you, a habit of gazing over your head, as if you were directly in his path, and the quicker you moved to one side and allowed him to advance without stepping on you, the better it would please him. Indeed, sometimes he would not speak to you at all. This was especially the case if he believed you to be "somebody"—the governor of the state or something of that sort. He respected the conductor and the president of the railroad, but beyond these he looked upon the human race as simply so many units to be baffled in their desire to have a seat turned or to learn the name of the next station ahead.

The brakeman's only visible dissipation was the consumption of quantities of tobacco, always of the "plug" variety. In a weaker man this might have been offensive, but in him it seemed merely part of his natural food. In fact, if we make no mistake, he always referred to it as "eatin' tobacker." He never sought to borrow this article of diet; but, properly approached up by the front stove, he would not, when it was offered him, refuse to take a generous bite from a passenger's personal supply.

But it was in action that the old-time brakeman showed to the greatest advantage. How he swung himself and twisted those brake wheels till it seemed as if they must come up by their iron roots! Old travelers can never be made fully to believe that this flimsy Westinghouse apparatus can set the brakes like the old-fashioned brakeman.

His announcement of the stations, in a deep bass voice, unintelligible but not unpleasing, was something worth hearing. It filled the car and woke up the sleeping passengers in the seat by the rear stove.

We regret to say that the early-day brakeman often, while standing on the platform, swore violently at things in general and in particular. We say "regret," though many worthy people often got much comfort from this habit, in precisely the same way as did the pious old lady in the storm at sea, who stopped in her prayer long enough to catch the profane remarks of the sailors and to say fervently, "Thank goodness, they are still swearing—they can't think it's very dangerous yet." When the car swayed around a sharp curve or bumped over a broken rail, the timid passenger clung to the fierce hexameter profanity of the brakeman on the platform and was reassured.

But our purpose was more particularly to speak of the present-day brakeman. What can we say of such a brakeman? Never before was there such degeneration in so short a time. Shorn of his usefulness by the air brake, he has been left a victim of evolution, an organ without a purpose. He is young, small, weak; he smokes cigarettes when off duty and knows no more about the use of tobacco than a sperm whale. He answers a passenger's question in a courteous, disgusting manner and announces the stations in a soprano voice, often so that the name can be understood. His sole active duty is to keep the ventilators shut. He does it, but the old brakeman used to nail them shut before the train started and thrash the first man he caught looking at them as if he didn't approve of it. The present brakeman could no more twist a brake till the chain creaked and the sparks shot from the car wheels than he could go into Wall Street and twist a railroad 'til the stockholders creaked and the dollars shot from their pockets.

The American passenger train brakeman of today offers a constant temptation to the old traveler to get up and take him by the ear and lead him away into the baggage car, out of sight.

—"An Instance of Degeneration," *Harper's Weekly*, July 15, 1893.

*Before the "degeneration" of
his breed, an able-bodied brakeman
could twist until sparks shot from the wheels.*

CHAPTER FIVE

Head End, Left Side

I

*"I grabbed the handhold and climbed
out onto the board, clinging there
for a dizzy moment, trying not to fall."*

IN THE SLANG of old-time railroading, a fireman was a "tallow pot." He took his name from his most exciting function, which was to climb out onto the boiler of the moving locomotive, carrying a long-nosed pitcher of liquid tallow, and oil the valves. The fireman's other duties, euphemistically called "handling black diamonds," were so abysmally dull and toilsome that the chore of oiling stood out as a moment of high adventure.

For pure drudgery, low pay, chronic danger, and debased social standing, the job of firing a steam locomotive was hard to beat. No one even bothered to record the name of the first practitioner of this grubby vocation, although he was the victim of an unforgettable accident. He was a black man, a plantation slave, and he had been put to work stocking pitch-pine logs into the *Best Friend of Charleston,* the very first operating locomotive in North America. (Two other engines, the *Stourbridge Lion* and the *Tom Thumb* ran earlier, but they were experimental models and never got into the regular business of hauling passengers or freight.)

In June, 1831, a full five months after the *Best Friend* had made its first run, the safety valve got stuck, and the boiler blew up with a concussion that shook the farmhouses of South Carolina for miles around.

This event was far from hilarious to the participants. The engineer, a white man, was badly scalded; and his name, Nicholas Darrell, has been sympathetically recorded in the annals of railroad disasters. But the mental picture of Ol' Black Fireman Joe, or whatever his name was, hurtling through the air with a look of astonishment on the remains of his dusky face appealed immensely to the minstrel show risibilities of several generations of railroad historians. Somehow, the tradition developed that the fireman, himself, had caused the accident (tee hee) by tying down the safety valve in order to stop its annoying sound.

The truth or falsity of this outlandish and defamatory story can never be proved, of course, because Ol' Black What's-His-Name was killed. In any case, nobody would have thought to ask him, peace to his soul. No one ever paid attention to the fireman. The locomotive engineer was a public hero—but his perspiring assistant was a nonentity.

In view of this general scorn, it is difficult to understand why every novice railroad man—every callboy, rear flagman, and roundhouse engine wiper—longed to become a fireman. Surely, the attraction could not have been intrinsic to the job. How could anyone hanker for the privilege of sweating for ten or twelve hours a day in front of a voracious firebox? Firing had to be some sort of formal ordeal, equivalent to a doctor's internship or priest's novitiate; and like those other, highly ritualized forms of initiation, it must necessarily have involved a deliberate self-abasement to prepare the neophyte to receive the chalice.

The ghostwritten memoirs of Joseph Bromley, a trainman on the Lackawanna line, provide some authentic answers, not only to the question of why a kid wanted to become a fireman, but also to such minor mysteries as, Why did engineers wear long hair? and How did engineers keep their false teeth clean?

WHEN I WAS WORKING as a callboy on the old Black River line in Utica, New York, in 1880, I dreamed almost constantly of the happy day when I would become a student fireman. Just let the master mechanic once send me out on an engine as a "tallow pot," and it would be no time at all before I would have an engine of my own, pulling freight over the hump of the Adirondacks and down the valley of the St. Lawrence, hauling timber from the mills of Watertown, or carrying summer people to Cape Vincent and the Thousand Islands!

Among the engineers I used to summon to work, the most imposing was a man called Baldy—a big, handsome man, the image of Buffalo Bill except for his naked skull. He had been a steamship captain on the Great Lakes, and you could see tattooing on his arms: women in tights and in nothing at all, American eagles, flags, and stars. Whenever I would knock at Baldy's door, he always said politely, "Thank you, Nobby. Won't you come in and get warm?" But I would shake my head, embarrassed by his imposing presence.

I was working in the shops, cleaning the flues of a boiler one morning when Baldy came in, spotless as ever in his clean white shirt and freshly laundered overalls. (He never hid his snowiness under the denim jackets that are the working uniform of trainmen.) With him was John Bailey, the master mechanic.

"How about putting my grate in for me, Nobby?" Baldy asked.

His engine was a little beauty, the newest on the road, but the firebox was so small a big man couldn't crawl inside. Usually, Baldy's fireman, a lean fellow who could have squeezed through a knothole, would get inside to set the grate; but he had fallen off the tank and was home with a hurt back.

While I was inside the engine, a dazzling idea leaped into my mind. It was fantastic, I knew; but Baldy liked me, and it was just possible that he might let me fire for him! As I wriggled backward out of the door, I heard John Bailey saying:

"You know he's too young, Ed, but it's your responsibility. If you get stuck on the hill, don't wire me for a helper. Your passengers can walk to Watertown."

And, turning suddenly, John Bailey told me to go home, get something to eat, and be back at four o'clock.

I ran all the way. While I gulped my dinner, my mother laid out my best blue-and-white checked shirt and black bow tie. With my hair plastered with water and my shoes shined, I hurried back to the roundhouse.

Number 22 was already on the turntable, spitting steam. In a few minutes Baldy came in. He and the conductor compared watches and picked up the orders, and we all climbed aboard the engine, with the two brakemen riding on the steps. Baldy gave her a whisper of steam; we slid into the yard to take on wood and water. At the woodpile the whole crew turned a hand, piling logs into the tender. Baldy stacked wood in the gangway, and I filled the firebox. Then we backed gently into the train—four bright yellow coaches, trimmed with black, a mail car, and on the end, a "combo" express and baggage car. The head "shack" dropped the coupling pin into the double link that connected us to the train, and we rolled proudly into the station.

Peering over Baldy's shoulder, I could see the passengers waiting on the platform. There were fashionable ladies in bonnets set above frizzied bangs, skirts trailing and parasols fluttering; and men with broad hats and waxed mustaches. But I felt I was every bit as grand as they, for I was not yet seventeen and was firing the fastest scorcher on the line.

We got the highball and Baldy eased her out, picking up the slack in the couplings without a bump. He nodded toward the steam gauge.

"Now, Nobby, you keep your eye on the steam and see to it that we carry a hundred and forty pounds. If she gets high and ready to pop, you can open the door a little. But the minute she begins to drop, get to work. You'll have to fire like hell to pull us up the hill to Remson."

Didn't I know it! At every short, impatient stop—Marcy, Stittsville, Holland Patent—I took advantage of the respite to stoke the fire.

Although we had no air brakes, we always coasted to a fine stop. The baggageman and the two shacks manned the hand brakes, and they were so well trained that they turned their wheels the instant Baldy whistled for brakes. It was my job to tend the tank brake. As we slid into a station, I would grab a tough little hickory club, shaped like a baseball bat, stick it through the brake wheel, and give it a wrench that clamped the shoes tight on the resisting wheels. At Marcy I set the brakes so hard that Baldy had to climb down from his seat and throw his whole weight on one end of the club before we could get them loose.

Baldy didn't pay much attention to me or say anything, except to call out orders, until we had gotten up the hill to Remson. Then, as we were hooting on the outskirts of the town, he suddenly shouted, "Open the firebox door!" I threw it open and watched anxiously while the steam went down.

"It's all right, boy," he explained. "Got to leave the door open to lower the steam pressure when we come into a big station. If she spits and pops, she's likely to scare the horses."

*The train crew,
like the engine,
appreciated water stops.*

Scribner's Monthly, 1888

I had never seen Remson at train time, so I leaned out the window and watched the people walking up and down the platform. There was a great bustle of climbing on and off the coaches. Cabbies were shouting, and people were milling around the hacks and carriages that stood beside the hitching rail. Just opposite me, a girl with long curls under her flower-covered bonnet was standing beside a pony cart. I waved, and she smiled shyly back at me.

"Look, Papa," I heard her saying. "That's just a boy." And the man beside her glanced at me and smiled, too. As we pulled out, I shouted good-bye and waved again. Baldy laughed.

"Some punkins, eh, Nobby?"

We stopped again at Alder Creek to take on wood and water. All the crew got off and helped, even the deadheads riding the cushions with the passengers. Just beyond the station was a siding into which we used to run to get out of the way of the "regular" in those dim, distant days a few months back when I was helping on the gravel train. I remembered that siding well, and also Boonville, with its abandoned locks, decaying saloons, and fancy houses, left from the busy days when timber boats used to come down from Carthage on their way to the Erie Canal. But, after that the route was new to me. We followed the twisting river through the hills to Carthage, then rode gently down the high timber toward the St. Lawrence.

Downgrade, I did not have to fire so steadily, and Baldy also relaxed. After Port Leyden, he leaned back in the window and called in an imperious tone, "Boy? My teeth!"

I was eyeing the steam gauge, and when I turned around I almost tripped over the slash bar. Baldy was holding out a set of false teeth, dripping with tobacco juice.

"Wash them," he ordered, indicating with a nod of his head the tap on the water tank. I put the teeth under the spigot and washed them off. Baldy returned them to his mouth, smiled, and smoothed his beard in the little mirror hung on the front wall of the engine. Four times on our run from Utica to Watertown, each time he finished a chew of tobacco, he would hold out his teeth to me with that lordly gesture.

"What a man," I thought. "What fastidiousness!" And I burned with admiration.

As I examined Baldy, sitting there on the high seat, solid and handsome, his heavy white arm along the window, with the sleeve meticulously folded back, cutting off the head of a tattooed lady, I could find only one imperfection in his magnificent person: a row of little pits around the base of his neck. It seemed as though he had been marked by smallpox there and nowhere else; and what hair he had left, he wore long to conceal those scars. All locomotive engineers, I had noticed, wore their hair uncut on the back of the neck; and, before we got to Watertown, I knew why. Those pits were scars made by red-hot sparks that flew down into their collars.

We were shooting through new country now, whistling for way stations, and swooping down on little white villages. Outside Lowville, Baldy cut off the steam and told me it was time to oil the valves and cylinders. That meant I was to climb out on the running board of the moving engine and open the cocks so that oil could be sucked from the cups into the steam chest. It was an operation that looked simple enough when an engine was standing on the roundhouse track.

From the shelf of the boiler head I took down the tallow pot. It was a handsome one, with a spout like a teakettle and shiny brass bands around its mouth of black iron. The tallow was warm enough to pour. I grabbed the handhold outside my window and climbed out onto the board, clinging there for a dizzy moment, trying not to fall onto the ribbon of ballast below me or against the hot jacket of the boiler. The grade was not steep, but the rails were swooping down and around a hill. The runners pounded in my ears, screeching as they took the curve. Holding myself there, with the wind cutting my face and blowing my hair, I felt as if I was riding a runaway. I glanced back and saw Baldy in the cab, resting his arm on the edge of the window. He smiled. This was nothing, nothing at all. Shutting the cocks, I climbed back inside the cab and nonchalantly threw a couple of logs in the firebox.

The rails were playing tag with Deer River. Scuttering under the willows, we drove into Carthage. We lost two coaches that were going on to Ogdensburg and took on others bound for Watertown. By the time we had wooded up and taken water, it was dusk. Baldy called me to bring a piece of clean waste and polish the glass of the headlights. As he lighted the whale-oil lamps, the beam fanned out along the roadbed in a yellow glow.

All I could see of the Great Bend was the two rails curving and running away from the cone of light. At Black River a shack held a couple of lanterns while we wooded up. I opened the firebox door to throw light into the tender.

When we got to Watertown it was completely dark. Baldy patted me on the shoulder as he climbed out of the cab and went to wash up. A quarter of an hour later, he waved good-bye and went uptown, a resplendent figure in his derby and his black town clothes. He was a spender, the boys in the roundhouse said. After a big dinner at the hotel, he would sit around all evening in a game of poker with the other lords of the road.

The conductor, the shacks, and the baggageman drifted away, with their shoes blacked and their hair plastered down. Everyone had some place to go. I washed up and came back to sit on the engine step, the pride oozing out of me. There was no one else left in that dim, smelly barn except the roundhouse man. He was cross and lame, and when he came around to wipe off the engine after the fire had died, he seemed put out that I was just a boy.

I helped the wiper go over the rods and running gear. At last he seemed to feel sorry for me, and he asked if I would like to see the town. But the cobbled streets were lined with railroad stores and beer parlors. I had only a quarter in my pocket; and all I really wanted was to get to my engine, my own Number 22, which would be friendly and clean.

I climbed up into the dark cab, laid Baldy's cushion on the deck, and curled up as much of me as I could manage.

It was a long time before sleep came. My veins boiled with exultation, and I saw myself firing an incredibly big engine, pulling up a mountain in the night, her runners pounding like thunder and her stack belching a plume of sparks as long as a comet's tail.

—Adapted from *Clear the Tracks*, by Joseph Bromley, as told to Page Cooper. Copyright 1943 by Joseph Bromley. Reprinted with permission of McGraw-Hill Book Company.

II

"It is no trouble at all for the engineer to 'knock out' the best fireman that ever handled a shovel—and I had been 'knocked out.'"

IN THE LATE 1920's, when economists all over the country were shaking their heads with dark forebodings about the future of the railroads, the Brotherhood of Locomotive Firemen and Enginemen published a thick volume of statistics, charts, and fictionalized anecdotes to show that the forgotten man on the left side of the old-fashioned steam engine was one of the most valuable servants of mankind.

The book had an ulterior motive, of course, which was more or less related to the declining health of the railroads. Reading the text was supposed to inspire an active sympathy for the firemen in their many disputes with railroad owners over wages, hours, and automatic stoking machinery.

Whether or not the book achieved its didactic purpose, only the Brotherhood of Locomotive Firemen and Enginemen knows. But it did fill a literary gap, for it is practically the only volume in our language devoted to the praise of firemen. Hundreds of thousands of men worked as locomotive firemen during the era of steam, yet the general public knows only two things about them: they were apprentice engineers, and their work consisted of feeding fuel into the insatiable furnace of the Iron Hog.

That this shoveling might total hundreds of tons of coal in a single journey, that the work might have subtle complexities of technique, that the apprenticeship might continue for decades without advancement, that the fireman was subservient to and dependent upon the goodwill of the engineer—

none of these possibilities occurred to anyone outside the railroad profession.

An illuminating account of one fireman's struggle with a hostile engineer appears in Herbert Hamblen's autobiography, *The General Manager's Story,* first published in the 1890's. The Brotherhood of Firemen might have done well to give it renewed circulation. But, then, what point this anthology?

I T WAS MY FIRST DAY on the job, my first job in Chicago, my first trip as a fireman. Phelps, the roundhouse foreman, pointed out the oil room.

"Git yer supplies and git right onto 227."

As I stepped up onto the locomotive tender and opened the oil box to get the cans, however, the most disagreeable-looking face I ever saw presented itself at the opposite gangway, and a thin, squeaky voice called out:

"Hey! What are ye up to? What ye doin' there?"

I asked him if he was the engineer.

"Who d'ye s'pose I be, ye blamed fool? The president of the road?"

"No," said I, "I thought you was the board of directors."

"The hell you did! Well, now you git down out o' there, and direct yourself somewheres else."

"Say, Pap," said I, "I don't know nor care a continental who you are; but I'm going to fire this engine tonight, and if you don't like it, now's your time to kick."

That made him mad. He shoved his oilcan and wrench up into the tender, and away he went across the yard shouting, "Hey, Phelps!" But Phelps kept out of his way.

When I got back from the oil room, the old engineer was in the cab waiting for me. The instant I set the cans on the footboard, he rang the bell and gave her a vicious jerk back; but as a brakeman I had climbed too many flying freight cars to be disturbed by that. I swung myself lightly aboard and gave him a black look, which didn't mend matters any. I was satisfied that he was a crank. It would be poor policy to knuckle to him, although in those days a locomotive engineer was a much more important functionary than he is now.

At last we got our train and got out on the road. We didn't have a very heavy train. I was satisfied that I could keep her hot without any trouble—and so I would have done if he hadn't worked against me in every way. He would let her blow all her steam and water away until he struck a heavy grade. Then, putting on his pump full head, he would drown her, running the steam down so that we stalled, had to "double" up every little hill, and delayed the Fast Mail fifteen minutes—an unpardonable sin.

He also "dropped her down a notch" for me so that she threw a constant stream of sky rockets out of her stack. As I told the master mechanic when he had me on the carpet the next day, a steam shovel couldn't have kept coal in her that night. As a consequence of the engineer's maneuvers, we ran out of fuel before reaching the end of the division and had to stop at the freight coaling station and coal up—a thing that had never happened to that train before.

The first time she "dropped her bundle"—which occurred less than halfway up the first hill and before we had gone five miles on our way—the engineer shut her off, slammed the reverse lever down in the corner with a bang, and, folding his arms, leaned back in his seat and ripped out the most horrible string of profanity I ever heard, every word of which was a curse at me personally.

Being a stranger on the road and not having the fear of Old Joe's displeasure properly engrafted on my mind, I waited until he got through; then, stepping over to his side, I grabbed him roughly by the shoulder, twisted him half round on his seat, and said:

"See here, you foul-mouthed old beast, I've got something to say to you now. In the first place, it's your fault and not mine that we're stalled here, because you don't know your business a little bit. Where I came from they wouldn't give you a job wheeling ashes out to the dump. And one thing more: If you open your head to me again while I am on this engine to say one word, good, bad, or indifferent, I'll split you wide open with this shovel, and if you have any doubt about it, you can satisfy yourself right away."

He didn't say another word to me; but the trip was a record-breaker. We got to the end of the division nine hours late, had four hours layover, and returned, repeating the performance even worse than on the up trip, for part of the return run occurred during the forenoon when the inward-bound passenger trains were thick on the road, and he managed to lay out three of them.

Before we started on the return trip, the conductor came up to the engine while I was taking water and said:

"Say, young feller, the head braky tells me that you set old Joe's packin' out for him in mighty good shape last night. Is that so?"

"Oh, I don't know," said I. "Why?"

"Because if you did, you've made a friend of every man on the division except Joe himself; and as you couldn't make a friend of him, anyway, that's no loss. But, of course, I s'pose you know you're discharged. No man could lay the whole road out the way you did and go out again. But don't you be in any hurry to leave town. If you ever want any assistance from anybody on this road, all you've got to do is to say you are the man that made old Joe Grinnell take water, and the boys won't be able to do enough for you."

All in all, it was a tough initiation for me, and I found out the reasons behind it afterwards. It seemed that old Joe had powerful influence in high quarters, which made him, to a certain extent, independent of the master mechanic. He did pretty much as he pleased, and being of a low, mean disposition, he pleased to abuse everybody who came his way. All the firemen feared him. Several of them had left the road to get away from him, and he had got several others discharged. On this particular occasion, when it became known that Joe's fireman was sick, all the others had made it a point to be away when the caller made his rounds; and it was to this combination of circumstances that I owed my job—such as it was. For the first time in his life, I suppose, old Joe got a fireman who had the audacity to talk back to him—to *him*, Joseph H. Grinnell. Who ever heard of such a thing? Is it any wonder that he determined to cut short my career on that road?

When we got back, we got off the engine and found the roundhouse foreman waiting for us. He said the master mechanic wanted to see us both in the office at once.

"Well, Mr. Grinnell," said the master mechanic, "I have a report here from the division superintendent, in which he informs me that the road wasn't big enough for the 227 last trip. What was the matter with her?"

"Nawthin'," said Grinnell.

"Nothing? What do you mean by that? Something must have been the matter."

"Yes, somethin' was the matter, an' a damned sight the matter, too. Look here, Mr. Seely, I want you to understand that the 227 is a first-class engine in every respect, an' that I'm a first-class engineer; but Phelps has got a notion of fishin' up all sorts of canallers an' truck-drivers an' sendin' 'em out to fire for me, an' I'm jist about sick of it, 'n don't want no more."

"Do you mean to tell me, then, that you laid out the whole road just because the fireman didn't suit you?"

"No, I don't. What I mean to say is that I didn't *hev* no fireman—only a cow-boy that never fired an engine before an' threatened to split me wide open with the scoop jist because I told him he'd hev to keep her hot or we'd never git there."

"Did you threaten Mr. Grinnell?" said Mr. Seely to me.

"Yes, sir," said I.

"Oho! You did, hey? Is that the way firemen talk to their engineers where you came from?"

"No, sir," said I. "But our engineers were men, while this old brute is a———"

"There! There! That will do. I don't want any quarreling in my office. You can call in tomorrow and get your time."

So here I was discharged. It was very discouraging, but then I could expect nothing else, for Joe was an old engineer on the road, and what was I? Merely a straggler who had been picked up in an emergency.

It was, unfortunately, a typical example of the relations that exist between engineers and firemen, and a true demonstration of the status of the fireman.

In some respects, the fireman is the most important man on a train. Not only do all engineers invariably depend on him to perform many of the duties properly belonging to themselves, but he it is who bends his back and hustles to make steam to get the train in on time, frequently with miserable fuel and an engine that ought to be in the scrap heap. When time is lost for the want of steam, it is on the fireman's head that the wrath of the engineer, master mechanic, and superintendent falls, even though it be evident that the coal is 70 percent slate and the valves and pistons blow like sieves. At the same time, no fireman can keep an engine hot except with the strictest cooperation of the engineer. In order that the engine shall steam, it is imperative that the engineer cut his steam off as short as possible and run his pump according to certain rules well known to the fraternity. In other words, it is no trouble at all for the engineer to "knock out" the best fireman that ever handled a shovel—and I had been "knocked out."

I would have left Chicago pretty bitter with discouragement had not the foreman of the roundhouse offered to set me wiping until another firing job came up.

For fifteen months I wiped engines, turned the table, shoveled ashes, washed out boilers and tanks, helped machinists to lug and lift, in fact, did all manner of the dirtiest, hardest work that has to be done about a railroad roundhouse. During those fifteen months I became, from constant association, perfectly familiar with all the outward and visible parts of the locomotive. I saw them taken to pieces by the mechanics and also learned enough about the mysterious properties of the slide valve to enable me to take part in deeply erudite discussions among the firemen. I became—in my own opinion, at any rate—an authority on "lap" and "lead," "compression," "expansion," and "cut off."

Wipers are severe critics of the engineers. They know whose engine is always in first-class order, nuts and bolts all tight, wedges never down, and everything where it ought to be. In our roundhouse, some engineers depended on the wipers to look out for broken spring leaves and hangers, cracked equalizers and eccentric straps, and nearly everything else; but there were others who looked their engines over with the greatest care. One of the careful type was old Joe Grinnell. He didn't want any help from anybody and was quite free in saying so, too; but I was lucky enough to discover something that he had missed one day, and it did me a world of good.

He couldn't help seeing me about the roundhouse. I was nearly always at work on his engine when he came to get her ready and to see that the repairs he had reported were done properly; but he never took the slightest notice of me. I was too far beneath him to be even worth damning.

One day I noticed that the male center casting of old Joe's engine truck was broken. Only one bolt held it, and that very slightly. I supposed, of course, that he had reported it, and I expected every minute to see the man come along with the jacks and jack her up to put in a new one; for although there is a kingpin down through both castings, no one would ever trust to that alone. Rounding some curve she might shear that kingpin off, shoot out at a tangent, and leave the track.

What was my surprise, then, as the time drew near for her to leave the house, to see that no attempt was being made to repair the damage. The hostler came and took her out across the table.

I had been long enough in the roundhouse now to get the hang of things pretty well, so I hunted up Mr. Phelps and told him what I had discovered.

"Is that so?" said he. "Are you sure?"

"Yes, sir," said I. "There's no doubt about it."

We walked rapidly to the hook on which the machinists hang the engineers' work reports after finishing the job and marking them OK. Mr. Phelps hunted the hook until he found the 227's report, signed, "Grinnell," OK'd, and signed by the man who had done the work. There were several petty jobs reported, but not a word about the center casting.

Mr. Phelps's eyes sparkled with pleasure. He saw old Joe had tripped at last.

"Damn him," he said. "If there was only him to think of, I'd let him go out with it. But there are good men who would have to suffer, too."

From where we stood we could see Joe oiling. No time was to be lost. We didn't want him to discover it—though even if he did, it would be too late now to save himself from censure. But we wanted to catch him as foul as possible.

Turning to me, Mr. Phelps said, "I'll get the Old Man out an' walk him past the engine. You be close by, an' just as we get to Joe, you tell him his center castin's broke."

"All right, sir," said I. Away went Mr. Phelps to fetch the master mechanic, while I sauntered out in the direction of the 227.

Joe was oiling his engine truck boxes, and I was in a flutter for fear he might look underneath and discover the broken center casting. But fortunately, another engineer came along just then and engaged him in conversation.

When I saw Mr. Seely and Mr. Phelps coming in our direction, I got within about ten feet of old Joe, and just as they were passing I called out loud enough for everybody to hear:

"Mr. Grinnell, your engine truck center casting is broken all to pieces and just about ready to fall off."

Joe's face was like a thundercloud. He told me to mind my own damned business, if I had any.

The officials had heard. Stopping short, Mr. Seely asked Joe what was the matter with his center casting.

"Nawthin'," said Joe. "This wiper's found a mare's nest. I guess I'm competent to look after my own engine without any help from the wipers."

Mr. Seely, however, looked under the engine himself. Seeing that I was right, he ordered her back into the house and a spare engine got ready in a hurry. Then he read the riot act to Mr. Joseph H. Grinnell in a manner that the oldest plug-puller on the road had never heard equaled.

He told him he was the most ignorant, useless, conceited fool he had ever seen. He told him he was neither an engineer, man, mouse, monkey, nor anything else. He said it was only old Joe's influence at headquarters, not his ability, that had caused the road to be cumbered with his useless carcass as long as it had.

Engineers, firemen, wipers—in fact, everybody about the place—came running from all directions to hear old Joe get his tongue-lashing. The downfall of that old brute was gorgeous and satisfactory to everybody—except Joe. As a grand finale, the Old Man, after calling him everything but a first-class engineer, sent him home for ten days, charged with incompetency.

After that old Joe could seldom go near the roundhouse without hearing from behind some engine the derisive cry of "center casting," "mare's nest," "wiper's reports," or something equally suggestive of the day he got what he had been so long aching for.

The next morning when I came to work, Mr. Phelps told me to go home again and return at six o'clock to relieve a fireman on one of the switch engines. My wiping days were over.

I fired nearly four years; and though firing is the hardest kind of work, I look back to those four years as the happiest of my life.

I never again came across quite such a crank as old Joe Grinnell, for as a rule the engineers were fine fellows. Every man jack of them, having served his apprenticeship at the scoop-shovel, realized the drawbacks and discomforts of the fireman's position and tried to make it as endurable as possible.

—From Herbert E. Hamblen's *The General Manager's Story*.
The Macmillan Company, New York, 1898 and 1907.

*Both fireman and engineer were blown to bits
when a boiler exploded on the Harlaem Railroad
in New York City on Independence Day, 1839.*

Howland's *Steamboat Disasters, 1840*

CHAPTER SIX

Hogger at Work

I

*"It was the first time I had had an opportunity
to make up time, and George and I determined
to make the best of a Heaven-sent chance."*

MARQUIS JAMES, the southwestern historian and biographer, has written of a journey he made years ago on a minor branch of the Rock Island line with an engineer called Ol' Gilroy in the cab.*

In the course of the trip from Oklahoma into Texas, the porters, waiters, news butcher, and conductor all spoke about the engineer's awesome reputation as a "fast roller." The train was late, but Ol' Gilroy whooped along, scorching the banks of the Canadian River, twenty minutes between stations that were scheduled half an hour apart. The passengers began to count on getting to Fort Worth on time.

Suddenly, however, a damper seemed to close on the engine. Ol' Gilroy turned cautious. A porter explained, with evident regret, "They putt the orders on him."

At the terminus, James walked up to the front end to have a look at the hogger whose personality had insinuated its flavor the length of the train. It turned out that Ol' Gilroy was not old at all; in fact, he was rather young looking for an engineer, and slight of build. But he looked the way James thought a "fast roller" ought to look: "His red bandanna was about his neck, his striped, long-visored cap was cocked rakishly. He walked with a swagger."

A switchman commented sympathetically, "Putt the orders on you, didn't they, Mr. Gilroy?"

---

*The *New Yorker* magazine, May 29, 1950.

"You mighty right," said Gilroy, with a wave of his hand and a smile, "or I'd brung her in here on time."

And there you have a clear, if fading, snapshot of the steam engineer: self-confident, adventurous, and debonair—a hot pilot, speed racer, and T-formation quarterback, all in one—swaggering toward the lunchroom in Fort Worth. Switchmen, porters, and traveling historians looked at him in open admiration. Was it any surprise that young boys saw him as a sort of deity? He took directions from the conductor, the dispatcher, and a number of minor "theys" who might "putt the orders on him"; but obviously he was the most important and interesting man on any railroad.

In the primitive days when every locomotive had unique dimensions and features that distinguished it from every other locomotive, each engineer was assigned to a single machine. He kept his engine oiled and polished, operated it in a form of competition with other locomotives, even selected its color scheme. (The sprightly taste of hoggers ran to yellow spokes, blue boilers, red tenders, and gilded animal heads.)

Later, when engines came to be manufactured in massive, identical families and engineers were assigned to run them on the principle of first in, first out, trains lost some of their individuality, but engineers did not. Every hogger continued to bear a nickname out of the classic assortment: Windy, Baldy, Smoky, Bony; Pop, Dad, Blue Line Dick; Snub-Nose This, Sour-Puss That, Ol' Man So-and-So. Every hogger had a distinctive whistle call, a unique style of running, a particular burden of superstitions and periapts, and a private stock of stories of way-back-when.

Not many stories were as self-effacing as Ted Custer's account of his experiences as an apprentice engineer in the 1880's. But, then, Custer had not stayed in railroading. He had no need to protect his reputation as a "fast roller."

FOR MANY YEARS after my apprenticeship in Altoona, Pennsylvania, there was a saying among the railroad men on the Pittsburgh division that was applied whenever a man was doing something particularly absurd, like stealing second base with the bases full or running through the red board: "He is making the stop at Greensburg." The phrase was always delivered in a high squeaky voice, and it grew to be the very essence of ridicule. The origin lay in a small incident in my career as a railroad man.

I had been sent on the road to learn firing and running a locomotive. There was a regular fireman and engineer on the locomotive, and at first I was only permitted to carry oil, tallow, and waste, and act as chambermaid. I polished the brasswork, sprinkled and swept the cab, cleaned the windows, and made things tidy. In a short while, after learning to throw coal into the front corners of the firebox, I was initiated into the finer art of keeping steam. It was quite a trick to spread the coal evenly over the fire and a still greater one to keep down the smoke. Soon I was doing all the firing while the regular man sat on the box and criticized my technique.

We helped drag freights up the hill from Altoona to Gallitzin—"snapping" they called it. When we helped passenger trains, the time was faster, and my work was cut out for me: I shoveled 4,400 pounds of coal into that insatiable firebox in twenty-six minutes. We made four trips a day, and I received twenty-five cents a trip.

There was a fascination about railroading that hard work and low pay could not dim. The thrill of holding up steam on a laboring locomotive with the throttle wide open never became commonplace. The flying switch at the summit held more than a hint of disaster, and the ever present threat of a broken freight train running wild down the grade against us was only too often transformed into a reality.

Six months of firing brought me a transfer to the righthand side, where I received instructions in running. By this time I had become quite familiar with the handling of the locomotive and had run it many times to and from the coal wharves. At the end of the run, the engineer and fireman would drop off and leave me to bring the locomotive to the roundhouse. Here, I turned in the engineer's report (a very reprehensible proceeding, even in those free and easy days). As I became surer in my handling, the engineer occasionally would move over to the left side, leaving me in complete charge.

But the crowning glory came when I went on the passenger run—that was the life!—an exciting series of adventures, punctured with cold meals out of a tin bucket and short periods of uneasy sleep in which I dreamed of stopping and starting, air brakes, and gauge cocks. I read orders, committed rules to memory,

The crew prepares for an undesirable confrontation.

Scribner's Monthly, 1888

grew oracular on the way to save coal, and held pronounced opinions on train dispatchers. In the roundhouse, I sat in on the quizzes where engineers asked what to do when any part of the locomotive broke down in service.

"What would you do if you came around a curve on a single track at fifty miles an hour and saw a train coming at you at the same speed?"

Answer: "Jump."

These hard-boiled railroaders affected a withering scorn for any engineer who would stick to his post when there seemed no chance of stopping. But when emergency actually came to them, they would go into the wreck, fighting for every inch. In all my experience with thousands of engineers, I saw only one who left his post when there was the slightest chance of stopping his train.

Two engineers alternated on the passenger run between Altoona and Pittsburgh. As the fascination grew on me, I would make the round trip with one or the other every day. Both engineers were first-clas runners who took every opportunity to coach me. Brady was my favorite, probably because he gave me longer stretches at running than did Burbank, who was cautious and rarely moved across the cab. Brady seemed perfectly willing to leave me alone after he had watched my work for a few weeks.

The Western Express left Altoona at 4:20 A.M., and as a rule it was late. Train rules forbade any attempt to make up time up or down the mountain, but after scooping up water at Sang Hollow, there was plenty of opportunity for fast running. When we were on time, Brady would motion me to his seat.

"Get up and watch for cows," he would say. It was his favorite expression. I made such a good fist at it that Brady felt safe in taking one or two trips to the baggage car. The mornings were cold, and the baggage car was warm. He could take a smoke there, something he never did on the locomotive.

The morning that stands out in my memory was cold, and the Western Express was twelve minutes late. At Johnstown the order board was down. We slowed to pick up the flimsey.

"Number nine will stop at Greensburg to let off passengers."

Brady read it, passed it to George, the fireman, who glanced at it and handed it to me. I was supposed to read it out loud, which I did. Hence there was no likelihood of the order being misunderstood.

Although we were late, Brady motioned me to the seat of honor after we had taken water at Sang Hollow.

"Get up and watch for cows," he said. "I'll be back shortly." Then he climbed back over the tender and disappeared into the baggage car. It was the first time I had had an opportunity to make up time, and George and I determined to make the best of a Heaven-sent chance.

Twenty minutes went by, and no Brady. At Florence we had made up four minutes. We howled through Derry yard only six minutes late. If only Brady would stay in the baggage car a little longer, I would have something to brag about for the next year!

Latrobe! George did a hoedown on the deck plate and held up two fingers.

We both yowled triumphantly. Oh, if Brady would stay another five minutes!

As we pitched over the hill to Greensburg, we were running at least seventy miles an hour. The rods were whitish blurs, the exhaust a continuous roar. It was a terrific speed for sixty-six-inch drivers. As I reached for the whistle rope to blow for the tunnel directly east of Greensburg station, I partially turned and saw Brady's head rise over the coal pile in the glare of the fire. Like a blow in the face it struck! We had forgotten the stop at Greensburg!

It was done in a second—I slammed the lever into reverse, jerked the sand lever wide open, and twitched the brake valve into the emergency. The shock was terrific. George landed on the hot lamp tops and Brady—did you ever see a street-car plowing through deep slush at a high rate of speed? That's the way Brady came through the coal pile.

Every passenger made an effort to butt into the berth ahead. With every wheel locked solid, the Western Express skated a train length past the station. The lone passenger for whom the stop was made had stepped into the aisle. He and his satchel rolled swiftly between the berths into Compartment A.

When the train came to a jarring stop, Brady was sitting on the apron, completely loaded with coal, bulging like an alderman, his right arm dangling uselessly.

I was jerking the reverse lever back and forth in an effort to shake the brake shoes loose when Dan Kearney, the conductor came running up to the gangway. Blood was streaming from his nose and mouth.

"You curly headed so-and-so! What the hell you trying to do?" he sputtered.

There was nothing to say. God knows I felt bad enough.

"I was making the stop at Greensburg," I squeaked.

They carried the disembarking passenger into the station.

Most of the wheels were flattened, and the rest of the run was like running over a corduroy road. George tied a pick handle onto Brady's broken arm. He gloomed on the left side while George ran the engine and I fired. We had several earnest talks before Brady was taken to the hospital at East Liberty.

Late that afternoon, George and I stood in front of a flat-topped desk. Robert Pitcairn, the division superintendent, trim, keen, and incisive, sat facing us. He asked a few questions and referred to some notes. He was an old friend of my family. I felt rather hopeful.

"Now, young man, tell me how this thing happened—few words as possible."

I leaned over the desk with my most engaging air of candor. At all odds I must protect Brady.

"It was this way, sir. Mr. Brady was showing me how to take water at Sang Hollow, and I guess I held the scoop in too long. It flew back and broke his arm."

R.P. nodded.

"We fixed him up the best we could, and I ran the rest of the way. Until I made the stop," I added apologetically.

"Where was Brady all this time?"

"Fireman side, sir. He was feeling pretty bad."

"And you both forgot to stop?"

"No, sir. We were running pretty fast—behind time, you know—and when I first put on the air, the brakes didn't seem to take hold. I got a bit excited when I saw how near we were to the station and shoved the handle over. They went on with a chug."

R.P.'s eyes never left my face during the recital. Then he pulled out a big crumbly cigar and struck a match.

"You have the makings of a first-class railroad man," he said between puffs. "You can lie with the best of them. About two weeks will fit your case."

It was a long, long time before I heard the last of that small event.

—From Edgar A. Custer's autobiography, *No Royal Road*, H. C. Kinsey & Co., New York, 1937. Copyright 1936 and 1937 by Edgar A. Custer.

A visit to the superintendent's office
was called "dancing on the carpet."
Scribner's Monthly, 1888

II

"Pop liked to have plenty of coal."

THE TROUBLE WITH FOLK HEROES is that they never do any work. Like errant knights, they move directly from one crisis to another, with scarcely time to lace their boots between encounters. No bread-and-butter letters for them to write. No bank statements to balance, no committee meetings to attend, no garbage to take out.

Folkloric engineers are as elusive as lizards when it comes to the daily grind. They always are busy jousting with holdup men, runaway locomotives, Indian raids, prairie fires, floods, and avalanches. You never catch a folklore engineer fretting over a steam gauge or waiting out a blizzard in a dormitory in Carlin, Nevada. Consequently, it is impossible to find out whether he is really any good at his normal job—or what his normal job *is,* for that matter.

To see the technical side of an engineer's life, one has to dip into such unromantic documents as Herbert Hamblen's autobiography, *The General Manager's Story.* Hamblen was well aware that all engineers are heroes, but he also knew that some engineers are incompetent. In the heyday of steam, the hogger's skill make a significant difference in the profits of the railroad: a freight train pulling forty cars would burn from forty to two hundred pounds of coal per mile, depending not only on the quality of the fuel and the difficulty of the run but also on the technique of the engineer.

SOME ENGINEERS, while meaning well, had failed during their apprenticeship to learn how to run and feed (pump) the machine to the best advantage. They made hard work for the fireman to keep up steam. Those engineers we called "pounders." As a rule, they were the very men who would take no hints from their firemen but instantly became dignified and talked loftily about how *I* pump and run *my* engine.

Shortly after I was promoted to fireman on a run out of Chicago, I was sent to fire for old Pop Fickett, a jolly soul, easygoing as an old shoe, who would often on a cold night get down and fire himself for a dozen or twenty miles to get warm, while I sat on his seat and played engineer, blowing for crossings and watching the water.

Unfortunately, old Pop was hard to fire for, because he was a pounder—

but I had not been at the business long enough to know that. I shoveled away for dear life, ignorant and happy.

With old Pop at the throttle, I always had to bend my back as soon as he pulled her out and had to keep the shovel and the firebox door swinging as regular as the pendulum of a clock. I wouldn't have a chance to stop shoveling until Pop shut her off. No need to worry myself by looking at the steam gauge; for, as Pop said, he could take care of all the steam I could make.

There were two coaling stations on the division, each about twenty miles from either terminus. We never passed them—indeed, we sometimes had trouble reaching them, even though Pop had had sideboards put on the tender to increase its capacity, saying he liked to have plenty of coal. When other engineers would brag about how many water plugs they could pass, Pop would remark sagely that he "allus liked to have coal and water enough"—and he did, too.

One trip Pop reported sick and an extra engineer took her out. As a rule, firemen hate to see an extra man get on the engine; he has different ways from the man you are used to, and railroad men get set in their ways.

This extra man, however, was a genuine and pleasant surprise to me. I began as usual to ladle in the lampblack until we were about five miles out, when he called me up to him and asked me if there was a hole through the front end of the firebox.

"No," I said. "Why?"

"What is the trouble, then? Is there somebody buried back there, an' you're trying to dig him out?"

I stared at him, wondering what he was talking about. Seeing that I didn't understand, he said, "For heaven's sake, man, get up there on your seat an' sit down! I never saw anybody shovel coal like you do. You've got enough in there to run to the next water plug right now. I can't put any more water into her till we get there, so crack your door an' let's have a smoke."

I did as he told me to, but I was worried. At last, when I could stand it no longer, fearing that my fire would go entirely out, I stepped down and picked up my scoop again.

"Say," said he, "hand me that scoop a minute."

I did so, wondering what he wanted with it. He threw it onto the footboard in front of him, and he told me if I didn't sit down and rest myself until we got to the water plug, he would report me for wasting the company's fuel.

The trip was a revelation for me. We not only ran by half the water plugs and the coal station, we also made the run in two hours' less time than usual, arriving with nearly half a tank of coal left.

Next day I asked the extra engineer how it was done. He took me to his side of the cab and showed me a notch in the quadrant that was worn smooth and bright.

"That is the notch Pop runs her in," he said. Then he showed me where he ran her, and gave the most lucid explanation of early cutting off, running expansively, and its effect on the coal pile and water tank that I have ever heard.

During the week that Pop was laid up with rheumatism, I gained several pounds in weight. I had such an easy time that, although I was fond of the old man, I began to dread his coming back.

"Why don't you tell him how to run her?" the engineer asked. "Pop's a good old feller. He won't get mad. You'd be a blamed fool to keep heaving coal in there for him to throw out the stack."

Well, at last the old man returned to work. He looked poorly, and I could hardly find it in my heart to speak to him, for he was a very old engineer and had been running just that way long before I ever thought of railroading. Still, I had sympathy for my own back. I broached the subject and made up my mind to fight it out with him if necessary.

Speaking rather diffidently, I told him the whole story, to which he listened very patiently, and when I got through, he said:

"My boy, I don't want to break your back. I know there's something in what you say, for I've had firemen kick before, but none of them in such a decent way as you have. Now, I'll tell you something that no man on this road knows but me.

"I am a machinist by trade, and I never fired but six months in my life. When this road opened, I had a letter from a big man. I asked for a job and was given an engine at once. Of course, I wasn't fool enough to decline, and I've been running here ever since. That's twenty years ago, and you're the first fireman that I would trust enough to tell that to.

"Now, show me how he ran her, and by gum, I'll do the same, and we'll see if we can't run by those water plugs and coal stations."

I showed him, and away we went. At first he was afraid she wouldn't make time, cut back so fine, but when he saw how she was going past the stations, he was as pleased as a child with a new toy. When we neared the first water plug, he sent me back to measure the water. We had nearly half a tank, and he wanted to stop; but I assured him that it was perfectly safe to go on, and so it proved to be.

Pop was delighted when we wheeled into the end of the division after the fastest trip he had ever made in all those twenty years. He never relapsed into his old style of running, and no fireman on the road had an easier time of it than I.

—From Herbert E. Hamblen's *The General Manager's Story.*
The Macmillan Company, New York, 1898 and 1907.

III

"I have been fifty-two hours on duty. Do not call me until I have had eight hours' sleep."

THE SELECTION THAT FOLLOWS requires an apology. It is so out-of-date, so recherché, so freighted with obscure technical details that it is almost incomprehensible. Can anyone nowadays be expected to understand the operation of water plugs, coal sidings, and crossover switches?

The answer is no; the apology is given. The editor's excuse for this impertinence is that he is haunted by the strangely familiar quality in this story of mechanized frustration on a midwestern railroad close to a century ago. It is like hearing the Monday morning tirade of a friend who spent ten hours on a drive that normally takes four hours, all because his car broke down on the freeway, the repair shops were closed, the children forgot their skis, the radiator boiled, the off-ramp was closed at Truckee, the road was blocked by a snowplow, the skid chains broke, and, after all that, the water pipes had burst in the cabin, and———

In short, this is a story of technological breakdown. The machine happens to be a large, coal-burning locomotive, the route is a pair of tracks, and the exasperated, exhausted human being is an engineer. But the subject matter, alas, is contemporary.

OUR LIVES AS RAILROAD MEN were not all made up of accidents, by any means. They were varied by long spells of semi-idleness when freight was slack, or of being worked to death when it was running heavy. At times of heavy traffic it is not admitted that men need rest or sleep; and I have had a roundhouse foreman indignantly ask: "What's the matter with you, that you register for rest? You've only been at work twenty-four hours! Some of you fellows ought to get a job clerkin' in a drug store."

On one occasion, arriving at the end of the division after a particularly tedious trip, I was ordered to return at once sixty miles down the road to bring up thirty cars of coal as fuel for the engines. "And hurry up with it! We want it."

I protested that I was tired out, unfit to go. But there was nobody else to take the run; so I coaled, watered, oiled up, got the caboose, and started.

You might think that after having hauled a heavy train over the road, it would be a snap to go back with nothing but the caboose; but, in fact, it is terribly hard riding on a heavy freight engine with no train to hold her down. She shakes you up like a die in a box, with a peculiar sidewise motion that affects the loins and back. Before I got halfway, my back ached like a hollow tooth. But I was anxious to get there, get back, and get some sleep; so I ran her right up to the speed limit—and a little more—regardless of my lame back. When I got there, I found four hours' switching (for which you don't get paid) to get my train together.

One of the important things for an engineer to do is to figure out where to take water most advantageously, for this job causes considerable delay, and you should do as little of it as possible; yet it is a high crime to run out of water, so lots of brain-fag is expended on this item. On my trip back I had a hill to climb. No one had ever taken thirty cars of coal up that hill, but I didn't know that. (If I had, I would have allowed for doubling the hill,* both in my water calculation and in estimating my time ahead of the passenger trains.) I did know that it would be a hard tug, so I cautioned the fireman to get a good welding heat on her. I got as much water into her as she would stand; and, after oiling the cylinders, I took a run for the hill.

But no sooner was the engine on the slope than the conductor came running over the train, waving his hat and yelling for me to stop. Not knowing what might be the matter, I shut off. When he came up, he said he had a hotbox on the last car! Perhaps I didn't read the riot act to that conductor, to stop me right at the foot of the hill for a hotbox! If he knew anything, he would have realized that long before I could get up there, he would be able to walk alongside the car and pack his hotbox.

The damage was done. I told him to cut the train in two. I would take my end up while he packed his box. By the time I got my train together again on top of the hill, I had barely water enough to reach the next plug. The fire was in bad shape, and not many miles behind us there was a mail train. With barely water and time enough—and a poor fire—I needed to make an extra good run of fifteen miles. I was far from happy and, furthermore, could see the steam dropping, although the fireman was working like a slave. About halfway to where I had to go was a little station with a crossover switch. I humored her all I could to get over the little hump to that station, for then my immediate troubles would be over. But the engine gave one expiring gasp and died before reaching the summit.

The thing to do now was to back across, out of the way of the mail, which was nearly due; but there was also a train due on the other track. Their time of passing this station was only about five minutes apart. The conductor, in obedience to the rule made for such emergencies, walked over the hump to the station telegraph office to find out if either of the trains was late. (If one was late, we might take advantage of that fact to avoid delaying them both.)

---

*That is, dividing the train into two sections so that the engine can haul them up one by one.

They were both on time. While the conductor was telegraphing both ways to ascertain that fact, the mail came up behind us and stopped.

In a big hurry now, the switches were opened and I was signaled back. As it was slightly downgrade, I merely gave my train of cars a little kick, and away they rolled. As I went past the conductor, I asked if he had a man on the rear car to set a brake and stop them after I got across. He said yes; but he lied. I thought so at the time.

When the engine was over all clear, I called for brakes, but I got no brakes. They were rolling faster than ever. In the meantime, the other passenger train had arrived and stood facing me. It was now dark. All I could see was lamp signals. Again and again I called for brakes, but there was no one on the train to set them; the mail had gone, and I ought to have been crossing back again out of the other fellow's way. If I stopped my cars with the engine, the chances were ninety-nine to a hundred that I would break the train in two. As gently as I could, I checked them and pulled my whole train across out of the way; but, alas! the caboose and two cars broke off and rolled away down the grade; so I had to back up again, clear of the switch, cut off the engine and go back after those cars. There was nobody on them, and the caboose lights had not been lit. It was a hunt in the dark. I had to go very carefully. All this time the passenger train stood there, waiting.

At last I got my cars and pulled them across in a hurry, although, to be sure, it was hardly worthwhile to hurry now. After the passenger train had gone, I shoved the cars back over the switch again, pulled up the train, shoved it over, coupled them all together, and pulled them back onto my track again.

I was now nearly out of water. In less than an hour the limited would be on top of us. The next water plug was five miles away. I cut the engine loose, ran for the water plug, took half a tank as quickly as possible, and started back after my train.

In cases where an engine has to come back after a train in the night, the rules require that a man be stationed on the head car with a lamp to signal the engineer back; but I had no faith in my conductor, so I didn't dare to come back very fast. Every minute I imagined I saw the head of the car looming out of the blackness.

I was right in not trusting the conductor. Although I came back whistling for a signal, the first thing I saw was the station lights. The trainmen were all inside, having a smoke—"didn't expect you back so soon."

I tried my best to stop, knowing I must be close to the train, but I hit hard enough to break the drawbar in the car. By the time they got *that* fixed up, there was no earthly hope of getting to the next siding ahead of the limited. Once more I backed over that crossover—but not until I saw a man swinging a lantern on the last car.

After the limited got by, we pulled across once more. By this time, it was doubtful I had water enough to get to the siding. As we had all night before us now, I let her take it easy. We got there with the tank dry and the boiler not much better. I got down to oil while the fireman was taking water and discovered that the link-lifting spring was broken; and, while I was looking at it and wondering how that could have happened without my knowing it, the head brakeman came up with an order for me to weigh that coal.

My back was almost broken; I was more than half dead with fatigue and worry; and now I had to weigh thirty carloads of coal without a lifting spring. The big cast-iron links and long eccentric rods must have weighed at least two hundred pounds, and as it is necessary in putting cars on the scale to move the engine back and forth continualy, I saw what a nice time I was going to have handling that old reverse lever.

I telegraphed the dispatcher, telling him how I was fixed and asking permission to use another engine to weigh the coal with. The answer was short: "Use the engine you have."

Back I went to the yard and weighed that coal. In order to back the engine, I had to brace both feet against the front of the cab and, pulling with all my might, raise the heavy links. If I had the misfortune to move the cars half an inch too far, I would get a signal to go ahead a bit. As I unhooked the lever, it would fly forward with such force as to nearly jerk me through the front windows. (Remember, I was nearly dead with fatigue and hunger when I started on this delectable trip.) Somehow I got the coal weighed and coupled on. The conductor, coming ahead, began to tell me how far we could go if we hurried up and got out ahead of Train 12. I cut him short by telling him to go into the office and tell Chicago I couldn't go another foot until I got five or six hours' sleep. Off he went, grumbling that we'd never get anywhere that way. Back he came in a few minutes.

"Chicago says, 'All right. Go to sleep.' "

I pulled into a convenient siding, picked as smooth a lump of coal as I could find in the tender, upholstered it with waste, and, spreading my coat on the foot-board for a mattress, I dropped the curtain and curled myself into the short, hot, dirty cab for a few hours' rest (?) to the tune of the fireman's grumbling.

This fireman was the toughest man I ever saw on a railroad or anywhere else. He didn't get fat on hard work—there was no more flesh on him than there is on a birdcage; but he could stand more grief than the old engine herself. He had been right with me ever since we left Chicago, the day before, shoveling fine feed into the old kettle—and she had an appetite like a stone crusher—yet now he kicked because I wanted rest. He said we might better go on in; it was only two or three hours' run, and then we could get proper rest and a good sleep. He couldn't sleep on an engine; so he kept his clack going until I begged him to be quiet and let *me* sleep, anyway. With that he got off, and I was in hope he had gone back to the caboose.

My back ached so, I was so tired, and my position was so cramped and uncomfortable, that it was some time before I could even doze. Just as I began to drop off, I heard someone step up into the tank. Glancing through a hole in the curtain, I saw that it was the fireman returning. He had a cigar in his mouth. I knew he must have been in some gin mill, as no other place would be open at that time of night. With ponderous caution he approached my side of the engine, making a clattering stumble over the fire hook, which he had left underfoot. Raising the corner of the curtain, he peeped cautiously in.

Not caring to be entertained by his idle talk, I breathed heavily as though sound asleep. It was an effort to take long breaths of the distillery perfume that he wafted into my ill-ventilated chamber, but I was suffering in a good cause: if left to himself, I felt, he must eventually go to sleep. Not he. He stood in the tender, looking around awhile and scratching himself. Then, carefully, he picked up the hook and laid it with a clink on top of the tank; opened both the oil and tool boxes, and looked into them vacantly for a while; shut each of them with some noise, just enough to be irritating, and at last got down.

"Thank the Lord," thought I. "He's gone to get another drink. Maybe he'll stay till morning."

Not at all. I soon heard a peculiar hissing, grating sound that told me he was pulling the flue rod from the tank truck bolsters where he aways carried it. So the flues were to be bored! I knew that would put the everlasting veto to my hopes of getting any sleep that night. Although I might have forbidden his doing it, I was so astonished at this display of endurance that I was ashamed to say a word.

The fireman went at his job with the most elaborate precautions against making noise, but he only succeeded in making more. I lay there and watched him through the hole in the curtain, his face shining with perspiration in spots where he had wiped off the coal dust, as he squatted in the coal and peered into the furnace, ramming, twisting, partly withdrawing, then savagely thrusting in the old flue rod. Listening to the monotonous scrape of the rod across the bottom of the door, at last I dozed off. It seemed about a minute.

Somebody was shaking my shoulder and saying, "Hey! hey!" I looked up, dazed and wondering, into the fireman's grimy face. "Seven's just gone, an' if we foller her, we c'n go right in," said he. "I've got the flues all punched out an' a good fire. Hurry up!"

With great difficulty I extricated myself from the reverse lever and seat box and crawled painfully to my feet. I couldn't realize at first where I was or what was going on. It was just getting daylight, a lovely morning, and as I looked about the yard, trying to locate myself, my eyes fell on the coal train. Memory returned with a rush.

I asked the fireman what it was he had said. He repeated it, and I answered sleepily, "All right."

Seven was the midnight train out of Chicago. If she had gone, there would be ample time for us to get in before the first morning train arrived. I was too dead to look at my watch, so I took the fireman's word for it and whistled for the switch two or three times. Nobody showed up, so I gave her a little steam to stretch the train out and then reversing, gave her a setback to shake up the rear end crew in the caboose, at the same time calling for the switch. I did this three times before the fireman, watching back on his side, said somebody was coming. It was the conductor, mad as a hornet. What in hell was I trying to do?

"Trying to wake you up so we can get out of here. You was in a terrible pucker to go last night when I wasn't able to, but now I'm ready."

"Well, you needn't smash everything all to pieces, jest cause you're ready!" he said. "The first time you set back you upset the stove an' all the pipe an' fire was rollin' round in the caboose. Then, while we was tryin' to pick it up an' git the fire out, you come back twice more an' broke all our dishes an' sot a lot of our clo'es afire. I don't see nothin' so almighty smart about that—are ye ready ter go?"

"Yes, yes! Get that gate open and let us out. Have ye got a flag out?"

"I'll tend ter the flag." Grumbling about the damage in his caboose, he opened the switch. We were soon jouncing along at a fairly good gait. I was still sleepy and dead, had to keep my head out in the sharp morning air to stay awake at all. Arrived at a water station about halfway, I told the fireman he had better fill the tank, as there could hardly be enough in it to take us through. While I was oiling, the conductor came up and asked if I was going to sidetrack there. I looked at him a full minute before I could get it through my head what he was driving at. Then I said, "No, certainly not. Why should I sidetrack here?"

"How fur ye goin' against Seven?"

"All the way."

"What time's she due here?"

"Fifty-seven."

"What time ye got now?"

I looked at my watch. It was forty-eight.

I jumped on the engine. With the conductor giving a backup signal, I jolted those cars into the siding as fast as it is safe to go. I called back the flag just in time to prevent Seven's engineer from getting a sight of it.

The fireman and I then had a little argument as to what it was he saw when he thought Seven passed us in the yard. I was now fairly well awake and was able to figure the time back. The only passenger train on the road at that time was one going the other way. After I had proved it by the timetable, the fireman finally admitted that "By gum, he guessed mebbe I was right."

"Well," said I, "we've only got about twenty miles farther to go. I hope we'll live to land this train in the yard—I've been with it so long that I take a kind of fatherly interest in it."

That unlovable damsel, Misfortune, had at last tired of worrying us. After Seven got away, we proceeded to our destination without further mishap, shoved the train away, and gave up the engine to the hostler. Having been fifty-two hours on her without rest (for the short spell of comparative quiet in the yard could not be so termed), I entered on the register this request: "9:30 A.M. Have been fifty-two hours on duty. Do not call me until I have had eight hours' sleep." I then crawled slowly and painfully over to the hotel and went to bed.

I was so completely fagged out that it was some time before my aching back would allow me to sleep. I had just dropped off when I was rudely shaken by the caller and saluted with, "Hey, hey! Are ye awake now? I've been callin' ye fer ten minutes! You're wanted for a stock train."

When I got my wits collected enough to realize who I was, who he was, and what he was talking about, I asked him the time.

"Ten-fifteen."

"What! Have I only been forty-five minutes off of that engine?"

"That's all."

Without another word I tumbled back on the pillow and pulled the bed-clothes over my head. But the callboy understood his business; he had been calling unwilling railroaders for four years and wouldn't be denied. For a while he shook and pleaded with me. Then, realizing the seriousness of the case, he snatched off the bedclothes. That was the last straw. I jumped out of bed and made a dive for him, but he was outside the door before I could reach him. With a parting shot through the crack of the door—"Hurry up now! They're waitin' fer ye"—he left.

I gathered up my bedclothes and again crawled uncomfortably into bed. The clothes somehow resolved themselves into inconvenient knots and lumps. My extremities and certain prominent parts of my anatomy were exposed to the disagreeable temperature of the contract-built hotel bedroom; but I was too sleepy and inert to attempt to straighten out the angle. I lay and shivered miserably. A more or less well-defined idea oozed through my soggy brain that I hadn't seen the last of that caller.

Sure enough, just as I was beginning to get my ideas into a pleasant state of haziness once more, the door was fired open with a bang. Rolling over, I beheld the exultant countenance, safely outside the door this time. He was holding up for my inspection a sheet of dirty yellow-colored paper, which I knew was a telegraph form.

"Read that now, an' see if ye'll get up or not!"

I took the paper and read: "Engineer M——, don't you delay this stock train. W.S.B."

A combined order and threat from the train dispatcher, signed with the division superintendent's initials, was a peremptory order, to be unquestioningly obeyed. I borrowed the caller's pencil and wrote underneath the order: "W.S.B. —I have been fifty-two hours on duty, am unfit to take stock train or any other train. J.B.M." I handed it to the caller, and, telling him that if he disturbed me again for any reason, even though the house should be afire, I would brain him, I once more retired. Although I had no doubt that I had signed my death warrant, I slept the sleep of the utterly weary.

I got my medicine—thirty days suspension for refusing to obey an order. I was lucky to get off so easily. The superintendent told me that all that saved my job was the fact that an engine came in off the branch opportunely and brought the stock train through.

—From Herbert E. Hamblen's *The General Manager's Story.*
The Macmillan Company, New York, 1898 and 1907.

*Railroad officials bought up all but one picture of
this bizarre head-on crash, and the public never
found out where or how it had happened*

Scientific American, 1876

CHAPTER SEVEN

Roundhouse and Shop

I

"The murky atmosphere...the faint light...
the constant racket...created an unreal sensation."

THE FIRST RAILROAD SHOPS, unlike other portentous developments in the Age of Steam, began without fanfare or festivity. Strictly speaking, they did not *begin* at all, but rather evolved out of older establishments—carriage-makers' sheds, wagon factories, livery stables, and iron foundries. Perhaps a few inland shipyards, formerly devoted to shaping and caulking canalboats, switched over (those were gloomy days along the towpaths).

Many of the early shops were leafy, rural places, like the village smithy's atelier under the chestnut tree. Mount Clare Farm, on Amity Road in Baltimore; West Point on the Hudson.... It was years before they took on the ugly, dramatic characteristics one associates with railroad shops nowadays, smoldering and glowering under clouds of soot and steam at the nether edge of some nondescript, middle-sized town that slinks away in grayish-yellow murk beyond the nearest hills.

The Philadelphia & Columbia, a horsepowered short line that became the germinal road for the vast Pennsylvania system, built its first repair shops in 1833 out in the fields of Chester County, midway between its two terminals, on a farm that belonged to John G. Parke.

Parke, a wealthy, influential man, was annoyed that the P&C had run its tracks between his house and his barn without paying adequate compensation for damages. He offered to sell the railroad several acres of his violated pasture as a site for its shops; and the railroad, to placate him, accepted the deal, laid out a town, and called the place Parkesburg.

In truth, the managers of the railroad were eager to put the shops out in the pristine countryside in order to keep the shopworkers away from the pernicious influence of trainmen. Trainmen were dastardly fellows in those days, and the management had little choice but to hire whomever it could recruit; but there was no point in corrupting innocent mechanics.

By the time Joseph Noble took on the task of maintaining a tidy roundhouse for the Santa Fe in southern Colorado some eighty-five years later, the shops exerted a corrupting influence of their own—or at any rate, they looked sufficiently malignant that even a practical railroad man found them unappealing.

I HAVE BEEN IN SOME rather cheerless surroundings from time to time during my railroad career, but if I were required to name one to head the list of disagreeable places, it would be a roundhouse on a cold, wet day.

The murky atmosphere, filled with smoke and steam, with water and scale spilled on the floor, the faint light filtering through grimy windows supplemented by dim incandescent lamps on the posts and walls, the constant racket—riveting hammers going, engines popping off, bells ringing, occasionally a blast from a whistle—and the shadowy figures of men working at the front end of the locomotives with kerosene torches—it all created an unreal sensation that I do not recall having experienced anywhere else.

Trying to keep such a place looking spic and span, which was part of my job at La Junta, Colorado, in 1919, was a very difficult assignment. In fact, it was just about impossible. But when we would receive word that some important officer was going to inspect the terminal, a manful effort always was made to improve appearances. The windows were washed. The walls, trusses, posts, and undersides of the roof were sprayed with whitewash; and, sometimes, part of the floors and the engine pits were even given this beauty treatment. When I saw one of these purifying operations underway, I always asked, "Who's coming?"

The questions that the officials asked during the general inspection usually were concerned with possible reductions of the force, how soon Engine Such-and-Such would be out of the shop, and so forth; but once in a while someone got more inquisitive. Once the general manager, who was heading the inspecting group, stopped at a fire hose and asked if it had been inspected at the required six-month intervals. He was assured that this particular hose had been taken out and tested only two weeks before. He then pulled the hose off the rack and shook a peanut out of the nozzle, which he had planted there six months previously during a similar inspection trip.

A roundhouse at a good-sized terminal had about thirty-six stalls for locomotives. In order to get all those engines in and out of the house, a turntable was provided. This consisted of a steel girder supported on a center bearing. It was long enough so that a locomotive could be run onto the girder and balanced for turning. There were wheels at the outer edges of the table, and these carried part of the weight. The power was supplied by an electric motor or compressed air.

Coal-burning locomotives, of course, produced large quantities of cinders, and the disposal of these before the engine came into the house was something of a problem. At coaling stations, the ties were sometimes covered with steel sheets to protect them from burning, and the engines would shake out cinders while taking on coal. But at terminals like ours, the arrangements were more elaborate. Our cinder pit was a concrete tank filled with water. Tracks ran over this on steel beams. Engines on their way to the turntable ran over this, and their pans were dumped into the water. Later, the cinders would be removed from the pit by a locomotive crane equipped with a clamshell bucket. The cinders were used for widening and restoring banks, surfacing track, and repairing washouts.

When an incoming engine left the cinder pit and was ready to move into the roundhouse, the turntable operator lined up the rails of the table to match those on which the engine was standing. He locked the table into this position. Then a hostler moved the engine onto the table, the table was turned to face an empty stall, the tracks were locked in place again, and the engine moved into its stall.

While a turntable was relatively simple, things could and did sometimes go wrong. If the operator failed to lock the table in place, it might shift enough to derail the locomotive. Usually all this did was to mark a few ties; but if the engine struck a girder, the table might be badly damaged. It makes me shudder to think of the racket that could develop when we got a turntable wrecked with thirty-five or forty engines bottled up in the house.

Sixty or seventy years ago, turntables were so small and light they could be turned by hand. There were two long wooden handles that were inserted in sockets on each end of the table, and men pushing on the handles swung the engine around. Children and other trespassers sometimes tried to use the turntable as a merry-go-round. The ensuing lawsuits, known as the "Turntable Cases" are legal history.

Progress, of course, has taken care of this particular hazard. A child could not push a modern turntable any easier than he could a locomotive, but I don't suppose many children would want to, anyway.

—Adapted from *From Cab to Caboose: Fifty Years of Railroading*, an autobiography by Joseph A. Noble. Copyright 1964 by the University of Oklahoma Press, Norman, Oklahoma.

II

*"I worked 118 hours the first week, 120 the second.
All that saved me from a solid day-and-night
third week was a fall into the roundhouse pit."*

IF CASEY JONES was the apotheosis of the railroad engineer, Sam Vauclain, of Altoona, Pennsylvania, was the ultimate roundhouse mechanic—a towering hero-worker (capitalist variety), in greasy overalls and oily boots, with a mallet and chisel in his hands, a cold apple pie in his lunch bucket, and a heart overflowing with love for mechanical contrivances: turntables, steam hammers, metal lathes, compound pistons.

Sam belonged to his geographic setting on the smoky main line of the Pennsylvania Railroad in the heartland of coal and steel and locomotive factories as naturally as Daniel Boone belonged to the Wilderness Trail or Bat Masterson to Dodge City. His father had been a roundhouse foreman for the Pennsy in Altoona; and when Sam was growing up, his papa used to reminisce about how he had helped build the locomotive *Old Ironsides* in Matthias Baldwin's watchmaking plant in Philadelphia back in 1832, when most people thought the future of transportation was in canalboats and six-horse coaches.

Naturally, Sam wanted to become a railroad man, too; but it never occurred to him to be a locomotive runner, any more than it would occur to a born auto machinist to take a job as a bus driver. Under the moist, carboniferous aroma of the roundhouse, Sam could detect the scent of true adventure.

At sixteen, he started work as an apprentice in the Pennsy shops in Altoona. In those days (1872) apprentices got fifty cents a day for the first year, seventy cents a day the second year, ninety cents a day the third year, and a dollar a day the fourth year. Sam learned to turn bolts, repair locomotive water pumps, and cut keyway slots in piston rods. He shaped and smoothed iron shafts with hand tools—bits and chisels, hammers and files—until the palms of his hands were worn down to the tendons and the third and fourth fingers of each hand gradually (and permanently) curled inward.

By the time he was twenty, and already turning gray, Sam was the boss of his own crew. He was a tough, demanding, custom-built taskmaster, infused with self-righteous prejudice in favor of his own virtues: early rising, hard work, and a robust appetite. His formula for success was "to eat plain food and plenty of it, get exercise and plenty of it." Hearty meals and heavy toil would bring you happiness, health, and prosperity; and those, in turn, would inspire others with confidence in your abilities.

That Sam Vauclain inspired confidence in the men who worked with him, we have on the eyewitness testimony of Edgar Custer, another Altoona lad of surprisingly similar spirit and background, who began his apprenticeship in the shops a few years after Sam.

Ted Custer was a relative of the celebrated general of the Little Big Horn. Like the general, he was bellicose and reckless, and like most Altoona boys he felt the magnetism of the railroad. He was natural material for Sam Vauclain's crew. Their association, as Custer recalls it in his autobiography, *No Royal Road,* published in the 1930's, was enriched by the mutual love of hard work, the excitement of large projects, and the joy of accomplishment.

It was an era of important technological innovations in railroad operations, and the Pennsylvania Railroad led the world in adopting new improvements. The shops were expected to maintain the locomotives in perfect condition. This practical, unaesthetic objective absorbed the energies of Vauclain and Custer as totally as the energies of Pierre and Marie Curie were consumed by the process of extracting radioactive material from tons of pitchblende. When Ted Custer followed his slaver to the Baldwin Locomotive Works in Philadelphia, the objectives grew closer, clearer, and more rewarding, but the drudgery was, if possible, even greater.

In time, Custer left the locomotive shops and became an executive in a manufacturing business. Sam Vauclain, having invented a compound engine used throughout the world, stayed with Baldwin. In three decades, he worked his way up from shop superintendent to president. The company, during this period, developed into a massive industry, turning out more than a thousand locomotives a year.

To Sam Vauclain and his protégé, the whole outcome was plain evidence of the power of square meals and hard work.

IN SEPTEMBER, 1877, shortly after I had been graduated from high school, I entered the shops of the Pennsylvania Railroad in Altoona and was put under the tender care of Bill Grindle, a mammoth of a man, who was the gang boss in the erecting shop. My overalls were about four inches too long in the arms and legs, to allow for shrinking, and the excess cloth was turned up in wide, stiff folds.

Bill Grindle took me in hand. He furnished me with a hammer, six rough files, and a number of unsharpened chisels. My first work was to sharpen the chisels on a large grindstone, a job that took me the better part of a morning. Up to that time I had never done a stroke of useful work, so the going was hard. The chisels slipped and the stone gritted the skin from my knuckles. Often, the grind-stone tore the steel from my hands and wrenched me cruelly.

Finally the job was done, ready for Bill's inspection. He looked the chisels over with some distaste and took them back to the grindstone. I followed with trepidation. With a few deft touches, Bill made the shapeless ends smooth and sharp. I was seeing a mechanic.

After dinner, Bill put me to work chipping off the ends of one-inch bolts that protruded through the nuts on a locomotive bumper. He cut one as an ex-ample—three swift blows that sank the chisel deep into the bolt close to the nut; then a sharp rap that broke off the surplus metal, a gentle smoothing off, and that was all. Altogether, he used about two minutes on the job.

At five o'clock that afternoon, I had cut off just one bolt. Gnawing it off would better describe my efforts. My left hand was swollen and bleeding where the hammer had missed the chisel; my right arm was aching like an ulcerated tooth. Dirty, disheveled, heartsick, I leaned against the locomotive pilot, over-come by the realization that I would have to work like this all the rest of my life.

A workman guffawed in glee at the sight of my woebegone face, but he stepped away hastily when I moved into a battle crouch and tensed toward him. For a moment I stood irresolutely in the middle of the shop. Then I brushed past the watchman with a bitter curse and entered the executive offices where my father worked.

"I'm done with that job," I said. "I want to be a surgeon."

"You will go to work at seven o'clock tomorrow morning," my father said. It was he who had given me the choice of a medical education or mechanical engineering—three or four years in the shops, to be followed by Stevens or Cor-nell. And it was I who had made the decision—and then shown the white feather.

In the days that followed, I developed what would now be called an inferi-ority complex. I showed a specious braggadocio, an eagerness to come to blows—anything to show my superiority and wipe out the stain that troubled me. But Bill Grindle handled me with fine disregard for my complex and my father's position. He gave me the dirtiest jobs in the shop and threatened to cuff me when I snarled in resentment. Scraping grease and old paint from the locomotive frames was about the highest class of work assigned me. Only my natural com-bativeness and a genuine love for the better railroad work saved me from sinking to the level of an ordinary laborer. Often Bill Grindle, missing me from my scraping job, would find me in the firebox of the locomotive, lustily "busting" flues with the boilermakers, vastly proud of my ability to swing a heavy hammer with either hand.

I gathered a gorgeous collection of small tools. These I obtained by making a tour of the shop with an empty wash bucket. Every loose file or chisel, hammer or caliper that I saw was dropped into the bucket and exchanged at the toolroom for the tiny files, chisels, and hammers that are the delight of budding mechanics. In a short while, the men hid their tools when I came into sight.

In the master mechanic's office I was the subject of a long discussion. Bill

Grindle figuratively threw up his hands. He'd had enough of me. He told what I had been doing instead of scraping grease.

Sam Vauclain, another gang boss, closed the conversation.

"Send him to me," Sam said. "I can use him. What's more, I'll see that he does what I tell him."

Bill Grindle waved his hand disparagingly.

"Wish you luck," he said.

Sam looked over the collection of tools I had accumulated, threw out the useless ones, and added a number of high-grade scales and calipers from his private store.

"You will be the leader on Number 4 track," he said, while I stared at him in dumb astonishment. He could not have amazed me more by announcing I had been appointed master mechanic. "My job will be to see that the work gets to you on time, and yours is to get it on the engine." He beckoned to two strapping fellows. "These are your helpers. They know their business."

He flourished a huge red bandanna, blew a trumpet blast, and walked away without a further word. In the days that followed, I learned that the trumpet blast meant get back to business. When it had echoed down the aisles, the subject was closed.

A wonderful vista opened before me. Yesterday I had been scraping grease, my hand against everyone and everyone's hand against me. Today, the best work on the locomotive was mine. The hours flew. I was surprised when the bell rang at six o'clock.

I learned a lesson very early under Sam's tutelage. We were finishing up a crack passenger locomotive and I was putting the last loving touches on the crosshead guides—quite the most prominent feature of the running gear. Bars, bolts, and supports glistened with a luster that rivaled a plate-glass mirror. Not a scratch or blemish marred the beautiful surfaces.

Sam came along on his final inspection.

"Fine job, Ted," he said, "but the bolt heads are not quite square. Slip a wrench on them and square them up with the bars." He walked away.

The switching engine was waiting to move the locomotive. The time was short. I would have to knock out the bolts, turn the heads, and tighten them up again with a wrench, and it would spoil that beautiful polish. I told myself no one would notice them at sixty miles an hour. I waved to the crew to go ahead and couple up.

The next morning Sam came to where I was working and without a word grabbed me by the ear and started for the roundhouse. I went along with wild leaps and wilder curses: I had to keep up or lose an ear. When we reached the locomotive, he shoved my nose almost against the guides, just the way you punish a puppy that has wet on the parlor rug.

Boiling with rage, I exhausted my blasphemous vocabulary while Sam turned his back and strode away without a word. Then I hunted up a wrench and a soft hammer and squared up the bolt heads.

One day Sam handed me a blueprint and told me to go out to the blacksmith shop, three miles east, and lay out some foundations for a heating furnace and boilers. I examined the print after I got to the smith shop, but it was all Greek to me, utterly incomprehensible. I started back to the main shop for additional instructions. Sam saw me coming down the long line of lathes, blueprint in hand. He stepped into the aisle and made an emphatic backward signal. Like a flash I whirled around and started back. Sam had given me a job, and he expected me to finish it.

Sam was as relentless with himself as with his men. When the big steam hammer broke down and needed a general overhauling, the master mechanic was of the opinion it would take six weeks to do the work. Sam promised to have it ready within a week.

He divided his gang into two shifts, day and night, and began tearing down the hammer. He gave me the job of running a temporary line of shafting from the wheel shop, two hundred feet away, to drive a boring bar that would true up the cylinder of the hammer. With my two helpers, Tom and Jack, I robbed the shop and storeroom of every piece of shafting and every shaft hanger in sight. We hung these from the roof trusses with spikes, bolts, and clamps.

It was Saturday morning when we began. By Sunday afternoon the shafting was in place. Sam, who had been on his feet since we started, had brought us a midnight lunch of hot beefsteak sandwiches and coffee. He and I took Sunday breakfast at his home. On Sunday night he sent Tom and Jack home with instructions to report back on Monday morning; but he kept me at work with him.

Without rest he drove day and night, and the only sleep I got was filched when I was driven by necessity to take a moment away from work. After the second day, we ate every four hours, and these large meals kept us going.

I was tending the boring bar on Tuesday afternoon, perched on a small platform among the rafters, when Stratton, the master mechanic, came into the shop with Sam. The boring bar was groaning in rhythmic waves as the tool cut into the cast iron, but there were no men about, the day gang doing machine work on the hammer.

"You don't seem to be doing much, Samuel," said the M.M. "I thought young Custer was working on this job."

Sam pointed me out in the dim recesses of the roof. The M.M. stepped back to look. I was so black with dirt and grime that it was hard to see me against the smoky roof. One of my hands was on the bar feed; the other held a paper-backed book. A thin line of smoke curled upward from a Sweet Caporal stuck to my lower lip.

Stratton was a disciplinarian from top to bottom of his five-feet-two, and he was no friend of mine. Words failed him. He had seen an unforgivable sin against his organization boldly flaunted in his face—an apprentice smoking during work! He stamped out of the shop. Sam laughed and went about his business, and the boring bar groaned and chattered as if in derision.

On Thursday night at nine o'clock we finished the work. I helped knock out the supports of the scaffolding and then ran for home and crawled into bed without taking off my shoes or overalls. I slept the clock around. Sam was at work at seven the next morning.

That was an amazing year under an amazing man. Sam's capacity for work was abysmal, his endurance stupendous. By the time I transferred to the lathe shop, he had made me a mechanic in everything but years.

Almost a decade passed before I worked for Sam again. I had been out of railroading, trying my hand as a cartoonist and newspaper reporter, and Sam had risen to the position of superintendent of the Baldwin Locomotive Works in Philadelphia. I wrote and asked him for a job.

"Come down and see me next Sunday," Sam wrote. "Wire me on what train you will arrive."

Sam met me at the train at nine o'clock Sunday morning.

"Why did you wait until the middle of the day?" he asked.

We walked up Broad Street to the works. Sam had invented a compound locomotive and was getting it ready for preliminary trials. The erecting shop was too small. The smith shop would have to be remodeled. A radial stay locomotive firebox, cast steel to replace cast iron—all the concerns of his active brain were paraded, but not a word about a job for me.

We went to Sam's house for dinner. He asked about my life in Cleveland. Later, he walked to the station with me. My train was to leave at three o'clock. The time came to shake hands, and still not one word about a job. Just as I was about to step onto the train, he asked:

"When are you coming to work?"

"Next Friday, the first of February."

"All right. I will start you at twenty cents an hour."

My heart sank. That was a third of what the drawing board had paid me. Sam dragged out the red bandanna and blew a mighty blast.

"All right," I said. "I'll be there."

There was no perceptible difference between the Sam I had known at Altoona and the general superintendent of the largest locomotive works in the world. When I arrived at Baldwin's, carrying a rolled bundle of overalls under my arm, the whistles were blowing for seven o'clock. Sam looked up from his desk and called in Charley Herman, his pet gang boss.

"This is the young man I was telling you about. Give him the Pike's Peak engine."

Charley led the way. The place was a bedlam. Men were swarming over a small locomotive, like ants on a pile of sugar. The floor was littered with locomotive parts in apparent disorderly confusion. No one paid a particle of attention to us.

I had kept my overalls from Altoona as a matter of sentiment. They were faded almost white: the badge of service, a notice to the other men that I was one of them. I slid into these old friends with a strange feeling of confidence.

Late that afternoon, Sam came to the gang and took me to work on the new

Baldwin Works had dozens of locomotives under construction
in the erecting shop (top), boiler shop, and wheel shop
(center). Steam hammer (bottom) walloped kinks out of steel.

Scientific American, 1884

compound locomotive. We worked until two in the morning, and I have an idea that we would have kept on if Annie, Sam's wife, had not come down to the shop and fairly dragged him away. Day and night on Saturday, Sunday until eight at night, he drove himself until he was satisfied with the progress of the work. I worked one hundred and eighteen hours the first week, one hundred and twenty the second. All that saved me from a solid day-and-night third week was a fall into the roundhouse pit one black night. That bunged me up somewhat, and I lost considerable time. Sam deplored my hard luck. Anything that kept a man from work was hard luck.

The next week I found forty cents an hour in my pay envelope. The new locomotive was now ready for road trials. Every night we would take the brute out on the road, and every night it would break down. Then back to the round-house, where we would work all night making repairs or substituting new designs for the defective parts.

Sam was on hand every minute. I slept on the coal pile in the tender, ate ham sandwiches and raisin pies (I am now off raisin pie for life), and washed in a bucket of water blue with the soap and dirt of many lavings.

One night we got as far as Wilmington, Delaware, only to have our soaring hopes dashed by broken valves. Sam wakened a farmer and drove madly on to Wilmington, where he caught a train back to Philadelphia. Arriving at the shop at two in the morning, he plunged immediately into the work of making an improvement in the design. As for the locomotive, it was hauled back to the shop with me dead to the world on the coal pile.

That afternoon the new valves were ready. A gang of men woke me up with the racket of installing them. We made fifty miles that night and limped back with a broken crosshead. The next night we broke a valve stem, and the night after that, a valve cage. There seemed to be no end to our troubles.

On the night when we finally made the run to Baltimore and back without a mishap, Sam took the victory quietly. It was I who made shrill cries and war whoops.

"We'll go home for breakfast," Sam said—it was four in the morning. "You don't have to wash up. Nobody will be out of bed. Then you can come back and go over that compound from back bumper to smokestack. I'll send a gang to you at seven o'clock. Go over the valves, set the pops—oh, hell, you know what to do."

Sam's Irish cook clumped down the backstairs, pulling her clothes into some semblance of decency. We washed our hands and faces at the kitchen sink and then sat at the kitchen table while Nora kept a stream of bacon and eggs, coffee, and griddle cakes rolling steadily toward us. Neither of us had eaten since noon the day before. When we could eat no more, I lighted up a Sweet Caporal, one of Sam's abominations, and leaned back in the chair to think over our triumph.

"No sleeping!" Sam shook me awake. "Time to go. I think I can take out the *Royal Blue* this afternoon."

Day was breaking over the silent city, splashing bits of color on the high stone walls of the Eastern Penitentiary across the way. Down in the close-lined streets, a baker boy hurried in the half-gloom, dropping unwrapped loaves of bread on the residential doorsteps. Over in the roundhouse, the compound was panting softly. A group of workmen were discussing its unusual features.

"Same old story," said a grizzled engineer. "Bigger engines, more cars, fewer engineers. Not for me."

I was under the engine when our gang came in at seven o'clock. We slaved in perfect amity until afternoon, when Sam came in and announced that the compound would take the Baltimore & Ohio's *Royal Blue.*

"Get something to eat and hurry back," he said. "We leave in an hour."

The compound backed softly against the long line of blue and gold Pullman cars. The air hose was coupled, the brakes tested. The conductor stood with watch in hand, waiting for the last signal.

"Blue Line Dick" was at the throttle—a highly capable, hard-running, black-mustached pirate of an engineer, swaggering and verbose, and one of the best men on the division. When the go-ahead signal came, he eased her gently out of the station shed. We were off on the trip that would make or break the reputation of the Vauclain compound.

Sam and I sat on the toolbox back of the coal pile, where the smoke soon painted us a deep sepia color. It was a hard place to ride, but here we could watch all the operations and see the color of the smoke at the top of the stack.

Blue Line Dick was whooping it up, sixty, seventy miles an hour. This 924 was possibly the roughest riding locomotive ever foaled at the Baldwin Locomotive Works, but she hung to the track, bucking the curves like an unbroken bronco, and taking the straight stretches like a frightened greyhound. At Camden Yard we were ten minutes ahead of time. We crept slowly the rest of the way to the station.

When we had uncoupled and were backing into the coal wharves, Sam suggested we could look her over and then hitch onto the nine o'clock express. We examined every rod, tried each separate nut, crawled over and under to do all the multitudinous tasks that every locomotive demands at the end of a hard run.

At nine o'clock we coupled up to the express. The engineer was a solemn-faced chap named Harry Burrell, who wiped his way into the cab with a bundle of waste. Very precise in his talk was Mr. Burrell, the direct antithesis of Blue Line Dick. He was a man in his early thirties, tall, slender, with large brown eyes. His beard was trimmed to a Van Dyke, with a carefully kept mustache. Absolutely nothing about him suggested the wickedest runner who ever pulled a throttle.

"He doesn't look like much of a runner," Sam whispered.

"Nope, he don't," I said. "Probably you will have to give him the prod before we go very far."

Ten miles out of Baltimore we were held up by a freight at the crossover, and we got away twenty minutes late.

Mr. Burrell then proceeded to give us an exhibition of fast running that raised streaks of goose flesh up and down our spines. He would wipe off the throttle handle and gently move it out a few notches. Then he would clean the reverse lever, and the locomotive would jump like a scared rabbit when he dropped it down. We roared, pitching and swaying, through stations and yards, and we slid into the B&O station in Philadelphia on time to the dot.

"I'm going to hire that fellow," Sam said admiringly as we walked toward home. And he did.

—Condensed from *No Royal Road*, the autobiography of Edgar A. Custer, H. C. Kinsey & Company, New York, 1937. Copyright 1936 and 1937 by Edgar A. Custer.

In 1884 the Baldwin Works built this
"Standard Passenger Engine."
Scientific American, 1884

Baldwin's "Standard Freight Engine" was built in 1884.
Scientific American, 1884

CHAPTER EIGHT

Railroad Town

I

*"With all its beautiful environment, the town
was deadly uninteresting and almost squalid."*

To a trainman, a "railroad town" is almost any division point where he can
buy supper and find a bed for the night. In common usage, the meaning of the
phrase is more precise. It refers to a peculiarly aromatic, soot-and-vinegar
community, unlike the towns begotten by any other industry.

The quality that sets a railroad town apart is not merely the influence of a
railroad. If it were only that, you could apply the term to Baltimore, where
trains go bumbling through the major streets and most of the land around the
harbor is railroad-owned; or to Chicago, "the Nation's Freight Handler," with
its long, thick webbing of silvery track and its dark, gaping stations, squatting
like gigantic spiders at the end of every filament. You would surely give the
name to that salubrious community that was located by pounding an engineer's
stake into the red soil at the projected meeting place of two rail lines in the
pine forests of Georgia—a station first called Terminus and later known as
Atlanta.

But Baltimore, Chicago, and Atlanta are not what one would call "railroad
towns." A town can be spawned by a railroad and dominated by a railroad
without belonging to the genre. The so-called cow towns of the Kansas plain
—Abilene, Ellsworth, Newton, Dodge City—do not qualify, although it was
the presence of the tracks, not of the cattle, that brought each of them into
existence.

As for Pullman, Illinois, a town locked in churlish servitude to the railroad industry, it was a unique specimen. The twelve thousand residents of this
factory-owned, factory-planned workers' utopia on the shores of Lake Calumet,

In a railroad town, everyone depended on the railroad.
King's *The Southern States*, 1875

just south of Chicago, lived in brick villas (for executives), row houses (for gang foremen), and apartments (for laborers), which were built and managed by a company that also built and managed railroad sleeping cars. The company trimmed the lawns, pruned the trees, selected the books for the library and the plays for the theater; but Pullman, withal, was a proto-fascistic company commune, not a railroad town.

A true railroad town must depend *directly* on the railroad for not only its creation and its current prosperity, but also for its mental, cultural, and spiritual existence. One thinks of Roseville, California, or even Ogden, Utah. But no place qualifies so perfectly as Altoona, Pennsylvania.

The seventy thousand people of Altoona huddle close to the main line of the world's largest railroad. They staff the Pennsy's major repair shops, which at times have employed as many as twenty thousand men.

Railroad engineers laid out Altoona in 1849, while the Pennsy was under construction. As soon as the tracks, building eastward from Pittsburgh, reached the town in 1854, it became a major division point, a shop center, and a thoroughgoing railroad town. Its years of vitality, its admirable strength, its simplicity, and its indifference to the gentle, noble, and enduring aspects of the human spirit, testify to all that has been good and bad about the railroad as a creative institution.

ALTOONA IS A RAILROAD TOWN, planned by a railroad draftsman. The avenues run parallel to the railroad tracks, and the streets are at exact right angles to them. There is no variation in the symmetry of the design except where the Old Plank Road, starting at Twelfth Avenue and Seventeenth Street, makes a most distressing break as it turns toward the county seat, seven miles south.

In the late 1840's, the Pennsylvania Railroad selected this site at the foot of the Alleghenies for their principal repair shops, when it became evident that the constantly increasing business demanded a more efficient method of moving passengers and freight over the mountains than was offered by the inclined planes of the Portage Railroad. The new road started at the edge of a large duck pond and immediately began the climb into the mountains to the west. It was a wonderful engineering feat at that time, and even today Horseshoe Curve, five miles west of the town, is one of the highlights of railroad travel.

The approaches to Altoona were of rare beauty, surrounded by towering mountains that dropped sharply to brawling trout streams or tiny patches of cultivated land. It was as if the designer of the town felt there was enough beauty in the surroundings to make parks and breathing spaces unnecessary. The town was simply a place where men would work, eat, and sleep. As befitted a railroad town, it was economical of space. The shops were built along the line of the new railroad, and the dwellings clustered around the shops as closely as possible. There should be no time wasted in getting to work. The duck pond was filled up, and the stately Logan House was erected on its site.

With all its beautiful environment, Altoona was deadly uninteresting and almost squalid. Outside of a dozen or so houses that the railroad built for its officers and higher workmen, the dwellings were all makeshift, wooden affairs, most of them painted a dull drab, unrelieved by any trimming. The streets were unpaved, and in the springtime they became almost impassable at crossings. A stream of liquid mud a foot or so deep filled Twelfth Avenue, the main business street, from walk to walk, slowly flowing eastward. Workmen carried planks to throw across the mudholes on their way to work. There were but four avenues that were comparatively level; the cross streets climbed the steep hills that rolled away to the mountains.

Even at the close of the Civil War, when I was a boy in Altoona, there was no sewage system. The waste water ran in the gutters, always choked with rank weeds that rose above the sidewalk. One of the diversions of the town boys was to build dams, which overflowed and transformed the streets into a highly odorous mass of mud and sewage. With all its twenty thousand inhabitants, there was only a solitary constable to keep the peace, and he was above concerning himself with the doings of small boys. It was a railroad town.

In time, Altoona acquired a brick opera house. Signor Blitz picked silver dollars out of the air, and Paul du Chaillu told about the ferocious gorillas in Africa. Other than an occasional concert or a series of lectures, that was about the extent of the amusements offered.

Still, with all its absence of diversion for the adults, the town was never dull for us boys. There was the excitement of the train wrecks that occurred almost daily on the steep mountain grades, the sanguinary battles of the railroaders in Whiskey Row, and the rivalry among the baseball teams of Altoona, Johnstown, and Hollidaysburg. We town boys invariably stoned the outside teams from the railroad station to the ball grounds and return; and in pursuit of this amusement, the rival gangs of the neighborhoods forgot their quarrels and joined in common cause.

Above all, there was the railroad, with its fascinating freight trains lumbering up the mountain, each train with three locomotives belching black smoke that covered the town with a sepia pall. Under this accommodating haze, a boy could steal a ride. The town boys became expert in jumping on and off moving trains, not always with entire success. Brother Will missed his jump and would have been killed had not Sam Tuck dragged him miraculously from under the wheels; and, as it was, he lost a couple of toes and limped to the end of his days.

No, Altoona, for a boy, was never dull.

—Condensed from *No Royal Road*, the autobiography of Edgar A. Custer, H. C. Kinsey & Company, New York, 1937. Copyright 1936 and 1937 by Edgar A. Custer.

II

"Few of them ever came back a second time unless they just happened to be passing through..."

IN SPITE OF IMPRESSIVE EVIDENCE that most railroad towns are dull and respectable, popular opinion cherishes the belief that division points are dismal swamps of depravity and construction camps are portable sinks of iniquity.

This entrancing notion was spread around more than a century ago by Samuel Bowles, a Massachusetts newspaper editor, who visited some of the end-of-track settlements spawned by the Union Pacific along its transcontinental tracks in 1868 and described what he saw as "hell-on-wheels." Since then, innumerable journalists have passed through these prosaic little towns—Julesburg, Colorado; Sidney, Nebraska; Corrinne, Utah—have looked in vain for vice and violence, and have sighed regretfully for those ungodly, awful scenes that used to be.

A reporter for the San Francisco newspaper, *Alta California,* who went up to Utah in May, 1869, to witness the joining of the tracks from east and west, was among the last of his craft who would have the opportunity to visit a real, honest-to-G——, Union Pacific, hell-on-wheels railroad town. Fully prepared to be horrified—and to *tell all*—he climbed into the wagon with the construction superintendent of the Central Pacific and rode over to the rival Union Pacific side.

As WE APPROACHED the Union Pacific posts, we were met by a party of white men who appeared to be in a state of unusual hilarity. There was a look in their eyes which indicated that, in their own estimation, they had just accomplished some very creditable and glorious enterprise. The thought struck me that probably they had just laid, or were about to lay, ten miles of track; but a short distance farther on, I found that they had only been laying out one of their own number.

The wounded man was stretched out in a pool of blood on the side of the road. Some Central Pacific engineers, who had a little camp in the vicinity, were attending to the wounded man. They said the party we had met along the road had fallen on this fellow with rifles and pistols. Shots had rained on the Central Pacific tents, and one of the engineers had crawled behind a water barrel for safety. Thirty or forty shots had been fired at the unfortunate wretch, and as he ran, one entered the left side of his face and came out at the other side, and another penetrated his leg. A rumor passed later in the afternoon that the party who had made the assault, finding that the man was not dead, were preparing to return and hang him; and he was accordingly sent back on a wagon to his own place. I met him on my return, lying on top of a load of flour, and bleeding like a stuck pig.

About two miles farther on is a little village of white tents. It is located in a picturesque spot in the Great Salt Lake Basin, with a portion of the lake visible in the distance. It looks smiling and calm enough, but a drive through its streets revealed that every house is either a rum-mill or a grocery. If their character were no worse than this, it is possible that the scenes of riot and bloodshed which are so often enacted here would not have such tragic terminations; but these places are kept by desperadoes who have been expelled from neighboring territories by vigilance committees. They have crawled along with the advancing army of workers from the East. Most of the earnings of the laborers of the Union Pacific have gone into their clutches.

I subsequently learned that the man upon whom the murderous assault had been committed was one of these predatory camp followers. He had mortally wounded someone else in the early morning. The windup of the affair, according to subsequent information, was the killing of five men.

—Excerpted from the San Francisco *Alta California*, May 1, 1869.

HELL-ON-WHEELS, however exaggerated its claims to infamy, at least had bowed out with pistols blazing. Imagine, then, the disappointment of a writer for the edifying columns of *The Chautauquan* who visited end-of-track on the Denver & Rio Grande in Colorado in 1882 and discovered that the major railroad town in the construction area was merely "a group of board shanties with canvas roofs, a wretched huddle of groggeries and boarding tents." This settlement had appeared overnight when the headquarters of the railroad stopped moving for a few days; then, it had withered away when the road moved on.

At the new end-of-track, deep in the Black Canyon of the Gunnison, the reporter found a real railroad community that was far less exciting than the riotous stereotype.

I STOPPED AT THE BOARDING TRAIN, which stood opposite a rock tower a thousand feet in height. The sunlight fell upon its pinnacle, gilding a huge profile carved by nature, but the canyon depths were all in shadow. Here was the temporary home of four hundred men. A little beyond was the working train at the very end of the rails. All along the dump, or roadbed, gangs of men were busily unloading and placing ties and rails.

Presently a whistle blew. Six o'clock had come, and the men, leaving their tasks, scrambled aboard the flatcars, and the train rumbled back to the "Hotel on Wheels." Long before the car stopped, the men were hustling each other like a flock of stampeded sheep in a wild race for supper. The seats were limited in number, the laborers many, and none had any idea of waiting for "second table."

A toilette was a trifling matter. The next morning would be time enough for soap and water. There were swarthy Italians, Irishmen with carroty locks— men of a score of nationalities, begrimed, tattered, gnawed at by the appetite given by labor in the bracing Colorado air. They swarmed into the old freight cars which had been fitted up with long planks for benches and tables. On the tables were tin pannikins, iron knives and forks, and pewter spoons. Mounds of coarse bread, pans of some strange stew, and pots of rank black tea appeared and disappeared. Words were not wasted. Every act had a bearing upon the business of satisfying hunger. . . .

One by one, the men rose from the table. There was nothing to be said. They had been fed, and for the time they were content.

But, presently, the social instinct reasserted itself. They lighted black pipes and drew together. Some rudely mended their garments; others produced stained playing cards or gathered to talk. A few clambered into the narrow board bunks in the cars and drew their blankets up over aching limbs.

It was a glimpse of a hard, cheerless life that I had seen; but as I turned to go back to the construction train, someone struck up a rollicking Irish song, and others joined until the canyon walls gave back the chorus.

—Excerpted from "At the Head of the Rails," by Ripley Hitchcock, published in *The Chautauquan*, June, 1889.

Harper's Weekly, 1883

Northern Pacific offered "Hotel-on-Wheels"
accommodations to its construction workers.

A CAMP AT END-OF-TRACK, whether it was a wicked little hell-on-wheels or a proletarian boxcar hotel, was populated entirely of railroad men, undiluted by outlandish vocations and unredeemed by domesticity. Most other railroad communities had to suffer the presence of persons who were loosely allied, unaffiliated, or even hostile to the road.

Among themselves, railroad men divided into "home guards" (those who stayed with one road) and "boomers," who moved from place to place as season or opportunity persuaded. To further complicate the social structure, there were towns that harbored a substantial core of "home guards" part of the year and then played host to a mob of boomers in flush seasons.

Laurence Bell's superb evocation of his boyhood in a railroad boomtown, which appeared in the *American Mercury* in the late 1930's—during Lawrence Spivak's tenure as editor of that once-brilliant monthly—is a unique picture of railroading in the Southwest half a century ago.

A LL THE YEAR LONG, from January through the late summer, the Texas town in which I sojourned as a youth would be so dead you almost could have emptied a machine gun down Main Street without hitting anybody. The railroad, whose freight terminal and repair shops were the sole reasons for the town's existence (it had been laid out in two days in a cotton patch when the railroad came through, and every once in a while a stalk of short staple pushed up through the sandy earth in one of the side streets), would be running only two or three trains a day: the regular manifest freights, one each way; and the locals, which took three or four days to complete a trip because of stopping at every cowpath to drop off a case of overalls or pitchfork handles consigned to some country store. Nine-tenths of the railroad men would be on the extra board or laid off altogether, and they would spend most of their time sitting in the Athens Cafe, drinking black coffee, swapping lies, and debating their respective prowesses at firing boilers, smelling out hotboxes, or whatever other feats by which they gauged efficiency.

During these months everybody lived on credit. The stores didn't do enough cash business to pay the help. They would all be deserted save for the loafers, who seemed to be included with the fixtures, and the occasional farmers come into town to buy something that was too much trouble to raise themselves. Even the bootleggers extended credit, this gesture being due not so much to a spirit of benevolence as to the pressure of competition. After the Volstead Act had extirpated the solid block of saloons that had adorned what was known as the "Lower End" of Main Street, the surrounding county had become famous for its moonshining industry, and there was considerable truth in the popular joke that corn production thereabouts was estimated by gallons rather than bushels. At least a third of the farmers operated stills, and since they were out for every dollar they could lay a hand on, no ethical compunctions restrained them from selling a quart or half-gallon, at wholesale prices, to anybody not in the way of the enforcement agents. As a consequence, the two dozen bootleggers who had replaced the town's two dozen saloons had either to give tick to steady customers or lose them altogether to the farmer-distillers, who would accept discarded clothing, second-hand automobile parts, or even a persuasive argument in lieu of cash. Such debts were rarely beaten, however, whiskey being too important as a cure-all. Not only was it efficacious for bodily ailments, scotching malaria in the summer and pneumonia in the winter, but for maladies of the psyche as well: without regular doses of the stuff, most of the railroad men would have found the town intolerable, and decamped forthwith. Thus, while the grocers, drygoods merchants, and even the banks were rooked from time to time, the bootleggers could be assured of collecting their due when the railroad's business picked up in the fall.

The railroad was a short line, owned jointly by two of the big trunk lines and treated by both as a sort of stepchild. They forgot about it nine months out of the year, letting the tracks rust while everyone dependent upon the road for a living got along as best he could. But in the fall, when the wheat had been harvested in the North and West, the owners would remember their neglected little railroad, because it was fifty miles shorter to the Gulf ports than any other line in the state. Then they would send down a couple of dozen big "900" locomotives to replace the little dinkies that pulled the regular trains, and the town would come to life. One day everybody would be sitting around, bellyaching about hard times, and then Jiggs Hall, the peg-legged callboy, would come clumping into the Athens or the Pastime Domino Parlor, looking for a couple of crews to take an extra north.

"The fust wheat's comin," Jiggs would announce. "A hunnerd cars already waitin' in the yards at Fo't Wuth now, and the goddamn place will be lousy with it inside of a week."

In two or three days the men on the extra board would all have regular runs. Old Man McCormack, the general superintendent, would start sending wires to all the men on the seniority list to report back for duty. He would wait until the last possible source of help had been exhausted before he began hiring "boomers," as migratory trainmen were called. He regarded the boomers as unreliable and was given to saying that they were a passel of no-good bums who couldn't tell a coupling pin from a mule on the right-of-way.

Old Man McCormack was partly right: a lot of amateurs managed to hire out each fall by using bogus service papers bought from a document forger in Fort Worth; but they seldom lasted more than one trip. The real boomers—experienced railroad men who just couldn't or wouldn't stay in one place—had nothing but contempt for these greenhorns, although they themselves included railroading among a variety of pursuits that ranged from hoboing to training race horses.

The boomers' versatility, along with their inclination to quit right in the middle of a boom, was the real reason for Old Man McCormack's reluctance to hire them; his sneers at their lack of experience were largely bombast, and he knew it. The Old Man had spent thirty years in the service of one of the big roads, working his way up from engine-wiper to master mechanic, before he had been made general superintendent of the short line, and he simply couldn't understand why everybody else wasn't filled with love of railroading.

Every fall brought a new and strange horde of boomers. Few of them ever came back a second time unless they just happened to be passing through that part of the country and were particularly hard up for pocket money.

Eventually, despite Old Man McCormack's prejudices, he would have to hire boomers. Most of the men on the seniority list would have reported, but still the yards would be jammed with loaded cars. Sometimes trains would be tied up on the main line, waiting for the tracks to clear, and the Old Man would be running up and down the yards, cussing loudly enough to be heard a quarter-mile away, while the crews would sit back and take things easy, drawing overtime without having to hit a lick. This would go on for a week or two, with the Old Man sending wires all over Texas trying to borrow men from other roads. He would even persuade men he knew to take leaves of absence from their regular jobs and come to work for him.

But he still wouldn't have enough hands to run the trains. After hearing everybody from the yardmaster on down complain that they were going crazy trying to keep the main line clear, he would give in, first delivering a tirade against tramp railroaders that would last for an hour or more. "All right, then," he would yell, "Goddamn it all, go ahead and hire every Dallas bootlegger and jailbird that comes in here claiming he's a railroad man! Maybe if a couple of hundred shows up, maybe there will be a dozen out of the lot with sense enough to just set still and pretend they know what they're doing."

The dispatcher would wag his head all the time the Old Man was letting off steam, and after he had stamped out of the office the dispatcher and the telegrapher would laugh for a long time. The Old Man always blew up, every year. Then he would start hitting the bottle every thirty minutes instead of every hour or two, and he wouldn't get completely sober until business had fallen off enough to cut the board clear of the last boomer.

So the call would go out, and the next day the boomers would begin swarming into town. Some of them would arrive on the passenger trains, having been hired in Fort Worth or Houston and given free transportation, but hardly any of them would have anything in the way of baggage but the clothes on their backs. They were accustomed to the deduction-order system of buying what they needed, this being a universal practice in railroad towns, and they seemed to expect to get skinned. Once they had their names on the payroll, most of them would head for the commissary, as they called the clothing store that was favored with the deduction-order franchise, and doll themselves up in blue serge suits and tan shoes and black hats, wearing the latter uncreased, high-roller style. They paid for their lodging and meals the same way, and they all boarded at the Athens Cafe, which would take on two or three country girls as extra waitresses during the rush. Getting lodging was more difficult. Most of the rooming houses either wouldn't take boomers in, or else would charge outrageous rates, so they had to choose between the Terminal Hotel and the Commercial House. The Terminal was an ancient two-story frame house that a self-respecting farmer wouldn't have used for a barn, and the Commercial was run by an old maid named Green, who was more than a trifle eccentric.

When Old Lady Green first came to town and took over the Commercial, she had refused to rent rooms to railroad men, regardless of whether they were tramp brakemen or officials who rode up and down the line in private cars. She despised railroad men because the noise from the switch engines working in the yards made her guests refuse to take rooms on the side nearest the tracks, and she let down the bars only when a fireman blew into town and recognized her as the former madam of a bawdy house in Montana. The fireman denounced her to her face, charging that she had made every dime she had by catering to tallow pots and switchmen, and moreover, had hogged the profits of her girls. In the face of this accusation, which she knew everybody in town would believe whether true or not, the old girl started taking in the rails, although she was always snooping around the halls at all hours of the night, hoping to catch one of them violating the house rules against gambling and having girls in their rooms. This latter taboo was rather inconsistent, inasmuch as there were always two or three prostitutes putting up at her place, plying an untrammeled trade among commercial travelers and high school boys.

A few of the younger boomers considered themselves hot sports. Instead of hanging around the Athens Cafe or the yard office, they would ease up Main Street and take position in front of the Palace Confectionery, competing with the local dudes in their flirtations with the young girls who flocked downtown every afternoon when school let out. No girl who was considered nice would have anything to do with the railroad men, except on the sly. But many girls who were old enough to be allowed to drive the family cars up and down Main Street in the early evening were known to have picked up collegiate-appearing boomers and taken them driving, being careful, of course, to do the picking up in a side street. One girl, whose father was the owner of a large clothing store, fell desperately in love with a young brakeman. He looked and dressed like a vaudeville tap dancer, but to her febrile imagination he was a composite of all the great lovers of Hollywood. She took the young man to her home and introduced him to her parents, telling them that she met him at a dance down at the state university. Pretty soon she was telling all her friends in confidence that she and the brakeman were going to be married. The brakeman got fired one day when Old Man McCormack caught him with a bunch of other rails taking a drink in the switch shanty, and he left town, telling the girl that he would send for her later. He was going to New Orleans, he said, to collect some money that had been left him by a relative.

After a few weeks the girl began to be afraid that she was pregnant. When she received a postcard from the brakeman, giving her an address in New Orleans, she took her mother's diamond rings, sneaked fifty dollars from the store's cash register and followed him. Her parents heard nothing from her for a few weeks, and then they received a letter, written on the stationery of the St. Charles Hotel and saying that she was married and very happy.

But the old man was a stingy old codger. Since the girl hadn't sent back the fifty dollars and the rings, he went to New Orleans to see what was what. He came back in about a week but refused to say anything about his daughter's marriage except that she was "doing fine."

The true story leaked out through their cook. The girl hadn't been registered at the hotel at all, and the father had had the police look for her. They found her in a house on Basin Street, loaded with whiskey or dope; and when the old man went to see her, she threw the diamonds and a wad of money in his face. After the story got out, people who knew the old man's reputation for being a tightwad said he was probably so glad to get his money back, and be relieved of supporting his daughter, that he had offered to sell her seducer all his suits at cost.

Most of the boomers, however, were clannish fellows who stuck pretty closely to themselves. They had little use for the town people, whom they called hayseeds and home guards. On their rest, they stood together in little groups, talking. Nearly all of them had known each other from other places they had worked. They didn't bother much with women, beyond kidding the country waitresses or dating up the Commercial House girls, and they were on the whole more conversant with the fundamental decencies than were a majority of the townfolk who decried their lack of morals. One time when a fellow who had hired out as a switchman was discovered to be sharing the earnings of a girl he had brought to town and installed in the Commercial House, a couple of brakemen gave him such a working over that he was three weeks getting out of the hospital. Thirty or forty citizens, who had been enthusiastic spectators, became indignant complainants when they cooled off and realized that the main street of their city had been the scene of a brawl between men who were probably fugitives from justice; and the brakemen were arrested and fined for fighting, disorderly conduct, disturbing the peace, and drunkenness.

The brakemen actually weren't drunk, but it was the custom to add drunkenness to any other crimes for which boomers might be hauled in, partly because of the town's pious conviction that boomers scorned all nourishment save booze and narcotics, and partly because the arresting officers and the trial judge each received a percentage of the fines as their fees. This system resulted in bitter competition between the city marshal, whose prisoners were tried by the mayor, and the precinct constable, who haled his victims before the justice of the peace. Sometimes the rival peace officers would cooperate, as in bringing to book the participants of a Negro dice game or the operators of a still; but most of the time they operated independently, as the fees were too small when split so many ways. Somehow, it never occurred to them to file charges in both courts, which not only would have inflicted double punishment on the miscreants, but also would have made collective criminal hunting profitable as well as convenient.

Rather than work together for the commonweal, the two divisions of the law would each deputize two or three of their relatives during the boom seasons. These deputies were for the most part loutish countrymen who made a pretense of farming but actually subsisted by selling white mule to high school boys who couldn't buy the stuff from reputable bootleggers. During their tenures as deputies, they received a cut of the fines, the same as if the marshal and constable had split the money between themselves, but the money stayed in the family; besides, the kinsmen deputies continued their regular bootlegging, using a Negro or another relative to perform the actual contacting of customers. It was considered not only ingenious, but quite ethical for a deputy's agent to drum up a sale to one of the boomers, who would then be arrested by the deputy himself for possession of intoxicants and, naturally, drunkenness and disorderly conduct.

Sometimes the boomers would not submit peaceably to this unique shakedown. One night the constable and his brother-in-law (a deputy) tried to arrest a fireman as he sat in the Athens; and the fireman, a gigantic red-haired man who said afterwards that he had done a little heavyweight prizefighting at various times, almost killed them both before the marshal and his staff came reluctantly to the rescue. Two other boomers waded in to help the fireman, and there was a free-for-all that lasted for nearly an hour and virtually wrecked the restaurant. The red-haired fireman was still going strong, though he had been struck with chairs, gun butts, and God knows what else, when Old Man McCormack came running and called him off. It turned out that the fireman had worked for the Old Man for a long time on another railroad, and the Old Man knew him to be a teetotaler: He merely had bought some whiskey for his ailing roommate and had taken it to their room before the Law grabbed him.

The fireman and the two others who pitched in with him were bounced, because the company regulations called for the automatic dismissal of any employee who became entangled with the Law; but the Old Man hired them back two hours later under aliases. Though he didn't have a very high opinion of rails who wouldn't stay put, the Old man had even less tolerance for the constabulary, whom he designated, with vast contempt, as "hawkshaws." He would not allow them to set foot on railroad property. When he caught the constable and his nephew-deputy pulling a couple of kids off a freight, he had the yard bull arrest the "hawkshaws" for trespass, ordered out an extra, and shipped them over to the county seat, locked in an empty refrigerator car. He was unaware (or so he swore when the men stumbled from the train two hours later with their clothing frozen to their bodies) that the car had been iced that afternoon, preparatory to being loaded with dressed veal. The constable made a lot of threats when he thawed out, but the Old Man threatened in turn to have the five-hundred-odd employees of the road remove him from office by petition. The constable quieted down, pleaded guilty to a trespass charge, and paid a fifty-dollar fine.

Because of the Old Man's attitude toward the police force, the railroad yard was the favorite gathering place of the town's sporting element and was generally livelier at night than Main Street. There would always be at least one game of crap or poker underway in one of the cabooses, and on paydays there would be a dozen or more. The boomers got in the habit of doing their drinking at the yard. They would line up along the edge of the freighthouse platform, with a half-gallon fruit jar for a wassail bowl, while the police force hid in the adjoining lumber yard, hoping one of the celebrators would get drunk enough to stagger out of the neutral zone, whereupon he could be seized and dragged into court. The boomers became pretty cagey, however, so the Law usually had to content itself with sending in an emissary to see if the jug didn't need refilling.

The boom generally stopped as abruptly as it had started. Crews reporting for duty would find that their trains had been cancelled and the board had been cut. When the ax fell, the boomers would drop their company-issue tin lanterns, give their gloves to the Negro roustabouts, and stampede the timekeeper's office to draw their pay. They evinced little if any regret at being cast loose from toil, having worked for two or three months with no time off excepting the eight hours rest between trips that the law required. On receiving their wages, or what was left of them after various deductions had been made, they would celebrate their emancipation.

The boom's end brought a climax to the antagonism felt mutually by both the rails and the townsmen, and there would always be a dozen or so fist fights. The town people feared that the rails might get out of hand and take the town apart, while the rails felt that they were entitled to at least one retaliatory gesture, having been persecuted by the constabulary, bilked by the tradesmen, and held up by the parents as horrible examples of what happened to young men who chose railroading as a career.

On these nights the Law would absent itself from town, knowing that the rails, with no jobs to hold, would accept jail sentences rather than pay fines. Then, too, there was the memory of one Wichita Joe Leamon, who came to town one fall and got himself hired as special deputy marshal on his word that he had been a Texas Ranger and practically single-handed had cleaned up Burkburnett during the oil boom days.

Wichita Joe carried two guns and a blackjack and made himself particularly disagreeable. On the day the board was cut, he swaggered down to the entrance to the yards and yelled in to the men waiting for their pay that he would pistol-whip any of them who were still in town after the passenger trains had pulled out. None of them said anything. At eight o'clock that night there weren't any drunks on the streets, and Wichita Joe took up his stand in front of the Greek's and began bragging about how he had cleaned up the town single-handed. He was going strong, getting tougher every minute, when from around the corner leading to the depot there came a racket that sounded as if fifty people were being skinned alive.

Wichita Joe whipped out both his pistols and headed for the corner, yelling over his shoulder for the crowd of loafers to stand back and not interfere with the Law. The onlookers saw him turn the corner. A minute or so later, they heard two shots fired. After a judicious interval, an adventurous group followed along to see what had happened. They found Wichita Joe lying in the alley, but they were able to identify him only by his two empty holsters. His guns were gone, and he was as bloody as a stuck pig. After that, the law-and-order agencies always observed the end of the boom by temporarily repealing the Eighteenth Amendment and taking to the tall timber.

Two days after the boomers had cleared out, the town would go back to sleep, but there would be evidences of the parting celebration in the form of moused eyes among the local champions. Several plate-glass windows usually would be broken from having had somebody knocked through them. The consanguineous police reinforcements would disband, resuming their normal pursuits of selling white mule to minors; and the citizenry, solvent once more, would sit back and do nothing for the next nine months or so. Barring drummers from Dallas and St. Louis and a handful of summer visitors who came only if they were unable to get themselves invited elsewhere, there wouldn't be a strange face in town until the next boom rolled around.

—"Railroad Boom-Town," by Laurence Bell, from the *American Mercury*, March, 1938. Copyright 1938 by the *American Mercury*.

III

"The boardwalk of Auburn, the place to show new hats and dresses, was the depot platform at 4:30 P.M.*"*

STRICTLY SPEAKING, Auburn, California, is not a railroad town. It is what guidebooks call a "retail and administrative center for an extensive agricultural region." This is about like saying that no one can put his finger on a specific reason for Auburn's existence except that it has been there for a long time.

When the tracks of the Central Pacific Railroad came through in 1865, Auburn already was there. It had started as Wood's Dry Diggings, a gold mining camp, in 1848, and argonauts from Auburn, New York, had renamed it for their hometown the following year. The "new town," up by the train station, did become a railroad town of sorts, although not exactly a hell-on-wheels in the opinion of young Clarence Wooster, the station agent.

Wooster later worked for the Central Pacific and its successor, the Southern Pacific, in other, livelier parts of California, but he made his living and his reputation developing and selling farmlands.

IN 1876 THE TOWN OF Dutch Flat, in the foothills of the Sierra Nevada, practically staggered with prosperity. At sixteen, I was freight, passenger, and telegraphic agent for the Central Pacific Railroad, all-around flunky for the general store, and chief messenger for the Wells Fargo Express.

I was getting along swimmingly, becoming acquainted with the sturdy men and broad range of business activities of Dutch Flat, when a telegram came from J. A. Fillmore, the division superintendent, offering me the ticket and telegraphic agency at the important station of Auburn. The job was a promotion, a compliment to my improved proficiency in telegraphy; but it involved a different way of life. Instead of alertness and ceaseless activity, I now had to adjust myself to the lonesome art of killing time. It was necessary only that I keep within hearing distance of the telegraphic instrument, sell tickets and check baggage for a morning and an evening overland train. A lazy man's job, indeed!

Mr. Willmot, the freight agent, occupied a building across the track. I boarded at Jimmy Borland's Auburn Hotel, close by. The main town, however, surrounded the Courthouse, down in a hollow a mile away.

Grandma Crandall brought me books from her voluminous library, and she helped acquaint me with many of the good folk of that very wholesome little city. All of these I was pleased to meet, and they were permitted inside the office when they came to meet the train.

The boardwalk of Auburn, the place to show new hats and dresses, was the depot platform at 4:30 P.M., when the eastbound overland came along. This was the event of the day, and an opportunity for all. (The westbound overland passed Auburn about eight in the morning.)

Two hackmen would always meet this train. Tommy usually arrived from the town, a mile away, first. He would poke his head through the ticket window and ask.:

"Is she on time this morning?"

"No, sir. Twenty minutes late."

"Hear what the trouble was?"

"No, sir."

"Guess maybe she pulled out a drawhead."

"Maybe so."

Then the second hackman would poke his head through the ticket window and exclaim:

"Tommy says Number 2 is twenty minutes late. Is that so, Agent?"

"Yes, sir."

"Hear what the trouble is?"

"No."

"I'd think they would fix them drawheads so's they would stand the gaff."

"They ought to do something."

"Yes, or change the time card."

Then Jimmy Borland's head would come through the window, with a smile on the front of it.

"Morning, Wooster. Is she on time this mornin'?"

"No, Jimmy. Twenty minutes late."

"Vell, some more bad drawheads. I come back."

A passenger would step up to the window.

Passengers were unwelcome intruders in the
controlled bedlam of a village baggage room.

Scribner's Monthly, 1888

"Ticket for San Francisco. Is the train on time?"

"Twenty minutes late, sir."

"After hurrying to get up and rushing through breakfast, here I have to wait around this depot for twenty minutes."

"Sorry."

Every passenger and human being on display would visit the window for a confirmatory report, nothwithstanding his having been repeatedly informed by others. This occurred every morning and served to appease my conscience for accepting a salary for loafing.

Once I printed a sign and put it in the window. Then they all asked, in turn, whether that sign was intended for today. I resigned myself to the inevitable.

—Adapted from "Railroading in California in the Seventies," the reminiscences of Clarence M. Wooster, in the *Quarterly of the California Historical Society*, XVIII: 4 (December, 1939).

IV

"I decided to stop sleeping on coal cars and treat myself to a bed in the Grove Hotel."

THE GLOOMY, RED-BRICK TOWNS of upstate New York are probably the least hellish of all settlements touched by the corrupting influence of the railroad. Joseph Bromley's account of night life at the Grove Hotel in Binghamton exudes an almost beautific sweetness along with its aroma of musty corridors and unchanged beds. Regrettably, the influence of an amanuensis is evident in Mr. Bromley's memoirs, like the busy hand of an interior decorator remodeling the attic; but it probably is safe to assume that no ghostwriter, only a bunch of railroad men, could have thought up the Utica Room.

IT WAS MY FIRST TRIP up to Binghamton, New York, hauling a load of Pennsylvania anthracite on the old Black River line. After we passed the junction with the branch to Syracuse, Boney Young, the engineer, turned and asked me where I was going to pound my ear that night.

"Mother thought perhaps I could go with you, Mr. Young," I answered, polite as I knew how.

Boney shook his head. "Kid, I'm as free from money as a turtle is from feathers. I ran against a full house with a flush last night. Now, if you have two bits, you can go over to the Grove Hotel in Binghamton, get the key to the Utica Room from Dennis, and I'll meet you at the side door. We'll be gone in the morning before he opens up."

I didn't understand about the Utica Room, Dennis, or the side door, but I didn't have to confess my ignorance.

"Mr. Young," I told him, "I'm free from feathers, too."

"Never mind, kid," Boney said. "We'll get along."

After we had turned the empties over to the yard goats and run the engine into the roundhouse, Boney told me to get the cushions from the cab and leave a call for the McKinney House. I followed him across the tracks to a coal yard with "McKinney" painted on the office shack. We climbed a high ladder to a trestle that led over a number of coal cars waiting to be unloaded. Scrambling from car to car, we finally reached one filled with rice coal.

"It fits your body like a feather bed," Boney said.

After we had settled ourselves, I opened my dinner pail and we ate Mother's sandwiches and pie to the last bite. We faced the next day without a crumb or a nickel between us, but Boney was untroubled. He rooted into the coal and began to snore.

I didn't stay awake long, either, in spite of my aching arms and the smarting of my thumb where I had broken a water blister. But I felt I never could learn to love the overnight accommodations in the McKinney House.

When the Old Man put me on the regular schedule, firing a local freight that ran to Binghamton and back, I decided to stop sleeping on coal cars or the floor of the caboose and treat myself to a bed in the Grove Hotel. On the first night in, I went across the tracks to the faded, square, shabby old building, in front

The waiting room was a place for talking,
parading new fashions, and asking questions.

of which a flock of railroad men were already gathering, filling the row of slat-backed chairs that stood side by side, nailed to a long plank, with their backs against the wall.

Pushing through the battered oak door with its panel of sanded glass, I entered the lobby. This was the first time I had seen the interior of a hotel, any hotel, so I looked curiously about the big room, with its dado of varnished yellow oak, topped by a band of faded paper. A row of split-bottomed chairs near the window, a large china spittoon filled with sand and cigar butts, and a chandelier dangling two fly-specked oil lamps, were the only furnishings, except for a gaudy advertising calendar above the counter that served as a desk. Behind the desk, a short, querulous man was looking at me with an unhappy air.

Hoping he would not know how green I was, I swung my lunch pail carelessly as I went over and ordered a room.

"Where do you work?" the man asked, giving me a hostile eye. Not satisfied by my answer that I was a fireman on the railroad, he demanded to know where I came from, and when I told him Utica, he glared at me and danced a sort of turkey strut behind the counter.

"Utica!" he shouted. "Utica! I wouldn't trust a Utica man, no more than I'd trust my life to the devil."

The men on the front porch stuck their heads through the windows. Glancing over my shoulder, hoping that my engineer and conductor were not witness to this humiliation, I saw Gander Schnell ambling through the door. Gander was a conductor on the Black River line and famous in all the yards for his Adam's apple, which bobbed up and down like a monkey on a string when he was angry.

Gander made an accurate shot at the spittoon and leaned across the desk.

"Pipe down, Denny," he said. "It ain't no crime to be from Utica. This kid's all right. He has fired for me. You ain't got anybody in the Utica Room. Go ahead and give it to him." He gave me a friendly pat and went back onto the porch, and the heads dropped out of the windows.

Grumbling, Denny took a big iron key from the board, led me down an unlighted corridor to Number 23, and opened the door to a bare room containing a couple of kitchen chairs, a washstand, and two nicked iron beds. One of the beds had fancy curlicues and a single, dented brass knob, stuck on at a cockeyed angle. The others, I guessed, had been knocked off by Utica men.

"I may have to put someone else in the other bed," Denny said. "You see, this room has an outside door so you railroad men can leave when you are called in the middle of the night, without waking me. That's the reason you have to pay in advance."

After I had washed up, I ate one of Mother's good beef sandwiches and a piece of cake and walked down Henry Street to loaf on a corner and watch the girls. The young bucks of Binghamton braced up the lampposts, waiting for the girls coming home from the cigar factories.

"Hello, sister. Got any scrap?" And the girls would dig into their two-foot deep pockets for the tobacco that they had saved for their favorite beaus. In those days the girls could carry home all the scrap they wanted, but later the companies sold it in five-cent packages. One big Irish girl, with red hair and the greenest eyes I ever saw, smiled at me and taught me how to crumble the scrap and roll it into cigarettes. We spent several hours walking to her home, which was a couple of blocks away.

When I got back to the Utica Room, the other bed was still empty. That was luck. I settled in for a good night's sleep. But I had scarcely buried my ear in the pillow when there was a scratching on the outside door.

"Joe, Joe?" came a squeaky whisper through the keyhole. "It's me, Andy." Andy was hind brakeman on our freight. "Thanks, pal," he said when I opened the door. He had stripped off his overalls and climbed into the other bed before I had the door locked. I bumped over a chair in the dark, found my own bed, and turned my face to the wall, hoping Andy wouldn't snore. I had not gone to sleep when there was a rat-tat-tat of knuckles on the outer door.

"Hold it, kid," called Andy. He jumped out of bed and whispered through the keyhole. "It's Bert Clark, a shack on Number 6," he announced, and he opened up. Bert Clark got into bed with Andy, and all was quiet again, though not for long.

Again a rattle of the door. This time Bert got up. It was like a game—last man in, first man out. Before one o'clock, we were seven—the two shacks and a fireman in Andy's bed, and a couple of shacks from the coal trains in mine. With all the whispering and bumping in the dark, we roused Denny.

"Sh-h, there's the old man," the brakie next to me groaned, as we heard bare feet flapping along the corridor. Denny pounded on the door.

"How many have you in your room, Bromley?"

"Nobody but me," I answered.

"Open up while I look."

Andy whispered: "Tell him you can't find the key."

"Can't find the key," I shouted.

"All right," called Denny, "I'll go down and get mine."

There was a scramble in the dark, overturned chairs, thumping of boots, screeching of the outer door. When Denny came back, carrying a round-handled glass lamp that threw a yellow light into the room, my bed was empty of all but me, and Andy was the only other man in the room.

"I didn't want to get you up so late, Denny," Andy said, grinning at the indignant Irishman. "Throw me my jeans and I'll give you the two bits for the bed."

Denny took his money and slammed the door.

"Poor Denny," Andy said, chuckling as he turned over to pound his ear. "He gets it going and coming. He goes through this performance almost every night."

—Adapted from *Clear the Tracks!*, by Joseph Bromley, as told to Page Cooper. Copyright 1943 by Joseph Bromley. Reprinted with permission of McGraw-Hill Book Company.

CHAPTER NINE

Bucking Snow

I

*"If you have never before ridden behind the plow,
there comes over you a sickening sense
of utter helplessness..."*

DURING THE LARVAL PERIOD of the American railroad, the green years of
wood-burning boilers and grasshopper pistons, there were many indolent railway managers who hoped to limit their exertions to daylight hours in the
summer season. Almost immediately, however, a few aggressive operators
introduced the notion of full-time, all-year performance; and from that moment
on, working on the railroad involved an annual battle with the North American winter.

In the mountains of Pennsylvania, deep snowdrifts filled the cuts. In
Maryland and Virginia, ice formed slippery patches on the metal rails. In
northern New England, locomotives and even whole trains froze to the tracks.
The scoop shovel, the overshoe, and the rescue sleigh became standard items of
railroad equipment.

On the Camden & Amboy Railroad across New Jersey in the early 1830's,
three or four inches of fresh snow were enough to stop all traffic. To get the
line open again, an engine would creep forward at two or three miles an hour
with a brace of muscular Jersey boys perched on the cowcatcher, pushing ordinary snow shovels along the tracks. This method of hand plowing was fairly
effective so long as the edge of a shovel did not catch on one of those curling
metal bands called snakeheads, which would spring up whenever an iron
strap broke loose from the top of one of the wooden rails. Catching a snow
shovel on a snakehead was like "catching a crab" with your oar in an eight-man
rowing shell: you were lifted off your seat and flipped tangentially through
the air—a dampening, humiliating, and often painful experience.

Before long, clever railroad managers began fastening a wedge-shaped scoop of heavy sheet iron to the cowcatcher of a strong engine, and this arrangement happily relieved innumerable adolescents from the misery of being catapulted into the snowy right-of-way of the Camden & Amboy several times each winter. Every well-equipped roundhouse soon had several locomotives equipped with pilot plows.

But as railroads stretched across the northern prairies and into the high passes of the Rockies and the Sierra Nevada, even pilot plows proved to be ineffective against the immense snowdrifts. It was here that necessity mothered the bucker plow, a huge, steel-reinforced wooden car, shaped like an enormous box with a wedge-shaped front and pushed by two, three, or even half-a-dozen locomotives.

When the snow was too deep or heavy to be shoved off the tracks by an ordinary plow, the bucker came into service. This formidable battering ram, pushed by its string of engines, would take position a mile or so away from a drift and charge at full throttle. Usually, the bucker plow broke through—sometimes after several runs—heaving great chunks of compacted snow up onto the sides of the cut. Often enough, however, ice and snow got under the wedge, lifting the wheels and derailing the engine, while the string of locomotives jammed into one another, end to end, with a merry smashing of glass, crunching of metal, and groaning of crew members.

Of all the accursed assignments to bedevil the soul of a locomotive engineer, driving a bucker plow was probably the most hellish. If the subject seems to inspire a certain nostalgia in the following account, one should bear in mind that the author, E. W. Hadley, was living in retirement in Santa Barbara, California, far from the northern plains, when he wrote this piece for *Scientific American* in 1897.

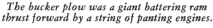

The bucker plow was a giant battering ram thrust forward by a string of panting engines.

Harper's Weekly, 1883

D URING MY MANY YEARS as a division superintendent on several hundred miles of Dakota and Minnesota railroad lines, I used to spend six or seven months out of every twelve in a ceaseless battle with snow. Like "the days of old, the days of gold, the days of '49," those days will come no more, for the advent of the rotary snowplow has robbed the blizzard of its worst terrors. Still, I think I can give you an idea of our old-time warfare—for it was nothing less than that—by describing one of our snow-bucking expeditions.

The Dakotas, Minnesota, and northern Iowa are the haunts of the blizzard and the home of the Storm King. Winter commences in September, and with no uncertain sound. I have seen water pipes inside the brick walls of a steam-heated building frozen solid on the twenty-fifth of September. In the shops and round-houses at division points on the great northwestern railroads, the last days of summer are devoted to putting the snow fighting outfit in trim. Engines are over-hauled, plows buckled on, "flangers" and "white wings" got ready. Lists of engineers and conductors are carefully scrutinized, and those men of most ex-perience, best fitted for this arduous service, are told off to run plows and "drag-outs."

As September creeps away, the division superintendent surveys the yards from the watchtower of his office. He listens without complete attention to the ceaseless click of the instruments in the next room. The connecting door opens, and the chief dispatcher looks in long enough to say that Medicine Hat has just reported a blizzard coming up.

Now, Medicine Hat is the weathermaker of the Northwest. The genuine blizzard is born there and comes thence a thousand miles to pile up the snow on your own particular track.

Again the door opens. "Medicine Hat says blizzard getting worse."

Outside, there is brilliant sunshine. The trains are all on time. But the superintendent goes to the phone, calls up the roundhouse, and tells the foreman to "put a fire in 321 and a couple of the lighter plows."

A few hours pass. A subtle change comes over the weather. The sun doesn't seem to shine so brightly. There is a haze in the air.

Suddenly, there is a change. The sky grows dark and leaden-colored in the northwest; the thermometer drops a few degrees, and there is a trace of fine snow in the air. Then, with a rush, the wind comes howling out of the northwest, filled with fine snow. In almost no time, the wind is a hurricane of forty miles an hour, and the air is so full of snow that it is impossible to see the length of a telegraph pole.

Now all is hurry. The superintendent takes up his quarters in the telegraph office. Together, he and the dispatcher watch the progress of the few trains still out upon the road and devise measures to get them under cover. No. 1, the Night Express, which left the southern terminus several hours ago, has run into the blizzard and is making slow progress. She left Colgate a full hour ago, but has not yet shown up at Pinto, the next station north. Her usual running time between the two is about twenty minutes.

At this moment, Pinto calls up the dispatcher and ticks off a message from the conductor of Number 1. He has just walked in. His engine has blown out a cylinder head three miles south of Pinto. She is short of water, and he has "killed her."

In swift succession, the superintendent sends orders to hold at terminal two branch-line passenger trains now due to leave. Then he orders the engineer of Plow Engine 119, which has been held in reserve at Fairmount, to run up to Pinto, flagging from there to the point were Number 1 is stalled, to try to get her out. The chances of getting out Number 1 before midnight look very slim. The superintendent sends a message to the conductor of the snowbound train, instructing him to hire any available sleighs at Pinto, load them with fuel and provisions, and get back to his train. This order is hardly off before the wire goes down and all communication is shut off.

Now comes a period of forced inaction which grows many a gray hair on the superintendent's head. What of the two hundred passengers on Number 1—the women and children out on the trackless prairie, exposed to the full force of the blizzard? What of the carloads of cattle and horses on the first section of Number 17?

There is nothing to be done until the blizzard will have blown itself out. The superintendent finds a vent for his activity in preparing for the coming fight. Putting on his buffalo overcoat and snow boots, he visits the roundhouse to see that everything is in readiness. Plow engines are abundantly supplied with oil, tallow, waste, and steam hose. Water cars are cleared of ice and filled; and a couple of boxcars equipped with stoves, tables, and chairs are loaded with provisions. Engine and train crews are notified to keep within instant call, and messengers are dispatched to gather an army of snow shovelers.

Toward morning of the third day, the superintendent is awakened by the caller. A message from the night dispatcher reports that the blizzard shows signs of dying down. It is welcome news, and a few minutes more finds the superintendent at his office ready for the start.

The dispatcher has not been idle. By the time the blizzard shows signs of dying down, the yard is full of snow equipment. Two heavy freight engines carrying iron plows stand ready to be launched against the drifts on branch lines. The outfit for the main line is even more ponderous. An immense Congdon plow, faced with wood and shod with steel, is backed up by two 17-by-24 engines. The pilot has been removed from the rear engine so that it may be coupled up close to the front one. The face of the huge plow rises almost to the top of the engine stack. In order for the crew to see ahead, a small cupola has been built on top of the engine cab. Here the conductor can ensconce himself and give directions to the engineer. On the main track, a few yards behind this immense plow, stands the drag-out, a 19-by-26 ten-wheeler. Coupled to it is a train of three or four coaches, some cooking and provision cars, a water car, a coal car, and the conductor's caboose. The coaches carry a crew of two hundred navvies.

The wind has almost completely died, and the thermometer has fallen to thirty-five below. All the men moving around wear shaggy fur overcoats, fur caps, and felt boots an inch thick. Nothing but the matted hair of the buffalo, a native of these barren prairies, could withstand this intense cold. The gray dawn comes and, with it, the conductor with yellow copies of his orders fluttering in his hand. He climbs aboard. There is a shrill blast of the whistle, repeated by the second engine, and the plow is off.

If you are in the cab of the forward engine, climb up on the fireman's side and brace your feet against the front end of the cab. The fireman will hand you a small piece of greasy waste. You can keep the frost off the window and gain a glimpse ahead. The engineer opens her up a little. We strike a thirty-mile gait. Nothing is in sight but the boundless prairie, looking like a frozen sea. The contour of the land is rolling, and on some portions of the line, cut succeeds cut on an average of ten to the mile.

All at once, the engineer, without waiting for a warning from the conductor, slows down. He knows he is close to a long, curving cut that will probably be full of snow. Close to the beginning of the cut, he comes to a full stop. Conductor, superintendent, and roadmaster unbuckle the snow curtains, get out and walk ahead. The crystals of snow are small and angular, like meal, and the driving wind has pressed and fitted them together with a solidity that is but little short of ice.

The long, shallow approach to the cut is the most dangerous part, for there the snow is hardest and yet not deep enough to guarantee that the plow will stay on the track. The roadmaster is sent back on the run to hustle out his shovel crew. Hailing the drag-out, which has now come up, he summons a force of husky shovelers. With the tact of a general disposing his forces, he soon has them scattered over the snowdrift. Some shovel away the shallow snow and put a "face" on it, as it is called; others cut trenches through the drift in its deepest parts.

When the entrance to the cut is partly clear, the superintendent orders the drag-out to back out of the way. The plow engine pulls back several miles to gather momentum for a run. Time is at a premium. Every hour that the road is blockaded means a heavy financial loss. Standing on the highest point of the drift, the burly roadmaster urges on the efforts of his men with hoarse shouts and commands.

From the distance comes the piercing whistle of the plow, announcing that she is ready. The roadmaster gives a final glance at the face of the cut. Is it properly undercut to hold down the nose of the plow? At last he climbs to the highest spot and signals that he is ready.

Now, back in the fireman's seat, you begin to get a sense of flight. The throttle is wide open. The engineer is giving her notch after notch. If you are an old hand, fear is swallowed up in the excitement of the mad rush; but if you have never before ridden behind the plow, there comes over you a sickening sense of utter helplessness. Flashing along at sixty or seventy miles an hour, you catch a glimpse of the lines of navvies on either side of the cut. Then you plunge into complete darkness. You feel as if you had dropped into deep water. The engineer throws her forward and, with almost human struggles and efforts, the tremendous machine pushes her way through the snow. As she strikes trench after trench, the wheels take a fresh hold on the rail, and the plow plunges forward a few feet farther. At last, with a final whirl of the drive wheels, you come to a stop. The engineer pushes back the sliding sash on the side of the cab. With a gasp of relief, you find that you are on a level with the top of the drift. Crawling out the window, you find the plow almost completely buried in snow. The drag-out has followed close behind, and the roadmaster has every available man hard at work digging around the plow.

Now the ponderous, ten-wheel drag-out is brought up, and proceeds by main force to haul the plow out of the drift. No sooner is the plow out of the cut than the shovelers are back into it, putting a new "face" on the drift, clearing the rails that lead up to it, ready for a new run. Back again, five or six miles, goes the plow. This time, you watch her as she comes out of the distance, growing rapidly in size, picking up a few shovelfuls of snow and throwing it off the plow in graceful curving rainbows. With a hoarse scream, she dashes into the cut. For an instant, it appears as if a mine has exploded under the drift. At first, the snow is thrown high in air; then, as the engine loses speed, the white mass rolls out of the cut in immense chunks, weighing tons. The drift has been skillfully trenched. The engine pushes forward, bursting out of the diminishing drift. With a growing feeling of confidence, you start ahead for the next struggle.

The next large cut is four hundred feet long, ten feet deep for some distance, and full of hard snow. The superintendent sends his men to critically examine and probe with a bar to detect any stratum of ice which might run through the cut. Finally, he decides to set the plow on a long, hard run to get through without spending time in trenching.

The plow rushes toward the snowdrift with a will. But the cut is deep and narrow, and the snow is hard packed. It is like running into a stone wall. The plow, moving at sixty-five miles an hour, stops with a mighty shock. Snow bursts through the cab windows and comes pouring in like an avalanche. Tons of coal in the tender surge forward, breaking the gate and sweeping against the boiler head. The cab is filled with escaping steam and falling glass. Wildly, you search for some means of escape.

Again, the plow is dug out. The snow is shoveled out of the cab, boards nailed over the windows, and the engineer, tying a handkerchief around his forehead to stop the flow of blood from cuts made by the broken glass, sounds a retreat. But he backs the engine with a grim vow to "put her through this time or break a steam pipe."

And so the fight goes on, day after day. It may be ten days before the line is again open to traffic. Dead engines are found and resuscitated, their crews having taken refuge in the nearest farmhouse. The passenger train is discovered, completely buried in snow, with a fence board stuck in the engine stack to indicate its grave. The train crew have managed to keep their passengers from freezing or starving by drawing on scattered farmhouses for provisions, and by using the coal from the tender to keep the cars warm. The broken telegraph line is found and repaired. The superintendent's first message sets other plows at work from the southern terminus. The two outfits finally meet, and with triumphant whistles and a few brief words of congratulations, the snow-bucking expedition is over.

I had just returned from a ten days' snow-bucking expedition when the first rotary in the Northwest was turned over to me. With feet still wrapped in bandages from the effect of frostbite, I painfully climbed from the old plow into a comfortable chair in the front end of the rotary. With a sense of complete triumph and deep satisfaction I saw this "whirling wheel of fortune" (as the machine was instantly dubbed by a quick-witted conductor) hurl my ancient enemy high in air beyond the right-of-way.

Yet, I am obliged to confess that if snow bucking with a rotary had lost almost all its discomforts, it had at the same time deprived me of a source of keen enjoyment.

—From "Fighting Snow on the Railroads of the Northwest,"
by E. W. Hadley, in *Scientific American*, July 10, 1897.

II

"We used to take out an extra insurance policy and say good-bye to our friends."

IF THE PLAINS WERE BAD for winter operations, the mountains were almost impossible. Struggling through its first winter in the Sierra Nevada, the Central Pacific Railroad used dozens of hastily constructed snowplows, hundreds of construction workers, and an army of 2,500 shovelers to keep the track open. Still, traffic was halted for various periods that totaled about two weeks.

Ultimately, the Central Pacific had to build thirty miles of almost continuous "galleries," or snowsheds, to protect its rails across the crest of the Sierra between Cisco and Truckee. The Canadian Pacific, similarly plagued with slides, drifts, and immense snowpacks on its trail through the Selkirk Range of southeastern British Columbia, built nearly twenty miles of sheds.

Outside the sheds, pilot plows worked day and night during a storm; and between 1865 and 1885, the Central Pacific shops in Sacramento built some of the largest bucker plows in the world—great, bargelike vessels on wheels, loaded down with twenty or twenty-five tons of pig iron. The plow boss would stand on an iron-railed platform atop the plow, giving directions with hand signals to the engineers behind him. On some occasions, there were as many as eleven locomotives hitched up to push the bucker.

In a really bad storm, even the largest plows sometimes got stuck, as Cy Warman recalled.

I HAD MY FIRST EXPERIENCE in old-time snowbucking on a mountain division of a western railroad in the mid-1880's, when we used to take out an extra insurance policy and say good-bye to our friends as we signed the call book. For twenty-four hours a pilot plow and flanger had been racing over the thirty miles of mountain, up one side and down the other. Each time they reached the foot of the hill, they received orders to "double the road."

It was Sunday afternoon when the caller came for me. Another engine was being ordered out to help push the snowplow through the great drifts, which were getting deeper every hour. Ten miles out of the division station, at the front of the mountain proper, we sidetracked to wait the return of the plow.

The hours went by; the night wasted away. Monday dawned, and there was no news of the snow brigade. All we could learn at the telegraph office was that they were somewhere between Shawane and the top of the hill, presumably stuck in the snow. All day and all night they had worked and puffed, pushed and panted, to no purpose. Then, giving up all hope of getting through, they had attempted to back down; but that was equally impossible. The heavy drifts in the deep cuts were not to be bucked away with the rear end of an engine.

Tuesday came and found us still watching and waiting for the snowplow. Other engines came up from the division station, hauling a work train and a great army of trackmen with wide shovels. A number of railroad officers came, too, and everybody shoveled. We had no plow on our side of the hill and had to buck with naked engines. First we tried one, then two, then three engines coupled together. The shovelers would clear off a few hundred yards of track, over which we would drive at full speed. As our engine came in contact with a great drift, eight to eighteen feet deep, she would tremble and shake as though she was about to be crushed to pieces.

Often when we came to a stop only the top of the stack of the front engine would be visible. The front windows of the cabs were boarded up to prevent the glass from being smashed. For three or four days the track was kept clear behind us, so that we could back out and tie up at night where there was coal and water.

All this time the snow kept coming down, day and night, until the only signs of a railroad across the range were the tops of the telegraph poles. Toward the end of the week, we had a terrific storm, almost a blizzard. This closed the trail behind us; and we were forced to camp on the mountainside. We had an abundance of coal, but the water in the tanks was very low. By shoveling snow into them, we managed to keep them wet.

For three or four days—sometimes in the dead hours of the night—we had heard a mournful whistle away up on the mountain, crying in the waste like a lost sheep. This was a light engine, we learned later, which had started down the hill, but had gotten stuck in the storm. For four days and nights the crew had been imprisoned in the drifts. They had only a few pieces of hard bread, which they soaked in snow water and ate. More than once during the fourth day, they had looked into the tallow bucket and wondered if they could eat the tallow.

On Sunday morning, just a week from the day on which I had signed the call book, the sun shone. The big pilot plow had reached the summit; but now a new danger confronted the lone engine whose lost cry had gone out in the night. The big plow was coming down the hill with two locomotives behind her; and if the light engine and her crew remained on the main line, they would be scooped into eternity.

When the storm cleared away, however, they found that they were within a few feet of a switch. If they could shovel out the snow and throw the switch, it would let them onto a spur track, so that the oncoming plow could pass. Hungry and weak as they were, they began with the fireman's scoop to clear the switch and shovel away from the wheels so that the engine could start herself. As they shoveled, they could hear the whistles of the three engines that were coupled behind the pilot plow, now whistling down brakes, then back up, then go ahead, hammering away at the deep drifts.

At last the switch was forced open, and the engine was in the clear; but not a moment too soon, for along came the great plow, fairly falling down the mountain, sending a shower of snow over the lone engine on the spur.

We, too, had heard and seen the pilot plow coming and had found a safe siding. When the huge plow came to the clear track we had made, the heavy engines, previously held in check by the snow, bounded down the steep grade at a rate that made us sick at heart. Each of the locomotives on the sidetrack whistled a warning; but the wheels of the descending train were covered with ice and snow, and when the engineers reversed their engines, they seemed to slide as fast. Fortunately, at the next curve there was a heavy drift, so deep that the snow train drove right through it, making a complete tunnel arched over with snow. Thus, after eight days, the road was opened. Eight sections of a passenger train came slowly and carefully down the mountain and passed under the arch.

—From Cy Warman's *Tales of an Engineer*,
Charles Scribner's Sons, New York, 1895.

Harper's Weekly, 1883

III

"Strung along the mountain in small groups, the men groped blindly. The snow drifted faster than it could be shoveled away."

IT WAS THE INVENTION of the rotary snowplow that finally relieved railroad men of the worst hardships and terrors of winter operations. The basic idea of the rotary plow—an immense revolving fan mounted at the front of a railroad car—had occurred to several imaginative men in the 1860's, among them J. W. Elliot, a Toronto dentist, and Charles W. Tierney, an employee of the Pennsylvania Railroad in Altoona, Pennsylvania. Elliot's "Revolving Snow Shovel" was a small-scale, hand-operated model, and Tierney's was a flatcar with a big revolving screw at the head end. Another early rotary, the Hawley, was displayed at the United States Centennial Exposition in Philadelphia in 1876.

In the end, none of these proved out. The inventor who perfected the rotary was Orange Jull, a flour mill owner in Orangeville, Ontario. Jull had been puttering with idealized snowplows for years, but he did not take his basic patent for a cutting wheel mounted on a whirling fan to fling the snow away until 1884.

Jull assigned his patent for manufacture to John and Edward Leslie, who operated a machine shop in Orangeville. They made certain innovations that became the basis of a prolonged patent suit years later, and, eventually, the Leslies and Jull wound up as competitors. In any case, their Jull-Leslie plow, tested first by the Canadian Pacific between Toronto and suburban Parkdale, was an undisputed success. Union Pacific bought the first commercially produced Leslie rotaries, and later the same model was bought by railroads all around the world.

The rotary came none too soon for the crews of machine shop workers, section hands, farmers, and schoolboys who used to muster to dig snow in the midst of the January blizzard. According to Edgar Custer, who was working as an apprentice machinist in the Pennsy's shops at Altoona in the late 1870's, just before the rotary came along, there was nothing particularly delightful about removing snow the old-fashioned way.

During severe winters,
railroads hired
thousands of men
to shovel through
drifts twenty to
thirty feet deep.
Harper's Weekly, 1881

IN THE WINTER when the snows lay thick on the Alleghenies, the whole shop was called out to keep the railroad tracks clear. Each man was given a scoop shovel and ordered to dress warmly. A long train of passenger coaches dropped gangs of men at strategic points. In a short time, two thousand men were strung along the road from Norcross Cut to the Gallitzin Tunnel,* every man shoveling for dear life. They had to shovel or freeze to death.

Every four hours, two baggage cars equipped for making coffee and broiling beefsteak were hauled up the mountain. At each stop the men crowded into the warm cars and thawed out while devouring huge beefsteak sandwiches and cups of scalding coffee. The stops were short; there were many men to feed. The bitter wind howled down the mountain gaps, opaque with frozen particles that cut our faces and drifted the tracks almost as fast as we shoveled it away.

One night, just as we had cleared the tracks and were waiting for the train, a fresh storm swooped down, shrieking in fury. It caught the railroad authorities unaware. The food cars had been shunted onto the home siding; the crew had started on the road home. The relief train ran into a drift and stalled before it had gone a mile.

---

*The 3,612-foot long Gallitzin Tunnel, eleven miles west of Altoona, was the highest point on the main Philadelphia-Pittsburgh line of the Pennsylvania Railroad—2,161 feet.

Strung along the mountain in small groups, the men groped blindly. The snow drifted faster than it could be shoveled away. Our party was stationed near the top of Horseshoe Curve, where the wind had a clear sweep. It was impossible to stay there, so we struggled down the tracks to the lee of the mountain shoulder. Here we dug holes in the drifts and huddled together for warmth. We had heard that one could be quite comfortable in the coldest weather under a snowbank, but the bitter wind searched us out and chilled our very marrow. It had been a long time since the food train had visited us, and now we were ravenous.

"We will freeze to death if we stay in these holes," shouted Jim McConnell, our leader. "Get out and shovel. Come on!" Guided by the tracks, we shoveled a path down one and up the other. Then we dog-trotted in single file, arms swinging and feet stamping to start the blood circulating. When we had warmed up, we again huddled in the holes until the cold drove us to monotonous tramping. Some of the men refused to come out of their holes, but these were dragged into the open and manhandled until they staggered with the rest.

Toward morning we heard a long-drawn whistle across the ravine around

*The new rotary steam snow shovel
took all the fun out of winter.*

Scribner's Monthly, 1889

which the tracks curved, nineteen hundred feet away. The storm was raging worse than at the start. We could not see fifty feet into the murk, but we stood facing the sound and shouted. The whistling became almost continuous. Evidently there were a number of locomotives at work. We could hear the sharp "off brakes" whistle; the mighty coughs of the exhausts as the engines gathered speed; the gradually decreasing tempo as they struck the drifts; and then silence.

The silence sent a shiver of fear through us. We had been cheering madly; now, suddenly, we were cold and disheartened again. All signs indicated that the rescue train was stuck in the drift. Again we started our dogged tramping. Back and forth we plodded, until a faint light told that the dawn was near. Some of the men were completely exhausted and no amount of prodding could stir them to effort. Jim McConnell started down the track in an effort to reach the train but came back only to report that the tracks were drifted level with the mountain slopes.

Two long whistles followed by a roaring flurry of exhausts broke the silence. Again we flogged our waning hopes. We would hear them drive into the drifts, stall, back off, and drive again. Nearer they came, and before we realized their nearness, five big freight locomotives pushing a short snowplow broke through the drifts below us. They had crossed over to the eastbound track where the drifts were lower and roared past, almost burying us with snow as we huddled against the mountainside. Back of them, two engines dragged a long string of coaches, the windows bright with the new Pintsch gaslights. The train came to a stop, and we wearily climbed aboard.

The car seats had been laid lengthwise, making a bunk of sorts on which the exhausted men lay. Doctors worked over them while hot food was served to those suffering only from exposure and hunger. Very few of the men escaped frostbite. The train followed the snow-breaking engines, picking up men until the last one was loaded.

We had been out twenty-eight hours, fifteen without food, in the worst blizzard in the history of the road. As we were paid straight time, I drew the sum of one dollar and ninety-six cents. Is it possible in these days to imagine a body of men working under such conditions with no overtime, no bonus? Our gang did just that and did it willingly. When the train arrived in Altoona, the men, crippled and uncrippled, piled out of the cars and dragged their shovels over the brick pavement in a clangorous din. Up the street they marched, lustily singing the Snow Shovelers' Song.

Hɪ-ADDLE-DE-INKTIM, DE-INKTUM-ADDLE-TY, INKTUM-ADDLE-TY,
Hɪ-ADDLE-DE-INKTUM, DE-INKTUM-ADDLE-TY — BANG
(crashed shovels on the bricks)

—From *No Royal Road*, the autobiography of Edgar A. Custer. H. C. Kinsey & Company, New York, 1937. Copyright 1936 and 1937 by Edgar A. Custer.

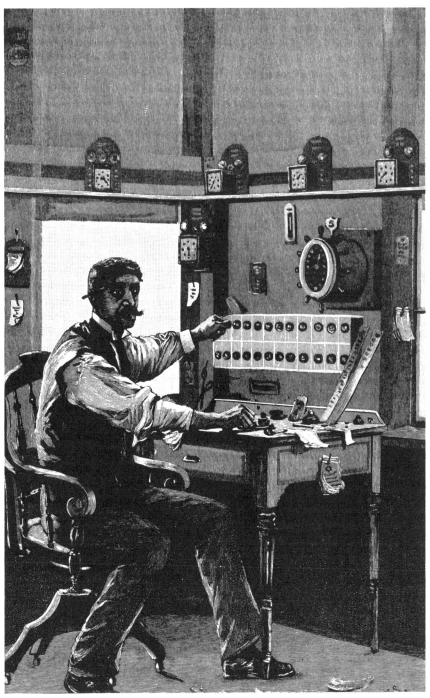

*The dispatcher at the telegraph key controlled
a scattered army of station operators.*

Scribner's Monthly, 1888

CHAPTER TEN

The Kingdom of the Keys

I

"Turning to the key, Tom McGuire called Kearney and told them he was surrounded by the Sioux."

THE WEDDING OF THE railroad track and the telegraph wire, which occasioned Samuel F. B. Morse's famous message, "What hath God wrought!" was a technological marriage made in heaven. Like other divinely arranged matches, it created a new entity that was better than the sum of its parts. Neither the railroad nor the telegraph, alone, could have developed half so quickly as both of them did together. Without the telegraph, the railroad might have been limited to use in industry and mining. Without the railroad, the telegraph would have lacked a right-of-way, a supply of operators, and a steady customer.

The basic idea of telegraphy had tantalized scientists for years; but the technique eluded them until the 1820's, when Joseph Henry, the leading experimental physicist of that time, discovered how to transmit an electrical impulse over a long, thin wire. The trick, Henry found, was to use a battery of small electric cells instead of a single large cell as your source of energy. A few years later, Sam Morse, a moderately successful, fortyish portrait painter, contrived the first crude telegraphic apparatus and made up a simple code of pulses and pauses with which to send electric messages.

Morse always had been a versatile man, thinly spread, and he proved to be a formidable lobbyist and promoter. While the back benches rumbled with disapproval, Congress appropriated thirty thousand dollars to exploit the Morse telegraph. An experimental line was strung from Washington to Baltimore, along the tracks of the Baltimore & Ohio Railroad, which gave its permission to use the property providing the tests should be conducted "without injury to the road or embarrassment to the operations of the company."

On May 1, 1844, Morse transmitted the timely (if nugatory) news that the Whig National Convention in Baltimore had chosen Henry Clay and Theodore Frelinghuysen as its presidential and vice-presidential nominees. Three weeks later, the line was complete from the B&O's Pratt Street Station in Baltimore to the chambers of the Supreme Court in Washington. Surrounded by senators, justices, and other federal dignitaries, Morse sat at his telegraph key and tapped out:

.__   ....   ._   _

....   .__   _   ....

__.   .   .   _..

.__   .   ..   ._   __.   ....   _   (!)

What God had wrought, among other things, was that there henceforth should be an intimate association between the railroad and the telegraph, not merely on the route of the B&O but all over the world. Within a few years, wire and track would become so mutually·dependent that almost every Morse telegrapher would be a railroad man and almost every railroad station agent, a telegrapher. By the time the transcontinental railroad was pushing its way across the great plains in the late 1860's, wire and track had become twin weapons in the national campaign to improve communications between the Atlantic Coast and the Far West.

The transcontinental wire was completed in October, 1861, almost eight years before the railroad was finished. At the celebrated "Last Spike" ceremony at Promontory, Utah, on May 10, 1869, Leland Stanford swung a mallet that had been wired to flash a telegraphic signal on contact with the spike. Stanford missed, or struck a glancing blow, and a telegrapher had to press the Morse key to notify San Francisco and New York that the moment for public celebration had arrived. But the point had been made. Not only was the continent spanned with track, the marriage of track and wire was again intact.

Many railroad men regarded service to the Morse key as a form of slavery, but to a young man aspiring to a railroad career in the 1870's, telegraphy was a natural first step. Out in western Nebraska, Wyoming, and the Dakotas, the position of operator in a small station also offered unique opportunities for heroism. The Sioux were at war, revenging themselves on the railroad for the white men's intrusion into buffalo grass country. The lone station agent, at the outer limit of the frontier, frequently had occasion to transmit a warning and sometimes even found himself the target of attack.

The scalp-lifting possibilities of this situation inspired the most dramatic episode in Cy Warman's novel *The White Mail*. As in most Warman stories, the cloak of fiction lies loosely and not very comfortably on a substantial bulk of real experience. That cloak seems transparently fragile when one considers that many telegraphers endured ordeals precisely like this one.

L OOKING INTO THE FUTURE, young Tom McGuire saw the necessity of learning the language of the wire that had just been stretched across the plains. There were schools of telegraph in Omaha, but he chose the office. Having shown good letters and a disposition to work, he was given employment—or rather, an opportunity to learn the business; and, as soon as he had mastered the key, he was duly appointed station master, ticket agent, operator, yardmaster, head switchman, and superintendent of a windmill and water tank at Plainfield, far out on the plains.

Carefully and tenderly, the superintendent of telegraph broke the news to the young man that he would have to sleep in the depot and would, until some enterprising caterer opened a hotel, be obliged to do his own cooking. The depot had "filled" walls, the superintendent said. Upon inquiry, McGuire learned that this meant the station was built of boards, outside and inside, with four inches of sand between them.

"What's that for?" asked McGuire.

"Oh, to keep out the cold and—things. But you must not rely wholly upon that. You must work and sleep in your six-shooters and keep your rifle in easy reach, day and night."

McGuire believed, until it was too late to back out, that the superintendent of telegraph was only having fun with him.

Three days later, when the westbound passenger train stopped at Plainfield, McGuire stepped off. The express messenger kicked off a bundle of bedding and a few boxes of supplies, some flour and bacon, and a small cookstove.

McGuire cast one sweeping glance over Plainfield, and turning to the brakeman, asked: "Where's the station?"

For answer the brakeman gave him a withering look, and then, putting his gloved hand upon the little board shanty that stood beside the track, said: "Johnny, you mus' be goin' bline! Here's yer station, see? Right here."

At that moment the train pulled out, and when McGuire had glanced up and down the track and out over the plain on either side, he realized that the brakeman had told the truth for, if we except the windmill and the water tank, this was the only "improvement" at Plainfield.

Down the track he could see the rear end of the departing train, contracting and sinking nearer and nearer to earth. Faint and far away came the roar of wheels, and even as he looked, the last car dropped below the line of the horizon and the sound ceased. He listened for other sounds, but there were none. He looked to see some living thing, but there was neither bird nor beast in sight. He glanced along the level plain that lay cold and gray at the end of autumn, but there was not a living, moving thing upon the earth, not even a snake.

A timid man would have been helpless with fear, but young McGuire was one of those rare beings who never knew that feeling in the least. What impressed him was the unutterable dreariness of the place. His whole being filled with a sense of loneliness, hitherto unknown to him. Seated upon one of the boxes, he was gazing at the ground, when, to his great relief, a little brown animal with dark stripes down its back came from under the shanty, sat on the end of a tie, and looked at him. It was no larger than a small rat, but it lived and moved, and it was welcome. Now, if this thing could live in this desert alone, a man ought to exist. McGuire took heart.

Fishing a key from his pocket, he unlocked the big padlock and pushed the door open. As he did so, he noticed that the door, which was also "filled" and as thick as the door of a refrigerator car, was full of holes. Walking around the house, he found that the outer walls were perforated. He remembered that the superintendent of telegraph had said the sand was put between the walls "to keep out the cold—and things." The holes, he deduced, must have been made by things.

He went inside. The place had been occupied before. There was a chair, a table, and some twisted wire; but the telegraph instrument had been taken away. A small coal stove, red with rust, stood on the floor. The floor was also rusty. No, it was not rust; it was blood. So the agent, too, had been taken away. McGuire examined the walls and saw with a feeling of satisfaction that none of the things had penetrated the inner boards.

In a low lean-to he found fuel. He decided to unpack and make the best of a hard layout. With a rusty hatchet that he had unearthed in the shed, he opened his freight. The first long box contained a rifle, two six-shooters, and many rounds of ammunition. Another held sugar and coffee. From a third he got a neat medicine chest that contained cotton bandages and liniment. Scenting the biscuits and bacon, the little brown squirrel came nosing around. McGuire appreciated the company. He gave the squirrel bits of cracker and gained a companion.

McGuire's first task was to examine his firearms and load them. He was not an expert with a rifle; but he had spent three winters in St. Louis, and he reasoned that a man who could hit a snipe on the wing with a shotgun ought to be able to hit a Sioux on his doorsill with a six-shooter.

When he had carried all his belongings into the shanty and the shed and spread his bedding upon the board bunk, he sat down on an empty box to think. The sun, big and red, was burning down the west at the end of a short, squaw-summer day. Out of the east the night came creeping across a sea of sagebrush, and the station agent turned to contemplate the glory of the sunset. Far out on the plain, a long, lean animal that looked to be part sheep and the rest dog limped across the face of the falling sun and disappeared in the gloaming.

McGuire entered the shanty and in the fading light tried to connect his instrument to the broken wire on the pine table. Tomorrow a man would come from Kearney and fix it for him; but McGuire was lonely. If only he could talk to Omaha, two or three hundred miles away, the operator there would be company for him. He worked patiently until it was dark and then lighted his lamp. He became so interested in the wire that he forgot to cook supper. At last he made coffee and ate some crackers and a short roll of indefinite meat. Presently, he heard the roar of an approaching train. He opened the door. The rails were clicking as though they were out in a hailstorm. Suddenly they began to sing, and a moment later the fast mail crashed by, showing her tail lights to Plainfield station.

It was eleven o'clock when the young operator got his instrument connected and in shape to talk to Omaha. The next moment brought an answer to his call. A great load was lifted from the young man's mind. He no longer felt lonely, for he could hear the wire talking to him. He called up station after station. They all answered cheerily and gave him welcome. All along the line the operators knew him for a new man. When the wire was free, they began to jolly him. Kearney advised him to take off his boots when he went to bed, so as to avoid the chance of dying with them on. North Platte told him to put his hair outside the door, so the Sioux could get it without waking him.

"Oh, you'll like the place," said Lincoln. "Good night."

McGuire made no answer to these shots. The situation, from his point of view, was far from funny. Having barred the doors and placed his firearms within easy reach, he rolled up in his blankets and tried to sleep. Far out on the desert he heard a lone wolf howl. That, thought he, is the shadow that crossed the sun.

He welcomed the return of day with all the enthusiasm of his youthful nature. He almost enjoyed the novelty of preparing his own breakfast—bread, bacon, and black coffee. A long freight lumbered by. The conductor, hanging low from the corner of the way car, dropped off a delay report. McGuire scanned it eagerly. When the caboose had dropped from the horizon, he sat down and told Omaha that a dragging brake beam had ditched a car of ore. He was glad, for it gave him something to do; but he didn't send that sentiment over the wire.

During the morning, he busied himself putting things to rights in his bachelor home. It was noon before the day seemed fairly begun. When the westbound passenger train came by, its express car gave up a full kit of tools—an ax, a hammer, a saw, a pick and shovel—and a case of eggs. McGuire watched the train, as he had watched each train since his arrival, until the rear car sank below the level of the plain.

While he was preparing his supper, his little friend the ground squirrel came out and sat in the door and ate crumbs. McGuire watched the twilight deepen on the dreary plain. Between him and the glow in the west, he saw the same gaunt shadow that he had seen on the previous evening. Still farther away, a horse was outlined against the pink sky. On it sat a bunchy, bareheaded being that might have been half-man, half-bear. This creature wore a blanket and feathers and was gazing at the little station.

McGuire was aiming a rifle at the wolf just as this Indian appeared. To show that he was armed, the telegraph operator let go at the wolf. It was a long shot, but the wolf leaped high and fell dead. The Indian, having marked the performance, turned his horse's head and rode slowly away to the north.

McGuire knew that government troops had been battling the Sioux over on Pole Creek. He had no doubt this was a scout from a dangerous tribe. Sitting there in the twilight, he wondered what he should do if this Indian came back with a few hundred followers. He might bar the door and kill a few while they stormed the station, but if they should kindle a fire under the shack, he would perish in the flames. He determined to go to work on a more substantial fortification.

Dreading the darkness of the house, he sat outside until the gold had faded from the sunset and the little brown squirrel went away to bed. "God takes care of the squirrel," mused McGuire, "and he'll take care of me as well." And he, too, went to bed, but not to sleep. He lay awake, planning how to fortify the place. After dwelling on and then dismissing many schemes, he decided to dig a tunnel from beneath the floor of the shed, under the railroad track and across to the water tank. If the Sioux came, he could make a hard fight, then take to the tunnel and hide in the tank. They would not be apt to burn that, having their eyes upon the station, watching for the agent to come out.

His first plan was to dig the tunnel without disturbing the surface of the ground; but he soon realized that would take too long. He would have to work from the top, making a short section each day and covering the ditch with boards and dirt as he went along. If any Sioux should come scouting about, they would not know of the tunnel.

Away off to the west, McGuire heard a wolf howl. The cry was answered by another nearer the station, then by another and another, still farther away. Presently he heard a low scratching on the outer shed door. After a long time, he fell asleep.

The sun was shining when he woke, and the brown squirrel was sitting in the center of the room, waiting for his breakfast. McGuire ate his morning meal, reported the through freight on time, got out his pick and shovel, and began his tunnel. First he made a trap door in the floor of the shed and excavated a place to drop into. Going out, he measured off the distance to the tank. It was sixty feet. He set himself the task of doing twenty feet a day.

On the second morning he was stiff and lame. His hands were so sore that he could scarcely close his fingers on the pick handle, but he worked on. By nightfall he had the tunnel completed under the track. At the end of the third day he went inside the shed, dropped into the tunnel, crawled through, and came out at the base of the water tank, which was boarded up from the ground to the tank proper. Before retiring, he carried across a good supply of cartridges and stored them in the framework of the tank near the top. Then he sat down to watch the sunset. The same glory flooded the west; and when the sun was down, the same gaunt shadows came out of the gloaming. They had begun to scent the food supply at the station. McGuire had by this time determined that it was only a waste of ammunition to shoot them, and since he showed no fight, the wolves came so near that he could have reached them with a stone.

As he was about to go inside, he thought he heard the distant roar of an approaching train. The muffled sound grew louder, but looking along the shining threads of steel, McGuire could see no break on the horizon. Sweeping the plain with his eager eyes, he saw only a low black cloud, just rising from the earth on the northwest. McGuire thought of sudden storms that he had read about; but the quiet sky gave no sign of storm. The growing cloud came nearer each moment, yet it still lay close to the sagebrush. It grew broader but no higher, while in its wake, a gray fog rose, like the mist that hangs over a swamp on a summer morning. The gray cloud mounted higher and higher, trailing behind the black one. In a little while, it covered the whole west, shutting off the light of the pink sky. The wolves lifted their heads to listen. The darkness deepened, and the roar of the cloud increased.

With his rifle resting on his arm, McGuire stood and stared across the plain. A moment later, the head of the cloud swept across the track like a regiment of cavalry, and he could hear hoofbeats rattling on the rails and crossties. This was no cloud; it was a band of buffalo. He could see neither the beginning nor the end of the herd. Raising his rifle, he began firing into the flying horde. With a great crash, one of the animals drove its head against the base of the water tank and then lay still. The roar of ten thousand feet, the wild snorts of the wounded brutes, the mad rush of hooves so excited McGuire that he ran forward, firing as he went. Suddenly, the noise began to die. The dark cloud was vanishing.

When the dust had fallen, McGuire found a fine calf that had driven its poor head against the tank and broken its neck. There was not a scratch upon its hide. All his bullets had gone wide of the mark or had been carried away under the shaggy coats of the buffalo.

Still, here was fresh meat. But before he could remove the animal's robe, the hungry wolves were pressing about in the twilight. They grew so bold that McGuire was obliged to take what he could carry and fly for the house. Before he could reach the door, the wolves were snapping and fighting over the carcass. Their howls and cries attracted a great band; and after they had finished what was left outside, they came clawing at the shed door, demanding the station agent's share. It was many hours before McGuire could find relief from the din in unquiet dreams.

By now, McGuire had been at Plainfield for a month, and he had begun to believe the place was not so dangerous after all. One evening as he was watching the sunset, however, he saw a speck on the horizon. It was a shapeless bunch—too big for a wolf and too small, he thought, for a horse. While he was watching, it moved along the plain to the northwest and disappeared.

McGuire was still seated on his box at the door of the depot when a big black bunch showed up. Nearer and nearer it came. Finally it stopped a few hundred yards from the shanty. Two horsemen road out and approached the station. They had feathers in their hair and rifles on their arms. McGuire brought out his rifle and let it rest on his lap.

A hundred yards from the station, the two men stopped and called out in a strange tongue. McGuire made no reply. The two Indians rode slowly up. They made sign for drink, but McGuire stood at the door and shook his head. They would eat; but McGuire refused to understand, and one of the Indians started to enter the station. McGuire sprang inside, slammed the door and shoved his rifle out through a small hole in the center of the shutter. The Indians climbed on their cayuses, wiggled their heels, and rode slowly back to where the band was waiting.

McGuire listened at the shed door. In a little while he heard the unshod feet of the Indian ponies beating the dusty plain. They seemed to have separated. Peeping through the small portholes, he could see a dark line of horses closing in on the little shanty.

Turning to the key, McGuire called Kearney and told them he was surrounded by the Sioux.

McGuire opened the exercises, firing first from one side and then the other to show the enemy he was numerous and well armed. The Indians returned the fire. Lead fairly hailed upon the house. Once, they charged the station; but some of the horses were hit by bullets fired from behind the well-stuffed walls, and the Sioux fell back.

They had no thought, however, of abandoning the fight. Before McGuire had succeeded in reloading his firearms, the Indians charged again. This time they reached the shanty, and, dismounting, beat upon the sand-filled doors in a vain effort to batter them down.

McGuire had been almost panic-stricken at the sound of the first volley that rattled like rain upon the boarded sides of the little depot, but now all feeling of fear had left him. Dodging from one part of the building to another, he kept pouring lead out through the narrow portholes until the Indians were driven away again. Many were wounded, some were dead, and the rest were desperate. Leaving their horses out of range of the agent's rifle, the Sioux concentrated their efforts upon the front door. By the sound of the bullets that hailed upon the house, McGuire could tell that they were coming only from one direction; so he kept his place at the side of the shanty nearest the track. He could hear the Indians ripping boards from the framework of the water tank and beating these against the heavy door. On the low table, McGuire had arranged boxes of cartridges. Now he stood in darkness, loading and emptying his revolvers. The noise of the assault on the outer walls of the wooden building became deafening.

Suddenly the besiegers hit the door a blow that shook the walls and the very floor of the house. They had succeeded in loosening a crosstie from the railroad and were using it to ram the shanty. At the same time, McGuire became aware of smoke in the station. Instantly he started toward his tunnel. The Indians had fired the shed at the rear while assaulting the house from the front. The smoke almost choked him as he groped toward the opening. Through cracks in the roof, he could see the fire. The end of a crosstie smashed through the ceiling and fell in a shower of sparks and burning splinters at his feet.

The front door gave way under heavy blows. As McGuire slipped into the tunnel, he heard a yell of victory from the wild band.

In a few moments, exhausted and gasping for breath, he found himself at the base of the tank. When he had rested, he climbed to the top. Peeping from a small window, he could see the painted warriors prancing over the plain, waiting impatiently for him to flee the burning station. In the light of the flames he could see them plainly. He longed to make targets of their feathered heads, but he was afraid to attract their notice.

As the flames devoured the little pine house, the heat grew less intense. The Indians peered into the ruins. Finding no sign of the late occupant of the place, they began circling around, searching the sagebrush. Satan seemed to have inspired one of them at this moment, for, taking a brand from the ruined station, he ran and placed it against the tank. McGuire aimed and shot.

The moment he had fired he realized his mistake. Those of the Indians who had heard the shot and seen the Sioux fall ran toward the tank, looking for the agent. One of the savages stopped and pointed toward the top. A great crowd had collected. They jabbered about the dead Indian, the tank, and the telegrapher. Then, raising their guns, they sent a shower of shot against the wooden structure. McGuire crouched against the water tub and held his fire. He heard them batter down the door, and, a moment later, he knew that they were climbing the narrow ladder. When the first feathered head showed above the landing, he brought the barrel of his rifle down and a Sioux fell. Leaning from his hiding place, McGuire emptied a six-shooter into the confused band. Sure now of the whereabouts of the white man, the Indians determined to have him at any cost. While the major part trained their guns on the tank, a half-dozen Indians carried firebrands and heaped them against the framework. The splinters of the broken door were used for kindling. Soon the flames were running up the side of the tank, lighting up the plain for five hundred yards around.

With a sinking heart McGuire saw the semicircle of light drive the darkness from the desert, and he knew that in a little while he must choose between this burning refuge and the band below. The fight had all gone out of him. It became a labor to breathe. His limbs grew leaden. His rifle was so heavy that he laid it down, and, leaning over the top of the tank, he ran his fingers through his hair and was surprised that it was tangled and wet, like fine grass heavy with dew. Clasping his empty hands, he lifted his eyes to heaven to ask for help. His glance was arrested at the horizon where a big star burned above the plain. As he looked, the star grew brighter, and he was reminded of the story of a world that had been as hopelessly lost as he seemed now, when a star burned in the east and the world was saved. Suddenly behind the star a yellow light flared, fan-shaped, from the earth, and he knew that the star was the headlight of a locomotive, and the flash was from the furnace where the fireman was shoveling coal. The rails were glistening in the glare of a headlight; and, bridging the darkness to the burning tank, the rails began to sing. The Indians heard, took warning, and fled.

"Too late, too late!" said the captain of the scouts, who was riding in the cab.

The engineer made no reply. He tugged at the throttle, which was already wide open, and kept his eyes fixed upon the burning building.

"That will do," he said to the fireman. He made a motion with his left hand as of a man drinking, and the fireman put on the lefthanded pump to save the boiler; for the water was low in the lower gauge.

"Too late, too late!" McGuire said, as the flames climbed to the top and a red tongue lipped the edge of the tank. Until now he had not thought of trying to escape, for only death had waited at the bottom; but, seeing the Sioux hunting cover, he peered over the edge. The smoke and flames were all about the ladder.

Now the first burst through, and the smoke came up, blinding and hot. He took a last stand on the narrow bridge that ran across the top of the water tub. As he climbed, his hands touched the water in the tank, which until now he had not thought of. The tank was level full. With his hands he began to scoop the water out. In a while, he checked the fire that was eating toward the rear; but it was too far advanced in front, next to the track, to be put out so easily. With a great effort he managed to reach the rope that was fixed to a valve in the bottom of the tank, and when he opened it, the water rushed out and deadened the fire. Lying in the bottom of the empty tank, McGuire was able to survive until the captain of the scouts and a couple of Pawnees reached the top of the charred structure and carried him, almost lifeless, into the open air.

"Little emergency runs like that," said the superintendent to the engineer afterwards, "make men appreciate the value of time."

—Abridged from Cy Warman's *The White Mail*,
Charles Scribner's Sons, New York, 1899.

II

"A good operator could easily have protected those trains, but I was very young, very careless, and very forgetful."

EVERYONE WHO LIVES IN AMERICA NOWADAYS, surrounded by telephones, radios, and television sets, takes it for granted that information moves faster than the swiftest vehicle. It is almost impossible to imagine the exactly opposite condition that prevailed when the first railroads were built; for in those days, absolutely nothing could move faster than a train. A train was always ahead of *everything,* even the news of its own departure. After the engine had left the terminus, there was no way to warn anybody along the route that the train was on its way. Nor was there any means by which to alert the train crew to a change in plans, a quirk of the weather, or a dangerous obstacle on the tracks.

To control the movement of opposing trains along a single line of tracks, each railroad established its own elaborate system of priorities. An "inferior" train would retreat onto a siding at a scheduled stop and wait, sometimes for hours, until a "superior" train came past. The system provided reasonable safety so long as every train remained on schedule; but if anyone forgot or ignored the priorities, there was deadly danger of a head-on collision. As an extra measure of security, the management of the Boston & Worcester Railroad used to station teams of horses at five-mile intervals along the line to rush back to the main terminus and report emergencies.

Despite such inefficiencies, railroad managers were proud of their schedules and suspicious of telegraphy, which struck them as some sort of nefarious interference. One of the early presidents of the Michigan Central dismissed the idea of putting a telegraph line on his right-of-way with the words: "Why, I had rather have one handcar for keeping my road in repair than all the telegraph lines you can build." As for the capitalists who might have sponsored

Despite the inertia of early railroad managers,
New York's Grand Central Depot developed
an intricate system of telegraphic controls.

telegraphy, they burned with a singular itch to build more railroad lines and had no enthusiasm or money for other innovations.

An exception, as always, was Charles Minot, the superintendent of the Erie Railroad. Minot scrutinized the progress of Ezra Cornell's first commercial telegraph line through Erie territory in 1849, and before long the railroad manager sensed a sympathetic vibration in the telegraph wire. He asked his board of directors to grant Cornell a right-of-way along the Erie track from New York to the Great Lakes. To quiet the board's objections, he suggested an arrangement that later became the standard of most railroads: clerks and depot masters would serve as telegraph operators so that there would be no extra cost to the railroad for unlimited use of the telegraph line.

Under Minot's direction, the Erie began using telegraphy to report transfers of fresh milk from Orange County, New York, fresh strawberries from Suffern, fat livestock from Pennsylvania; and in June, 1851, the Erie used the telegraph to revolutionize the dispatch and control of trains.

It happened that Minot was aboard a westbound express ("inferior") that had been waiting for several minutes on a siding at Turner's, New York, for an eastbound express ("superior") to meet and pass. Impatiently, Minot stepped into the commercial telegraph office at the station, wired the operator up ahead at Goshen, fourteen miles west, and asked whether the eastbound train had come through. It had not come through.

"Hold eastbound train for further orders," Minot wired. He handed the conductor of the westbound train an order to run to Goshen regardless of the rights of the opposing train.

The engineer, terrified, refused to obey the superintendent's written order. He jumped out of the cab and huddled in a seat at the back of the rear car. Minot took over the cab and ran the train to Goshen. The eastbound express had not yet arrived. Again, Minot wired ahead, learned that the train had not yet reached the next stop, issued a second "hold" order, and rattled along, full steam, to Middletown. At Middletown he checked Port Jervis, issued another "hold" order, and pushed on.

Simple as it was, the procedure had never been used before. Within weeks, every train on the Erie was controlled by the telegraphed orders of a train dispatcher. By 1855 many other railroads had adopted the telegraph, as used on the Erie; and during the next ten or fifteen years, the Morse apparatus was accepted almost everywhere as an essential to safe operations.

Even the miraculous telegraph, however, was subject to human failures: inexperience, laziness, inattention. The late Harry Bedwell, a professional railroad man whose many stories and novels are notable for accurate detail, confessed to several personal derelictions in his first published article, which appeared in 1909.

Y REAL REASON for taking up the study of telegraphy was that I was just a little lazy. In my ignorance, I thought that all my troubles would be over if I could once learn a trade and get a position. Poor, misguided young heart! I was not quite eighteen years old.

It was nearing the end of a term of high school. Examinations loomed up in the near future. I quietly stepped out a side door, entered the depot of the only railroad that ran into our small town, and began to learn to railroad.

My first responsible position was very nearly forced upon me. The traveling auditor came to the station to make a transfer of agents, and before he left, he asked me if I did not think I could hold down the station. I answered that I did not think I could. The auditor laughed softly.

A short time after this I received a telegram from the chief dispatcher, ordering me to go to a small station on one of the branches and begin work as agent. The auditor would meet me at the station and make the transfer. As there was no examination to pass which would reveal what kind of an operator I was, I decided to take the job.

I arrived at the station all right and the transfer was made. After giving me some fatherly advice, the auditor left me alone.

For a time I got along all right, because there was little work to be done. But I lived in great fear of the dispatcher. This particular dispatcher could send a lot of words in a minute. It was his delight to frighten "hams," as he called students and young operators. Every time my call sounded, I began to tremble. If it was the dispatcher on the wire, I had to go outside and walk around the station to quiet my nerves sufficiently to manipulate the key.

For perhaps a month I got along this way. Then, one day, the engine of a passenger train broke down a short distance from my station, and I was compelled to copy some train orders from the wire. No one could have read them. What copies they were! Half was omitted. When I repeated the order to the dispatcher, I had to guess at most of what had been sent me. Then, I recopied the order before delivering it to the trainmen, and, in my state of nerves, I left out part of the order.

Think of leaving out part of an order to a passenger train, governing its movements against other trains! But the company was short of men. Almost any kind of a telegraph operator would do. It was a road that paid poor wages, and good men avoided it.

Surely the god of all fools watched over me, for most of my mistakes were trivial. But there was so little work to do at this small station that I did not improve at all. When I was ordered to a place I shall call Noel to take the position of day operator, I was hardly equal to the job.

There were two other men working in the Noel station: the agent and his assistant. I was a kind of assistant to both of them. I did whatever work they could not find time to do.

I still had to recopy the train orders after I received them over the wire.

This kept me very busy at times, for the dispatcher sometimes sent three or four orders, one after the other. I would string all of these out on a piece of "clip," omitting some parts when the dispatcher got too fast for me, and filling in when I copied the orders on the manifold.

Two branches ran into Noel from the north, but to the south there was only a single track over which the trains of both branches ran. After two miles, the branches again separated at a little junction where there was nothing but a shack containing a register and a telephone connected to our station at Noel.

All trains were supposed to stop and register at this junction, for the trains on either branch were dispatched from separate offices, and neither branch knew what the other was doing. On arrival at the junction, northbound trains would call me up on the telephone if they needed orders or instructions; and I, in turn, was supposed to ask the dispatcher if I was in doubt. All this took time, however, and the trainmen generally preferred to take a chance on a clear track.

Sometimes, when a train was in a hurry, the conductor would neglect the formality of registering. He knew that the telegrapher at Noel was supposed to keep close watch and could protect his train. In truth, a good operator could easily have protected those trains. But I was very young, very careless, and very forgetful. Sometimes a conductor at the junction would call me up and ask me to hold an outgoing train until his own arrived at my station. Twice I let a southbound train by me after I had promised to hold it back. It was a close call both times, but fortunately, the outgoing train sighted the incoming train before leaving the yard.

The agent at Noel was a middle-aged man, old in the service of the company. He seldom came down to the depot on Sunday, and on that day his assistant, Hills, and I ran things as we pleased. On Sunday we had only two passenger trains to meet, and these came near the middle of the day. The rest of the day, Hills and I were free. One Sunday evening we were loafing around the depot with nothing to do when Hills suggested we run down to the next town, six or seven miles away, and see what was going on.

There was a handcar down in the yards. Its wheels were chained together and locked; but both of us had switch keys. Hills claimed the acquaintance of a young lady or two in the town. After a little delay, he got one of them on the phone and made an appointment.

We found the handcar and, with some difficulty, got it onto the track. It was hard work climbing the two hills on the way to town, and we were not what you would call in trim condition; so it was more than an hour before we saw the switch lights of our destination and stopped to open a switch. As we pumped slowly down through the yards, we saw the headlight of an engine that was drawn up before the depot.

Inside the office were the trainmen of this extra. The station operator sat at his table repeating an order. When the order was completed, a message came in from the dispatcher, addressed to the conductor of the extra, ordering him to pick up five loads of time freight at Noel.

When I heard this, little shivers began to run up and down my back. Suddenly I remembered well enough those five cars of freight, and I also remembered that I had not left the register and waybills outside. If the conductor found no bills in the box, he would not take the loads; and when the chief dispatcher learned of this, he probably would tell me he did not need me any more. How to get back to Noel with the handcar before the extra got there—*that* was the question.

Hills and I drew away from the depot, discussing the question. The young ladies were forgotten.

"The only thing to do," Hills said, "is to hitch the handcar onto this freight train."

I had doubts, but there seemed no other way out of it. We rushed down into the yards, as anxious to get out of town as we had been to get in. Lifting the car onto the sidetrack, we ran down to the main line switch, then pumped back to the rear end of the extra.

We had brought the chain with us that locked the car wheels together. Somehow, we managed to fasten it to the caboose of the extra. I remember we had to lock the chain to the car with the switch lock to make it secure.

The jerk of starting lifted our light car clear of the track and sent it bouncing along after the caboose. Hills and I peered at each other through the darkness. Then Hills said "We had better sit down, I think." I thought so, too. We crouched down on the floor of the car, out of the way of the rising and falling pump handles.

As we passed the depot, two trainmen swung aboard the caboose, but they went directly inside without seeing us. In our haste we had forgotten to reckon what the trainmen would do if they discovered us.

"I wish we had disconnected the handles from the gear," Hills said.

"I wish we hadn't started at all," I said. The train was gathering speed, and the handles, close to our heads, began to pump up and down with dangerous frenzy.

"And those girls!" Hills cried. "What will they think of us? I wish you could remember to leave that register out."

I could think of nothing to say just then.

It was upgrade for a little way out of town. Then came the downgrade. The ride was bad enough while the train was climbing, but when the cars began to file over the top of the hill, the speed increased drastically. Our little car jumped and bucked and threatened to leave the track at any moment. I thought the car was off at least half of the time, and I do not understand to this day how it stayed near the track at all.

We lay flat on the floor, hanging on with all our might. Above us, the handles swished up and down viciously, and a harsh, rasping sound came up from beneath. Our feet hung over the rear edge of the car, and our faces were at the front end. There were few places to hold on, and little room for our bodies anywhere.

"I'm going to try to unlock the chain," Hills cried in my ear.

"No you won't," I yelled in a panic. "You'll break your neck!"

Hills must have come to the same conclusion. He did not try to free us from the caboose.

I do not know how we managed to hold on to that lurching, bouncing car. At any moment, it was bound to turn turtle, and there was no telling where we should land. I put my arm over the top of my head, hoping to protect my skull if I lighted on it.

Then the engine began to climb the next little rise and the speed slackened. I began to breathe easier, hoping for the best, when suddenly there was a grinding, rending crash. The car careened violently and seemed about to fall to pieces. My wits left me for a few seconds, and I seemed to be floating in air. Finally, I realized that I was still on the car and that the car was still bumping along the track. I could see the dark shape of Hills' head and shoulders.

"What happened?" I gasped.

I was trembling so that I could hardly keep my hold on the car.

"I think we must have run into the caboose and broken the handles off our car," Hills said at last.

I noticed then that the vicious swish, swish above my head had ceased. Hills was right. When the train had slowed down on the grade, our car had bumped into the rear end. The handles probably had struck the drawhead.

The car ran more smoothly now. As we hummed along up the grade, I had time to think about the next descent. So did Hills.

"We had better watch out when we come to the bottom of the next hill."

I saw the point of this at once. With the handles gone, we would run *under* the caboose and collide with its rear wheels, and that would mean derailment, and probably death.

The speed began to increase. We knew the engine had topped the hill. Then the whole train slid over and we swept downward, our little car dancing and humming along, but hardly so much as before. When our car began to gain on the caboose, we put out our hands and braced ourselves against the drawhead to keep from running underneath. It was dangerous and wearisome, and we were nearly exhausted when we came to the last incline.

Soon we reached familiar landmarks. As we approached the first switch, we hauled the handcar up to the caboose, cut ourselves free, and, with much exertion, dumped the handcar off the track and out of the way. Shivering with cold and fright, we ran after the slowly retreating taillights of the caboose, caught up and swung aboard. When the train had nearly stopped, we dropped to the ground and ran ahead again, reaching the depot before the conductor got off the train. Before any of the trainmen came up, we had put the register and waybills into the bill box and slipped back into the depot. We waited in the office until they had switched the five cars into the train and departed. Then we lit a lamp.

Hills and I looked at each other for a few moments in silence. We were both begrimed with dust and ashes.

"Why, where is your hat?" I said at last.

Hills clapped his hand to his head. Then he grinned.

"Where is your own?" he said.

I stayed at Noel about two months and was then transferred to another station. For a time, I was sent from place to place as relief agent, which is not very desirable; then one day I was brought up on the main line. My previous career seemed as peaceful as a parson's compared with my first few weeks on the main line.

First of all, I could not telegraph fast enough to keep warm. I had never seen real trains before. Why, it seemed to me the trains moved by in droves! It kept me going all the time to keep them moving.

Then there was the block system. I never could work it right. Generally, I pulled the wrong lever and stopped a train when I had intended to give it a clear signal. I still had to recopy orders.

I began to realize that if I intended to become a railroad man, I had better learn the trade.

I wanted to go west, and in time I left the main line, journeyed westward as far as C———, and there got a position. My first place was as night operator. There was not much work to do—nothing, in fact, save watch the trains go by and copy an occasional order.

About two o'clock one morning, the dispatcher gave me a Form 19 order to be delivered to a westbound passenger train. This is the kind of order that does not require the signature of the conductor—in other words, it may be delivered without stopping the train.

This was before the road began using "hoops" to deliver orders with. The station operator had to pass the order up to the conductor and engineer by hand. This took some nice calculating. The operator had to stand far enough away from the track not to be struck by the engine, yet close enough for the trainmen to take the order from his hand.

It was still dark when I heard the train coming. I stepped out onto the platform with a lantern in one hand and the order in the other. When the train was close, I swung the lantern high as a signal that I had a "19" order for them. But the engineer did not respond with two short blasts of the whistle, as is customary. Neither did he slacken speed as he approached, which is also customary.

I took up a position at about the right distance from the track as the train swooped down upon me, but I kept edging farther away, for I did not like the speed at which he was traveling. The engine shot by me, but no one reached for the order. I got a fleeting glimpse of the engineer in the cab window as he passed. His head and shoulders hung over the sill; his head was rolling from side to side.

Farther along the train, someone reached for the order, but he only brushed my hand. Then the train was by and had whisked out of sight around a curve, leaving me a little dazed by the suddenness of its passing.

That was the first time I had ever seen an engineer asleep on a moving train. The man had probably been on duty so long that he could not help it. I do not know where the fireman was all this time.

Soon, the train came backing into the town. The conductor had been out on the platform steps when his train passed; it was he who had brushed my hand, trying to get the order. He had thought his engineer had caught his copy of the order in passing but was not sure. He signaled to stop. When there was no response, the conductor knew the truth. He repeated the signal until the engineer awoke.

I was still bound for the land of the setting sun, and thither I drifted. This time I did not stop until I came to the Pacific. One day I walked into the office of a chief dispatcher.

"How are you fixed for operators?" I asked.

He thought he could use me, he said. He asked the usual questions about previous service, then started me on the examination: a small yellow pamphlet in which were hundreds of questions. These questions were all answered in the book of rules—in other words, I was supposed to know the book of rules by heart. Observing the doubtful look on my face, he brought out a copy of the book of rules and handed it to me. He did not wink when he did it, but I understood that he was badly in need of men, and I set to work to copy the book of rules. It took lots of time and patience, but I finished it at last. After I had passed the physical examination, I was told to go to a certain station and begin work as night operator.

There were a few tickets to sell for an evening train, a few train orders to copy during the night. For the rest—nothing. In fact, there was too little work to do. I got in the habit of sleeping most of the night.

One morning an hour or so before I went off duty, I heard a station some distance to the north reporting that the engine of a southbound extra had "died" there. It should be explained that the usual cause of "death" of an engine is leaking flues. The water leaks out so fast that it is impossible to keep up steam.

After a little time I heard the dispatcher ordering out a light engine from division headquarters to take the place of the "dead" one. He also ordered a change in the meeting place between the "dead" train and other trains bound in the opposite direction and gave right-of-track to a northbound extra that was approaching our station from the south.

The day operator relieved me at seven o'clock as usual, and I went to get some breakfast. Afterwards, I returned to the office for a few minutes' conversation before going to bed. While we were talking, the "dead" train, southbound, arrived with its fresh engine. It did a few minutes' switching, then pulled it out. The day operator reported them out to the dispatcher.

"I think you are mistaken," the dispatcher replied over the wire. "Look again and see if they aren't at the lower end of the yards."

The day operator looked. I looked. The agent, who happened to be in the office, looked. No train could we see. The day operator told the dispatcher.

"Is the northbound extra in?" the dispatcher asked.

It was not.

"Then those fellows have overlooked an order," clicked the dispassionate wire. "They should have waited there until the northbound extra arrived."

The conductor of the once "dead" train had received the order giving right-of-track to the opposing train so long before that he had forgotten about it, as had his engineer. They had pulled out of town right in the face of the other extra.

"The northbound extra ought to be nearing Blank about now," went on the dispatcher. "One of you try to get Blank on the phone, and tell him to hold the northbound extra. I'll try to get CS (a station between us and Blank) to stop the southbound train." And he began to call "C–S, C–S, C–S . . ." steadily, persistently.

The agent jumped to the telephone and called the station at Blank.

"Is that northbound extra by you yet?" he asked.

"It is coming right here, close," answered Blank.

"Stop them!" ordered the agent. "This is the agent at B——."

"What for?" asked the operator.

"Stop them!"

"Can't," said the operator mildly. "The engine has passed my signal."

"Put out your signal and get outside and flag the conductor as the caboose passes. He'll stop the engineer."

"But I'd like to know what you want him stopped for," persisted Blank.

The agent was almost tearing his hair, but he managed to answer: "To keep them out of an extra south that's got away from us!"

"Oh, good heavens!" cried the operator in sudden terror. "I can't stop them now. They are by me and out of reach!"

We turned to the telegraph table, where we could hear the dispatcher's strong, steady call. "C–S, C–S, C–S . . ." went the sounder evenly, dispassionately, with hardly a hint of the importance of an answer, save in the oft-repeated "19" which might mean any one of a dozen things.

"Why doesn't he answer?" I asked angrily. The strain was telling on all of us.

"He's not due to begin work until eight-thirty," said the agent, "and it's only eight-twenty now."

Still we sat there waiting, unable to help in any way, listening to the dispatcher's steady call. CS was a small place and had no telephone. It was like sitting at a sickbed, listening to the seconds ticking off the time which would bring a change for better or for worse.

At last came the answer "I, I, C–S," equally dispassionate.

"Anything coming?" buzzed the dispatcher.

"Extra south coming close," was the prompt answer.

"Stop them!" snapped the dispatcher.

"S–D," was the simple answer. Those two letters told us that the trains were safe. They mean, "Signal displayed." Without hesitation or question, the operator at CS had stopped the southbound train.

—From "The Mistakes of a Young Railroad Telegraph Operator," by Harry Bedwell, in *American Magazine*, November and December, 1909.

CHAPTER ELEVEN

Section Gang

I

"Section men are not supposed to work."

A FEW YEARS AGO, when everyone in America traveled by train, there would have been no need to explain the meaning of the term "section gang." A section gang, as every alert railroad passenger knew, was a group of men—muscular, sunburned, streaked with dust and sweat—who stood along the railroad right-of-way, leaning on crowbars and mallets, and peered at you through the windows of the lounge car as the train slipped cautiously over a newly repaired stretch of track. Section gangs were—and still are—the maintenance crews, the housekeepers of the railroad. All summer they chip away at their alloted five or ten miles of roadbed, weeding, spraying, burning, resurfacing, reballasting, repairing the ravages of frost and rain. When a train comes past, they step aside; and their faces flicker past the windows, gazing curiously in while the passengers gaze curiously out: glowering faces, shadowy with anger and hostility; cheerful, animated faces, bright with the pleasure of good health and outdoor work; callous faces, empty of thought; challenging faces, keen with ambition; furtive, covert faces, reluctant to be known.

To any passenger with normal curiosity, the section gang is a small mystery. Where do these men come from? Where do they go? Do they occupy those battered, brindle-colored boxcars on that abandoned siding, all overgrown with weeds and hollyhocks? Are they college sophomores working a semester? Or new immigrants learning the country? Or old failures condemned to hard labor? Do they work in hope, in agony, in apathy, in despair?

The questions are never answered. The train begins to gather speed. The traveler yawns and turns away. The section captain calls his men, and the gang goes back to work.

Fortunately, in view of all this dangling rhetoric, the section gang is one of the few departments of railroading that has been successfully penetrated by literary men. Over the years, a surprising number of writers have blistered their hands in the interest of smoother roadbeds and afterwards have recorded their impressions of this type of toil. The reactions are wonderfully varied. To a young Macedonian immigrant in a crew of his old-country compatriots on the route of the Great Northern, the section gang was a harsh but necessary initiation into his adopted country. To a knock-about kid with literary ambitions and taped fists, it could provide a lugubrious illustration of proletarian futility. To a displaced Londoner doing a summer tick in Alberta, it was—well, a sort of Wild West fresh-air school: field sports, light work, polyglot companionship.

I N THE MID-1880's, I was one of a gang of men employed on a section of the Canadian Pacific Railway. A section, I must explain, is a stretch of railway, or "track," presided over by a ganger (in western parlance, "boss"), who has under him a complement of men. The section I belonged to worked on the lonely prairie within clear view of the Rockies, blue and snow-capped, to the west.

We lived in one of the frame-built houses, all on the same model, which are stationed along the track at intervals of twenty miles or less. In each are lodged two gangs, one keeping the line in repair ten miles east, the other ten miles west. The head of one of them has the additional duty of keeping the section house and boarding the men. Our boarding boss was an Englishman, a frank, straightforward fellow, whose buxom wife, besides her maternal duties, did the cooking for both gangs. Her work, moreover, was often increased by the quartering upon us of the surface gang, a large roving detachment that worked sometimes on one section, sometimes on another, as their services might be required.

Our pay was a dollar and a half a day, but our fellow gang received two dollars, not owing to any difference in their work but to its lying west of ours, labor being of more value in that direction. The line had been drawn, as ill luck would have it, at our section. Four dollars a week was deducted from our wages for board. Considering the excellence of the fare, the charge was moderate: beefsteak and potatoes, beans and bacon, porridge (or "mush," as it was called), bread and butter, sweets, pies, and so forth, with the unvarying accompaniment of tea. We were certainly fortunate in our boarding boss and his wife; but as far as my experience went, the other sections fared equally well.

Our gang was a strange mixture, headed by a genial, burly Austrian, called for shortness "Joe," whose knowledge of English was very limited. Under him were two young Prussians, brothers who, having been prospecting in the Rockies, had lost their outfit in attempting to cross the Bow River; an old Irish-Canadian whose chief characteristic was a strong disinclination for any sort of exertion save talking; a young Chicagoan who was something of a dude and evidently greatly dependent on the toothbrush that ostentatiously protruded from the outside breast-pocket of his coat; and two Englishmen, of whom I was one. An old army-pensioner, a native of Dublin, was with us for a time, overflowing with amusing reminiscences of his soldier-life in India. But section work was not congenial to him. One fine day, with his little bundle slung over his shoulder, he bade us good-bye and tramped east. Nor should I forget our Birmingham man, who, cut adrift from civilization, clung desperately to his last vestige of it in the shape of a dingy linen collar, which he persisted in wearing long after it had ceased to be an ornament.

The sections, indeed, are made up of all sorts and conditions of men, including almost every nationality. The gang that boarded with us was no less curiously composed than our own. The most noticeable member of it was a young Creole, a somewhat mysterious subject to our old Irish-Canadian, who would allude to him indiscriminately as "that Kamchatkan," "Norwegian," or any other out-of-the-way designation that might occur to him, furthermore expressing his belief that, quiet though "the nigger" now appeared, he only wanted opportunity, backed up by some of his own people, to work havoc in our little commonwealth and perhaps murder the whole lot of us.

On a section not far from ours was an old man, a quondam London clerk, who had come over to the States to better his fortunes. Failing in this, he had

*A dollar and a half a day was good wages
in a section gang on the western plains.*

drifted out here into section life, for which his previous habits and shattered health rendered him wholly unfit. It must not be supposed, however, that the work was particularly hard. To the ordinary British navvy, it was nothing. I once heard such a one, who had been a section hand for some months, assert that during all that time he had not done one good day's work. Seeing me putting too much weight on my shovel, this easy soul advised me not to exert myself, for "section men are not supposed to work"—and he appealed for corroboration of his statement to none other than the boss, who turned off the question with a half-deprecatory chuckle.

We would rise at six in the morning, awakened by the stentorian cry, "Come, arouse!" of the boarding boss. Breakfast followed, and at seven (nominally, for it was often later) Joe would summon us to our duties with a "Now, poys, all aboord!" This referred to the handcar that we rode to the scene of our labors, which was sometimes close by, sometimes several miles distant. (In the latter case, we would occasionally take our dinner with us, and the excursion would be facetiously called a picnic.)

The handcar was nothing more than a flat, open truck on wheels, which raised it about a couple of feet above the rails. It could be lifted on and off the track by four men, two at each end, and it afforded comfortable standing-room for six, though more were often crowded on. The men stood up to pump the handles by which it was propelled. To the genuine old railroad man, this little machine is an object of much interest and care. There is a sort of dirge-like chant concerning it, each verse of which concludes:

>   ... *And, Jerry, go ile the car!**

—a duty which was always conscientiously performed by Joe.

Our work consisted in keeping the track in good level order. We used a jack to raise the sunken rails, shoveling earth beneath the ties to keep them in place. Sometimes, after we had raised a length of track and had not yet finished tamping it, a train would come thundering along, making the ties heave up and down in a manner remarkable to behold and necessitating our doing the work all over again. When a piece of work had been accomplished, Joe, regarding the job with a critical eye, would remark, "Dot's pooty goot. Leetle rest now." And reloading his pipe, he would bring himself comfortably to anchor. We were not slow to follow his example, rising only when we heard "Shoofels on de car!" which meant that we were to gather up our tools and prepare for our homeward journey.

---

*In his novel *The White Mail*, Cy Warman gives one verse of this Irish-American ballad:
>   Wid a big soljer coat
>   Buttoned up to me troat,
>   All danger I would dare;
>   Thin jint ahead an' cinter back,
>   Oh! Jerry go ile th' kayre!

The version quoted by Carl Sandburg in *The American Songbag* concludes:
>   And it's joint ahead and center back
>   And, "Jerry, go and ile that car."

The monotony of our work was now and then enlivened by some incident of prairie life, such as a party of Indians coming up and gravely shaking hands all round after a gruff but cordial salutation consisting of one word, "Nichee" (good man), which, with admirable impartiality, they bestowed on all alike. I remember a young buck, far above work on his own account, who was greatly interested in the mechanism of our jack. He handled it with guarded curiosity, as if not knowing what dangerous properties it might conceal.

Once (but this was in the section house) we were honored by a visit from no less a personage than the ex-chief of the Crowfeet—a splendid, savage old man, such as Walt Whitman would have delighted in, yet not unused to the ways of society, judging from his courtly bow in shaking hands. He showed us an exquisitely finished rifle, a gift of former days, allowing us to examine it while he looked on as a mother might do who had consigned her offspring to strange hands.

In autumn we took our own guns with us on the car and had many a shot at the prairie chickens, as they were called, though no chickens in size. Wonderfully tame birds these, or else weary of life, for they seemed absolutely to enjoy being shot at. Approaching to within a dozen paces or so, they would come to a dead stop, watching us stolidly. One of them once took its stand close to the telegraph operator's shanty, and it was ludicrous to observe that gentleman potting away at it with his revolver while the bird regarded him with contemptuous indifference. At each shot, the telegrapher stealthily advanced a step. He might eventually have accomplished his purpose had not one of the young Prussians rushed out, shotgun in hand, and dropping on one knee, put an end to the telegrapher's game and the suicidal fowl at one and the same moment.

When there was nothing in particular to be done on the section, we would drive the handcar to a spring several miles off and fetch home a barrel of good water. Not far from the section house was a small pool from which all the water used for cooking and drinking purposes ordinarily was obtained. But in ladling it out, we had to exercise some care to avoid taking up tadpoles and other small fry; so that our sallies after a purer supply were not quite a labor lost.

It was pleasant, too, driving over the track in fine autumn mornings when the oppressive heat, with its swarms of mosquitoes, was over. Around us stretched the illimitable prairie, its air of loneliness relieved perhaps by a cavalcade of Indians, moving slowly over the plain, with their squaws and papooses attached in some ingenious fashion, along with the rest of their household goods, to the trailing ends of their tepee poles, and their yelping dogs bringing up the rear. Now and then we would scare a gopher out of the track, where it had been burrowing a hole, or a badger would be spied making along as fast as its unwieldy body would permit. The sight of a badger never failed to cause intense excitement among the gang, most of whom, armed with shovels, would jump off the car, and haste to the massacre of the unoffending beast, towards whose species they seemed to entertain an inexplicable but deep-rooted spite. If one of the luckless creatures succeeded in reaching its hole in time to elude its pursuers, they used the shovels with which they had hoped to smash its head to earth up the opening of its lair, stamping the ground down to make sure of their prisoner. It was our two Berliners, I must in justice state, who were the perpetrators of this gentle deed.

More rarely a fox, tail in air, would bound flashing over the prairie. In the twilight an owl would now and then alight on the rail, waiting till our car was nearly on her, then sluggishly flying a few paces ahead and repeating the maneuver in solemn fashion, as if impelled by some mysterious impulse.

Later in the season the ground would be covered with snow. The frosted rails glistened brightly in the clear sunshine, giving forth a cheery ring beneath the wheels of our car. Away we would spin, pumping leisurely on the level, with greater vigor up the long, steep grades, and resting at the summit, leaving the little car to rush down the slope, the keen air whistling in our faces.

Occasionally, we would be surprised by a train. Then we were forced to pump our hardest, straining every nerve to reach a handy spot where we could get our car off the line, perhaps just in the nick of time. One incident of this sort nearly cost us our lives. We had received orders from the roadmaster to unload a gravel train which, he said, would stop about a mile up the track at eight o'clock that evening.

Toward that hour, seeing the light of an approaching train, we got our car on the rail and drove down to meet her. Joe was in an excitable mood. Urged on by his repeated injunctions to "poomp," we made our car fly over the frosted rails.

The night was dark, and we did not perceive until it was too late that the train was coming upon us, her red light looming dangerously near. Joe made frantic efforts to stop the car, pressing heavily on the brake. In tones of concentrated energy, he cried "No poomp!" (somewhat needlessly, as may be imagined). But the rails were slippery, the car was going down an incline, and the train was on us in a flash. We had barely time to leap off to the right and left before the cowcatcher struck our car and sent her flying. A broken splinter hit our old Irish-Canadian in the back, though without serious injury. The trail pulled up immediately, and we discovered that it was not our expected gravel train, but a pay car, freighted with the men's wages, which had been long overdue.

In the midst of our confusion, the pompous paymaster appeared, resplendent in snow-white shirt, followed by the engine driver, lantern in hand. Joe responded to their remonstrances in a strange new jargon, neither Dutch nor English, which did not throw much light on the affair.

When the train had vanished into darkness, we disconsolately gathered together the fragments of our shattered car and piled them in a heap at the side of the track. Then, sadly shouldering our shovels, we marched home, a crestfallen band. Poor Joe, on whom was thrown the brunt of the catastrophe, had to bear the incessant nagging of the old Irish-Canadian, whose shoulder smarted. Our fellow gang, to whom the news had traveled, accused us of having attempted to wreck the paycar that we might enrich ourselves with the booty. It was not until the following morning that the gravel train arrived.

Our new handcar (for of course the old one had to be replaced) nearly came to grief shortly afterward. We were working away leisurely one breezy morning, never thinking of our car, which we had left on the rails, when one of our men noticed that she had given us the slip. The wind had set her going down the sloping line. There she was, about a mile off, placidly continuing her course, and —alas for the cussedness of things in general—a train was rushing up to meet her. We overtook the runaway just in time to lift her off the track before the train went past.

These were not the only tricks our handcar played. Once, as we were going rapidly over a switch, one of her wheels came loose, and she toppled sideways, sending our gallant chief flying—alighting on all fours. Another time, when we were returning home laden with firewood, a log fell off on the rail, and the car, bumping over it, gave a violent jerk that forced me, without an instant's preparation, into the performance of a complete somersault.

There were often heavy rainfalls in the summer. In my time, it once rained three consecutive days, during which we occupied ourselves with card-playing, reading, or doing nothing—the pay going on as regular as clockwork. Moreover, if a man wanted a day off for any reasonable purpose, he could get it for the asking. Nor would a cent be deducted from his wages if he was laid up through sickness for a time. Among a party of men who had tramped from Montana and joined the section there was a Swede who almost immediately complained of rheumatism. Fully a month he stayed inside the house, on the flat of his back for the most part, losing never a day's pay. When his health improved, he was employed in light housework.

Besides the regular pay, we made overtime when there was any special work to be done, as the unloading of gravel trains. Occasionally we worked on Sundays, greatly against the principles of our old Irish-Canadian, who asserted that money thus made never did one any good. His scruples, I suspect, fell in with his love of repose.

One evening towards the end of summer we extinguished a prairie fire, beating the flames out with our serviceable shovels; and for this exploit, which occupied us scarcely over an hour, we were booked for a half a day's overtime. Thereafter, it fell to our regular work, when the wind suited, to burn the grass to within a distance of about sixty feet on either side of the track to guard against fires kindled by sparks from passing engines. Joe would march ahead, trailing a bundle of lighted rags saturated in oil and fastened to a wire. With this he fired the grass while his trusty gang followed him in single file, each armed with an old sack with which to smite out the flames.

These precautions had been neglected on the section west of the house and a fire broke out in that direction. Speeded by the wind, it made straight for our abode. We were working at some distance off, and the other gang was miles away. It became a race between us and the fire, and we were not in time to burn around the house. In this extremity, we had to rely almost solely on buckets of water which the good wife supplied from a barrel at hand, handing them to us quick as lightning, with never a word, not for one moment losing her presence of mind. We owed it to her that the house was saved. As it was, two fine haystacks, worth some sixty dollars each, were destroyed. And, if it had not been for the forethought of one of the young Prussians, who drove the two squealing pigs to a place of shelter, our boarding boss would have sustained still further loss.

Very sparing were those Prussians, as I discovered afterwards to my cost. In an evil moment, I yielded to their persuasions to set up housekeeping with them in a miserable little hovel of their own construction. Here I learned how far the force of economy could go. We took turns to cook, but their watchful eye was rarely off me. If I were to put what they considered a grain too much sugar in the cakes, or committed any like extravagance, one or the other of them would be sure to jump up excitedly and stay my hand, exclaiming, with an assumption of playfulness, but in tones vibrating with genuine solicitude:

"*Du bist verrückt, mein Kind!* Know you not dere vas von hundred cents in von dollar? Yah, it all counts oop, I tell you."

From having had enormous appetites in the section house, they became abstemious to an almost dangerous degree. At dinner time the younger of the two would frequently throw himself on his couch, light his pipe, and assert that he had "no hoonger."

This was in the fall. Such close quarters during the hot season, with the windows shut against the mosquitoes, would have been unbearable. If a window were left open, they would swarm in by myriads, rendering sleep utterly impossible. On one hot night several of us sought refuge outside, where we made a dense smoke by burning a pile of dry plants, the only way to keep our tormentors off. An old cow immediately made for the fire and eagerly thrust her head into the smoke, as grateful as we were for the relief it afforded.

Besides the plague of mosquitoes (though fortunately not in their numbers, or nothing of us would have been left), there was a species of large black fly with a pair of huge mandibles and a voracious appetite. Sharp and sudden was the onslaught of this monster—one hasty nip, as from a pair of scissors, leaving a drop of blood.

One broiling summer's day, I ventured to bathe in a marshy lake near the section house. Not one of these flies was visible when I reached the water, but no sooner had I got well out beyond the sedgy border than one came hovering near me, my unprotected state no doubt presenting most unusual attractions. I flicked it off and was sharply bitten in the rear by another. Gradually the number of my assailants increased—flick here, bite there. In vain I sought refuge in the shallows of the lake—my head was still at their mercy. Desperate, I groveled altogether beneath the surface—want of breath forced me up again. Sore discomfited, I beat an ignominious retreat, closely followed by my adversaries, who kept skirmishing to the bitter end.

Winter sets in early in the Northwest. From the commencement of the dark mornings, we never started to work before eight o'clock. Sometimes, after driving out to raise a piece of track, we would find the frosty ground impenetrable to our shovels. On such occasions, we were free to occupy ourselves as we chose, some of the men preparing traps for foxes or investigating the results of those they had set overnight. (Foxskins met with a ready sale.) Only a few of the hands were kept on past November, two on each section. The rest got free passes east, there being next to no work on the track until the frost breaks up.

It is in the spring that most of the laborers find their way to these parts. Many of these, fresh from the old country, probably know little of the sort of life awaiting them. The uninitiated pilgrim experiences a rough awakening when, in the innocence of his heart, he demands refreshment in the shape of beer. He is immediately supplied by an obliging bartender with a glass—fortunately a small one, though its cost is ten cents—containing a villainous compound, looking not unlike the genuine article at its muddiest. But the only effect of this concoction is to produce unlimited nausea, for the sale of intoxicating liquors is forbidden here. Such, however, is the force of habit that men will sit playing cards by the hour, the stakes being this delectable concoction, which they make believe to toss off with relish. Next to the pleasure of winning the game must be that of losing it!

The great drawback to section life, remote from any town, is the dreariness and monotony of its surroundings. Few of us were sorry to receive our discharge.

Late one bleak November night, the snow lying thick upon the ground, the train that was to bear us to Winnipeg came down from the Rockies, already nearly full of men that it had picked up from the sections on its way. Short time was given us to get aboard. The two young Prussians, who were to stay on with Joe for the winter, obligingly helped me in with my box, having, as I afterwards discovered, greatly lightened it of its contents. The last image on my mind was of Joe standing somewhat disconsolately watching our departure, his honest face illumined by the light from the telegraph operator's shanty. The scene of our sometime labors was soon far behind. On we sped, stopping at each section to take in living freight until the cars were crammed.

A motley crew we were, cooped up together through what seemed an eternity. The only diversion was the passing of the trainboy, offering his wares for sale, and the occasional quarreling of the men after we had reached the whiskey region.

—Adapted from "Section Life in the North-West,"
an anonymous article published in *Cornhill Magazine*, London, January, 1888.

*"As I touched the steel, linking one rail to another,
I was linking myself to the new country
and building my own solid road to a new life."*

DURING THE AGE OF STEAM, many railroad men looked upon the section gang as a form of mystical initiation into a profession that doted on starting from the bottom. After all, hadn't Daniel Willard, the great and renowned president of the Baltimore & Ohio, started his career in a section gang on the Vermont Central? Ninety cents for a ten-hour day!

Without being unduly cynical about this Horatio Alger fantasy, one can suggest that the section gang was never really an ideal place to commence a rapid climb to the presidency of your favorite railroad. In truth, the section gang, even in the most rugged era of free enterprise and economic opportunity, was always the province of uneducated, unmarried, undemanding drifters and of young foreigners who could not speak English. Native Americans didn't choose to work for that kind of money, even in hope of rising to the top of the B&O.

Thus it was that the section gang came to be a sort of reception center and indoctrination course for thousands of new Americans during the 1880's and 1890's, when immigration from Europe reached its historic peak. This low-paid refuge for unskilled and unlettered laborers absorbed wave after wave of bachelor immigrants, held them together for a few seasons in little ethnic enclaves, transported them across the country into the vast, underpopulated regions of the West, and eventually scattered them into the republic like seeds from a bursting pod. Apparently, very few section hands stayed with the railroad in any capacity, much less rose to the presidency; but that is not to say they did not find success in other careers.

State Senator Stoyan Christowe of Vermont went through his adaptation to the culture of the New World in a section gang composed of immigrants from the Balkan Peninsula. Born in Macedonia in 1898, when that unhappy area was torn by almost incessant warfare among Turks, Greeks, Serbs, and Bulgarians, Christowe had emigrated to the United States with his father in search of the freedom and peace that was impossible in his own country. After becoming an American citizen in 1924, he worked as a newspaper correspondent and became an expert in Balkan political affairs, a widely read author, and a successful politician; but it was his experience in the section gang that stood out as the pivotal episode in his Americanization.

In his autobiography, *My American Pilgrimage,* he describes in simple, profoundly moving language his ordeal of cultural adjustment while working on the railroad.

CHRIS, THE STRAW BOSS and interpreter, set the fourteenth of March as the day of our departure for Montana. Chris had arrived in St. Louis around the middle of February. He had been sent by the Great Northern Railway to gather a large gang for the Montana Division of that line. With an array of "self-writing" pens and pencils in his vest pockets, and a notebook, he went around signing up people.

Men who worked in factories and foundries, in steel mills, packing houses, and roundhouses, gave up their jobs and signed up with him. It was not entirely the prospect of money that made them do it. Some of them, especially the younger ones, made as much as three and four dollars a day as chippers and coremakers in the steel mills, while the pay on the railroad would be much less. It was more the release, perhaps, from these heavy, sweaty tasks, the getting away from soot and grime and smoke and ashes and grease, that made them sign up for Montana.

With some it was the distant sorcery of the West, the freedom and mobility. They had come four thousand miles from the hearthside to where they were, and they would go still another thousand miles or more in their search for America.

Chris made no extravagant promises about wages, living conditions, or special privileges. He said that of all northwestern railroads the Great Northern was the largest and had the best reputation for "treating good" its employees. He was a good-hearted, well-meaning man. Although it would endanger his own position as a straw boss–interpreter, he signed up some men who could—as the saying goes—buy and sell him when it came to knowledge of the English language. He turned down no one. He did not bat an eyelash when Vasil, who had a reputation as an "agitator" and a "gang-buster," proffered his five-dollar shipping fee.

As our train glided out of the shed and twisted through the yards, the coal chutes, ashpits, roundhouses revolved into the background. Some of our people who worked in the yards stood on the tracks, in their greasy overalls, their mummers' faces grinning as they waved to us. Once I had stood there like that, watching the trains and wishing I were traveling through America. Now, I kept my face to the window. A sudden deafening roar, galelike, blasted in my ears, and my view was blocked by another passenger train going in the opposite direction. The train on which I rode went ahead, carrying me forward into a new life.

But I turned my face from the window and there, beside me, was my old life. My father was asleep, the old cap on his head. The ponderous watch chain at his vest seemed tied to my own neck as it was to that old Turkish watch, bulging in his vest pocket, ticking away the old life. And that wasn't all. I was riding in an American train, going across the heart of America—but as a member of a Balkan community-on-wheels, as one of a hundred people who held their nationality in the palms of their hands, like old coins. In the three coaches set aside for the gang, the talk, the music, the memories were Balkan. The Old Country was quarantined here, and I was of it.

Occasionally my father would wake and lean over to the window. For a minute or two his sleepy eyes would gaze listlessly at white farmhouses, cathedral-like red barns with cupolas on their roofs, and circular towers, like campaniles, attached to them. He would shake his bewildered head and close his eyes again. I knew he was unhappy, and it hurt me.

Yet I had only to look out the window at the fields and farmhouses and the clumps of trees rotating backward to regain my sense of separation and forward motion. Broad, flat earth rolled away with American prodigality. And my being yearned to be one with it.

Section gangs lived on the tracks they had laid.

Harper's Weekly, 1875

Strung upon the line, our section gang looked like a tribe of pygmies lost in a glacial region. With puny bodies, cumbrous in heavy wraps, and with steel implements, we defied the skin-cracking cold which gripped the plain. There was nothing tame or gentle about this Montana country. It was one vast desolation. The snow was not deep, for blades of last year's grass stuck above it. But the cold was all-pervading.

The track ahead was but a thin stripe upon the earth's white expanse. And upon this band of steel the hundred men, like animated tumbleweeds, bent and twisted, bored and scratched. Upon the white bosom of American earth we engraved a necklace of steel—set in tie plates, clasped with bolts and angle bars, brocaded with spikes. And there it lay secured to the earth, immovable.

I had always thought that the building of a railway was a complicated business, as mysterious as the building of a steamboat or a locomotive. And I had believed that we would be carrying the steel while others—Americans—would be doing the skillful work. Now a hundred erstwhile plowmen and shepherds tore off the old track and built it anew as fast as they tore it up, and the whole thing struck me as too simple to be true. There was the feeling in me that the hundred men, adults though they were, were just children pretending to be building a railway, over which maybe a toy train could pass, but no real one.

There was not an engineer in sight, nor an American, to lend credence to this thing, to impute reality to what was being done. The boss was an Irishman with the fantastic name of Pat—just Pat. Could a man named Pat build a railway? Wrapped in a bearskin cloak which reached to his galoshes, and with a beehive fur hat upon his head, Pat walked up and down the track, from the claw bars to the spike malls, doing nothing, saying nothing.

Around eleven o'clock, when some sixty or seventy new rails had been strung upon the line, Pat called a stop. The men lay huddled like a flock of sheep while Pat and Chris took over the business of temporarily closing the track. This was the first chance I had had to see Vasil, who was on a spiking team in the rear.

"Is this all there is to building a railway, Vasil?"

"It's simple enough here in a straight line but gets plenty complicated on curves, bridges, and switches."

"Why did we close up?"

"I think for the Fast Mail. That's the train which carries the U.S. mail from St. Paul to Seattle. It's the fastest train on the line. If Pat stopped it for one minute, we'd have a new boss tomorrow morning. Freight trains you can hold."

"So a train will pass over this track we just built?"

"And how!"

"Why is it forbidden to hold the Fast Mail?"

"Because it costs the Great Northern one thousand dollars for every minute the Fast Mail is late getting into Seattle. It's in the contract. It comes cheaper to the company for us to wait a whole day than for the Fast Mail to be one minute behind schedule. Nobody can hold the Fast Mail."

Chris and Pat walked up and down the track. The ground wind, which had winnowed the snow, had died down, and the plain, as if in hushed expectation of the Fast Mail, lay in frozen quietude. Only the telephone wires moaned continuously.

"We're getting paid for doing nothing," I remarked.

"It's the only rest we get," replied Vasil. "Except when we come to switches and the Irishman will be scratching his head to figure out the position of the frog and the head block. But switches here are far apart. In the summertime there'll be more trains—stock trains, fruit trains, specials. Stock trains you don't hold either. They're as important as the fastest passenger trains. The animals lose weight in travel and the faster you get them to Chicago stockyards the more money they bring."

The things this Vasil knew!

Pat's thin voice announced the approach of the train. The men stirred, picking up their tools as they stood up. I looked up ahead to the east. And there, where the track vanished, a bundle of black smoke was visible. That and nothing else. But that was the Fast Mail. That patch of black smoke on the steel-gray horizon began to rouse the plain. We could detect a faint sound emitted by the rails.

By and by the bundle of smoke assumed the shape of an inverted cone, with its apex spinning on the edge of the plain. And soon I saw the engine, a black point upon the rim of the horizon. There was now a distinct vibration upon the rails, with the emission of an occasional sound as when you pick at an over-stretched wire.

The men, holding claw bars, line bars, line wrenches, spike malls, adzes, tongs, and standing upon the embankment, looked like an armed savage tribe watching a vessel steam up to the shore of their island. The approaching train seemed the only living thing upon this broad expanse of lifelessness. I watched the locomotive grow bigger and bigger as it left more and more of the plain behind it. With reduced speed the locomotive rolled on, the head of it rearing higher and higher.

Pat stood in the middle of the track signaling to the engineer to continue on with caution. Two short blows of the whistle acknowledged Pat's signal, and he stepped out onto the embankment.

The engine appeared immense. Its cowcatcher was sculptured in ice, but its stack belched smoke, for there was a fire in the heart of the engine which no cold could stifle. And as long as the wheels stayed on the rails, the engine was a mighty power. It moved with earth-shaking ponderosity. The pistons shuttled like gigantic arms bending at the elbow to propel the wheels.

The locomotive was still over old track, and the wheels turned slowly, cautiously, feeling their way, as if suspicious of the new track ahead, laid by us. The engine itself sniffed, scented, its many valves spurting out jets of vapor.

The men withdrew farther down toward the ditch, and I too stepped back with them; but my eyes were on the front wheel, watching it come closer and closer to the point of connection. High up in the cab the engineer had slid open a section of the glass that enclosed him, and his goggled eyes held the rail below like a pair of binoculars.

My heart thumped as the front wheel turned onto the switch point. The next instant it was on the new rail, and then upon the joint which I had made secure with bolts and fishplates, and on it rolled, over the new track.

I gave out an involuntary cry and brandished my line wrench like a mace. And then a chorus of a hundred voices waked the plain from its frozen lethargy. There was warmth and cheer in every voice, as if the locomotive were a rescue party from a peopled world come to us forsaken upon the nakedness of a cold and desolate America. The engineer gave out a prolonged, heartening whistle, and the train gathered speed upon the new and firmer track.

I watched the Fast Mail disappear into the unknown West. I felt less alone now, less cold.

"All right, men, rip her up now," Pat yelled in his high-pitched voice.

A new energy seized the workers. The claw bars clamped the spikes with iron fangs and jerked them out like frozen worms. The tongmen slung in the new thirty-three-foot rails with the lightness of sticks. I unclasped the metal hooks of my sheepskin-lined coat so as to breathe more freely, and I took off my mittens that I might touch the steel with my bare hands. And then I felt as if a candle were suddenly lit inside me, glowing within me and warming my body. In crowded St. Louis I had never felt so close to America as I did now in this pathless plain. I knew that as I touched the steel, linking one rail to another, I was linking myself to the new country and building my own solid road to a new life.

On a warm sunny June day which had brought the gophers from their holes, the roadmaster dropped a message from the rear platform of the Skidoo, and before Pat had had a chance to read it the men began to shout, "We're moving."

"All right, men," Pat announced, "we are moving. We close up right away."

It was to be the longest move yet, more than a hundred miles to the west. Moving was always exciting. It meant an interruption in the monotony of work; it meant riding across new country, to a new campsite, perhaps near a town where there might be a store, or close to the Missouri, in whose muddy waters one could take a bath on Sunday. We moved in the daytime, and as a rule by freight trains, occasionally by a work train. That meant slow going. The men liked it, even if it wasn't comfortable riding, because we got paid the same as if we had been at work on the track.

By four o'clock in the afternoon, tools, handcars, push car, switch point, and other equipment were loaded on the flatcar, and the camp was ready to be picked up at a moment's notice. With still two full hours before dinner, the men took advantage of the interval to indulge in hobbies and devote time to their personal appearance at the company's expense. Some took out their musical instruments, some organized card games on the grass flat before the cars, others set down backgammon boards and reclined on the ground. There were two professional barbers, and they both set up shop in the open, trimming hair at twenty cents a throw to earn a few extra dollars. The cook was heard to argue with those who had lined up before the kitchen door with basins for hot water for shaving.

"We need the hot water for the dishes," the cook complained. But he kept filling the basins which were held out to him. "Why do you have to shave? Where do you think you're going, to Great Falls?"

I took soap and towel to the tank to save lugging water in pails to the wash-stand in the bunk car. I was drying my face when I heard the ring of the gong, an old fishplate hanging at the door of the kitchen.

"Is it for dinner?" I asked a man standing in a doorway.

"It's for a meeting, for not to move at night."

All through camp the men were stirring. A score or so were already gathered before one of the dining cars, clustering around Vasil. I climbed into our bunk car, hung the towel on its nail above my bunk, put on a clean shirt and was ready to go. Then I turned to my father, who was lying down.

"You coming to the meeting, Father?"

"No, I'll just rest. Let them thrash it out."

"Don't you feel good?"

"I don't feel bad." His voice sounded feeble. He had the easiest job in the gang, carrying shims in a two-pound lard pail and holding one at the end of a rail as the next one was set in place by the tongmen. A child could do what he was doing—still, he was perpetually tired.

When I got to the meeting, nearly everybody was there. The discussion was underway and I heard a young man say, "Work animals get better treatment."

"Work animals have better sense than some of us." This was said by a dusky fellow with straight, coal-black hair, who was a spiker.

"I never heard of any place where they paid you while you slept," declared an elderly man, who as an adzman did work that was play compared to spiking.

"That's just the point," said Vasil. "You won't sleep. These freight trains average about fifteen miles an hour, and that means you'll be banged and bumped all night long. And you should be paid for it."

"That's too bad. Are we made of glass? It's unreasonable to demand pay for lying in your bunk. Whether you sleep or not."

"Here comes Chris," someone said. The straw boss—interpreter was seen coming out of Pat's car.

"Are they going to move us at night?" Vasil asked Chris.

"We'll be picked up around ten tonight." Chris's straw-colored hair, freshly combed, was wet and stiff. He fingered the gold heads of several pens and pencils in his vest pockets. On hot days he would remove his jacket, but never his vest, which he would wear unbuttoned.

"What about time?" demanded Vasil.

"Pat's got no authority to give time for night moving."

"Has he asked for authority?"

"There's no use telephoning. The answer will be no. It's the rule."

"The answer may be *yes* if Pat says the gang'll *strike*."

"Who elected you spokesman for the gang?" Chris jerked out one of the fountain pens from his pocket and waved it at Vasil.

"Nobody did," a thin voice chirped. "He rings the gong on his own. Now he says we'll strike. We've got something to say about that."

"When a worker's not paid for his time, his time's his own," argued Vasil. "And nobody has the right to budge him from his home."

"Don't forget there's wheels and rails under your home," Chris answered. "Your home belongs to the company and the company can move its own property as it pleases."

"That's right," several voices echoed Chris. "That's right."

"That's not right," said Vasil calmly."We're in the cars, see. And that makes a lot of difference. We're not property, we're human beings; not freight either. Look here, men, for myself I don't care. A dollar one way or another don't make much difference to me."

"It don't to us either."

"All right then, it's not the dollar. It's whether it's right or wrong for workers to be pushed around without compensation. The company owns the cars and the tracks, it's true, but the company don't own us, and shouldn't move us on our own time unless we are willing—"

"We're willing," screeched a short, stumpy man.

"We'll find out who's willing and who's not. We'll take a vote."

"It will do no good," counseled Chris. "We're all for pay. But we can't get it. St. Paul says no pay for night moving."

"We'll not vote for pay," declared Vasil. His words evoked some laughter. And his own face twisted into an ironic smirk. "We'll vote on whether to strike."

"What'll we strike for?"

"For straight time, or time-and-a-half, for night moving."

Many voices spoke up at once: "He's crazy. . . . He's a gang-buster. . . . He don't give a damn if we all get fired."

Then a single voice was speaking. "We came here to work, not to right wrongs. Whoever don't want to be moved at night, he knows what to do."

Vasil made a fresh start. "Look here, men. I know we came here to work. I'm not urging you to stop work. I am only trying to tell you that when we are not at work, our time is our own, and we shouldn't let ourselves be pushed around."

There was earnestness in Vasil's voice. If there was anger in him, he did not let it go into his voice or into his words: he let it escape through his hands, which worked continually, clenching and unclenching.

I felt Vasil's strong belief in what he was saying. His words, while not tense or loud, rang with conviction. They were like the strokes of his spike mall, precise, compact, well aimed. I saw the hostility in some of the faces, and the cold, steely eyes turned on him. And I could think of nothing to say which would carry any more weight than what Vasil was saying, yet I had a strong urge to add my own voice to his, and once or twice I did open my mouth to say something, but said nothing.

"Who are we, a bunch of Balkanians, to be telling the Chewtobaccos what's right and what's wrong?" someone said. "They really ought to charge us fare for carrying us to this new place of work. Still, if they were to do that, I'd say, yes, let's protest. But to ride on a train, just to ride on a train, and demand pay for riding on a train, I never heard of such a thing."

After much argument someone had sense enough to suggest, "It don't cost nothing to vote, so let's do it and stop this wrangling."

"Wait a minute. Why should a whole gang yield to Vasil?" This was said by the Avocat, a law student who had joined the gang wholly for reasons of health.

"You're not yielding to me. I'll abide by the majority opinion same as anybody else. We're simple people, and we wish to settle this matter by the simple method of voting."

"Then we're giving in to you," insisted the Avocat.

For perhaps a whole minute Vasil stood silent. Then he said, "Well, what do you propose?"

"I propose we first take a vote on whether to vote for a strike."

Many people scratched their heads, unable to grasp the fine point.

"I never thought of it in that light," said Vasil. "Let's do it that way before somebody asks for a vote on the vote whether to vote for a strike. Now understand, men, we're not voting on the question of a strike, but on whether we should vote for a strike. Those in favor of taking a vote for a strike raise your right hand."

All right hands went up, including the Avocat's.

"That settles that. Now we shall vote again, but this time it's whether to strike or not to strike. This will decide it."

"Just a minute," a voice spoke up. "It's not against the law to strike, is it?"

"We have a legal right to strike," assured the Avocat.

"I just wanted to be sure we're not breaking any laws."

"All in favor of striking so as to get time for moving at night raise your right hand," said Vasil.

At least a score of men were counting hands, some inaudibly, some loudly. Thirty-one hands were counted.

"Those against striking raise your right hand."

Fifty-three hands went up.

We moved on our own time, without pay.

"You'll soon get well, Father. You need rest and some good food. I'll go ask the cook if he's got something special."

On a nail above the bunk in which my father lay hung his old Turkish watch, with the winding key on the heavy silver chain. The watch looked out of place here in the boxcar but no more so than its owner, lying on his back and staring at the ceiling, his lips dry and cracked.

"I'll soon have no need of food," said my father weakly. "As for rest, that's for God to give."

"You'll get well. And as soon as you're strong enough to travel we'll go back to St. Louis. You shouldn't have come here in the first place. You've got to eat something to give you strength."

"I can't eat, my son." The voice was like the voice of a cracked bell.

"Then maybe we should send for a doctor. Pat said he'll send the section foreman with the motorcar to fetch a doctor. There's one in Glasgow. It's only twenty miles."

"To send for a doctor that distance! He'll charge a whole month's wages."

The next day Pat sent the section foreman for the doctor. It was August and a hot sun was beating down upon the roofs of the bunks, overheating the interiors. Still the sick man felt chilled to the bone. I put his coat over the blankets, and watched his dry forehead for sweat. There was no sweat.

"Pull the covers from my chest, my son." He had to stop between words for breath. It was labor for him to speak.

I uncovered his chest.

"Inside the vest, on the lining," he whispered.

On the left side of the vest against the lining there was a patch pocket with a flap over it secured by a small safety pin. I unfastened the pin and took out a wallet, shaped like an ordinary envelope. "Is this what you want?"

"Yes."

"You want me to keep this for you?"

"Listen, my son. Will you send one hundred dollars to my sister Kyra. And say to her that I did not forget her."

"Of course I will."

"That's good, that's good." He rested a moment. And then again in a faint voice, "Will you forgive me—my son—if I've been angry with you—and said things—in my anger—you are a fine son—will you—" The whispering faded.

When the Turkish watch on the wall pointed to half-past two I heard the cough of the section foreman's motorcar and went to the door. I climbed down the ladder and started up the bank to meet the doctor, who turned out to be surprisingly young, for a doctor. He could hardly have been thirty, had no beard, no mustaches, and wore a loose-fitting gray suit. The only thing to inspire confidence in him was the little bag he carried, a little black leather bag with a shiny metal clasp.

"I am Doctor Wainer," he said. "Is it your father who's sick?"

The examination was very brief. I stood by quietly, watching the doctor hold my father's wrist awhile, take his temperature, and listen to his breathing through a contrivance.

He put the listening contrivance back in his bag and clicked the bag shut. He then carefully pulled up the blankets to cover the sick man's chest and motioned to me to follow him.

Out on the grass he turned and spoke to me. It was as if some mechanism spoke and not a human voice. "You know what pneumonia is?"

I thought a moment. Then my mind supplied the unpronounced letter *p*, and I nodded.

"How long has he been ill?"

"Four days."

"Why didn't you send for a doctor the first day?"

I made no reply. There was nothing I could say.

"I can't take the responsibility of moving him to a hospital now. It's too late." The doctor spoke without emotion. He was not angry.

For a moment or two both the doctor and I remained silent. And then it was he again who spoke, but still without feeling, without sympathy, even without a tone of impatience in his voice.

"It may not have helped anyway," he said. "There's no resistance."

"Resistance?"

"Yes. Strength. The body has no strength to fight the sickness. Hard work. Bad food."

The doctor's phlegmatism extended even to the matter of his fee. Failing to think of the word fee, and aware of my inability to phrase my question more delicately, I asked, "How much you charge, Doctor?"

"It doesn't much matter. Ten dollars will do."

He took the ten-dollar bill and without bothering to look at it stuck it in a pocket.

"Keep him wrapped up and give him plenty of water. All he can drink." Then he walked up to the waiting motorcar, and the section foreman drove him off.

That night I stayed up, but there was nothing much I could do. My father would not even take a sip of water. His breathing, the only sign that he was alive, was so labored that every time he breathed out, I feared he would have no strength to take in sufficient breath to keep him alive.

After the others had gone to bed around ten o'clock, I kept the kerosene lamp on the floor and turned low so that the glare from it might not interfere with their sleep. I myself lay in my bunk, but awake, my whole being turned to my father's breathing, picking it out from the breathings of the others.

A little after midnight I fell asleep. When I waked, the first thing I listened for was my father's breathing. I tried to separate it from the other respirations, as I had done before, but I couldn't. I lay there quietly and listened intently. After perhaps a minute my ear picked up the clean, metallic tick of the old Turkish watch hanging on the wall above my father's bunk. That gave me a momentary reassurance. I could not conceive of that old watch ticking without my father's breathing.

I rose and picked up the lamp from the floor and turned up the wick. I put the lamp up on the narrow folding table between my father's bunk and my own. The flame cast a weak yellow light upon his face, which looked as if he had fallen into a deep, dreamless sleep. My father was not breathing.

I went over and touched Vasil, who lay asleep in the bunk next to mine. "Vasil," I whispered. Vasil sat up and stared in the semi-darkness. "I think my father is dead, Vasil."

"He died?"

"He's not breathing."

"God's been kind to him. Guess we should wake the others."

"Yes."

Slowly and silently the band of men moved across the open plain behind the coffin of rough pine boards borne by a farmer's cart. The farmer on the driver's seat, with his team of horses, alone seemed of this place.

I paced directly behind the cart, Vasil at my side. I was dressed in my brown suit and wore my felt hat, and I did not weep. In all the sadness that hovered about me, there was deep inside me an unsuspected sense of relief.

I was thinking how different my mother's funeral had been, which I remembered vaguely. The procession here through the treeless plain was unreal and unbelievable. There was something incomplete, unfinal, about my father's death, and about his burial. This was no way to return a man to his eternal resting place. No bell tolled; no priests in vestments swung fuming censers or intoned funeral chants. And there was no avenue lined with tall poplars and cypresses leading to a chapel shaded by ancient oaks and walnut trees.

My mind wandered to the Old Country, to St. Louis, and then would project into the future and would return to the plain, to the coffin. How my father would grieve if he knew that he had become the cause of every man in the gang losing a day's wages in order to bury him.

We carried him to a small burial ground fenced off by barbed wire to keep the cattle from tramping on the few graves. It was a lonely and remote spot, but a more fitting burial place could hardly be found, for scarcely fifty feet away was one of those mesas that rise sheer from the plains, like temples, to heights of two and three hundred feet. No one could be in the shadow of this majestic tableland without being aware of something mysterious and supernatural dwelling within its terraced sides. The group that gathered about the coffin, now set on the ground, was not impervious to the mystical spell which emanated from this natural monument. That in itself seemed to make up, in some measure, for the lack of religious rites.

—From Stoyan Christowe's *My American Pilgrimage*, Little, Brown & Co., Boston, 1947. Copyright 1947 by Stoyan Christowe.

III

"Sweat poured down our faces, burning our eyes and putting us in a savage humor."

ON MANY RAILROADS section work was neither a summer adventure nor a citizenship course, as is evidenced by a rulebook used on the Memphis & Ohio Railroad before the Civil War. In the interest of humanity and good personnel management, section foremen on the M&O were admonished to give "particular attention to the condition and health of Negroes under their charge" and deal with them in a firm, resolute, and temperate manner. "Chastisement, if required, must be administered in moderation, and within the bounds of the law, which is not to exceed thirty-nine lashes."

The rulebook specifically forbade the section boss to strike a Negro with a fist, a club, a stick, or any other heavy instrument.

"Should a Negro run away," the book continued, "notice of the fact must be immediately given to both the road master and assistant superintendent, stating the name of the Negro, date and cause of his running away, together with all attending circumstances."

Inevitably, the section gang attracted the interest of "proletarian" writers in the 1920s and 1930s, among them a young New Yorker named Erich Sonnichsen, who wrote for the *American Mercury.* Sonnichsen's prose has the artlessness of an autumn English composition on the dread theme, "How I Spent My Summer Vacation." But like Stoyan Christowe's reminiscences, his report rings with the clarity of real experience. Its inadvertent (or perhaps intentional) crudity exhales the sweaty fumes of "social realism," c. 1930.

When Sonnichsen did his stint on the Pennsy, he was a young man in the midst of his *wanderjahr,* which actually had lasted several *jahr.* He had spent eighteen months or so at sea, had hoboed across the United States, had boxed as an amateur, calling himself Eddie Sullivan, and had done other refreshing and educational things. In the 1880's, he might have enjoyed the section gang as naively as did the English adventurer who wrote for *Cornhill.* But in 1930, a summer on the rails no longer could be regarded as a fling. The men were different. Times had changed. The section gang was degraded and degrading.

Readers of the *Mercury* were relieved to learn that Mr. Sonnichsen had given up railroading and was planning to go to college.

Sonnichsen's experience in the gang was not without intellectual value, however, for he discovered the answer to one of those gnawing questions about section men, namely, Why do they always stand so dangerously close to the passing train? Answer: the breeze cools you off.

W E WERE A SHABBY BUNCH. About thirty of us were in the last car of the local, puffing slowly across the New Jersey countryside. Dungarees, blue denim shirts, dirty caps. Some had suits—worn, frayed suits. At many of the stops men would get off. They kept dropping off till there were but fifteen of us. We were all going to the same place, a few miles from Princeton.

I sat on the dusty plush seat. My coat was off, my sleeves rolled up. A man across the aisle sat staring stupidly ahead. His bloodshot eyes, reminiscent of the previous night's drunk, would close momentarily, then open slowly. His hands, heavy, thick, work-stained hands, hung between his legs, lifeless. Another man saw the Sailor's Union pin on the lapel of my coat. He began talking to me. He seemed sickly and repulsive.

One young fellow who spoke in a loud tone was recounting his misfortunes to several others just ahead of me. He had driven from Florida to Baltimore, where his car had broken down. With a few dollars in his pocket, he had hitch-hiked to New York. Drifting over to West Street, he had shipped out on the railroad.

Several others stand out in my memory. One was Fred, a French-Canuck from Maine, a happy, laughing fellow.

The train pulled into the junction. We all got off. The railroad camp was a short distance from the station. At the camp a fat Jew took charge. He put down our names, ages, and whether we had worked for the railroad before. The camp was deserted. All the men were working, although it was the Fourth of July.

The crumb-boss gave each of us a blanket and a sheet. There were several old passenger cars on a siding. The red paint on the outside was cracked and peeling. Inside the cars, beds were double-tiered, twenty-four to a car. We walked along the cars, between the rows of bunks.

Each of us threw his blanket and sheet on an empty bunk. I had an upper. Slim, the loud-voiced fellow, drew a lower just across from me. I had two pairs of dungarees tied up in a bundle. Slim had two towels. We traded—a towel for dungarees—and began to make up our bunks.

At four-thirty the men began coming in from the tracks, hot, dirty, sweaty. They washed at a wooden trough in the wash house before battered, half-running faucets. There were more than a hundred men in the camp.

Six o'clock. The crumb-boss came out of the mess hall, a long, unpainted building, and with a stone hit the steel rail hanging from a stick. The men formed into a long line leading into the shed.

We took places on benches around the long tables. Mess boys passed around, filling our bowls with soup from a wooden pail. Flies buzzed around over the tables. There was no sugar, no butter. Coffee came in pots, already sweetened and with milk—coffee that was mainly chicory—vile stuff. The potatoes had black spots which one must cut out. The meat had an acrid flavor.

After supper, the Jew opened the commissary. He sold candy, cookies, tobacco, and clothes. The men, without money, bought what they needed and had it charged against their payday checks.

There were all sorts in the camp. Young and old. Many still in their teens. There were Italians and a few Russians, but mostly Irish—a laughing, singing crowd.

In the cars the men sat around talking. About nine o'clock we began to undress, lying in our bunks smoking.

My first night was a series of skirmishes with lice. Thereafter I took a tip from the other men and burned the springs of my bunk with newspaper.

During the night it rained. The roof leaked. In the morning I awoke wet and stiff. At six-thirty we ate breakfast. Oatmeal thinned with water. Evaporated milk. The eggs were cold and greasy.

On leaving the mess hall, the men passed by a huge basket. Each took his dinner or "nosebag" from the basket. There were four sandwiches in the paper bag—jelly, cheese, salami, and cooked meat.

The new men were divided into groups. I walked down by the station to the toolhouse with Fred, the French-Canuck from Maine, and several others. The section foreman, an Irishman, took our slips and our names. More men came to the toolhouse until about twenty-five were there.

Two straw bosses took immediate charge of us. One was a Negro, the other an Italian, Bennie.

At seven o'clock we were given large forks. We spread out along the tracks and sifted gravel from the dirt. We threw the gravel between the ties.

The heavens were kind to us. It clouded over. Splotches of rain fell. Then it poured. We began to grumble about working in the rain. The foreman's whistle called us to the toolhouse. We dropped our forks and ran.

Several men built a blazing fire in an old dilapidated stove. Others played poker. Most of us slept.

When the rain stopped we went back to work. Sometimes it stopped only long enough for us to get out to where we were working.

At twelve o'clock we ate dinner. The meat in the sandwiches was green. The cheese was rancid.

At twelve-thirty we went back to work. The Negro straw boss took ten of us down the track. We worked with picks, raising the tracks and tamping stones beneath the ties. It was back-breaking work. After twenty minutes I had to stand up to stretch.

At four-thirty we quit. We put our tools in the toolhouse, then walked the half-mile to the camp. My back was stiff. Blisters were on my hands. Worst of all was the hunger gnawing at my stomach, which seemed to have shrunk to nothing.

We sat around talking until the gong sounded for supper. There were many young fellows there. Andy, who had left his wife and lost a fine job through drink, Paddy, Scotty, Jerry—all young, knocking about from job to job. The end of a job was the signal for a carouse.

Sunday was boiling-up day. Men put their clothes in a big can and boiled the lice and dirt from them. The dead lice would float on the surface to be later thrown out.

It was the tenth of July, payday. The sun was beating down upon us. The men who were quitting that day loafed on their picks. The sweat, dried on our clothes, was white. It stood out like blisters on our red faces. The water boy, a lad of fifteen, kept busy running to a farmhouse a quarter of a mile away. We drank huge dippers of cold water and got cramps.

Construction workers favored plain water in 1868,
red wine in the 1920s.

The Negro sat farther up the track. When he saw a train coming he would blow a whistle and call to us. We would stand along the track. The breeze from the train cooled us, but the dust filled our eyes and mouths.

We quit work ten minutes early on payday. The men went to the ramshackle station for their checks. The pay was forty cents an hour, or $3.60 a day. The commissary bill was also taken from the check.

I didn't get a check. Next payday, July 25, I would have one. I had been working only five days. The railroad held back two weeks' pay from each man.

Payday usually saw a wild night. Many men would go to New Brunswick, where a man could get all the comforts he craved.

After supper poker games started, seven or eight in a game. A crap game began on the platform of a freight house. Only a few hours of playing and some men would be without a cent—two weeks' wages.

The camp seemed deserted that night. Only those wanting to get a stake or, like myself, newcomers, were in the camp. Old Gordon, one of the men in the same gang as I, treated me to some ice cream and a cigar.

When I turned in, many of the bunks were empty. Near one o'clock, I awoke. The single electric light in the middle of the car was lit. It cast dull light between the tiers of bunks. Two men were wrestling. They were Scotty and Paddy, both good friends of mine. Several others yelled, "Fer Christ's sake, cut out the racket." But Scotty and Paddy wrestled on.

Tiring at last, they picked up a gallon jug from the floor, half full of wine. Their procession down the car was followed by yells. Before their friends they stopped. Paddy woke the sleeper, Scotty offered the bottle. A long drink from the bottle shook the sleep from my eyes.

In two days the camp was back to normal. New faces took the place of those that had gone. Among the crowd of newcomers were two young fellows. One was a boxer. He brought gloves, bandages, headguard, and a victrola. He came to the camp to toughen up. He was a Cuban. I have since seen his picture in fight magazines as a promising fighter.

I have been interested in boxing for many years and have had some fights in the ring, so naturally I gravitated toward these two. They were glad to have another fellow to box. The first night we were to meet, the whole camp turned out to watch. It was about eight o'clock. Men sat on boxes, ties, and the tracks, watching us. The three of us were dressed in tights. The Cuban and I put on the gloves. I had seven pounds advantage in weight.

We boxed three rounds. I held my own.

There was a great deal of work to be done about the station. The ties at the switches needed tamping.

Our gang joined Bennie's gang to do the work. Sam, another straw boss and a brother to Bennie, brought his gang to help. None of the men liked Bennie. He tried to make them work harder than the other bosses did. When a man leaned on his pick for a moment to rest, Bennie would come rushing toward him, screaming broken English.

One day we were straightening the tracks. We had crowbars which we put under the track. At a signal we would all heave together, straightening the tracks an inch at a time. The sweat poured down our faces in the sun, burning our eyes and putting us in a savage humor.

Another fellow and I were heaving on a big bar together. The bar had been in a fire that had taken the temper from the steel. It bent easily.

"Hey, Bennie," I yelled, "look how we're bendin' this bar. I bet we're doin' all the work."

Bennie came over and looked at the bar. He ran his finger over the rusty steel. "No," he said. "You no bend da bar. It no good."

I laughed scornfully. "We're stronger," I said.

"What, you tink you stronger?" Bennie cried, all excited.

"Sure."

The men stood about, grinning, hoping for a fight. Two leaned from the open windows of the signal tower, listening.

This was too much for Bennie. "Aw right, you tink you strong, eh? Then you come tomorra mornin' early an' we see who carry the tie the mos'."

"G'wan," I answered. "There's other ways of showin' your strength."

"How you mean, eh?"

"Oh, by jumpin' around for a few minutes." I made a pass at any imaginary opponent.

"You wanta fight?"

"Yes, I do."

"Aw right, you come over da field." Bennie turned and ran around the corner of the signal tower, away from the tracks.

I followed, running around the corner where Bennie had disappeared. I ran up the embankment—and stopped short.

There was a path through the waist-high hedge. Bennie stood there, blocking my way into the field—his knife, a bright six-inch blade, in one hand, a rock, half the size of my head, in the other.

"You dirty wop!"

Bennie laughed. "C'mon an' fight, you son of a ———."

I kicked, trying to hit the hand that held the knife with my heavy boot. He jumped back, grinning, taunting me with words.

One of the other bosses came near. "Yuh might as well come back. Yuh can't do anythin' while he's got that knife."

I turned, reluctantly. Bennie followed, closing his knife.

"I'll get that guy some time before he has a chance to draw that knife," I boasted.

Feeling ran high among the men. Many advised me to report him to the police. Others told me to get him when he was going home, when he was off railroad property.

There was one fellow in Sam's gang whom I came to know well, by name Mulvaney. Every night after supper, Mulvaney and another fellow took a bucket of swill to Sam's house. Their reward was a quart of wine. Sam gave the swill to his pigs.

Mulvaney asked me to come with him one night. There were six of us.

Sam's house was a quarter of a mile down the tracks. It was a dirty house surrounded by grape arbors. His kids were dirty, but his garden was weedless.

Sam showed us his garden. We took the hint from Mulvaney and praised it—the size of his watermelons, his corn.

We spent an hour commending Sam on his garden. Several of us began looking inquiringly at Mulvaney. Then we sat down under the grape arbor. Mulvaney leaned over to Sam and spoke low. "Sam, let's have our quart now an' give us an extra one. We'll pay you payday."

"Sure, I sell you." Sam wasn't like his brother, Bennie.

One of Sam's restless brood of kids set cups before us. Sam put two quart jars of dago red on the table.

Two rounds and the quart bottles were empty.

The wine sent delightful shivers over me. I looked at Mulvaney. He spoke to Sam. Another bottle was set before us.

We had six bottles.

We stumbled back over the tracks, falling over the rails, tripping over the ties. No trains came along. Singing snatches of ribald songs, we came into camp. Men yelled to us to shut up.

One of the fellows suggested that I sleep in their room. I agreed. I rolled down the aisle to my bunk, talking, swearing, and left the car with my mattress rolled up in my arms.

We sang and talked until early morning.

There were many young girls in town. In the evening, when walking, we would try to pick them up. The girls ignored us—rigidly. We often felt the need for their companionship.

Slim came to me one day and asked if I would care to quit and go to the wheat-fields. I was sick of the tracks and agreed.

It would cost forty-five dollars to get Slim's car out of the garage in Baltimore. We were to pool our money and pay for the car. Then we would go to Canada, for the wheat-fields.

Five of us were going—an English fellow who had been to Canada before; Jim, an Italian gambler from Philadelphia; Andy, Slim, and myself. We spent several delightful days figuring up the money due us. Then Andy, tiring of Slim's loud talking, threatened to beat him up. Two days later Slim and I began calling each other names while lying in our bunks. We almost fought.

Payday came, the day we were going to quit. That night a big crap game started. Slim and Jim cleaned up more than a hundred dollars. Next day they left.

Others left too. Andy and Jerry disappeared. Three days later Jerry came back, without a cent and with a big head.

A few days later, Mulvaney and several others in our room quit. I missed them. New men came to the camp. Two fellows came to our car. One was small, a southerner. The other man was big and good-looking in a rugged sort of a way. He had deserted the army three weeks before after a year's service. He used an assumed name. Three days later he and the southerner hopped a freight train going west. Four or five new men came in, fresh from the Bowery.

Apples and other fruit were ripening. We would take trips after supper and on Sundays and come back with our shirts and pockets full. On Labor Day, my birthday, all of us in our car got corn and apples. Dutch and I built a fire. We heated a huge can filled with water. Frenchy threw the husked corn in. I took pictures of the men eating corn.

I went on nightly forays to neighboring gardens. There was one garden where I was sure of getting at least two tomatoes. Green peaches gave me cramps.

September 5 was hot. I felt disgusted. At noontime I went to the toolhouse, looking for the section foreman.

"I'd like to get my time today," I said.

"Get your board bill," he answered.

That night in camp, my last, I packed my few clothes. Frenchy gave me his name. I was to send him the pictures taken on Labor Day.

My last night in camp I felt somewhat softened. Forgotten were the hot days spent in the sun.

Next morning I ate breakfast in the mess hall. My train was due at a quarter to seven. I stood on the station platform. Men passed by going to work. I shook hands with many.

My train pulled in. Dutch and several others were on the platform.

"I'll see yuh on the Bowery," I called from the steps.

I went inside. I leaned from an open window. I waved my hat to others walking to work. Frenchy was trudging along to work across the tracks. I called. He waved, yelling something. The train was moving.

"Wha'd yuh say?" I called.

"Don't fergit the pictures," answered Frenchy.

"Sure, you'll get 'em," I answered.

I kept my promise.

—From "I Was Workin' on the Railroad," by Eric Sonnichsen, in the *American Mercury*, June, 1930. Copyright 1930 by the *American Mercury*.

CHAPTER TWELVE

Certainty, Security, and Celerity

I

*"On a cold, stormy winter night, it is no joke
to serve these small way stations with the mail."*

A FEW YEARS BEFORE the Civil War, the postmaster in Ontonogan, a village in northwestern Michigan, opened a freshly arrived sack of mail and found that a pair of mice in a labeled package had increased to a family of six while en route from Chicago, some three hundred miles away. According to the quaint but unreliable folklore of the Railway Mail Service, a letter of complaint from this postmaster caused George B. Armstrong of the Chicago office to think up the traveling post office car.

In any case, *something* started Armstrong thinking about how to speed up the distribution of mail, for he is generally given credit for having devised the system of sorting mail in transit that has been used in the United States for more than a century. Armstrong, who was a professional post office clerk and a distant relative of President James Buchanan, perfected his innovative ideas while struggling to administer an overloaded mail depot at Cairo, Illinois, during the War Between the States, and he paid the expenses of the first trial run of a post office on wheels between Chicago and Clinton, Iowa, on August 28, 1864. His name adorns a school in Chicago, his statue ornaments a post office there, and the date of his experiment is taken as the official birthdate of the Railway Mail Service, which has been known since 1949 as the Postal Transportation Service.

Armstrong's trial run on the Chicago & Northwestern line was by no means the first time the U.S. mail had gone by train. The government started shipping pouches of letters on railroads as early as 1834, and in 1838 Congress declared all railroads to be postal routes. "Traveling agents" of the Post Office

Department rode aboard government-built mail storage cars on the Washington-Philadelphia run, the Philadelphia–New York run, the New York–Boston run, and the Boston-Springfield run. These agents even did some minor shuffling of through and local mail; but the United States inexplicably failed to adopt methods that were in use in Great Britain to hasten the collection and distribution of letters at railway terminals. In the 1850's the delivery of a letter from Maine to Florida generally took two weeks.

Just before the Civil War began, the Post Office Department took some steps to improve service between North and South. These steps consisted simply of paying certain railroads to run mail trains from New York to Boston to carry southern mails without the usual overnight layover in New York. But the only in-transit sorting before Armstrong's scheme was the work of William A. Davis, a postal clerk in St. Joseph, Missouri. Davis would deadhead east on the Hannibal & St. Joseph Railroad as far as Palmyra, Missouri, board there the westbound mail car, open the brass-bound mail sacks, take out the California mail, and have the Pacific Coast pouches all sorted and bundled, ready for the pony express, when the train got to the distributing post office in St. Joseph. Since all this happened in mid-1862, there is a small school of historical interpretation which holds that Davis, rather than Armstrong, should be called the Father of the Post Office Car, if anyone is going to be called that. But the fact is that Armstrong suggested and executed a complete and permanent change in the sorting and carrying of the mail throughout the country.

To try out Armstrong's ideas, the Chicago & Northwestern remodeled a mail agent's car, installing several banks of letter cases with seventy-seven pigeonholes in each bank. A select group of letter-sorters and newspaper-flingers, and a cluster of businessmen and reporters got aboard to ride as far as Dixon, Illinois. Among the press representatives was Joseph Medill, the editor of the Chicago *Tribune,* who opined: "Why, Mr. Armstrong, your plan is the craziest idea I ever heard of in regard to mail distribution. If it were to be generally accepted by the Post Office Department, the government would have to employ a regiment of soldiers to pick up the letters that would blow out of the train."

Three days later, Armstrong's car began regular service on the Chicago-Clinton line. In October the Armstrong plan was tried on the New York–Washington route, and by the end of the year, traveling post office cars were operating on two more routes out of Chicago. Joseph Medill amended his comments and became an enthusiast of the post office on wheels.

When a correspondent for *Scribner's Monthly* boarded the Buffalo-Chicago mail eight years later to take notes for an anonymous report on the inner workings of a sorting car, the Railway Mail Service, which Armstrong headed until shortly before his death in 1871, had grown to fifty-seven lines,

*The station master's daughter, braving the danger of being
clobbered by an extended catching-hook, waited at a
western flag stop for the traveling post office.*

Harper's Weekly, 1875

covering more than fourteen thousand miles and employing 650 clerks. Postal cars were rolling more than twelve million miles a year, snatching up, sorting out, and flinging back mail all the way.

T HE WESTERN MAIL TRAIN leaves Buffalo at twenty minutes past twelve noon. Early in the morning, the railway post office clerks assemble at the city post office, where each head clerk (there are usually three clerks on a postal car—one head clerk and two assistants) receives the registered matter for points along his route.

The head clerk receipts for his registered packages—say two hundred in number—locks them safely in a pouch, and is impatiently waiting for a signal to leave. Soon the cry is sounded: "Chicago—all aboard!" Three or four clerks who are to make the journey pick up their traps, consisting of post office directories, maps, schedules of distribution, tags and labels, working clothes, blankets, lunch baskets, and so forth, and jump into the mail wagon, which is loaded to its utmost capacity with leather bags and iron-bound wooden boxes.

A fine pair of sorrels hastens us to the depot. Here a substantial but somewhat dingy car with the words U.S. RAILWAY POST OFFICE painted in large letters on the side is awaiting our arrival. We shall spend many hours in this sorting-room on wheels, long enough to get a perfect idea of the sort of work performed by the railway postal service.

We have singled out this line—the Lake Shore & Michigan Southern Railroad from Buffalo to Chicago—because it forms the highway, so to speak, over which the bulk of our western mails is transported. On this route, railway postal service is performed twice a day, and the number of letters handled on each trip of the postal car averages from fifty to sixty thousand. This makes about one hundred thousand letters for the round trip or two hundred thousand per day handled and distributed on this route alone.

Newspaper mail is quite a separate feature, averaging about three tons a day. Toward the middle of each month, when magazines are published and sent to mail subscribers throughout the country, the newspaper and package mail often reaches the enormous quantity of ten tons on a single trip. Wednesdays and Fridays, when the leading weeklies are issued, are also heavy days on the postal cars.

The post office cars used on this route show marks of rough service and are not the dainty, elegant coaches I have seen on some of the western lines.

(On the western lines, we meet the modern postal car in all its glory of fine upholstery, varnish, and gold leaf. One specimen that I saw on the Central Pacific Railroad at Ogden might justly have been called a palace postal car. It was built in the company's shops at Sacramento, California, under the advice of Messrs. Barstow and Alexander of the Post Office Department, and constructed in a very ingenious manner to economize space. It was bedroom, parlor, dining room and workroom combined. One end was taken up by a semicircle of large pigeonholes for newspapers and packages, each of which bore a label with the name of a station on the route. At the opposite end were a number of smaller receptacles for letters, all arranged in a certain order and labeled with the names of stations and connecting routes. In the middle was an apartment for the clerks, with washstand, wardrobe, beds, a table, chairs, and other conveniences, not unlike the cabin of a vessel. There was also a place where a cooking stove could be arranged for the convenience of the clerks, if they desired to keep their own menage. The remaining portion of the car was set apart as storeroom for through mail from San Francisco to Ogden and farther east, or vice versa, which does not require sorting on the road.)

On the Lake Shore line, however, postal cars are constructed with a view to hard work and durability, for they must resist the wear and tear of a speed of from thirty to sixty miles an hour, next to the engine and tender, and the concussion of numerous "catchings."

Arriving at our appointed car, our wagon is backed up to the door; the bags, pouches, and boxes composing our load are rapidly piled in; the clerks and ourselves jump after, and business commences in earnest. Such luxuries as hats, coats, and vests are dispensed with. Sleeves are rolled up. Leather pouches and canvas bags (the latter containing newspaper mail) fly about in all directions. The "through" sacks and pouches are piled up in one end of the car, while the matter for distribution along the road is stacked up in the working room in the fore and middle part of the car.

While all this is going on, we ensconce ourselves in a corner by the stove. Here, we are out of the way, and at the same time have a good view over the field of operations.

The head clerk commences by unlocking a pouch and dumping its contents —six or seven thousand letters, all tied up in packages of eighty to one hundred or more—out upon the floor. He picks up an armful, places them edgewise on the shelf in front of him, cuts open the strings holding them together, and squares himself for further operations, sorting the letters with a degree of dexterity that fairly astounds us. While the head clerk is thus engaged, one of his assistants has emptied out another leather pouch and is engaged in distributing the contents of this in a smaller case of pigeonholes on the side of the car, adjacent to the newspaper case. This is the "way mail," destined for delivery at points along the route. "Direct packages" are made up for all the stations along the line and also for connecting lines to points off the main-line track. Nearly every prominent station on our line forms a distributing post office for numerous smaller offices adjacent. The other assistant, who glories in the technical appellation of "paper jerker," is distributing the bulky newspaper mail in the other end of the car. He fires away at tiers of labeled boxes all around him, seldom missing his aim or "jerking" a paper into the wrong box.

Bags and pouches are rapidly thinning out. Others, filled with the sorted matter, are being locked, tagged, and dragged into the "through" room, ready for delivery at the larger stations. Indeed, we think the work is well-nigh over when a heavy pounding on the door attracts our attention. There is a wagon outside, loaded to the top and backing up against our car. The door is opened, and we are again flooded with mailbags and pouches, upwards of a hundred. This is the late New York mail, by the Erie road. The horses attached to the wagon are steaming and foaming. *Bump, bump!* In come the pouches, helter-skelter, one on top of the other. *Bang* goes the door. The receipt for registered matter is handed out through an open window. The gong sounds. In a moment, by some unseen agency, our car is attached to the train with a thud that nearly throws us off our feet. The bell rings; passengers are running to and fro on the platform; the whistle shrieks; a jerk, a grating, jarring noise, and we are off, slowly moving out of the depot, at exactly twenty minutes past noon, on our way to Chicago and intermediate stations.

Clap, clap, clap—how it jars and rattles as we rush along at thirty miles an hour! Two pouches already have been made up for delivery at Angola and Silver Creek—the two first stations on the road. As we dash past the depot at Angola, a bag is thrown off and another is caught without stopping. This is quickly opened and has been assorted long before the bell rings and we hear the brakemen shouting in the passenger cars: "Silver Creek!"

The mail for this place, once quite bulky, has dwindled down to a single pouch of rather slim proportions, and the bag that we receive in exchange is slimmer still. We stop only about two minutes and then are off again at a rattling rate, tearing along the shores of Lake Erie.

At Dunkirk, forty miles from Buffalo, we stop for five minutes and receive fifty or sixty additional bags of mail matter. "Dunkirk—all aboard!" shouts our head clerk. A letter pouch, quickly closed and locked, is thrown off, followed by two canvas bags of newspaper mail for Dunkirk City. In another minute, two more bags are made up, closed, and labeled for the Buffalo, Corry, and Pittsburgh line, which connects here. These are pushed off the car just as we are moving out of Dunkirk station.

Station follows station, but we do not stop, this being the through mail, or express train. Bags are thrown off at some places, and pouches are caught with a sudden jerk as we fly past. The interior of our car presents a more confused aspect than ever. The clerks, working in their shirt sleeves, scarcely speak a word. Bags and pouches are opened, emptied, distributed, with wonderful dispatch. The paper jerker is desperately battling with a veritable avalanche of newspapers and magazines.

The catcher now used by the Railway Mail Service is known as "Ward's catcher." It is remarkable chiefly for its simplicity and effectiveness. It operates in conjunction with a crane, on which the postmaster of a way station suspends the outgoing pouch shortly before the train is due. An apparatus attached to the postal car catches hold of the pouch and swings it aboard the train. The catcher consists simply of a large, two-pronged iron fork with one arm considerably longer than the other. The shorter arm is attached to the side of the car, just outside the door. When the catcher is not in use, both arms are placed against the side of the car. When it is ready for use, the operator turns a lever, causing the longer arm to project forward from the side of the car at an acute angle. This outthrust arm catches the pouch; then, the operator pulls the lever and relieves the pouch from the iron grasp of the catcher.

The apparatus seldom fails to do its work effectively; but great care and circumspection are necessary to be certain that nothing except a crane is in the way. It happens occasionally on dark and stormy nights that the catcher is thrust out at the wrong time, and very undesirable and embarrassing objects have been caught, such as telegraph poles, lamp posts, or switch lights. One of two things inevitably follows such a mishap. Either the catcher and appurtenances, including door, windows and sometimes a large portion of the solid woodwork of the car, are torn away; or some incongruous and occasionally injurious article suddenly enters the car.

While the mail train thundered toward Chicago,
things got dreadfully untidy inside the postal car.

To prevent accidents of this kind, the engineer always blows his whistle in a peculiar manner when approaching a catch station. Upon this signal the catcher is let down. If everything is all right, and properly timed, a mail pouch is the result.

The bag with the mail for the station is simply thrown through the open door while the train is passing. This operation is, to all appearances, simple enough; but, like catching, it requires considerable skill and not a little physical force. The pouch must be thrown just at the proper time. A few moments too soon or too late will leave it on the ground a considerable distance from the station. It must be thrown with force against the wind—otherwise, it will be blown under the cars and ruined.

On a cold, stormy winter night, it is no joke to serve these small way stations with the mail. At every opening of the door (and the catcher cannot be operated, nor can the way mail be delivered, unless the door is wide open) an avalanche of snow and icy sleet comes rushing in. The force of the wind, with the train running from fifty to sixty miles an hour, is terrific, and one must have a good, firm grip at the iron bars at the side of the door when leaning out to see how far we are from the station. Presently there comes a short, hoarse shriek from the locomotive. The door is thrown all the way back, the catcher quickly let down— *thud!*—a slight shock, and *bang* goes the door again, shutting out the wind and snow, while the pouch that has just come aboard is being rapidly unlocked. By the time this is done, the bag we threw off has been picked up by the messenger in waiting and is in all probability on its way to the country post office.

This American system of catching and delivery, notwithstanding its drawbacks, is an improvement on the system used in England. British postal cars have a net attached to the side, which, by some complicated mechanism, is supposed to open out and catch the mailbags at stations where the train does not stop. While the American catcher sometimes grabs too much, the English mechanism, it is said, often misses the mark entirely. For this reason it is being gradually abandoned, and other systems, more or less like our own, are being introduced. In India, the American system has been exactly copied; and it is now being introduced on the Australian railroads.

Arriving at Cleveland at seven in the evening, we stop twenty minutes for supper. Hastily the clerks throw on their coats. Before the train has come to a full stop, two of them may be seen at the bar of the restaurant, devouring cold ham, sausage, and pie at a terrific rate. Soon the gong sounds again, the bell rings, the conductor shouts "All aboard!" and off we go once more, the clerks busy at work opening a dozen or more new pouches taken on board at this point.

It is almost midnight when we reach Toledo. The three postal clerks with whom we made the journey all the way from Buffalo bid us good-bye, and another set comes aboard to take their places. All through the night, the work continues. Every once in a while a mail pouch is caught and another thrown off; but the stops are few and far between, and we tear along through dark pine forests where snow and hoarfrost glitter on the branches, illuminated by showers of sparks from the engine. The clerks courteously offer us the use of their berths. While they are at work, we retire and try to sleep; but all the time we are aware of our peculiar situation, and we hear the thud and jar of every catch.

As morning dawns, we approach Chicago. The clerks pack up their traps and prepare to deliver the last of their way mail and the pouches, bags, and boxes which have been stowed away in the "through" room. Precisely at a quarter of nine, we enter the depot in Chicago. Our journey in a railway post office is at an end.

—Excerpted from "Our Postal-Car Service,"
Scribner's Monthly, June, 1873.

II

"You can throw your watch in the clothes box now. You won't want it tonight."

THE PROFESSED GOALS of the Railway Mail Service were "Certainty, Security, Celerity," but the performance in the early years seldom came up to the mark. Consider the frustrations endured by George S. Bangs, Armstrong's successor as superintendent of the RMS. Bangs wanted to start a high-speed route between New York and Chicago. He urged William H. Vanderbilt, the vice president of the system then known as the "New York Central & Hudson River Railroad," to build the necessary new mail cars in return for an exclusive contract to carry virtually all mail in and out of New York City; and Vanderbilt agreed to the arrangement, despite the opposition of his aged father, Commodore Cornelius Vanderbilt, who shook his head and muttered: "If you want to do this, go ahead, but I know the Post Office Department, and you will, too, within a year."

The first "Fast Mail," consisting of four graceful new cars, painted white, stylishly trimmed with gilt and ivory, and named for the governors of four states along the route, left Grand Central Station on September 16, 1875, loaded with a festive cargo of deadheading newspaper reporters, mayors, postmasters, and other appropriate public personages. The Fast Mail was a dazzling critical and technical success. Apparently, the only objection anyone raised was that the train went *too* fast: the clerks hadn't time to sort the mail for post offices between New York and Poughkeepsie. Even this complaint died out after Bangs had two hundred sacks for close-in mail dyed red so that the clerks could pick out and sort them first.

But you know the government. Three weeks after the Fast Mail started, somebody in Washington ordered the mail for three states to be taken away from the New York Central and given to another railroad. Then a clerk of the second assistant postmaster general disallowed the dyer's bill for color-coding two hundred mailbags and sent Bangs a letter suggesting that such expenditures would be unnecessary if mail clerks would do their work properly. Bangs exploded all over the intradepartmental chain of command.

"Do you know the man who wrote this letter?" he shouted. "He is a wheezy priest, a fool, and a Baptist, at that!" (Bangs was wrong. The man was not a Baptist.)

Eventually, the dyer got paid. Vanderbilt's Fast Mail rolled, and the Pennsylvania Railroad began a similar service. But the following year, Congress cut back the rate of pay to trunk lines carrying mail, and the railroads retaliated by dropping the Fast Mail. By this time, the younger Vanderbilt presumably understood what the old Commodore meant about the P.O.

In time the Fast Mail was reestablished. It became a rich source of revenue to the railroads and an abundant treasury of romantic lore to the readers of dime novels. Even the long, silent routes through the lightly populated prairies west of Chicago began to produce a handsome return for the transcontinental lines. When the Post Office Department, toward the close of the nineteenth century, ordered the railroads to cut thirteen hours off the time between the Atlantic and Pacific coasts, the Chicago & Northwestern Railroad challenged the Burlington Route to an informal contest for the mail contract. If the Burlington, which held the existing contract, should fail to keep the new schedule, the C&NW would demand the prize for itself.

The editors of *Harper's Weekly,* learning of the rivalry, sent Cy Warman, the country's best-known writer of railroad stories, out to Chicago to ride the Burlington locomotive in the "great transcontinental mail race of January 2, 1899."

ALL DAY THE DRIVER of the black flier that was to take the Fast Mail out of Chicago worked about the big machine, going underneath, coming out of the pit, and working round and round. Every nut and bolt from the pilot to the tail was tightened or tested. There was not a spot upon her blue-black jacket that the fireman did not dust a dozen times; and then the wipers came, squatted on their waste boxes, and wiped her wheels and links and rocker arms.

The coal tender had been emptied and refilled with fresh fuel; the water tank had been washed out; and all the feed pipes and air pipes had been cleaned and tested.

When night came, the driver wiped his hands on a piece of soft wool waste and went away to supper. The night shift came and lighted lamps all about the black racer, and a watchman walked up and down, never losing sight of the engine. It was not that one railroad feared sabotage by the other; but there are always dangerous men around who may have been discharged for incompetency, or have a grudge against an official, or be jealous of the crew. A man could steal up to the side of an engine, loosen a set screw, and with a single blow of a copper hammer that could not be heard a hundred feet, send a key wedge so tight that

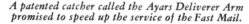

*A patented catcher called the Ayars Deliverer Arm
promised to speed up the service of the Fast Mail.*

Scientific American, 1897

the pin would be ablaze in the first five minutes out of the roundhouse. A small bit of soap in the feed hose could make the engine froth and sputter and lose the race that means more than a million to the management.

At eight o'clock the driver came back, threw the stub of a cigar into the pit, and put on his overclothes. The fireman was already in the cab. The driver touched the throttle, and the big racer stirred and moved slowly out of her stall. A moment later, she swung majestically around on the table, just as a great ship turns in a wide harbor, stopped, and backed away to meet her train.

Far back along the Lake Shore line, another engine was rushing westward toward Chicago. At noon, Superintendent Lewis L. Troy of the Railway Mail Service had called to say that the Lake Shore was running an hour and a half late. By 4:00 P.M., she was only thirty minutes late. At nine o'clock, it was down to fifteen minutes, and the Burlington officials agreed to wait.

But the Lake Shore was not fifteen minutes late; she came to a stop two minutes ahead of time. Hundreds of mailbags hurtled out into eighteen waiting wagons, and the horses left the station at a gallop, headed through downtown Chicago to the Burlington station. By the time the Burlington's black racer backed up to her train, most of the mail had been loaded, and a Pennsylvania Fast Mail had come in with sacks from Baltimore, Pittsburgh, Washington, and Philadelphia to increase the turmoil.

In an incredibly short time, the mail trucks were cleared and the signal was given. At 9:25 the wheels of our big black Baldwin began to turn.

A crowd had gathered to see the start. They cheered and waved their hats as the train pulled out. The rail was slippery from the constant dripping of over-oiled yard engines, and it was not until after we had passed the last crossing and left the lights of the city behind us that she was able to grip the rail.

"You can throw your watch in the clothes box now," said the master mechanic to the engineer. "You won't want it tonight." That meant he could go as fast as the wheels would turn. The driver held onto his watch.

We began to pick up speed. The sound of the big engine passed the *get-cher-bag-gage, get-cher-bag-gage* point, and the stack began to flutter incoherently. The general manager, who stood just behind me, shouted in my ear: "Thirty-eight miles, forty-two minutes!" We had made two full stops at crossings, but we were passing Aurora on time.

Well, it did not *seem* fast. A seven-foot wheel is deceiving. Its revolutions come as fast as a Frenchman can say, "zip, zip, zip, zip," and at each revolution she goes three feet farther than a six-foot wheel will go.

Burlington locomotives take water from standpipes and tanks along the way. At Mendota the driver closed the throttle. Amid a smell of brimstone, 130,000 pounds of steel and coal and water ground to a stop within one train-length. While the brakeman was filling the tank, the engineer and the fireman, each with a blazing torch in hand, darted around the engine, dropping a little oil here and there. In a few moments we were off again.

During the run to Galesburg, 163 miles out, the driver was actually killing time; but at Galesburg the general manager showed his good judgment by going to the rear. A handsome young man with less judgment and a sketching pad came and stood behind me in the cab. He would make sketches of the train crew as they worked.

In three minutes the young artist became uneasy; in four minutes he had shoved his apparatus between the waste box and the wall; and a moment later he was hanging on for dear life. Burlington, the next stop, lay at the foot of a forty-mile slope, and the driver had decided to give the deadheads a whirl for their money. A mile a minute on straight track is all right—but when you begin to hit curves and reverse curves at sixty-five and above, it is hard on the nerves. You find yourself straining until your sides ache to help hold the engine on the rail. First she goes around the curve, apparently on one rail; then, when she finds the tangent, you get another shock.

The artist kept asking me to guess how fast she was going. He had heard some prediction that we would hit ninety before we reached the Mississippi River. "Isn't that ninety?" he would ask; but I had neither the nerve nor voice to answer. On she went like a Kansas cyclone, swinging over culverts and bridges, turning now right, now left, following the bend of the low bluffs. The driver played with danger like a man who is unhappily married. The artist grabbed my arm again. "Now?" he asked. I nodded emphatically.

Presently, with a wild shriek, we shot out upon the long bridge. A moment later we were beyond the river and into the real West. My companion stole out of the car and into one of Uncle Sam's letter wagons.

Burlington is 206 miles and (on this run) four hours west of Chicago. The engine crew that had brought us the entire distance had earned their wages quickly, but, as the general manager observed, had earned them well. We said good-bye to them and took on another engine with a wheel four inches smaller. She moved a foot less at each *zip-zip* than did the other, but her zips came closer together. In a little while the rail was rushing beneath her throbbing throat like a swiftly running river.

The pale remnant of a moon, worn as thin as an old brake shoe, came out of the east and shone along the cold steel. I began to nod, for it was past midnight; but this engine soon began to roll just as the other had done. The cab window slammed up against my head, and immediately I was wide awake. The farther west we got, the harder these drivers hit the curves! The general manager said this driver had been on the Fast Mail a dozen years, but I should not care to hazard a guess that he will be there twelve years more, if he keeps up this gait. At one flag station, where we were four minutes ahead, we lost eleven minutes cooling a hot hub on the letter wagon. That left us seven minutes late, and seven minutes afterward the driver, having relighted his cigar stub, was swinging us around curves that were never meant to be used that way. There was a steady roar from the stack, a wild cry. The black flier leaped and rolled and plunged. The bell, driven by steam, hiccoughed and stammered until someone reached over and shut it off. As the green and white lights of a small station brushed past our windows, the driver yelled over the boiler head at me: "On time!" In twenty-six minutes we had made up seven minutes. We dashed into Creston, Iowa, two minutes before we were expected.

A fresh engine again, but it slipped and fretted. The driver touched the three-way cock to see that the air was off and opened the sand valve once or twice to drop sand on the frosty steel. Immediately we could feel the fine gravel crushing beneath her wheels, felt her lifting the train, with the west wind pushing hard against the cab; and we pulled our heads inside. But the steel was cold and hard and glassy in the January night, and now and again the engine would begin to slide. Her wheels would whirl so furiously that the driver dared not hold his throttle wide. The moment she slipped, he would grip the lever to help her if she failed to catch herself. At the same instant, a faithful fireman would open the furnace door to prevent her tearing holes in her fire and pasting her flue sheet with the molten fuel, which bubbled like black strap molasses inside the white-hot firebox.

Always, above the roaring of the wheels, you could hear the low burr of the injector, which was throwing thirty-five gallons of water a minute into the big boiler to cool her burning thirst. At times I would also hear the singing of the lefthand injector, which chirped in my ear precisely as a locust sings on a tree twig close beside your head.

More curves now, and reverse curves, and we are face to face with eternity. It seems impossible for her to hold the rail! For the first time in my life, I feel every hair on my head tingle at the roots; and then I hear the sweetest music that has ever smote my ear: the hiss of the three-way air cock as this daredevil lets off pressure and clamps the brake shoes to wheels that are whirling at a mile and a half a minute. *Sssss . . .*

Ah, that did me good! The driver, too, had felt her tremble, slam, and wrestle with a curve that was scarcely perceptible to the eye. It was a curve that would not even have been noticed by a passenger on board the Denver Limited,

*Catching the pouch (left) and sorting its contents
occupied clerks on the Lake Shore Railroad.*

Scribner's Monthly, 1873

but at this speed it became a curve so wicked and severe that it froze my blood. The driver saw that she had reached the limit, and he began to steady her. The clamp of the brake shoes brought her down to a smooth gait, and she trembled away through the night, with passenger trains, long creeping freight trains, and sleeping villages brushing past like ghosts.

Away out there in the dawn lies a long, gray line of fog, marking the trail of the Missouri. With a triumphant cry the big machine relaxes, slows down, and stops and stands quite still. Only the air pump, breathing softly, and the flutter of steam from the dome, and the burr of the injector cooling off the boiler show that she still lives. I feel like pulling out the pin and letting her go leisurely down and cool her feet in the Big Water. We have made a half-thousand miles in a little over ten hours, and that is not bad.

In the middle of the afternoon the Union Pacific Fast Mail, eastbound, comes over the long bridge and lays her cars, gray with the dust of Utah, Wyoming, and Nebraska, alongside our train. Deftly as a shell-man shifting the pea under the walnut hull, the handlers transfer the eastbound mail into our empty cars. At 3:55 we begin the long race back again.

The eastbound time is thirty minutes shorter than our schedule going west. We put the towns behind us as if the matter had been arranged by time card. Hour after hour, the general manager, the general superintendent, the master mechanic, and your correspondent sit watching the pointer on the speed recorder. It goes up and up and up, then down again, for even these fast trains do not ignore the small towns of the mid-continent. At almost every county seat we stop, pick up and discharge mail, take on water, change and oil engines. These stops take up so much time that on the runs between them, the pointer on the speed recorder has to play constantly around a mile a minute. East of Galesburg, when the indicator shows eighty miles an hour, the general manager and I try writing notes. They are not beautiful specimens of handwriting but are probably as good as either of us could do at our desks.

At 2:09 in the morning, when all the good people of Chicago are asleep, we slip into the great city, six minutes ahead of time.

Our Burlington Fast Mail has not been the only flier abroad tonight. A few miles to the north of our track, the Chicago & Northwestern's splendid locomotives, side by side and almost neck and neck, have raced us over this thousand-mile course. It is not a race to see who can go quicker from Chicago to the Missouri River and back; we have made the trip on time and so has our rival train, and that is as much as either of us has hoped to do. No one will really know the utmost limit of these black fliers, for that could only be determined by putting one of them into the ditch.

—Adapted from "The Black Fliers," by Cy Warman,
Harper's Weekly, January 21, 1899.

III

"If we are attacked ... there will be no use in using cipher."

IN THE RIPENESS OF ITS GLORY, before the advent of air mail (or "flypaper," as the railway mail clerks call it), the Railway Mail Service commanded a yearly volume of postal cars that would have reached, end to end, from Chicago to Kansas City. Practically every train carried a post office car; and there were many crack expresses, zipping along at eighty or ninety miles an hour, that carried nothing except mail.

Railroad postal routes rejoiced in whimsical, savory names: the "Thief and Crook," which ran from Thief River Falls to Crookston, Minnesota; the "Sin and Saint," between Cincinnati and St. Louis; the "Virginia Creeper," which slipped quietly through Arlington, Virginia, en route to Washington, D.C.; the Salt Lake City and Kanab, Utah, known as the "Polygamy Special"; the "Ketch and Show," from Ketchum to Shoshone, Idaho; the "Fish and Dirty Feet," from Salmon to Blackfoot, Idaho; the "Sowbelly," out of Kansas City; the "Tin Can," between Waco and Stamford, Texas; the "Kite," running from Albuquerque to Los Alamos, New Mexico. There were the "Galloping Goose," the "Leaky Roof," the "Macaroni," the "Old Man's Darling," the "Preacher," the "Pumpkinvine," the "Poor Boy," the "Rickety Bang," the "Pickle Vat," the "Wooden Axle," the "Dog House." *

And the clerks who followed these routes developed a racy slang within the vast and imaginative language of railroading: *nixie*—an unsortable, mis-addressed letter; *virgin*—a letter to be postmarked; *balloon*—a big sack of mail that expands hugely when dumped out; *bladders*—newspapers (German *blatter*); *sleeper*—an unnoticed letter left in the mail car.

For all its vitality, however, the Railway Mail Service was notorious for treating its employees with callous indifference. During the national impover-ishment of the early 1890's, railway mail clerks made their runs in cars built before the Civil War—rickety, unpainted, with wide glimpses of track and roadbed flashing through cracks in the floor. Sorters stood on piles of empty

---

*For an exhaustive list of these flavorful Americanisms, see Bryant Alden Long and William Jefferson Dennis, *Mail by Rail*, Simmons-Boardman, New York, 1951, p. 18 ff.

sacks and wore heavy overshoes to keep their feet warm. The temperature in the cars often fell below zero. Regulations for a time required that clerks save all bits of twine, knot them together, and reuse them. The employees on a route in Oregon sent their division superintendent a year's accumulation, rolled into a ball two feet in diameter. It was labeled: "First Annual Ball for the Benefit of Baled-Hay Widows and Unidentified Orphans."

When the Service was badly in need of favorable public notice, Superintendent James White received an unusual new assignment, which he described in his reminiscences published in 1910.

D URING THE EARLY YEARS of President Grover Cleveland's first administration, the United States slipped into a deep economic depression. Business was becoming more depressed daily; values were declining; and the financial outlook was overcast. The reserve of gold coin in the subtreasury at New York City gradually was reduced by shipments abroad and by redemption of gold certificates until in July, 1892, it totaled less than $43 million. The secretary of the treasury, with considerable anxiety, foresaw that this sum might prove insufficient to meet demands upon the government before the drift of business was reversed.

As a precaution, Secretary Charles Foster ordered the transfer of $20 million in gold coin from the subtreasury in San Francisco to the subtreasury in New York. For many years, it had been customary to send gold in amounts from $50,000 to $200,000 as registered mail from San Francisco to New York, enclosed in leather pouches, locked with brass locks, and sealed in rawhide trunks, and the secretary at first planned to follow this procedure, shipping a million dollars a day for twenty days. But his plan became known to the public and therefore had to be abandoned. After consulting his assistants, he held a conference with Postmaster General John Wanamaker as to the safest method of moving the entire sum in coin from one city to the other. As a result of this conference, I received the following letter:

> *Captain James E. White*
> > *Gen'l Supt. Railway Mail Service*
> SIR:
> > You will consider this as your authority to proceed to San Francisco, California, for the purpose of personally directing the movement by United States Mail, of a number of shipments of registered matter, particulars of which have already been furnished you.... Whatever details may occur to you as essential to the successful accomplishment of the service, you are hereby empowered to enforce. This office—by code—must be kept advised....
> > > Yours respectfully
> > > J. LOWRIE BELL
> > > *Second Assistant Postmaster General*

I left Washington on July 21, 1892, and made my first stop at Cleveland, Ohio, where I called on W. H. Canniff, general manager of the Lake Shore & Michigan Southern Railway, and had a confidential conversation with him respecting the trip to the Pacific Coast. The Lake Shore was asked to furnish one car to transport gold and guards eastward, also take care of all the treasury cars from the time they reached Chicago until transferred to the New York Central at Buffalo. Mr. Canniff agreed.

I had telegraphed Superintendents Lewis L. Troy, George W. Pepper, and Norman Perkins, of the Sixth, Ninth, and Tenth Postal divisions, to meet me at the Grand Pacific Hotel in Chicago on Saturday morning. They reported promptly and I explained the problem. To transport the coin from one coast to the other, five cars would be required, and that meant the detail of five officers and forty-five clerks. The officers, in addition to those present, would be Superintendents Samuel Flint of the Eighth Division and Assistant Superintendent Frank W. Vaille of Portland, Oregon. As for the clerks, great care must be exercised in making selections, with veterans of the Civil War to be given preference. The three eastern superintendents with their thirty-six clerks were to gather at Omaha the following Friday, July 29. Superintendent Troy would have charge until they arrived at San Francisco. I gave him inspectors' commissions for the thirty-six employees to use in returning east, but we deemed it best not to use commissions bound west because of the suspicion it might cause.

In order to preserve secrecy as to the object of the hegira, the superintendents were to tell the clerks that the Post Office Department wished to reward their good work in some unusual and attractive way. An outing to San Francisco with a few days for sight-seeing would not only serve this purpose but would give them an opportunity to meet the clerks in that far off section and discuss the service and the methods in vogue in their respective division.

As a matter of fact, these men made the trip to San Francisco without the least knowledge of the real object of the journey, nor did they learn the truth until they were taken down to the cars the last day in San Francisco to witness the opening of army chests containing Springfield carbines, cartridges, Colt revolvers, holsters, and cartridge belts to equip every member of the guard.

The memorandum of Second Assistant Postmaster General Bell had provided that I fix the code to be used between him and me. Mr. Bell contemplated that there would be five shipments of $4 million each, and the men in charge of each shipment would use the code to keep in touch with us. That night I drafted a letter in lead pencil on yellow paper and sent Mr. Bell this corrected copy in ink.

Chicago, July 25, 1892.

MR. BELL:

Thus far the arrangement is all right. . . . I will leave here tonight, and see Mr. Dickinson at Omaha tomorrow. Will try to get two cars and a colonist sleeper from him. If I can get it free, will; if not will get it at reduced rates. . . . The men will need sleeping accommodations going west, for they will have to rough it coming east. . . .

The CB&Q will provide the tickets over their line free. Coming back, we will use commissions. If we leave San Francisco as a second section, I will telegraph you: "Have engaged an old stagecoach for World's Fair." If five shipments must be made, will telegraph the day the first one leaves: "Syracuse and Cleveland division should be extended," which will mean, *Pepper in charge*. Second shipment: "Portland and San Francisco in good condition," which will mean, *Flint in charge*. Third shipment: "Vaille can be supplied from Los Banos route," which will mean, *Vaille in charge*. Fourth shipment: "Minneapolis and Chicago needs 40 foot additional," which will mean, *Perkins in charge*. Fifth shipment: "White's Bridge should be made a Post Office," which will mean, *White and Troy in charge*. I expect, however, that the whole shipment will come as a second section, and if so, I will be in charge.

Keep June schedules of Sixth and Eighth divisions and July of the Ninth before you. If anything happens such as hotbox, broken engine, repairs to track, some other train in ditch, I will telegraph: "See page 23.— Land slide at 2:05 A.M.," which would mean, *Delayed at Gold Run*. Any other time given in the telegram would indicate where the delay occurred. If we are ditched, will substitute for land slide: "Ruins at 2:05 A.M.," and the number following will indicate how many are unfit to defend.

If attacked, will substitute: "Strike on again at 2:05 A.M. in Idaho." After that, there will be no use in using cipher.

If you find it necessary to call a halt anywhere, you will know what to say. I will understand.

If everything moves right will telegraph from Reno, Ogden, Cheyenne, Union Pacific Transfer (Omaha), and Chicago: "Service in excellent condition."

Respectfully,

WHITE

Having finished and mailed the above, I took the train for Omaha. General Manager Dickinson of the Union Pacific agreed to furnish two cars: baggage car Number 1092 and express car Number 1242. Both were unusually well built. Number 1242 was plated throughout its interior with boiler iron, and its windows were heavily barred. Dickinson agreed to waive mileage on the foreign cars, issue tickets for the westbound trip, furnish a tourists' sleeper to San Francisco, and accept the cars, eastbound, from the Southern Pacific at Ogden, Utah, either separately or made up as a train with all the guards. This being accomplished, I took passage in the Omaha & Ogden Fast Mail that evening and, changing at Ogden, arriving at San Francisco at 9:45 A.M. Thursday.

I called on Vice President A. N. Towne of the Southern Pacific, who agreed to deliver the four gold cars as a second section of SP's eastbound Fast Mail, running ten minutes behind it, to Ogden, Utah. This resolved the question of whether the money would be dispatched in five separate shipments of $4 million each, or in one shipment of $20 million. To complete the train, Southern Pacific would furnish an officers' car with an observation end and facilities for making coffee.

It remained for me to call on the commanding officer of the Benicia Arsenal at Benicia, California, who had been directed to issue to me seventy-five rifles or carbines with 3,000 rounds of ammunition. I said I would prefer sixty Springfield carbines with 2,000 rounds of cartridges, fifty-one Colt revolvers with 1,000 cartridges, fifty-one cartridge belts and fifty-one holsters. The command officer said he thought that could be arranged, and while I waited, he received authority to make the change.

Meanwhile in San Francisco, Col. J. P. Jackson, the assistant treasurer of the United States, had set his force to packing the coin—five-, ten-, and twenty-dollar pieces—in five hundred substantial boxes. Eight sacks, each containing $5,000, were packed in each box, and the covers were fastened down securely with long screws. Each box weighed 160 pounds gross and contained 152 pounds of gold, worth $40,000. The entire shipment, including the boxes, weighed 80,000 pounds.

While these preparations were underway, Mr. J. A. Fillmore, the manager at the Southern Pacific, sent me a telegram requesting me to call at his office. It seemed that the wife of a known train robber had called at a baggage car in the Southern Pacific yard, handed the baggageman a letter addressed to her husband, and asked him to mail it. The baggageman accepted the letter and made a proper delivery, considering the circumstances. Although he knew nothing about the proposed shipment of gold, he did know the woman, the lawless occupation of her husband, and the losses his employers had sustained at the hands of these marauders. Mr. Fillmore read the letter with great care, first in the regular way, then between the lines, upside down, downside up, under a magnifying glass, and so forth, without finding that this wife was seeking to inform her "lord and master" of the largest jackpot ever heard of.

On Thursday morning, August 4, I gave my associate, Superintendent Flint of the Eighth District, money to purchase provisions—mattresses, campstools, chairs, tinware, and food for the journey from San Francisco to Ogden.

The gold coin had now been boxed and registered, and Southern Pacific had made up the train. The observation platform of the officers' car was coupled to the tender, which was narrower than the engine; and thus, the guards, sitting in front of the observation windows, could see the country and the steps on either side of the engine. Next followed the Burlington car, the Lake Shore car, and the two Union Pacific cars. The boxes of coin were to be equally apportioned among these four cars. A "dinky" car was hauled part way to accommodate the train crew.

First, the ordnance stores were placed on the train. Then, after the guards had been shown into their cars, the chests and boxes were opened and the weapons issued. After this, the registered boxes began to move across the city in heavy truck wagons from the subtreasury. As each wagon was loaded, a tarpaulin was thrown over the boxes. Two guards with concealed arms accompanied the wagon to the train. At Southern Pacific's Lower Transfer, the officers and guards placed the boxes on the floor of each car, one layer deep, on each side of an imaginary aisle. Packed this way, each car held just 125 boxes. On top of these were placed mattresses where the guards rested when off duty. There were nine clerks and one officer in each of the four cars carrying gold. In the first, or observation car, (sometimes called the "danger car") there were nine guards and two officers. Two squads in each car relieved each other regularly, but even those who were off duty were required to keep their carbines by their sides, the barrel resting in the inside curve of the arm and the revolver within reach. Those who were on duty had to occupy chairs and campstools near the doors and windows, wide awake, their revolvers in holsters belted on their bodies, their carbines in reach, and the doors bolted and locked. No one was permitted to enter any of these cars —not even the one to which he was assigned—without first giving the countersign "Grant," a name selected in honor of our old commander.

The provisions that Superintendent Flint had purchased arrived during the day and were placed in the cars. All this transpired in the business portion of the city, but no one except those officially concerned seemed to know anything about it. The postmaster of San Francisco had given a receipt to Colonel Jackson of the subtreasury for the registered boxes; and now, having checked off the last one in turn, I gave my receipt to Postmaster Backus for five hundred boxes, containing a total of $20 million in gold coin.

We left the Lower Transfer as a supposed silk train. (This fable served its purpose well, and it was repeated until we arrived at Ogden.) The guards were in their places, the doors were locked, and everyone was wide awake as we moved out into the Sacramento Valley. We had reached no farther than Sacramento City, however, when we were compelled to pause to repair a drawhead on car Number 695 before commencing the ascent of the mountains.

A half hour was lost in this operation. Then the train moved quietly into the plains, and the climb began. The higher we mounted, the more tense became the strain upon the couplings. In the extreme effort to reach the summit, the coupling between the engine and the observation car broke. Fortunately, the company had taken the precaution to reinforce the couplings at all points with chains, for, had the chain been lacking, the five cars would have started upon a ride to destruction, perhaps to death. Still, the loss in time at Sacramento, added to the delay in repairing the couplings at Colfax, put us more than three hours behind the Fast Mail. Furthermore, I noticed that our train was being side-tracked in favor of all trains moving west. I called on the conductor for an explanation. He said he had wired to his superintendent but no instructions had been received in return. I asked him to accompany me to the train dispatcher, who occupied a bungalow at one side of the track. After telling the dispatcher enough about the situation to interest him, I asked him to put me in direct communication with Mr. Platte, the assistant general manager of the system at San Francisco.

I telegraphed Platte that the train had been unavoidably delayed half an hour at Sacramento, repairing a drawhead; twice by couplings breaking while ascending the mountain; and once by a flagman who had placed a torpedo on the track and was waving his flag to stop the train before it reached the point where a gang of track men was making repairs. (When the torpedo exploded, the guards had sprung to their feet, arms in hand, but a quick inspection showed the harmless character of the disturbance and doubtless saved the flagman's life.) I told Mr. Platte that these different delays now added up to more than three hours. We had been expecting a contest with his regular schedule time, and we were surprised to be sidetracked to let freight trains pass us, especially in view of the agreement that the gold train was to run only ten minutes behind the Fast Mail. Since this was now impossible, I suggested he "cut us loose" so we could overtake the Fast Mail. This he promised to do, and we moved down the east slope of the Sierra Nevada at a spanking rate along the banks of the Truckee River.

At Wadsworth we stopped for water, then commenced speeding through a valley full of lakes and sink holes, vanishing and reappearing streams, until we passed Humboldt Lake, into which the Humboldt River, the longest in the state, disappears after running its irregular course for nearly three hundred miles.

When we reached the Humboldt's shores, our engine was aroused, and the tail end of the train cracked like chain lightning. This alarmed me somewhat, because the roadbed was as crooked as the river. We were running at sixty-five miles per hour, and I was afraid we might derail on one of the curves. I therefore sent one of my boys over the tender to the engineer to tell him that he was showing very little judgment in the handing of the train. My "cut loose" order was for New York, not eternity.

The engineer came back to the observation car at the next coaling and watering station. We spoke to each other pleasantly, and he said: "Your opinion of me is about correct. I ought to have known better than to run at such a rate of speed on such a track."

I replied: "When you strike a good piece of track, reasonably straight, you can let the engine go as fast as steam will carry her, so far as we are concerned."

After this, we moved along at the highest speed that safety would permit. We caught up with the Fast Mail entering the yards at Ogden. As our train pulled near the depot, we were greeted by the newsboys' call of Salt Lake City morning papers, announcing the shipment of gold coin from San Francisco, and by the sound of a gong announcing that breakfast was ready in the restaurant.

We had left San Francisco with enough cold food, canned meats, fruits, and such, in our cars to supply us until we arrived at Ogden. Now in order to insure warm meals to all and maintain thorough protection over our treasure, we allowed five guards in each car to turn over their arms to the remaining five and proceed in a nonchalant manner to the restaurant, eat quickly, and resume their posts. The second relief then proceeded to breakfast.

Forty minutes after reaching Ogden, we resumed our journey as the first section of the Omaha & Ogden Fast Mail. In Rawlins, Wyoming, where we stopped to change engineers and engines, the relief engineer protested against taking the train out. He had been held up twice near a big tree standing isolated on the plains. I assured him it would be impossible for a gang of outlaws to interfere while there were fifty-one armed guards in the cars behind him. He must make the run, paying no attention to signals, flags, or lanterns, until that tree was west instead of east of us.

Soon we were climbing the west slope of the Rockies. At Sherman we stopped at the very summit of the transcontinental railroad line. Hearing the low hum of voices and the shuffling of feet outside, I marshaled guards in front of two of the doors with their guns at the level. The two doors opened, the muzzles thrust through the openings, and we stared into the faces of some tramps who were seeking free rides on Uncle Sam's flying treasure houses, unconscious of the proximity of great wealth.

Our next stop was at Cheyenne, where one begins the long, gradual descent of the plains. We expected to make a fast run over the next five hundred miles of track, and we did make sixty-five miles per hour for some time. After passing into Nebraska, however, the engine slipped an eccentric, and we arrived at Omaha three hours late.

We left as soon as the engine could be replaced, intending to make up our lost time before reaching Chicago; but owing to hotboxes and a number of special trains we met carrying Knights Templar to Denver, we arrived one hour and twenty minutes late. For some reason, the Lake Shore & Michigan Southern did not make up any time—in fact, we arrived at Buffalo one hour and forty minutes late. But Vice President H. Walter Webb at the New York Central was determined to land the train in New York City on time. Engine Number 880 accomplished the work. The train moved without friction, no swinging or rolling, no disturbance, save at one point (east of Rochester, I think) when she came down with a tremendous jolt and bounded as if she had run against the end of a broken rail. Then she trembled and moved forward as before, her equilibrium restored.

There was nothing to disturb the peace of anyone, even as the train swept around the curves of the beautiful Hudson. We drank deep of the majestic and peaceful scenery. The sun rose as we were passing West Point and the Palisades. We had been in the keeping of Providence from the beginning to the end of our journey.

At 10:46 A.M., August 9, 1892, the "Gold Train" came to a stop in Grand Central Depot in New York City. We found waiting to welcome us a vast concourse that had come to witness something unusual and meritorious. I had the carbines, extra ammunition, equipment, campstools, mattresses, and so forth placed in the officers' car under guard. Then the doors on the discharging side of the cars were unlocked and guards stationed at each. Five wagons were loaded as quickly as possible. Two armed guards rode on each, with the driver, and the wagons left Grand Central at 11:50 A.M. At 12:40 P.M. the first group pulled up at the Pine Street entrance of the subtreasury. In a short time, five more followed, and shortly thereafter the last four were en route. When all were unloaded and their contents placed in the vaults, Postmaster Van Cott of New York City give me a receipt for $20 million in gold.

—Condensed from James E. White's *A Life Span and Reminiscences of Railway Mail Service*, Deemer & Jaisohn, Philadelphia, 1910.

Superintendent White's nervous journey was neither the last nor the largest gold haul made by the Railway Mail Service. The richest run of all carried $15 billion in a series of trains to the underground vaults at Fort Knox, Kentucky. Within a short time, most of the bullion was carried back out again.

The worst trip was a one-million-dollar transfer from Philadelphia to New York in 1914. Counting up the loot at the end of the run, Division Superintendent James L. Stice discovered that he had misplaced one of the fifty sacks of gold. It was located back at the Mint in Philadelphia, but Stice collapsed with a severe, though not fatal, heart attack.

Scribner's Monthly, 1888

CHAPTER THIRTEEN

A Cake and Coffee Stop

I

"The Coffee Stop in Winnetka"

AMONG THE MANY TECHNICAL PROBLEMS whose solution eluded the managers of primitive American railroads, none was more pressing, from the passengers' standpoint, than the matter of nourishment en route. Resourceful passengers would climb aboard the wooden carriages toting wicker hampers packed with baked hams, sunshine pickles, and marble cake; but those travelers who lacked the foresight to bring their own provisions had to endure starvation while jostling along, surrounded by the sight and scent of other people's eggshells, chicken bones, and apple cores.

Out in Pennsylvania on the Philadelphia & Columbia line, the engineer would stop the train every few miles to let the passengers slog across the velvety pastures of Lancaster County to some sedate old inn, renowned for years as a stagecoach stop, where one could take a glass of whiskey and a pipeful of tobacco and sample the specialties of the house: fresh doughnuts and coffee, apple pie with milk, chicken fricassee, waffles and fish, gingerbread and spruce beer. Few railroad routes could match the nutritional resources of the Pennsylvania Dutch country.

Happily, somebody thought of providing dinner stops, or "refreshment saloons," as they were called, at major junctions. The result, as of 1840, fell short of gustatory bliss, but it was insurance against starvation.

"At every fifteen miles of the railroads there are refreshment rooms. The cars stop, all the doors are thrown open, and out rush all the passengers like boys out of school and crowd round the tables to solace themselves with pies, patties, cakes, hard-boiled eggs, ham, custards, and a variety of railroad luxuries too numerous to mention. The bell rings for departure; in they all hurry with

At a Chesapeake & Ohio station in Gordonsville former slaves peddled "railroad luxuries."

King's *The Southern States, 1875*

their hands and mouths full; and off they go again until the next stopping-place induces them to relieve the monotony of the journey by masticating without being hungry."*

As for the concessionaires who took on the task of feeding the insatiable passengers, they regarded their work as a humane public service, fraught with the danger of moral censure.

W HILE I WAS STATION AGENT at Waukegan, Illinois, back in 1856, I established what was, if not the first, among the first railroad station eating houses in the United States. My wife, who was a thrifty New England housekeeper and noted for the excellence of her cooking, began to bake a few pies, a little cake, and some doughnuts for "the boys" who wanted refreshments. I had these articles set out on a little table for sale. One day the superintendent, W. S. Johnson, stopped at the station and noticed this lunch stand with its modest display.

"Who's this for?" he said. "A good idea. You can have one end of the station for a lunch counter if you want it, Charley."

---

*From *A Diary in America*, by Captain Frederick Marryat, Philadelphia, 1840.

So I fitted up a neat little refectory at one end of the dingy old station, and Mr. Johnson and the trainmen soon got into the habit of lunching there every time they stopped. The superintendent of the Chicago & Milwaukee road had the conductors and brakemen announce refreshments on their trains just before reaching Waukegan. It was not long before there was a large and regular patronage. Within a year, the place was known from Maine to Minnesota.

My passengers on the road were constantly doing kind things to help my eating house along, making suggestions or giving presents as occasions came up. Dr. V. C. Price, the originator of the famous Price's baking powder, gave me one of the first cans of powder he made. My wife always used this preparation in her cooking, and she attributed a great part of the success of our eating house to this fact.

My eating house caused a crisis in my church associations. For several years I had belonged to the Methodist Episcopal Church. My wife also was a member, and my children were in the Sunday school. Among the various articles for sale at our little refectory, however, was ale. A committee of church members waited upon me and informed me that I must stop the sale of this beverage at my place.

"Gentlemen," I said quietly, "I went into the church with ale, and I can go out with ale."

Shortly afterward, I joined the Presbyterian Church.

—From Charles George's *Forty Years on the Rail*,
R. R. Donnelly & Sons, Chicago, 1887.

II

*"Right after we pulled out, I started my campaign
by going through the train with salted peanuts."*

As SOON AS RAILROADS BEGAN to use telegraphy, the tempo of in-transit feeding accelerated. The conductor would walk through the train shortly before a scheduled stop at an eating place, count the number of passengers who planned to take nourishment, and telegraph ahead at the next way station to warn the cooks to get busy. At a well-run refreshment saloon, this could result in the sort of breakfast they served at Sidney, Nebraska, on the Union Pacific in 1882:

"There were given us eight little dishes apiece, containing hot beefsteak, two slices of cold roast antelope, a bit of cold chicken, ham and poached eggs, a couple of boiled potatoes, two sticks of sweet corn, stewed tomatoes, and four thin buckwheat hot cakes laid one on top of the other, to be eaten with golden syrup the last thing of all....

"Cold tea in tumblers with a quantity of sugar added seemed to constitute the popular beverage, if it was not cold milk. There was hot tea and coffee for those who preferred.... For this and every meal, except two, along the route of the Pacific Railroad from Omaha to San Francisco the charge is one dollar."*

Poughkeepsie, Altoona, and Springfield, Massachusetts, offered famous station restaurants, and the Fred Harvey houses along the Santa Fe were literally oases in the southwestern desert. But there was cause for complaint about the quality of most refreshment stops. As a rule, trains stopped for only ten or twenty minutes, and passengers seldom had enough time to eat a full meal. Sometimes the service was maddeningly slow; often the food was too hot. With reason, the passengers suspected that uneaten food was being carried back to the kitchen to be offered to passengers on the next train through. Meal stops fitted the schedule of the train, not the rhythm of human metabolism. Three meals might be offered within a few hours, or they might be spaced eight or ten hours apart.

One highly unsatisfactory alternative to the wham-bam service at the refreshment stops was to buy one's food from the peripatetic peddler, or "news butcher," a relentless young fanatic who hustled postcards, salted nuts, and miniature glass signal lanterns filled with pellets of colored candy.

The news butcher first appeared on the railroads of New England around 1850, hawking magazines, papers, and tobacco. Later, his descendants branched into an amazing number of commercial sidelines, limited only by their own imaginations and the patience of the suffering public.

Twelve-year-old Thomas Alva Edison, news butcher on the Grand Trunk Railroad between Port Huron and Detroit in 1859, augmented his stock of candy, cigarettes, and cigars with loaves of fresh bread, tubs of butter, and home-grown vegetables picked up along the route. William A. Brady, who was later to make his fortune as a prizefight promoter and theatrical producer, ran a movable general store aboard the transcontinental immigrant trains of the Union Pacific and Central Pacific in the 1870's, offering reading matter, groceries, toilet articles, hardware, candy, tobacco, bedding, guidebooks, and an assortment of useless souvenirs. On the Old Colony Railroad in Massachusetts in 1889, fifteen-year-old Harry Thomas found that his most popular product was drinking water, dispensed from a brass tank that he carried on his shoulder.

The news butcher was nineteenth-century American boyhood on the make.

---

*From *Through America*, by W. G. Marshall, London, 1882.

Robert Louis Stevenson wrote tenderly about the peddler on the overland route. Horatio Alger made a fictional hero of the newsboy on the Erie road.

All the same, the kid was an unbearable pest. To one English visitor, crossing the plains in 1885, he was the most irritating feature of travel in the United States:

"First he offers you yesterday's newspapers; next time he walks through the carriage he drops two or three handbooks, guides, maps, or magazines beside each traveler; the next trip he forces the choice of apples or pears, then oranges, California grapes, dried figs, maple sugar, including an advertisement; cigars—each item nearly requires a separate trip up and down the carriage; last, he brings his basket of peanuts, and throwing two or three into everyone's lap, he has completed the round, not for the day but for the nonce; he will begin again at the beginning, for sure, after dinner. This itinerant trader certainly should be suppressed; his prices are extravagant and his office unnecessary."*

Many news butchers would have agreed with this conclusion, for they were inexperienced, underpaid boys who had signed up for a difficult type of commission work expecting to find wealth and adventure. Among the disillusioned veterans of the trade was Ernest Haycox, a prolific author of novels and short stories, who told his experiences to his friend and neighbor, Stewart H. Holbrook.

I BEGAN MY BUSINESS CAREER as a news butcher on the old Sacramento Northern Railroad in California, and I believe I was unquestionably one of the worst train butchers on record. I also was given one of the worst runs in existence. It was from Oakland to Sacramento, with now and then a trip to Mount Diablo. Either run was too short. Few passengers felt the need to buy anything from the butcher, and I was little more than a silly intruder in the cars.

I could sell a few newspapers, of course, and, though the profit was small, the older butchers taught me how to increase the margin by the ancient and dishonorable method of short change. Say that the customer gave me a fifty-cent piece for a five-cent newspaper. I'd assume it was a quarter he had given me and return him twenty cents in change, meanwhile, however, retaining a quarter in the palm of my hand. If the customer noticed the discrepancy, why, I was quick to drop the quarter into his hand and say, "Sorry!" Half the time, at least, the customer didn't notice, and I was twenty-five cents ahead. My moral being unquestionably suffered injury to a much greater extent.

The runs I had were so bad that I could earn barely enough to pay for my meals and a room in a flophouse. After a while, I discovered a place in San Francisco where I could buy three packages of gum for a nickel. These I could

---

*From *Prairie Experiences,* by Major William Shepherd, Orange Judd Co., New York, 1885.

sell at five cents each, this making a profit of a dime on the deal, for this was not news-company merchandise, but my own sideline.

Then, there was Crackerjack, which sold for ten cents a box. Quite often, some kid would buy a box, and then his mother would prevent his eating but a little of it. My eagle eye, sharpened by want, never missed such a happening, and when mother and child got off the cars, I was on hand to snatch the Crackerjack. This I would inspect carefully, and if the contents were less than half devoured, and the general appearance of the package still passable, I would later, and in secret, open eight or ten boxes of the stuff, take a little from each to fill the depleted package, seal all the packages again, and return to the market with eleven instead of ten packages—and the assurance of a dime clear profit. It was only by such shady practices that I could earn enough for my modest living expenses.

Often, the railroad company would run an excursion up into the hills, where the Mount Diablo Dam was under construction. The first such event I attended was an Italian picnic. The news company seemed to think that this picnic would be a big killing. They loaded me up with six gigantic cans of ice cream, one thousand cones, and God alone knows what other stuff. The excursion train ran to nine cars, and every seat was taken by an Italian.

Well, right after we pulled out, I started my campaign by going through the train with salted peanuts. That was the style of merchandising the old-time butchers had taught me—first, get everybody in the train thirsty, then break out the soda pop and ice cream. So I went through with salted peanuts. I think I sold two five-cent bags in the entire train. Next I prepared a big tray of ice cream

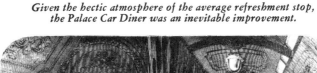

Given the hectic atmosphere of the average refreshment stop,
the Palace Car Diner was an inevitable improvement.

Harper's Weekly, 1869

cones and took them through. I did exactly that: I took them through the train and back again to my headquarters in the end of the first car. On that long, long day, and to that immense crowd of Italian folks, I sold four cones.

It was the same day I learned what my employers should have long since known—namely, that Italians traveling take with them sufficient food to last not only all day, but to last two or three days, in case the train should be delayed for that length of time. The Italians in this particular train carried enormous stocks of bread, cheese, sausage, and wine, all so well garnished with garlic that after one trip through the cars, my tray of ice cream cones, which I finally ate to prevent their complete disintegration, had a flavor I shall never forget.

It was quite a picnic, on which I made a total profit, if that is the term, of forty cents. It convinced me I was not cut out for the glamorous job of train butcher. I presently resigned, and I am sure the news company never missed me. Yet, my few months at the job gave me a professional outlook in the matter of news-butchering; and today, thirty years after, I never fail to note the butcher on any train I am riding and watch closely his technique. That, however, is as near as I care to be to one of the most difficult and hazardous occupations I can think of.

—Recollections of Ernest Haycox, as recorded by Stewart H. Holbrook in *The Story of American Railroads*, copyright 1947 by Crown Publishers, New York. Reprinted by permission of Crown Publishers.

IT WAS INEVITABLE that someone should build a refreshment car to accompany the ravenous passengers on their journeys. Railroad men started talking about the idea almost as soon as trains began to operate. The problem was, how to make money with a restaurant-on-wheels.

In 1863 the Philadelphia, Wilmington & Baltimore Railroad finally took a chance on this profitless undertaking. The first "dining car" was an ordinary, fifty-foot day coach, partitioned across the center to create a smoking room in one half and an eating bar with a steam table in the other. The PW&B used two of these proto-diners for about three years on its Philadelphia-Baltimore run. They lost money.

Late in the 1860's the first diner on which food actually was cooked came into service on the Great Western Railroad of Canada. The operator was George Mortimer Pullman, the Chicago sleeping car entrepreneur, who frequently had demonstrated his flair for perfecting, exploiting, and publicizing ideas that had failed to ripen in other hands. In this case, Pullman also demonstrated his shrewdness by turning the whole unprofitable business back to the railroads.

Dining cars provided comfort and conviviality to railroad travelers for a century; but they never did make any money.

Dance of Death
in the Switchyards

I

*"All through my employment as a switchman,
my sister kept one clean sheet for the express purpose
of wrapping up my mangled remains."*

THE HAZARDS OF RAILROAD TRAVEL during the early years of steam produced an enormous literature of admonition, indignation, and sensation.

In the beginning railroad disasters were an absolute novelty. Horrified witnesses noted down every painful detail of the world's first passenger accident, which took the life of a British official named William Huskisson on the inaugural run of the Liverpool & Manchester Railway on September 15, 1830. Later, when a wreck on the Camden & Amboy in New Jersey in November, 1833, claimed the first railroad fatality in the United States, historians recorded not only the name of the victim, one James C. Stedman, a jeweler from North Carolina, but also the names of other prominent passengers, including Commodore Cornelius Vanderbilt, who was injured, and ex-President John Quincy Adams, who was not.

In time it grew obvious that all railroad passengers rode at peril of their lives, and the reporting of accidents became a perfunctory matter. What with "snakeheads" popping up into the cars, boilers exploding, bridges collapsing, and angry bulls charging at locomotives, there was a surfeit of small mishaps to write about. Sparks rained down, setting fire to hats and clothing. Stoves tipped over and ignited wooden coaches. Passengers were crushed between link couplings while trying to walk from car to car, and derailments became so common that some companies printed on their tickets a warning that all able-bodied passengers would be on call to help put cars back on the rails. Only especially grotesque or bloody accidents merited attention in the press.

By the 1850's the number of deaths and injuries on the railroads had become alarming. In a greedy frenzy to create new routes, railroad builders laid out poorly ballasted and badly graded roadbeds, whacked together flimsy bridges and trestles, and crowded the rails with unsafe cars and engines. The Civil War temporarily diverted public attention from the question of railroad safety, but in the 1870's the political and intellectual leaders of the country belatedly realized that the unconscionable slaughter on the railroads had become a major national problem.

The most influential periodicals, the most persuasive essayists and orators

Night work in the switchyards quickened one's reactions and shortened one's life expectancy.

Scribner's Monthly, 1888

of the day awoke to the horror of carnage on the rails. Wendell Phillips, Lyman Abbott, Henry Adams, and others turned their eloquence and invective onto the unfamiliar subjects of slow brakes, loose couplings, and archaic methods of signal transmission.

One by one, the states established railroad commissions to set safety standards. The Westinghouse air brake, which was perfected and installed on most passenger trains in the seventies, was the most important innovation in railroading since the use of telegraphy to send train orders—or, at any rate, it was important for passengers.

The trouble was that none of the eloquence, the inventions, or the legislation had much effect on the safety of railroad employees. Six times as many railroad employees as passengers were killed every year, and almost ten times as many employees as passengers were injured.*

At least a quarter of the employees' deaths and a third or more of the injuries occurred during the coupling of cars. Passenger cars, which were fragile and expensive, were equipped with automatic couplers; but freight cars, which were heavy and cheap, diverse and numerous, were not. In railroad switchyards, where freight cars from all parts of the country creaked and clanged together along the spur tracks, brakemen darted out like *banderilleros,* trying to stab the necks of moving cars with metal spikes.

According to the recollections of brakeman Harry French, switchyard employees were haunted by superstition. The reason, perhaps, was that in coupling boxcars with a link and pin, no one was permitted to make more than one mistake.

D ICK MILES, THE YARDMASTER of the Hannibal & St. Joe† in Kansas City, had the reputation of being hard-boiled. His voice was a roaring bellow, invariably distorted by a huge cud of chewing tobacco. He was very proud of his "accuracy of disposal," employing a side tilt of his head to better aim at the sawdust-filled box that was part of his office equipment. Whenever he missed, he used a special roar to signalize the event. I had no way of knowing that all the bluff and bluster of his manner was a dodge to hide a heart filled with kindness.

"So y' wanna be a switchman w'en y' grow up?" he asked when I stated the nature of my visit.

"I want a job now."

---

*In 1888, the first year in which reliable statistics were kept, 315 passengers and 2,070 employees were killed; 2,138 passengers and 20,148 employees were injured.
†The Hannibal & St. Joseph, one of the earliest midwestern railroad routes to be conceived, was chartered by the Missouri legislature in February, 1847, and started four years later. It is now a portion of the Burlington system.

"G'wan—get outa here," he roared. "Come back w'en y' got some whiskers."
I got out, stayed out for ten shaveless days. Then I again walked into that
dingy little yard office. Mr. Miles looked me over suspiciously as I fingered the
scant crop of fuzz on my chin.

"Back, huh? Listen, kid, I can't put y' to work. Y' ain't old enough. How old
are y'?"

"Seventeen," I replied, stretching my age a year.

"Yeah—seventeen—goin' on fifteen. W'at makes y' think y' can cut the
mustard on this job?"

"I know all the signs. I can get on and get off as good as the next fellow.
Besides, I want to be a railroad man."

The yardmaster did not reply immediately. He tilted back in his chair, put
his feet on the desk, and spat expertly into the box. "Come 'round Monday
mornin'. I'll put your name on the board."

That meant I had been hired as a switchman by the Hannibal & St. Joe. I
rushed home to tell my sister of my good fortune. She firmly expected me to be
killed the first day I worked. All through my employment as a switchman, she
kept one clean sheet for the express purpose of wrapping up my mangled remains.

It is very difficult to look back to 1875 and give a clear picture of the conditions under which railroad men worked at that time. Link-and-pin couplings, of
course, for all cars. The MCB (Master Car Builders) coupler did not become
universal until about 1888. It was developed from the idea of a man named
Janney, and for a long time the coupler bore his name. The Janney coupler used
the principle of the hooked fingers of the human hand. A pin behind the knuckles
kept the coupler locked, and the pin could not be raised as long as the coupler
was under pulling strain. To unlock the coupler, all the trainman had to do was
to relieve the pull strain and lift the pin. It was not necessary for him to walk
between the cars to uncouple them. A lever at the side of the car made that dangerous job a thing of the past.

To couple cars with the old-time link and pin, perfect coordination of mind
and muscle were an absolute necessity. The link was first fastened with a pin in
one car. Then a pin was "cocked" at a slight angle in the other car to be coupled.
As the two cars came together, the trainman guided the link into its slot.
The impact of the coupling usually shook down the cocked pin, completing
the coupling. If the pin did not shake down, the trainman stepped in between the
cars and pounded it down with a spare pin. Oftentimes it was necessary to walk
between the two moving cars. Wary feet, an alert mind, and chilled nerve were
needed every instant. A man lived only long enough to make one mistake.

The uncoupling of the cars was always the most dangerous job. Often it
was necessary to uncouple with the cars in motion, especially in making some of
the more intricate switching movements. The switchman had the choice of running along between the cars and pulling out the pin at the proper time or of
lying on the beam that held the coupling slot. In the latter choice the danger was
equally great. There was not a great deal of room for a man's body on the coupling

beam. The handholds were seldom trustworthy. If there was any miscue, or if the pin could not be pulled, the trainman stood a fine chance of being thrown under the car.

Some railroads required that their employees carry specially made brake clubs which could be used to pry the coupling pins upward. Brake clubs were a standard part of a switchman's existence, but most of the patented clubs were nuisances.

Pins and links that broke during couplings and uncouplings took their toll in fingers. One of the most common marks of a railroad man in the seventies and eighties was a crushed hand or a shortage of digits. It was my luck to keep all my fingers and toes.

None of the switch frogs were blocked with wood as now. A careless foot that strayed into one of these traps was cut off before it could be jerked out. If the trainman was lucky, he lost one foot. The slanted switch had not yet been invented. Rail ends at all switches were open, presenting the same trap as the frogs. The cars themselves were unsafe. Regular inspection was unheard of. Some of the handholds were wired, some patched up with nails. All brakes were set by hand. When a brake chain broke (a common occurrence), the trainman had a fifty-fifty chance of being thrown under the wheels. I estimate that in 1875 there were from three to five men killed or badly crippled in the Hannibal & St. Joe yards each week.

In the switchyards of the mid-1870s, the death rate
was three to five men per week.

I was light and wiry, and, as I grew more expert, I was inclined to take unnecessary chances. A friend cured me of chance-taking. He was a fellow work-man by the name of Jack Foster. A cool, iron-nerved, skilled railroad man, Jack had been thoroughly trained in what chance-taking meant. He had been in construction work when the Union Pacific was throwing a web of steel across a continent. Much of the country crossed by that railroad was fought for, and oftentimes paid for, in blood. Rifles were always kept ready in the engines and cabooses. Side arms were kept ready for action and were worn constantly.

Jack Foster took a great deal of pains in coaching me in finer points of a switchman's duties. He taught me how to get on the swiftly approaching footboard with the least danger, how to get off and keep balance. He taugh me never to stand on the footboard in front of the cylinder head when the engine was under starting load.

"I saw a fellow get killed thataway," he told me. "The hogger didn't bleed his petcocks, and the cylinder head made a hole in his chest that you could throw a frying pan through."

It was Jack Foster who showed me how to cock my lantern at an angle so all the light would show on an approaching footboard when we were working nights. He showed me how to hold that lantern upside down to light it in a hurry. (There were times in after years when the quick lighting of a lantern made the difference between life and death.) Jack Foster would not stand for my having a drink before or while I was on duty. I obeyed him when I would have fought anyone else. He was more than a friend. He was a teacher, adviser, storyteller—my first coach in the game that was to become my life work.

One night we were making up a train. A light haze of rain made everything slippery. Only three more cars to couple and we were through. I took the first and, after some trouble with a pin that would not drop, succeeded in reaching in with another pin and beating it into place.

Jack took his turn at the next coupling. He carefully examined the two cars to be coupled. One car's coupling slot was considerably higher than that of the other, making necessary the use of a gooseneck coupling link. Jack stepped over to the linkbox and selected a gooseneck link. He fitted it into the low car, cocked the pin on the high car. Then he signaled the engineer to back up. Slowly the train slacked back for the coupling. The two cars touched firmly, but the difference in their coupler slot heights was so great that a coupling could not be made until the link was reversed.

Jack signaled the engineer to go ahead, intending to let the train draw away far enough for him to step between the cars and reverse the link. As soon as the cars separated, Jack signaled the engineer to stop. I had taken my post, ready to transmit any signal that might be needed. With the lantern on the crook of his arm Jack worked to release the pin in the slot of the low car. But the impact of the first attempted coupling had bent the pin; it would not free. Suddenly, I noticed that the cars were closer together. The rear section was moving. Slack was running back.

"Jack!" I screamed. "Slack running!"

He heard me. A glance told him of his danger. He tried to spring clear. There was a split second when it seemed he would make it. I can shut my eyes yet and see the tiny slip of his foot that defeated his attempt. His body was caught between the cars as though in a giant vise.

In making his jump for life, he had raised himself high enough to be crushed just below the ribs. One of the lower ribs protruded through the skin, and from this hole gushed black blood. At least it looked black under the light of my lantern.

I had jumped towards him when I realized his danger. When, in response to my frantic signals, the engine pulled the front section away, I caught the crushed body. Jack was still conscious. The engineer and another switchman went for a stretcher. Desperately, I tried to help Jack. I tried to plug that gush of blood with a bandanna handkerchief. Slowly Jack's head shook. "No use, Harry," he whispered. "I've seen too many like this not to know what it means."

"You'll get well, Jack."

Again that tiny shake of the head. Then with his eyes he motioned me nearer. "You're young," he whispered. "You'll live to teach others. Tell them— tell them always, safety first."

With tear-filled eyes I nodded.

But after Jack Foster's death, my interest in my work faded. Not that I was afraid. I was simply heartbroken. Jack Foster had intended to resign. He had planned to go to work for the Santa Fe as a brakeman. Had he quit when he intended, there would never have been the tragedy.

No superstition among the early railroad men was so prevalent as that against working after you have decided to quit. To do that was regarded as the acme of bad luck. Without making any claim as to whether or not it is unlucky, I believe there is a mental letdown that does cause accidents. I have seen the occurrence too many times to doubt. Few trades require as much concentrated attention on the job as that of a switchman. Getting on the footboard of a locomotive as it approaches, walking a swiftly moving car, making a sprint, securing a trustworthy handhold, swinging onto a moving car—all require undivided concentration. So do the coupling and uncoupling of cars, even with the automatic couplers now used. There is no room for any other thought than the particular job that is being performed. If a man has decided to leave the service, if he has another job, or is studying where such a job could be secured, such thoughts or plans are certain to lower his safety efficiency.

Thirty years later, when I was working as a freight agent at Kapowsin, in eastern Washington, I again experienced this dangerous phenomenon.

My work at Kapowsin threw a tremendous amount of responsibility on me. To me fell the inspection of all loaded cars, logs or lumber. I was the sole arbiter as to whether a car was properly loaded. Car repairers and hostlers were under my jurisdiction, as well as my own train crew.

The two brakemen under me were the cream of the crop. I trained them, and I protected them from being "bumped" by other men who might have a trifle more seniority. Under railroad rules the senior man—that is, the oldest in point of service—can bid in any job held by a younger (in service) man. I could not supersede this rule, but it was possible to drop a hint that a new face on my crew would be unwelcome.

Al Thompson, one of my brakemen, came to me one morning.

"Harry, I've got a chance to go to night school in Tacoma. I'm going to study telegraphy, typewriting, and shorthand. I'm going to quit."

"Fine, Al! I'm glad you're going to try to go on up. We can get by OK today. I'll have Walker send up another man for tomorrow."

"But, Harry, I wanted to work through until Saturday."

"Al, you know I wouldn't fire you. The only way I could think any more of you would be for you to be my own son. I'm telling you, if you've made up your mind to quit, don't work those three days—don't work three minutes."

"You know I'm not superstitious, Harry."

"I am, about quitting. I've followed this game right up from the link-and-pin days. I've seen it happen too often. You can work till Saturday if you wish, but I'd go down and pack my stuff—quick."

"I've made my arrangements, Harry. I'd rather work."

Al worked that day—worked Thursday. He met my protests with a grin. It may sound silly, but I was worried. Never could a man have been more careful than I was for those next days. Al had a brother, Jim, who was the hostler for our locomotive. I went to Jim and asked him to help me to get Al off the job before Saturday.

It was no use. Friday morning we made up our train getting ready to leave for Tacoma. The train consisted of about forty cars. Al had a coupling to make about halfway back. After he made the coupling, he was to walk along and inspect the air hoses to see that they were all coupled. The train stood on a sidetrack, which lay between the main line and a steep hill that came right down to the edge of the sidetrack.

Al was on the hill side of the track. He signaled the fireman to back up for the coupling. Then, apparently he decided to cross to the main line side in order to have better walking as he inspected the air hoses.

I had just handed the engineer his train orders when the fireman received Al's signal to back up. The engineer placed the quadrant in reverse and opened the throttle. The engine started to move backward for the coupling.

"Al's crossing on your side," the fireman called to the engineer. "Is he in sight?"

"I don't see him yet," the engineer answered.

All my foreboding broke at once. "Stop her!" I screamed.

I swung out of the cab and lit running. Back twenty car lengths, about a thousand feet, there was trouble. Never was I more certain.

Bill, the other brakeman, saw my frenzied run. He was closer to Al than I. We arrived together. Al was twisting in the grasp of the couplers. His coat was still hooked to a projecting bolt above one of them.

Desperately, frantically, Bill and I worked to get the link-bolt to rise. We tugged and pulled on the levers that operated the couplers. But the couplers were under the pull-strain of the engine. No power on earth could open them until they were squeezed together. That meant further crushing of that body in their viselike grip. Again I made the run back to the engine.

"Al's caught in the couplers. They've coupled on him. You've got to slack back against him. Watch my arm. When I give it, tip her over with everything you've got the other way."

Never was slack given as easy as that was. Back where the boy was held there was just barely perceptible movement. One thousand feet of equipment moved less than one-half an inch. Bill had his arms around Al, his huge shoulders braced against the car to take as much of the strain as possible off Al's hips.

At the first sign of movement backward, I lunged on the lifting lever. My arm flipped out, there was a thunder of exhausts from the head end, and the cars parted. Bill held the crushed boy in his arms. He carried him to the nearby caboose. The doctor at Kapowsin could do nothing but ease his pain. I wired for right-of-way over all trains to Tacoma and got it.

Telegraphy and block signal systems like this
Saxby and Farmer signal cabin lowered fatalities
but did not completely eliminate mayhem.

Scientific American, 1875

Al's brother Jim accompanied us on that trip to the hospital. We placed Al on a thick bundle of blankets to ease the shock of the rough-riding caboose.

At noon the next day, Al asked Jim to wire me that he had changed his mind—he wanted to return and work with me. Jim wrote out the wire and showed it to Al.

"That's all right," Al said. "Harry'll be glad to have me back. Turn me on my side so I can sleep."

Jim turned him on his side, and Al went to sleep forever.

—Excerpted from *Railroadman*, by Chauncey Del French. Copyright 1938 by the Macmillan Company, New York.

In 1893 Congress passed the Safety Appliance Act, requiring the installation of power brakes, grab irons, and drawbars of standard height, and outlawing link-and-pin couplings on all railroad cars and locomotives. The law did not become fully operative until 1900. Each of the safety devices specified had been known, patented, and manufactured for more than thirty years.

During those three decades, approximately 65,000 railroad men had been killed and more than 750,000 injured. In the decade after the safety law came into effect, the yearly death rate of railroad employees was reduced by more than one-half and the injury rate by more than two-thirds. It is easy to estimate how many lives and limbs might have been spared had the railroads been forced to protect their employees as diligently as they protected their expensive passenger cars.

Scientific American commented in an editorial on automatic coupling devices in 1896:

"It seems remarkable that all inventions designed to protect human life are adopted only after some stern statutory enactment, municipal, state, or national. Any invention containing features which fairly promise to protect property needs no support from the law-giving power of a community or a nation. The owner of a building will cheerfully equip it with fire extinguishers, but he rarely spends money for a fire escape until some municipal officer enforces a law to that effect.... This seems the natural result of human selfishness. Human life is cheap; property is dear."

CHAPTER FIFTEEN

Tickets, Please

I

"All he says is 'Ticket!'
and he utters the word in a dry, callous tone,
as if it would cost something to be cheerful."

THE AMERICAN AIRLINE STEWARDESS, uniformed in the colors and insignia of her corporate employer, masked with a frozen smile, and outfitted with an apparently limitless supply of bottled martinis, aspirin tablets, and airsickness bags, is one of the triumphant achievements of twentieth-century personnel management. She did not evolve, as did most of God's creatures, by a process of Darwinian mutation or divine manipulation; she was created whole, full-blown, to fit a predetermined role. She looks and acts the way she does because the airlines *wanted* her to look and act that way. Neither Pygmalion, carving his Galatea out of ivory, nor Zeus, plucking Athena out of his forehead, enjoyed such absolute control of his female material.

The American railroad conductor, on the other hand, grew as naturally as a thistle in a ditch. You might even say he got out of hand. From the very beginning of his career, he was captain of the train, elected by his fellow crewmen, a ceremonial figure, pompous and grandiose, whose magnificence put the most dignified passengers in the shade.

The conductor makes his first recorded appearance in the person of Mr. John T. Clark, "Master of Transportation" aboard a passenger train from Albany to Schenectady, New York, on an historic day in August, 1831. The occasion was the first passenger excursion over the newly completed, fifteen-mile Mohawk & Hudson Railroad, germ of the future New York Central system; the locomotive was the justly renowned *DeWitt Clinton;* the engineer was David Matthews, who had built the *Clinton* with his own hands at the

West Point Foundry; and the passengers were the bravest and brawniest citizens of upper New York, who had lined up at the hotel desks of Albany the night before to purchase tickets for the great event.

But it was Captain Clark, out of all the crew and crowd, who is remembered, stepping nimbly along a four-inch ledge that ran along the outside of the cars, collecting tickets, greeting friends, and finally mounting to a high buggy seat between the woodpile and a cask of water just behind the locomotive, where he drew from his pocket a small tin horn and blew a resonant fanfare that signaled the beginning of the journey.

The jerk of the locomotive on the loose couplings tumbled passengers to the floor. Blazing cinders of pitch pine from the furnace rained down on the open cars at the rear, lighting hats and coats and burning even the umbrellas that passengers raised as shields. Horses and oxen bolted through the meadows as the horrible smoking monster passed.

Still the Master of Transportation sat aloof on his perch. In the face of danger, discomfort, and exposure, he maintained a glacial majesty of bearing that would not be shaken through the years. In time, his frock coat would give way to a long-tailed cutaway of dark blue serge, trimmed with gold buttons. His silk topper would change into a billed cap, and he would relinquish the privilege of blowing a trumpet flourish or ringing a bell to announce the departure of every train. But he never would become, like the airline stewardess, a servant of the passengers: he was a representative of the company, if you please, with a heavy watch chain of white gold looped across his vest and his rank spelled out in silver letters on his hat.

In the East, conductors wore boutonnieres and answered to "Captain." Out west, one could meet a conductor on the Union Pacific who had yielded up his living scalp to the Sioux at Plum Creek and another who played angelically on a parlor organ in one of the sleeping cars. Everywhere, the conductor was a man of distinctive personality and independent behavior, worthy of respect.

When William Chambers, the Scottish biographer, encyclopedist, and publisher, toured the United States in the early 1850's, the conductor already had established himself as a powerful, if not particularly ingratiating, public figure.

AN AMERICAN CONDUCTOR is a nondescript being, half clerk, half guard, with a dash of the gentleman. He is generally well dressed, sometimes wears a beard, and when off duty passes for a respectable personage at any of the hotels and may be seen lounging about in the best company with a fashionable wife. No one would be surprised to find that he is a colonel in the militia. At all events, the conductor would need to be a person of some integrity, for the check upon his transactions is infinitesimally small.

One thing is remarkable about him—you do not get a sight of him till the train is in motion, and when it stops he disappears. I can account for this mysterious feature in his character only by supposing that as soon as he touches terra firma he removes from the front of his hat the word blazoned in metal, which indicates his office, and so all at once becomes an ordinary human being. The suddenness of his appearance when the train gets underway is marvelous. Hardly have the wheels made a revolution when the door at one end of the car is opened, and the conductor, like a wandering spirit, begins his rounds.

Walking down the middle, with a row of seats on each side, and each seat holding two persons, he holds out his hand right and left as he proceeds, allowing no one to escape his vigilance. All he says is "Ticket!" and he utters the word in a dry, callous tone, as if it would cost something to be cheerful. If you have already bought a ticket, you render it up to this abrupt demand, and a check in given in exchange. Should you have followed the ordinary practice and have no ticket to produce, the conductor selects the ticket you require from a small tin box he carries under his arm, and you pay him the cost of it, increased in price to the extent of five cents as a penalty for having had to buy it in the cars.

Within all the principal termini, there are offices where tickets may be procured, and there are likewise, in every city of importance, general railway agencies, resembling shops, where tickets for a series of railways may be purchased. These establishments are known by flaming placards hung out at the doors, and they distribute vast quantities of handbills, recommendatory of certain

Many passengers preferred to buy their tickets from the conductor.

routes as the cheapest and speediest. At the hotels these alluring advertisements are literally sown broadcast on the ground, it being nothing singular to see a lad enter with a mass of yellow- or pink-colored bills and throw them about on the tables, chairs, and floor of the bar, to be picked up and read according to pleasure.

Comparatively few persons, however, put themselves to the trouble of waiting to buy tickets at the stations, but unceremoniously enter the cars and take their seats even at the last moment, leaving the business of settlement to be adjusted with the conductor.

Having finished off in the car in which you are seated, the conductor opens the door at the farther end, steps across a gulf of two feet to the platform of the next car, and so goes through the whole train. In the van devoted to baggage, he has a kind of den for counting his money and cogitating over his affairs. But as there is no rest for the wicked, so there is no repose for a conductor. Just before the train comes up to a station, he makes his appearance and takes a deliberate survey of his customers, receiving checks from those who are about to depart. When the train is in motion again, the same ceremony is gone through—rather troublesome, it must be owned, but the conductor has a faculty for remembering who have checks for a long and who for a short journey, and he ceases to say "Ticket" more than two or three times to anybody.

When it grows dark, the conductor does not trust to the lamp that lights up each car; he carries a lantern with a strong reflector that enables him to scrutinize equivocal bank notes that may be tendered in payment. The lantern is made with a tin hoop beneath, and through this ring the arm is thrust so as to leave both hands disengaged.

The checks which are distributed and collected by the conductor consist of narrow pieces of pasteboard about three inches long. On one side there is a list of the various stopping places, with the intermediate distances in miles. Information in this form is very desirable, for there is a great deficiency of railway officers at the stations and the conductor is usually out of the way when you want to ask a question.

—From William Chambers's *Things as They Are in America,*
William and Robert Chambers, London and Edinburgh, 1854.

*An 1837 ticket
on the Boston
& Worcester Railway.*
Scribner's Monthly, 1888

II

"A conductor has to be alert to the tricks of passengers with a disposition to cheat the railroad."

THERE WERE INNUMERABLE CHALLENGES to the conductor's authority. Engineers, brakemen, station agents, passengers—even firemen asserted claims to boss the train. On a few railroads the crew at the head end usurped control, and the conductor was reduced to collecting fares, superintending freight and baggage, and shouting, "All aboard!"

According to a misty tradition, it was Captain Henry Ayres of the Erie Railroad who finally settled the issue in favor of the conductor. Ayres was a conductor on the Erie's forty-seven-mile run between Piermont-on-the-Hudson and Turner's, New York, in 1842. Time and again he had longed to be able to stop the train in the midst of a journey to put off some belligerent passenger who refused to pay his fare, and at last he devised a way to communicate with the engineer by running a piece of twine the length of the train and fastening it to a piece of wood in the engine cab. If Captain Ayres wanted the train to stop between stations, he would simply pull the string and raise the stick, commanding the engineer to close his throttle and whistle for brakes.

The engineer was a German named Jacob Hamel. Jacob Hamel wanted no orders from Henry Ayres. As soon as the train had left Piermont, he cut the twine. When Captain Ayres came up to the cab at the end of the run, Hamel said he proposed to run the locomotive without any interference from *dummkopfs* at the rear.

Next day, Captain Ayres rigged up the string and stick again.

"Jake," he said, "if that stick of wood is not on the end of this cord when we get to Turner's, you've got to lick me or I'll lick you."

On arrival at Turner's, Captain Ayres discovered that the string had been cut again. He took off his black frock coat and stovepipe hat, laid them neatly aside, and implored the engineer to step down from the cab. Jake declined the invitation, so the conductor climbed up and struck him a blow that propelled him out the other side of the cab. Thereafter, Jake Hamel responded to the tug of the conductor's leash, which in time became a bell cord.

To support the authenticity of this fable, every railroad passenger can offer evidence of the bellicose temper of many conductors. In other countries conductors are slightly more amiable; the American breed always has been notoriously grouchy. This trait may have resulted from the old-fashioned apprenticeship system, which required conductors to begin their careers as brakemen, a professional group renowned for pugnacity. Or perhaps it is attributable to the constant, abrasive contact with passengers, who are not only quarrelsome but also sneaky.

In his autobiography, *Forty Years on the Rail,* Charles George made a case for the noble conductor harassed by malicious and mendacious passengers.

THE DISTINGUISHING CHARACTERISTIC of the old-time conductor was his fine silk hat. Slouch and stiff hats were good enough for the ordinary citizen, but conductors followed their own taste in dress, usually selecting the best to be had. A leather strap, on which in silver letters was the word "Conductor," was buckled about the hat and taken off at the end of each run. As a lad, I never saw a more awe-inspiring sight than Levi Wright, of the Boston & Lowell road, with his tall hat and impressive dignity, waving his hand to the engineer and shouting "All aboard" in a tone worthy of a general. The first uniforms used by railway employees were on the Hudson River road, if I remember correctly. The Pennsylvania road next adopted uniforms; but it was not until the 1870's that they came into general use.

When I first worked as a conductor in the early fifties, we enjoyed a good

Slouch hats and bonnets were good enough for
ordinary citizens—but not for conductors.

London Illustrated News, 1861

deal of liberty in dress. Even our role as ticket-takers was still in an awkward evolution. At first, railroads had adopted the old stagecoach custom of "booking" passengers. No tickets were issued. The receipts kept by the booking clerk served as evidence that the fare had been paid. Later, the conductor used to make his rounds carrying a large tin box into which passengers dropped their fares in cash. One old conductor, who ran a train in Ohio, used to keep all the cash until Saturday night, then pay off himself and the boys on his run, returning the surplus earnings to the company. Conductors were great men in those times!

The first railroad tickets were simply thick, white cards, bearing the name of the company and of the two stations between which the ticket could be used. The agent at the selling point would write his name at the bottom to prevent counterfeiting.

Of course, these tickets were good only for local use on the railroad that issued them. There were no railroad pools or combinations. The cars of one line did not run over the tracks of another, and monthly balances between railroad companies were unknown. A passenger traveling beyond the limits of one road had to step off the train at the beginning of each new road and buy another ticket. Traveling from New York to Chicago, for example, the passenger had to leave the car at Buffalo and purchase a ticket over the connecting line that ran to Cleveland. There, he again went to the ticket office and paid his fare to Toledo. At Toledo, he bought his last ticket.

About the middle of the [nineteenth] century, the general ticket agent of the Lake Shore line hit on the idea of using coupon tickets from point of departure to destination. Each company would keep a division book, recording the amount due to and from other roads. At the end of a month, each road would make a statement to the others and pay up its balances. This plan, with some modifications in detail, made it possible for passengers to buy tickets all over the country.

A conductor has to be alert to the tricks of passengers with a disposition to cheat the railroad. Hundreds of pious people who would be horrified at the idea of stealing a penny from a neighbor seem to have no compunctions about defrauding a corporation—using limited tickets after they have expired, presenting tickets and passes made out to other persons, riding together on family passes when no relationship exists.

A common practice is to buy a ticket for a station just short of one's destination and then stay aboard the train, hoping the conductor will not notice. One day a man on my train rode past the station he had paid for. I suspected that there was something wrong, and after some argument with the passenger, I decided to pull the bell rope and put him off the train. When the man was on the ground, he turned around and said with an air of triumph: "This is all right. I live just over there." And he pointed to his house across a forty-acre lot.

Before the Interstate Commerce Bill [of 1888] limited the use of railroad passes, everybody who was acquainted with a railroad official found some pretext for asking for a pass. It is said that some of the eastern roads annually gave out twenty-five thousand free passes. Pass-holders sold their privileges to scalpers, and a dozen different persons might make use of a pass that was called "nontransferable."

A farmer once called on our superintendent and asked for a pass.

"I see yer cars are runnin' quite empty, and I thought you could take me 'long as well as not, there bein' so much room."

The superintendent explained that he could not give a pass on those grounds. The farmer thought a minute and then said:

"Wall, now, Mr. Superintendent, if I was a-drivin' 'long with my wagon in the country, and I had plenty of room, and you was walkin', and you should ask me to let you ride, and I refused, you would think I was a darned hog, now wouldn't you?"

The superintendent laughed heartily, turned around to his desk, and wrote out the desired paper.

A passenger once used his pass to torment one of my fellow conductors. This passenger, wearing ordinary citizen's clothes, boarded the train and quietly took a seat. When the conductor asked for his ticket, he said he had none.

"Then you must pay cash."

"I won't do anything of the kind, and you can't make me."

"We'll see about that," said the conductor, pulling the cord to stop the train.

"So you're going to put me off, are you?" said the man. "You can't do it. Here's my pass."

The pass was properly made out, and the conductor, though vexed enough to say something far from pleasant, left the car without a word.

After leaving the next station, the conductor came on a new passenger. The same conversation took place as before, and when the pass was produced, it was the very one offered by the other man. The explanation was that the passenger had drawn up his overcoat collar, hunched his shoulders out of position, put his hair and beard in disorder, and pulled his hat down over one eye, besides changing his seat.

Later in the trip the conductor saw, in the end seat by the stove, a new passenger, who had his coat off, wore a remarkable-looking checked shirt and a peculiar hat. As before, a ticket was asked for, then cash, and finally the cord was pulled. A general laugh arose in the car when the selfsame pass was produced and several people identified the man as the owner.

The man proved to be a veritable Proteus. He next disguised himself as a sufferer from neuralgia and rheumatism, had his face tied up and wore a huge muffler around his neck. The conductor was again deceived. His patience was all gone, but he held his peace and resolved not to be taken in again. He felt sure he knew his man.

At the next station a passenger got on board whom the conductor recognized at once as the practical joker who had worried him all day. Obviously, the man had got off one side of the train only to get on board at the other. As the conductor took up the tickets he passed by this man, giving him a wink and a broad smile. A little farther on, the man, who was really a new passenger, got off. As he left the car he said:

"I don't know what I've done to ride free, but seeing it's all the same to you, I don't care."

—From Charles George's *Forty Years on the Rail,*
R. R. Donnelly & Sons, Chicago, 1887.

III

"My friend, the chief dispatcher, told me frankly that enforcing the full fare would make me hundreds of enemies."

IF THE PRACTICE OF issuing free passes was a petty annoyance to conductors, it was a malignant monster to railroad managers. John Wilkinson, the president of the little Syracuse & Utica line in the 1840's, vowed to get rid of deadheading judges, militia officers, newspaper editors, and junketing charivaris such as "Aaron Burr's daughter's wedding party." In March, 1846, Wilkinson achieved one lustrous day without a single free-loading passenger; but no one could maintain the integrity of the Syracuse & Utica against the demands of seeping humanity. Wilkinson acknowledged in his diary that he had broken down and issued passes to "five mutes ... one poor crazy man ... six blind girls ... and a poor woman with a small infant. ..."

The main problem in limiting the number of deadheads was that most railroads could gain some sort of tactical advantage by issuing passes to legislators, cattle growers, manufacturers, and other men of consequence. Even men of no consequence carried passes that the railroads dealt out in the liberal spirit of bonhomie now called public relations. Aboard the Erie in its days of heroic legend-making, a conductor gave a lifetime pass to a Presbyterian minister who had talked the other passengers out of signing a petition against the railroad. The minister naturally suggested that all his brother clergymen should also get to ride free; and so the great and good-hearted Erie carried ministers year after year for love.

Sometimes it was the conductor himself who set up a system of reduced fares and free-loads without the knowledge of the company. A conductor on the Chicago & Northwestern in Minnesota in the 1880's boasted that he had accumulated twenty-five thousand dollars by knocking down the fares of cash passengers and pocketing a share of the coin. Spotters sent out by the company never succeeded in trapping him: he always received a timely warning when a spotter was aboard. An honest conductor who took over for a cheater had to face resentment and criticism. Harry French described some of the unpleasant consequences in his book *Railroadman.*

W HEN I BID IN AS CONDUCTOR on the Heppner branch of the Oregon Railroad & Navigation Company in the early 1890's, I stepped unknowingly into a pretty tough spot.

The fare over the branch was $2.25. That was the amount the OR&N was supposed to get. But the former conductor had used his own method of collecting fares. His proposition was that the passenger should pay him $1.50 cash and the railroad should never see it. The passenger saved seventy-five cents by not buying a ticket. Almost no tickets were sold by the local agents.

My first month's turn-in amounted to over five thousand dollars. It was an unheard-of amount to receive from that branch line. The sum was so great and so unexpected that it caused considerable comment at headquarters. I had a friend, the chief dispatcher, who told me frankly that enforcing the full fare would make me hundreds of enemies and that they would use every means to get me discharged. I did not worry about his warning, although I knew it was made in good faith. Had I wished to be dishonest, I could have played ball with any of several lawyers and had a large sum of money from my injuries. I had a lifetime job—what did I care for enemies?

One of the worst offenders was my own engineer—at first. He had developed a field of his own in passenger traffic. I told him I had no objection to a railroad man riding deadhead if he carried a card. But if this condition was met, that man did not have to ride the seat box with the fireman—he was welcome to come back and ride on the cushions as a railroad man should. I stopped the practice of people riding in the cab—but the engineer remained an enemy.

There was another factor I had not reckoned on. My policy caused a great number of ticket sales, and that meant a lot more work for the various agents. Inasmuch as these agents did not get anything out of ticket sales, I made a further number of ill-wishers.

But I did make a number of friends. After a couple of years on that run, I knew everybody in Heppner and in most of the stations along the forty-five-mile run to Arlington Junction. I knew prospectors and sheepherders, cowhands and wool buyers. With most of them I had more than just a nodding acquaintance.

Three of these sheepmen and a bank holdup at Roslyn, Washington, three hundred miles away, brought me a lot of grief. This holdup was staged by three men—desperate men, they turned out to be. They killed the cashier during the robbery. Several townspeople saw the gunfight and the shooting, and gave excellent descriptions of the men and their course of flight.

I was registering my train at Arlington when the wires began clicking off the story. I drew a pad toward me and wrote down the message:

> THE THREE SUPPOSED ROSLYN BANK ROBBERS ARE EXPECTED
> TO TRY TO CROSS THE COLUMBIA AT EITHER GRANTS OR ARLINGTON.
> THEY ARE HEADING FOR THE BLUE MOUNTAINS.

The rest was a close, detailed description of the three men. I wrote it all down. This message was intended for the sheriffs at Grants and Arlington. The sheriff at Arlington already had been given a description of the men and had departed for the hills in search of them. I could not deliver the message I had intercepted, but I kept the copy I had made.

When my train was about ready to leave Arlington, I noticed three men who were acting suspiciously. They kept moving about—not actually hiding, but keeping behind sheds, warehouses, and sidetracked boxcars until my train was ready to pull out. When I gave the "All aboard," they came over together, got on, and paid their fares.

Their acts in my train further drew my suspicions. I had seen them as a group of three around the warehouses; they had entered my train as a group of three; but when they selected their seats, they divided. Two sat in a front seat, which they had reversed to face the rear of the coach; the other sat in a rear seat facing forward. In this way, they could see everything that went on in that coach. All of them wore six-guns. (This was not unheard of in upstate Oregon, but it was uncommon. The casual cowhand might take his six-gun along with him to be used in cases of social necessity, but it would be carried in his war bag—not on his hip.)

The first station out of Arlington was Willows. It had telegraph facilities. I sent Sheriff Noble of Heppner a wire:

> HAVE THREE ROSLYN SUSPECTS ON MY TRAIN. BETTER MEET IT
> PREPARED FOR ACTION. ALL ARE ARMED.

I was not sure how far the men would ride. Two had paid fares to Douglas, about ten miles from Willows; the other had paid to Ione, about halfway to Heppner.

Arriving at Douglas, the two who had paid to that point decided to go on to Ione. The train was delayed twenty minutes or so at Ione, and I fully expected the men would vanish while I was absent from the coach. But, leaving Ione, I discovered I still had my three suspects. We were pretty well acquainted by this time. They told me jokingly that they had finally decided to go on to Heppner.

By this time I was pretty certain these were the bandits. They answered the description in every particular. I showed my copy of the telegraph message to my baggageman, Joe Helfrich, and asked him to take a look at the three men. Joe's look was just a glorified peek. He was about as scared as a man could be and still walk. He was certain they would try to carry off his strongbox—and there happened to be a large amount of specie in the strongbox on that trip. We reread the description and agreed that it tallied with the men in the coach. I mentioned writing this description on a pad at Arlington. Inasmuch as I was intercepting a message, I had no time to get a clean, new sheet. Along with the description, I had jotted down the numbers of some cars on the sidings at Arlington. I kept that piece of paper with the message and description. Why, I do not know. The hunch just came to me to hold onto it.

Our train, a combination freight and passenger, was a heavy one. Joe Helfrich and I talked over the possibility that the men might try to rob us on the stiff grade between Lexington and Heppner. Figuring that our job was to prevent a robbery if possible, I went into the baggage car as we approached the long grade. Joe supplied me with a six-shooter, and I belted it on. We covered the strongbox with other baggage and waited. As we drew close to Heppner, I unstrapped my six-shooter and went back into the coach.

My three suspects had gone. Passengers informed me they had gotten off when the train slowed down. A disappointed sheriff met my train. He and his posse left immediately in pursuit.

About two weeks later, pinned to the register at Arlington, there were three pictures and a note from the agent asking me if I had ever seen these men. The pictures were of three sheepshearers who had often ridden on my train. I knew these men—Hale, Kimsey, and Zachary—very well. They were rough, two-fisted, drinking men of a type that eastern Oregon still produces in quantity. I penciled under the note the single word, "Yes," and forgot about the inquiry.

A Tacoma detective now came to me and asked if I could identify the three men I had had on my train the day of the robbery. I told him how many times they had paid fares to me and how many conversations we had had. I was certain I could recognize those men if I ever saw them again. The detective told me three men were under arrest in jail in Ellensburg. One of them already had been tried and convicted of first-degree murder.

"Your evidence will convict the other two," the detective told me. "There is a two-thousand-dollar reward on the conviction of all three. That reward will be split three ways: you, Joe Helfrich, and myself." (Joe Helfrich had made the trip to testify under this man's urging. His testimony had been the means of convicting the first man.)

Arriving in Ellensburg, I was met by the attorney for the defense. He asked me to accompany him to the jail. A group of fifteen men were prisoners.

"See if there is any one you recognize, Mr. French."

I looked over the group. Imagine my surprise when I saw Hale, Kimsey, and Zachary. I shook hands with these men—called them by name. The defending attorney told me that it was my "Yes" on that note of the station agent that had caused the arrest of these men. Hale had been tried first, and the trial had resulted in conviction of first-degree murder.

"But these are not the men I had on my train that day!" I said. "They don't even answer the description that was sent out."

"Have you, by any chance, still got that paper with the message and descrip-

tion you intercepted?" the lawyer asked. Joe Helfrich had mentioned my intercepting the police wire.

I dug the message out of my wallet. Just a yellow piece of paper, but on it
were car numbers and the register check I had made that day, as well as the
message itself.

The defense lawyer was elated.

"Until now I have had no way of proving that they were framing those three
men. When you give your testimony tomorrow, you'll take the noose from around
Hale's neck."

Next day, I took the stand and the prosecutor plied me with questions.

"You were the conductor on the Arlington-to-Heppner train of such and
such a date?"

"I was."

"You intercepted a message at Arlington concerning the Roslyn bank
robbery?"

"I did."

"You wired the sheriff at Heppner that men answering the description were
on your train?"

"Yes, sir."

"You would recognize these men if you saw them again?"

"I am certain I would.

"Bring in the prisoners."

Hale, Kimsey, and Zachary were brought into the courtroom.

"Do you recognize these men, Mr. French?"

"I do."

"Are these the men who rode your train on that date?"

"Positively not."

"What?"

"Positively not."

"But you just said that you recognized them!" the prosecutor stormed.

"I do recognize them. They have ridden my train many times."

All efforts of the prosecutor to shake my testimony were useless. He asked
the court to have it stricken from the records. This the court refused to do. The
defending attorney brought out the fact that the three men on trial were hard
workers and that my penciled note to the agent at Arlington had nothing to do
with identifying the men as the Roslyn bank robbers. I was asked to produce the
original message I had written. It was submitted in evidence, and the court ruled
that it was acceptable. The defense scored heavily by bringing out the fact that
the description in no way applied to the men on trial. Under questioning, I estimated that the three men on trial had ridden my train a dozen times or more in
the two years that I had been on the Heppner branch. I had never seen them
armed. Furthermore, it was brought out that Joe Helfrich was badly scared when
he had his peek at the men he thought were trying to lift his strongbox.

The facts broke the state's case. All three men were eventually released. The

Roslyn case was cleared up in Idaho a short time later. In a bank holdup in that state, the robbers overlooked a cashier who happened to be an ex-cowboy and a fine offhand pistol shot. When the smoke of his six-shooter cleared away, one robber was dead, one dying, and one so wounded that he thought he was finished. In a statement that he imagined was his last, he confessed that he and his two partners had held up the bank at Roslyn and had killed the cashier, had taken a train from Arlington to Heppner, and had escaped into the hills at that point.

When his share of the two-thousand-dollar reward slipped out of his fingers, the Tacoma detective became my active enemy. It took him only three months to get his revenge, and I shall always believe that he had help in getting it.

I was discharged for the theft of thirty-six cents.

Although I was able to prove that my paid fares and tickets showed five more passengers than the report against me claimed, nothing could save me from the frame-up.

Framed, discharged, dishonored, I left the OR&N. It had taken a straight-shooting cashier in Idaho to clear me of suspicion of conniving with criminals to escape justice. I never had a similar chance to prove myself innocent of the theft of thirty-six pieces of copper.

—Excerpted from Chauncey Del French's *Railroadman,*
copyright 1938 by the Macmillan Company, New York.

King's *The Southern States, 1875*

CHAPTER SIXTEEN

Lord of the Pullman Car

I

*"On the first night I had to compel
the passengers to take their boots off
before they got into their berths."*

CONSIDERING THE DISCOMFORT AND DANGER of railroad travel during the early years of steam, it is difficult to understand how any passenger could have fallen asleep amid the horrors of the journey. Nevertheless, many travelers—fatalistic, steel-nerved, or exhausted—did indeed succumb to a sort of limp, half-conscious hibernation. Their heads lolled sideways on the wooden benches, their hats fell off, their mouths drooped open, and their eyes closed on the waking nightmare. When headlamps were invented and night travel increased, it was natural that. some aggressive railroad should provide these groggy customers with horizontal resting places.

The bellwether company was the little Cumberland Valley Railroad, which chugged among the Pennsylvania hills from Harrisburg to Chambersburg. The Cumberland's first sleeping car, introduced in 1836, was simply a day coach that had been split into several compartments, each one fitted out with two or three roughly padded shelves along one side of the car. There was no bedding (you were expected to bring your own blankets or lie down with your clothes on), precious little ventilation, and scarcely more privacy than is available in an army barracks. The car was heated with a wood-burning stove that was almost guaranteed to tip over and incinerate all aboard in the event of a wreck. Obviously, the sleeper was for men only; no woman would have ventured inside that foul-smelling, candle-lit dormitory with its creaking wooden floors, its row of brass spittoons, and its tiers of grumbling male bodies, laid out with their boots on like cadavers in a morgue.

Between the first appearance of this murky little coffin-rack and the emergence of opulent palace cars as designed by Woodruff, Wagner, Pullman, and Mann, American travelers passed twenty or thirty years of relatively painful nights stretched out on many varieties of convertible swivel couches, horsehair bunks, cane-bottomed berths, hinged shelves, and patented, airborne platforms. It was only when railroads began to reach across the vast distances of the mid-continent that the extra-fare, luxury sleeper for long-distance travel came to perfection.

The patriarch of the business was George Pullman of Chicago, whose name has become synonymous with railroad sleeping cars. Trained as a cabinetmaker in a small town on the Erie Canal, Pullman had gained a reputation as a practical genius in the Midwest by figuring out how to lift a large hotel several feet to a new street level. (He used thousands of jacks, manned by hundreds of workmen, to raise the building a fraction of an inch at a time.)

With the money he had made raising buildings along the boggy shore of Lake Michigan, Pullman undertook to convert two day coaches of the Chicago & Alton line into a new style of sleeping car. On its inaugural run, Pullman's first car was put in charge of a young conductor named J. L. Barnes—first of a new breed of railroad men: the Pullman car attendant.

The first Pullman car—a "primitive thing"—was called the Pioneer.
Scribner's Monthly, 1888

M R. George M. Pullman had an office on Madison Avenue just west of LaSalle Street in Chicago, and I boarded with a family very close to his office. I used to pass his office on my way to meals. Having read in the paper that he was working on a sleeping car, I stopped in one day and made application to Mr. Pullman personally for a place as conductor. I gave him some references and called again, and he said the references were all right and promised me the place.

I made my first trip between Bloomington, Illinois, and Chicago on the night of September 1, 1859. I was twenty-two years old at the time. I wore no uniform and was attired in citizen's clothes. I wore a badge, that was all. One of my passengers was Mr. Pullman himself. All the passengers were from Bloomington, and there were no women on the car that night. The people of Bloomington, little reckoning that history was being made in their midst, did not come down to the station to see the Pullman car's first trip. There was no crowd, and the car, lighted by candles, moved away in solitary grandeur, if such it might be called.

I remember on the first night I had to compel the passengers to take their boots off before they got into the berths. They wanted to keep them on—seemed afraid to take them off.

The first month business was very poor. People had been in the habit of sitting up all night in the straight-back seats, and they did not think much of trying to sleep while traveling. After I had made a few trips, it was decided it did not pay to employ a Pullman conductor. The car was placed in charge of the passenger conductor of the train which carried the sleeping car, and I was out of a job.

The first Pullman car was a primitive thing. Besides being lighted with candles, it was heated by a stove at each end of the car. There were no carpets on the floor, and the interior of the car was arranged in four upper and four lower berths. The backs of the seats were hinged. To make up the lower berth, the porter merely dropped the back of the seat until it was level with the seat itself. Upon this he placed a mattress and blanket. There were no sheets.

The upper berth was suspended from the ceiling of the car by ropes and pulleys attached to each of the four corners of the berth. The upper berths were constructed with iron rods running from the floor of the car to the roof. During the day the berth was pulled up until it hugged the ceiling; at night, it was suspended about halfway between the ceiling of the car and the floor. We used curtains in front and between all the berths.

In the daytime one of the sections was used to store all the mattresses in. The car had a very low deck and was quite short. It had four-wheel trucks and, with the exception of the springs under it, was similar to the freight car of today. The coupler was link and pin—we had no automatic brakes or couplers in those days. There was a very small toilet room in each end, only large enough for one person at a time. The washbasin was made of tin. The water for the washbasin came from the drinking can, which had a faucet so that people could get a drink.

—Reprinted from Joseph Hubbard's *The Story of the Pullman Car.*
Copyright by A. C. McClurg & Company, Chicago, 1917.

II

"A tip is not a humiliation, but a living salary would be preferable."

ALTHOUGH PULLMAN'S CONVERTED DAY COACHES were fairly successful, neither the Alton line nor the inventor was completely satisfied. Pullman went out to Colorado for four years and ran a general store in a mining town, meanwhile pondering lofty schemes for hinged upper berths and seats that could slither together by night to form beds of Medicean grandeur.

Returning to Chicago, Pullman formed a partnership with his boyhood friend, Ben Field, and spent the staggering sum of eighteen thousand dollars to build *Pioneer,* the first true Pullman sleeping car. It was a foot wider and two and one-half feet higher than any railroad car in America. To put the *Pioneer* in service, the Alton had to widen bridges and narrow station platforms the length of its route; but the carpentry was completed in time for the *Pioneer* to make two historic journeys—first with the funeral train that carried the body of President Lincoln to Springfield, then with the excursion train that hastened General Grant from Detroit to his home in Galena, Illinois.

It was not George Pullman's inventive spark but his zeal as a hotelkeeper and business strategist that made him preeminent in the sleeping car industry. He saw earlier than his rivals that a growing class of Americans would pay for cleanliness and comfort, and his exacting standards of quality set Pullman cars apart from other parlors-on-wheels. Not only did Pullman build cars, he undertook to keep them clean, staff them with trained attendants, supply them with bedding and linens, and put the stamp of his own name on every portable item. This complex and unprecedented service gradually evolved into an immensely profitable national business.

At one time traveling salesmen considered it the acme of wit to call Pullman porters "George," presumably after the paternal founder himself. No one knows precisely when or why Pullman decided that porters must be men of the Negro race; but for close to a century all porters in the United States have been Negroes. The first was probably a well-trained ex-slave, hired about 1867. Nameless in history, he filled his positions so capably that he established an exclusive field of employment for thousands of other black men, who gained education, mobility, and social status by working for the railroad.

H. Nathaniel Hall, who wrote this illuminating account of a porter's life for the *American Mercury* in 1931, was born in Alabama, the son of a Baptist preacher. He had worked in many non-railroad jobs, as a waiter, elevator operator, bootblack, bellhop, real estate salesman, and post office employee, but he found his vocation in the Pullman car.

I AM ONE OF THE SIX THOUSAND colored men who will be at the doors of your Pullman cars tonight, waiting to greet you and watch over you as a mother hen watches over her chicks. Before you are off your car, you will have every reason to believe that your porter knows his business.

The Pullman Company's first step toward service is the careful selection of its men. It prefers to discriminate, and it does discriminate. It recruits its porters mainly from certain states of the old South—chiefly Georgia and the Carolinas. Indeed, it almost limits its choice to certain counties within those states. It shows a decided preference for the sons of its employees; in fact, one might almost say that there are boys growing up down there in the cotton country who came into the world with the hope and expectation of becoming Pullman porters.

King's *The Southern States, 1875*

As soon as a rookie enters the service, he goes to school in one of the large railroad centers. A sidetracked sleeping car is his schoolroom. A retired porter is his instructor. First, he learns to swat the fly—to drive him from the car. Then he is shown the proper handling of the linen closet—the proper method of folding and putting away clean linen and blankets, the correct way of stacking in laundry bags the dirty and discarded bedding. A sheet, towel, or pillow case once unfolded cannot be used again, although it may be spotless. Technically, it is dirty and must make a round trip to the laundry before it can reenter the service.

The company's rule book stresses discipline. The instructors teach not only the art of making up and taking down beds, they also go into such finer things as how to call passengers. Noise is tabooed, and even a soft knock on the top of the berth is forbidden. A porter must gently shake the curtains on the bedding *from without.*

When the recruit has finished this schoolroom education, he goes out on the line. Under the direction of an old porter, he first comes into contact with actual patrons—comes to know their personalities and their peculiarities. After all, we porters are servants, and we realize that as such we must perfect ourselves, we must always do better, we must anticipate our patrons' desires.

After several trials with an old porter, the new man is turned out alone on his first trip, all excited. What an experience that first trip is! Mine was a nightmare. We left New York (where I took my schooling) at 8:00 P.M. and were scheduled to arrive at Buffalo at 7:30 the next morning. I had never experienced people yelling at me to hurry and make their beds when I was with the old porter on my trial trips over this line, for he had everything well in hand, and had his passengers in bed before the train arrived at Albany. But this night was far different. Passengers began calling for berths to be made up as soon as the train pulled out of the station. Grips were lying all over the aisles, and it seemed to me that everybody was calling and ringing the bell at once. My last passenger finally got to bed somewhere between Rochester and Rome, New York. (Anyone who has been on that line knows that it is daylight when the train arrives at those cities.)

Two gentlemen—and I mean *real* gentlemen—found out that it was my first trip and contented themselves with sleeping it out in the smoking room.

My eighteen years in blue have been full of experiences. I have met people in all walks of life, and I know at least two hundred of the big bankers and businessmen of New York and Boston. I know the Boston ones better—the ones who belong to the Somerset and Algonquin clubs and are Boston enough to pronounce Peabody "Pebbuddy"—and they know me. But it isn't just knowing them and being able to call them by their names; I've got to remember what they smoke, what they drink, and how many minutes to call them before breakfast.

I have been asked quite often who are the best passengers and tippers. That question is hard to answer, but my first choice goes to the regular riders, such as traveling salesmen, who ride weekly or monthly. These men know service; they are reasonable; and your tip, though only standard, is sure. Then there is the working class, who work a year to take a vacation. They have itemized every little detail for the two weeks' trip, and they never forget the porter. Newlyweds are also good. The groom tips fast and heavy, especially in the presence of the bride, and he is always in her presence. Women traveling alone are very conservative with their tips.

Baseball players are the limit: most of them are vulgar and uncouth. They tear up the linen, destroy the pillows in battles, and many walk out without even saying "thanks" for the service. One big league team in particular has this reputation. When a porter is assigned to its car, he is in for a miserable night, and all porters know it.

Among the most generous tippers of today are underworld characters. Drunks were once also among the best, good for tips ranging from five to ten dollars; but now, in this age of rotten liquor and bad beer, they're only good to lose something—a shirt, a suitcase, or a shoe.

Some actors and actresses are ill bred and like to impress their friends with their importance, but as a general rule they're pretty fair. Writers and reporters are a good bunch, all jovial, with a few exceptions. Boxers are also fine, Mr. Dempsey being the choice of the lot—a gentleman always. He never allows a porter to address him as Mr. Dempsey but always wants to be called Jack.

A wealthy traveler is always good when the service is good. He knows service, demands it, and pays for it; but if he is traveling with his valet or secretary, it is a bad proposition for us porters, for he leaves the tipping to his servants, and they are as a rule hard on porters. Often they keep part of what the employer allows for service. Sometimes, I hear, a valet tosses the money his employer allows for tips in the air. All that comes down he pockets, and all that hangs on the bell cord he gives to the porter.*

The better class of riders and tippers are in the East, and many of them seem to ride the New York Central. It is an old saying among porters that if you are not railroading for the New York Central, you are not railroading at all.

There are many trains a porter does not like to ride— for instance, one of the stag trains out of Chicago to Detroit. It leaves Chicago about midnight. It is always heavily loaded, and the passengers are regular riders who know every stop on the line. Three-fourths of them will not take any service, such as a brush-off or assistance with baggage, but will sneak off to keep from tipping.

In the days when I made that run, the porters became desperate. Caucus after caucus was held, scheme after scheme was tried, but nothing seemed to stop the sneaks. We tried locking the doors, but they would get through locked doors and swing off before the train came to a stop. Some would go up to the smoker and get off, and one porter declares that he caught a man trying to get through a transom. Most of those stag riders could make Houdini look small when it came

---

*Henry Tammen, one of the founders of the Denver *Post*, vouched that in his days as a bartender in the old Windsor Hotel he would toss up each dollar he collected: If it stuck to the ceiling, it belonged to the boss; if it fell, it was Tammen's.

to getting out of tight places. We finally found a remedy: we got wet towels and placed them in the doors. When those heavy steel doors swing on a wet towel, it's a job for a half-dozen men to open them. It's funny now to see the stags walk by and get their brush-off after they have tried to open the back door and failed.

Many folks will probably be surprised to hear that porters dislike crack trains. Tips as a rule are smaller, for the fare is much higher. Many people ride these trains just to say they have been on them; and after they pay the excess in fare, they are hardly able to tip. Then, too, you never know when you are going to have one of the road directors aboard, or a Wall Street banker who owns half of the company. Inspectors are on your neck every step, and write-ups are quite common. The world's biggest ride these crack trains, but common riders are best for the day-after-day grind. Their demands are less exacting.

The Pullman Company does not pay a porter very much for his work—in fact, not enough for him to live on if tips were abolished. A few years ago the late Robert Todd Lincoln, son of the Emancipator and at that time president of the Pullman Company, sat before the Federal Trade Commission in Washington and answered some pretty pointed questions as to the division of the porter's income between the company and the passenger.

The salary at that time was $27.50 a month for the first fifteen years of service, slightly increasing thereafter to $30. Today the porter gets $77.50 a month for eleven thousand miles service, and out of it $4.20 a month is taken for a group insurance policy and for membership in the Pullman Benefit Association. The former is compulsory. The policy provides no benefit if the porter is injured or killed on duty. When he is dismissed from the service, regardless of his years in the service, the policy terminates.

A porter is required to report to work—receiving passengers and seeing that his car is in order—two hours before his train leaves, and for this he receives no pay, since his time doesn't begin until the train departs. Many times he hangs around the "sign out" office from eight o'clock in the morning till eight or nine o'clock in the night, waiting to be assigned to a car. If he gets no car, he gets no pay. Porters are paid only for the time and mileage they make.

A recent survey made by the New York Labor Bureau showed that the average monthly tips of a porter came to $58 and that the porter was compelled to pay out $33 a month for food in transit and at terminals, and for two uniforms a year and shoe polish to shine passengers' shoes. Tips are uncertain, irregular, and often inadequate, but it seems that the system has fastened itself on the porter securely, and he must smile genially as he views what he thought was a quarter tip, only to find it to be a Canadian penny.

A quarter seems to be the standard Pullman tip. Some men give more; some, alas, less. A tip is not a humiliation, but a living salary would be preferable, for in these days tips sometimes run far below the most modest living standard. A porter whose run carries him from New York to Chicago and back nowadays averages around $45 a month in tips. For this he works pretty hard.

Take, for example, a porter who runs between New York, Chicago, and St.

Louis. He leaves New York shortly after lunch on Monday, having reported at his car nearly three hours before, so as to make sure that it is properly stocked and cleaned for its long trip. He is due at St. Louis near eleven o'clock Tuesday evening, though it will be nearly two hours later before he has checked the contents of the car and slipped off to the porters' quarters or made his own bunk in the smoking room.

On Wednesday evening at seven o'clock he starts east, due in New York about dawn Friday morning. He cleans up his car and himself, and gets to his home in Harlem some time before noon. By noon on Saturday he must be back in his car, making sure it is fit and ready by 2:30 P.M.—the moment the conductor's arm falls, and they're headed west again.

This time the destination is Chicago, which is reached about six o'clock Sunday night. The porter bunks that night in the Windy City, then spends thirty hours or more on a slow train, going back again to New York. He sees his home one more night; then he is off to St. Louis again, started on a fresh round of his eternal schedule. During these trips he has plenty of time to count the telegraph poles, think about the Hoover prosperity and the unequal distribution of wealth, and reflect on the mutability of men and things, for passengers are scarce today. But the porter is hard-schooled in adversity. Many are the times he gets back home from St. Louis or Chicago with a fifty-cent profit. This is likely to create an anarchist—or at least a socialist—under that black skin.

The Pullman Company collects revenue from passengers and a mileage fee from the railroad, even on a half or three-quarters empty car; but the porter's end of the business is a dead loss when his car is nearly empty. One cannot, of course, blame the company, for it is a business proposition, not a charitable institution, although many Negro boys have had to depend on it for the means to acquire an education, and thousands of Negro men and women have relied upon it for a living. In many fields the black man is shoved aside. Once the Negro servant was the pride of America. A black man stood at your elbow in the dining room of every great hotel. A colored butler was the joy of the finest homes along Fifth Avenue or around Rittenhouse Square. But those days have passed, and despite the vexing questions of tips, the Pullman Company might fairly be called our salvation.

One or two of the Canadian roads, which operate their own sleeping-car service, have employed white men as porters; down in the Southwest, the Mexican has been placed in the familiar blue uniform; and a few years back the Pullman Company tried out Filipinos. But none of them has been as satisfactory as the Negro. Many porters on Pullman cars today are college- and high-school–trained men who found the life on a Pullman pleasant and exciting. I, for one, left and attended high school and came back; left again for post-office work and came back again. The chance to meet people and see the country, and the opportunity to make a living in a pleasant way are magnets that draw us back.

Like nearly every other job, that of the Pullman porter has its hardships. If you do not believe me, just go upstairs some hot summer night to that rear

In the Pullman Parlor Car of the 1880s,
the saying was: "Let George do it."
Scribner's Monthly, 1888

bedroom—the little room under the tin roof that you keep for your relatives—and make up the bed fifteen or twenty times, carefully unmaking it between times, and placing the clothes away in a regular position. Let your family nag at you and criticize you during every moment of the job, while somebody plays a solo on the electric bell and places leather grips and shoes underneath your feet. Imagine that the house is bumping and rocking—and then try to keep a smiling face and a courteous tongue through it all.

Or do it on a bitter night in midwinter; and between every two or three makings of the bed in an overheated room, slip out of your linen coat into a serge one, and go and stand outside the door from three to ten minutes in the snow and cold. In some ways that is the hardest part of the porter's job. At all stops, we must be outside the car, no matter what the hour or condition of the weather.

What becomes of old porters? Sometimes, when the trains, the broken nights' rest, the exposure, and the hard work begin to be too much for them, they are rewarded with soft runs on parlor cars—a leisurely seventy or a hundred miles a day, or on sleepers on a side line, where travel is light. When the old porter is unable to hold even his soft run, probably he has saved enough for his dreams to come true: a small sandy farm on a Carolina hillside, where an old man may sit and nod in the warm sun and dream of the days when steel cars were new and went bounding over the rails—may dream and nod and then, in his waking hours, stir the grandchildren to the glories of a fast train and a fat run.

—Abridged from "The Art of the Pullman Porter," by H. N. Hall, *American Mercury*, July, 1931. Copyright 1931 by the *American Mercury*.

*In personal appearance the Brave Engineer
sometimes seemed more avuncular than heroic.*
Leslie's Illustrated Newspaper, 1872

CHAPTER SEVENTEEN

The Brave Engineer

I

*"I grabbed the whistle cord again and
frantically blew the 'broke in two' signal,
hoping it would warn someone that I was
coming through and couldn't stop."*

RAILROADS ARE LIKE THE GOVERNMENT. They are large, complicated, and useful, but year in and year out they are hard to love. In more than a century, the American railroads produced only one or two folk heroes. The wonder is not that there were so few, but that there were any at all.

A few near-heroes come to mind, but some unpleasant aspect blights each one. Think of the sturdy Irish tarriers, pounding spikes out in the desert of Wyoming, and your heart fills with admiration; but then think of the Credit Mobilier that the promoters of the Union Pacific set up to milk the public and corrupt the Congress of the United States, and an unbearable miasma begins to fill your nostrils. Think of tough old Commodore Vanderbilt, Jay Gould, Dan Drew, Jim Fisk—the picaroons of railroad finance—and you feel a certain wild, wicked glee; then think of the strangled commuter service into New York and Philadelphia on the conglomerate Penn-Central, and every pulse of sympathy for railroad financiers slinks away like the mistreated passengers of this huge and monolithic corporation.

In search of railroad heroes, it is best to think only of the Brave Engineer, highballing to glory, unsustained by the blotches on anyone's industrial image.

They handed him his orders at Monroe, Virginia,
Sayin', "Pete, you're way behind time.
"This is not Thirty-Eight, but it's old Ninety-Seven
"You must put her into Spencer on time."

It was Sunday, September 27, 1903, and the Southern Railway's Fast Mail, Number 97 from Washington to New Orleans, was an hour behind schedule. At the division point in Monroe, a new engineer, Joseph A. Broady, and a fresh crew boarded the train. They had a 166-mile run ahead, which normally took about four and a quarter hours.

He looked around the can at his black greasy fireman,
Sayin', "Shovel in a little more coal.
"An' when we cross that White Oak Mountain
"You can watch old Ninety-Seven roll!"

It's a mighty rough road from Lynchburg to Danville
And a line on a three-mile grade.
It was on that grade that he lost his average,
And you see what a jump he had made.

Just north of Danville, there was a high bridge called Stillhouse Trestle, spanning the ravine of Cherrystone Creek. Without cutting speed, Broady sent old Ninety-Seven hurtling down the hill and into a dangerous curve above the trestle.

He was goin' down hill making ninety miles an hour
When the whistle broke into a scream!

The engine leaped off the tracks and dived into the bank of the stream, dragging five cars behind. The two firemen, the conductor, a flagman, and eight postal clerks were killed. As for the Brave Engineer:

He was found in the wreck with his hand on the throttle
And a-scalded to death with the steam.

When a popular singer named Vernon Dalhart recorded "The Wreck of the Old Ninety-Seven" years after the event, hundreds of persons professed to have written the words. The United States Supreme Court finally ruled that they were the work of David Graves George, a Virginia farmer. George had once been a brakeman, and he had seen the smoldering wreckage of the Ninety-Seven shortly after the disaster. Setting his primitive poem to the tune of "The Ship That Never Returned," he sang the ballad to a group of his friends at the village barbershop.

Like most other enduring tales of the Brave Engineer, "The Old Ninety-Seven" is feeble in character development, elliptic in plot, unconvincing in dialogue, trite in theme, weak in motivation, inconsistent in idiom, coarse in language, and does not parse. It also is an almost perfect vignette of man and fate, a microcosmic drama of duty and destiny.

For a more intimate and introspective picture of the Brave Engineer in action, one has to look into the personal accounts of men who survived the classic predicament. In *The General Manager's Story*, Herbert Hamblen tells about a downhill run that could have turned out as badly as Joseph Broady's last trip.

M Y BOYHOOD HOME WAS near a heavy grade on the local railroad. I used to watch with great interest as the long freight trains slowly and laboriously puffed up the hill, the brakemen sitting (if it happened to be pleasant weather) on their brake wheels, with folded arms and hat brims flapping in the breeze.

But it was the down trips I preferred to see. As soon as the engine pitched over the crest of the hill, the engineer would shut off his steam, and the train, gathering headway from its own weight, would whirl down the grade at a great rate. The engineer would blow his whistle, and the brakemen, running lightly over the tops of the bounding and rocking cars, would twist up the brakes as though they could tear them out by the roots.

There was one fellow—a big, tall, strapping man, a perfect Hercules—who always rode near the middle of the train when going down the hill. I fancied I could see the train perceptibly slow down every time he set a brake.

One day his train broke in two a couple of cars ahead of where he sat. I noticed a gradually widening gap between the cars, and he soon spied it too. He leaped to his feet, let out a wild yell, pulled off his straw hat and swung it a full-arm vertical circle in front of him, and having thus signaled the engineer, commenced to set brakes with all his might. You see, when a train breaks in two on a downgrade, the head section at first draws away from the rear one, but then the lighter rear section, unless checked by the brakes, gains so much momentum that it will crash into the back of the head section—and this results in some of the worst wrecks known to railroad men.

When the engineer gets a signal that his train is broken in two—or discovers the fact himself, by looking back on a curve—he instantly "pulls out" and runs as fast as possible to get away from the rear section, at the same time giving the whistle signal for "broke in two" to notify the train crew, so that they can set brakes to stop the rear end.

In this case, the engineer either saw the brakeman's signal or discovered the break himself. I saw the head end dart away and heard four long blasts of the whistle, repeated again and again. The trainmen responded promptly and did their level best to stop their half, but the hill was so steep, and the train had got such headway on it, that even with all brakes set and fire flying from the wheels, they went down that grade like a stone dropping into a well.

At first it seemed as if the locomotive gained quite rapidly. By the volume of black smoke pouring out of her stack, I knew that the engineer was giving it all she was worth. After awhile, she seemed barely to hold her own, and then the rear section seemed to gain on the one ahead. This appearance might have been partly due to my perspective.

Anyway, I saw that the train crew finally got the rear part stopped. The engine, which was now half a mile or more ahead of them, backed up, coupled on— and away they went.

This incident, I afterwards learned, was a very common occurrence. In fact, it happened to me a few years later, after I had become a locomotive engineer in the freight service of one of our great railroads.

There was a mountain on our division, and the track down this mountain was about seven miles long. At the top was a tunnel half a mile long, opening onto a short curve on the downhill side. It was a handy place to look back and see if your train was all together. The road down the mountain was quite crooked, as such places always are, and so steep that to take a train up its entire length without "doubling," was a feat to brag about. Halfway down, and hidden by a curve from both directions, was a station with a freight house on the opposite side of the tracks. Nearly all inward-bound trains had cars to drop off at the freight house, and they had to cross over the outward-bound track to get to the freight siding. The switch to this siding was a "head-on" switch to the outward or downhill track. The whole place came under the "yard-limit" rule, requiring all freight trains to come in there dead slow; and, consequently, conductors had gotten in the habit of leaving the head-on switch open after they went into the freight siding, so as to be able to get back on the main track without readjusting the switch. The flagman would go around the curve to flag any oncoming train and stop it before it could run through the open track and into the siding.

On the day we broke in two, I had a heavy mixed train, including four cars loaded with railroad iron. As soon as my engine had plunged into the tunnel, I shut her off, for she would roll all too fast after that and would need a few brakes set. I knew the crew were apt to be asleep in the caboose—it was early on a summer morning—so I called for brakes to wake them up. Nothing happened. I looked back as I came out of the tunnel and watched the cars following each other out. About half the train came through, then no more.

I pulled out at once and blew the "broke in two" signal again and again, all the time looking back for the rear end of my train. We must have parted just on the crest of the mountain, and the rear section must nearly have stopped before it pitched over to follow us; for I had opened out a good train length and was beginning to think the crew had got their end stopped when they shot out of that tunnel like a comet, four cars of railroad iron in the lead.

Again I pulled out for dear life, blowing my signal. Not a man was out on the train. As the last of it came through, the caboose—a little four-wheeled affair—was flirted off the track by the whiplike motion of the train. Flying through the air, the little car dropped into a river more than five hundred feet below. The entire crew, head brakeman and all, went down to death in their caboose—a severe penalty indeed for going to sleep on the road.

Now I, too, was in a tight box, with not a living soul to set a brake on those free-falling cars. I told my firemen to close the firebox door and jump.

"We shall probably never get to the bottom of this mountain," I said.

The chances were that somebody would be working in the freight-house siding at that time of day, and the switch to the siding would be open. In that case, I was bound to go in there and wreck the whole outfit, for I couldn't stop any more than a three-year-old child could stop an earthquake.

My fireman looked at the fast-flying telegraph poles and didn't dare to jump. On we went, faster and faster, yet hardly fast enough. The old engine jumped and rolled so that we could hardly hang on to her. Coal was running out of each gangway in a steady stream, the lids of the tankboxes flew open, and tools and oilcans marked our trail.

I shall never forget that wild ride down the mountain if I live to be a thousand. When we struck a reverse curve about two miles from the tunnel, the fireman was thrown clear through the cab window and literally torn limb from limb as he struck the ground: I thought the train had left the track altogether, for she rolled almost over, hurling me across the cab and back again as she struck the reverse end of the curve; and she came down on her wheels with a crash that shivered every pane of glass and loosened every bolt and joint. The cab was as loose as an old basket, and it rolled around with every movement of the engine. If it should break away, it would surely take me with it.

I grabbed the whistle cord again and frantically blew the "broke in two" signal, hoping it would warn someone that I was coming through and couldn't stop.

I couldn't see ahead very well. It seemed as if the wind was blowing a hurricane. I raised such a cloud of dust that I couldn't even see the rear car of my own section. I just hung on desperately, blowing my warning signal and watching the steam gauge. As the steam went down, I pulled the throttle out a notch at a time. At length I had her wide open, hooked up within a couple of notches of the center, and the exhaust sounded like a continuous roar.

And now I saw ahead of me a man in the middle of the track, languidly waving a red flag. Yes—it was all over with me now: the freight-house switch was open. Mechanically, I blew the signal. Then, realizing that I had not more than a half dozen more breaths to draw in this world, I felt myself possessed by a kind of demoniac frenzy, a desire to do all the damage possible with my dying breath, to annihilate everything from the face of the earth. Clutching the reverse lever with both hands, I with difficulty unhooked and dropped it down a couple of notches. As fast as she had been going before, I felt her leap ahead. A fierce joy surged over me to think what a world-beater my wreck would be.

Looking ahead again, I saw the flagman drop his flag and run at breakneck speed for the switch. For a wonder they hadn't sent out the biggest dunce on the train to flag. He had sense enough to comprehend the situation and wit enough to know the only right thing to do, which was more than I had any right to expect.

Once more coward hope rose in my breast. If he could get that switch closed, the absolute certainty of instant death at that point would be over. The chances were one in a thousand. To spur him on, I again blew the despairing death shriek of the iron devil I was riding; and to give him every second possible, I shut off my throttle, with the immediate result that cars bumped up against the tender with a shock that nearly threw me over backwards. Hanging on, I watched the man as he flew toward the switch. What if he should stub his toe, as men so often do under like circumstances? It would mean death for me before I could close my eyes. I remember thinking, even then, how fortunate it was for me that, owing to the usual laziness of flagmen, he hadn't gone out as far as the rules required, but had stayed near the switch.

I saw him reach it, stoop down, clutch the handle, and at the first effort fail to lift it. Then I swept by like a cyclone. The man had got the switch closed just in the nick of time. The rush of wind from the passing train hurled him down a fifty-foot embankment, bruising him and tearing his clothes, but fortunately doing him no serious injury.

What did the company do to reward him for his heroism in preventing a disastrous wreck? They let him off with a reprimand for not having been out a proper distance with his flag, and they discharged him within thirty days for a repetition of the offense at the same place.

As I whirled by, I could see in the siding the engine that I had come so near to hitting. The engine and train crew were out in the field staring with blanched faces. Hearing a crash, I looked back and saw that the corner of the head car had rolled over far enough to break off the water crane that stood alongside the track. The result was a bad washout before they got the water shut off.

I breathed much easier now. With a light heart, I pulled up the lever again and gradually opened her out. I was running through a yard where the rules required me to reduce speed to six miles an hour, but a train going sixty-six could not have kept up with me. I began to almost enjoy my ride. After what I had passed through, it seemed as if there was no more danger.

There was a passenger station at the foot of the mountain, however. Looking at my watch, I saw that a train was just about due there. Again I began to blow my signal to warn them to look out. The station was on my side of the road, and passengers and baggage had to cross my track.

Yes, there she stood—a little three-car local. Again I blew to make sure they understood, although I could see that the track ahead of me was clear. The operator at the preceding station, with rare presence of mind, had telegraphed ahead that I was coming "broke in two." Fast as I went, the message beat me; and although I couldn't hear it for the roar and clatter, I saw two short puffs of white steam from the engine's whistle meaning, "All right, come along."

And come along I did, to the amazement of those passengers who certainly never saw a freight train wheeled at that rate before. The agent had a truckload of baggage ready to take across as soon as I passed; but the suction of the train drew the whole business under the wheels, and it disappeared. (The agent was discharged; the superintendent said he was a d—— fool.)

The engineer of the local told me afterwards that he saw the front end of the engine, with my face at the window. Then came a big cloud of dust and a roar, and that was all he knew about it.

I was now down the mountain, thank Heaven, and on level ground. But the rear section wasn't, and I hadn't the least idea of how far it was behind me. So I kept the old girl waltzing along as fast as I could—which wasn't very fast, as my steam was down to sixty pounds. I didn't dare get down and look at my fire, for fear of being killed if the rear section should catch me at that moment. A collision now was imminent. While I was losing way on the level ground, the speed of the rear cars had hardly been checked at all.

I began to think of jumping. If I had, it probably would have been the last of me, for the bank was a rock fill, formed by blasting out high rock on the other side of the road. I was still going thirty-five or forty miles an hour—and, besides, I was so shaken up by that terrible ride that I was as weak as a rag and lame and sore all over.

Suddenly, rounding a curve, I saw a man standing by the switch of a long siding. He was giving me a frantic "go ahead" signal. At that sight, my spirits rose about two thousand percent, for I knew I was saved. The runaway rear section would be switched onto the siding.

Giving an answering *toot toot*, I dropped my reverse lever down in the corner and pulled her wide open to get as far from the rear section as possible. I wanted to give him all the time I could to throw the switch and get out of the way after I darted past.

The siding was on a long curve. When I had passed alongside one quarter of its length, I saw that it was partly occupied by a number of loaded coal cars.

Here was another danger. There was going to be a wreck on that siding, and I might get caught in it yet. If I didn't get far enough past the point of collision, some of the cars might pile over on top of me. Then again, if I got to the further switch at the wrong time, the coal cars might be shoved out of the siding and ram me.

You see, it frequently happens on the railroad that you have to think of several things at once—and not be very long about it either. The result of my rapid thinking on this occasion was that I had done enough to save the company's property for one day and now was a good time to look out for myself.

As my steam was low, I concluded the engine would stop herself best if shut off. While I was waiting for her to slow down enough to give me a chance to jump on the left side, the crash came.

There was a great smashing and grinding and piling up round the curve behind me. On the portion of the siding nearest to me, the coal cars merely ran together with a great *ker-bump* and a rattling of links and pins that I could hear continuing on around the curve ahead.

After the noise stopped, I started to back up. Then, remembering that in all probability the track was blocked by wreckage, I ran ahead to the next station and notified the agent to hold all trains.

I reported to the train dispatcher by wire. He ordered me to cross over to the other track, run back to the wreck, find out how the tracks were, and report to him from the station. The agent would keep the track open for my return.

The agent helped me fire up, and back I went. As I had expected, both tracks were blocked. The wrecked cars were piled in heaps, mixed and tangled with the railroad iron that had been part of my train. Coal, flour, agricultural machinery, and all sorts of merchandise were scattered all over the ground.

Four lives and all of this property were lost because a train crew took an early morning nap.

—From Herbert E. Hamblen's *The General Manager's Story.*
The Macmillan Company, New York, 1898 and 1907.

*A wreck on Indian Trestle, North Carolina, in 1880 resembled
the Wreck of the Old Ninety-seven—but nobody sang about it.*
Leslie's Illustrated Newspaper, 1881

CASEY JONES, like the engineer of the Old Ninety-Seven, was a real man who died in a real train wreck. His name was John Luther Jones, and he was born in 1864 and grew up in Cayce, Tennessee, whence came his nickname (always misspelled). He was running the Illinois Central Number 1, the Fast Mail between Chicago and New Orleans on January 1, 1900, when he made his farewell trip to the Promised Land. In Vaughn, Mississippi, he piled into a freight train that was stalled on the main track. The engine overturned. Casey was found dead, the broken whistle cord in one hand and the brake handle in the other. No one else was killed or seriously injured.

Aside from historic curiosity, there is no particular reason to care whether Casey was real or imaginary. Brave Engineers are shadow figures in any case: undistinguished—or, rather, *indistinguishable*—among thousands of locomotive runners who face the same dangers.

Whether his name be Casey Jones or Joseph Broady, whether his story be myth or history, the Brave Engineer is only a common railroad man. He is not a unique specimen, *sui generis,* like Paul Revere, Jim Bowie, or Chief Joseph. It is gratifying, in view of his quiet heroism, to realize that when they made *one* Brave Engineer—or two, or three, or four—they did not break the mold.

Reading on the Railroad

THE LITERARY MONUMENTS of the railroading profession are obscure, scattered, and uneven. An essential guidebook to the most important landmarks in the field is Frank P. Donovan, Jr.'s *The Railroad in Literature: A Brief Survey* (Boston: Railroad & Historical Society, 1940). Donovan's survey includes short stories, novels, poems, and songs as well as biographies and autobiographies of railroad men. Although the author hoped this list might serve as the basis of a later, more detailed bibliography, it has had to stand as written, and it is short of references to periodical literature. Another weakness is implicit in the date of publication, thirty years ago.

If the Donovan survey were to be brought up to date, it undoubtedly would include Peter Lyon's *To Hell in a Day Coach*, (Philadelphia: Lippincott, 1968), an acidulous, witty, thoroughly readable chronicle of the long and agonizing deterioration of passenger service on the American railroads. Not the least of this book's many virtues is a carefully chosen, thoughtfully annotated bibliography.

Other valuable bibliographies: John F. Stover's *American Railroads* (Chicago: University of Chicago Press, 1961), a compact historical record with a good essay on sources; E. T. Bryant's *Railways, a Readers Guide* (Hamden, Conn.: Archon Books, 1968), which is British in authorship and emphasis but offers a selected list of standard books on American railroads; and Oscar Osburn Winthur's *A Classified Bibliography of the Periodical Literature of the Trans-Mississippi West, 1811–1957* (Bloomington: University of Indiana Press, 1961), which lists dozens of regional memoirs of railroading but does not attempt to appraise their value.

Most books about the Age of Steam deal with the history or rolling stock of a particular line, for example: Joseph L. Scott, *Rails across Panama* (Indianapolis: Bobbs-Merrill, 1967); V. V. Masterson, *The Katy Railroad and the Last Frontier* (Norman: University of Oklahoma Press, 1952); Richard C. Overton, *Gulf to Rockies* (Austin: University of Texas Press, 1953); James W. Marshall, *Sante Fe: The Railroad That Built an Empire* (New York: Random House, 1945); and Robert G. Athearn, *Rebel of the Rockies* (New Haven: Yale University Press, 1962).

Among the numerous accounts of the transcontinental railroad are Robert West Howard's *The Great Iron Trail* (New York: G. P. Putnam's Sons, 1962); Wesley S. Griswold's *A Work of Giants* (New York: McGraw-Hill, 1962); James McCague's *Moguls and Iron Men* (New York: Harper & Row, 1964); and George Kraus's *High Road to Promontory* (Palo Alto, Calif.: American West Publishing Co., 1969).

A beautiful evocation of life on the railroads is Simpson Kalisher's *Railroad Men* (New York: Clarke & Way, 1961). A brief, poetic text, transcribed from taped interviews with railroad workers, accompanies the portfolio of superb photographic portraits. Thomas Childs Cochran's *Railroad Leaders, 1845–1890: The Business Mind in Action* (New York: Russell & Russell, 1965) probes with scholarly precision into railroad life at the managerial level.

Many railroad books are too specialized to be of interest or value to general readers. Among the pleasant exceptions are the numerous pictorial volumes by Lucius Beebe and Charles Clegg; Freeman H. Hubbard's *Railroad Avenue* (New York: McGraw-Hill, 1945; revised edition, San Marino, Calif.: Golden West Books, 1964); Robert Selph Henry's *This Fascinating Railroad Business* (Indianapolis: Bobbs-Merrill, 1942); S. Kipp Farrington's *Railroading from the Head End* (New York: Doubleday, Doran, 1943), and *Railroading from the Rear End* (New York: Coward-McCann, 1946); and the Stewart H. Holbrook volume cited elsewhere in this book and entitled *The Story of American Railroads* (New York: Crown Publishers, 1947). J. B. Snell's *Early Railways* (New York: G. P. Putnam's Sons, 1964) is miles ahead of most picture books in the quality and variety of its lithographs.